# A Branch Without a Tree

Zigrid Vidners

*This book was printed in the United States of America.*
**ISBN**
**978-0-578-11718-8**

*For copies of this book, or to contact the author, please email:*
**vidners@sbcglobal.net**

Cover & book layout and design by
Kim Maynard, Kimbilt Graphic Design

LOGOS • BROCHURES • BUSINESS CARDS
ADVERTISING • BOOK LAYOUT, DESIGN
PRE-PRESS • PHOTO MANIPULATION & REPAIR
*typwiz@gmail.com • www.kimbilt.com*

# ~ *Dedication* ~

*This book is dedicated to those who fought and lost
trying to protect their homeland Latvia
and to the many Latvians, including my father,
whose lives were extinguished in the far reaches
of the Soviet Union.*

*My thanks and deep appreciation to my son
Maris Vidners and to the esteemed editor Jay Gallagher
who helped me to bring this book to frutition.*

# TABLE OF CONTENTS

## <u>Notes on Pronunciation</u>

Latvians use the European alphabet.

a = a *(as in "cup")*
e = e *(as in "let")*
i = i *(as in "in")*
u = u *(as in "put")*
o = o  or ua
*The dash above a vowel means it is a "long" vowel sound.*

## <u>Consonants:</u>

l,  n,  k,  g  — *with markings under them, soften the sound*
ļ, ņ, ķ, j  — *pronounced as if there was a "j" following
                    the consonant*
j = y *(pronounced as in "you")*

š = sh

ž = *as the french pronounce " j."*

*Accent is almost always on the first syllable, and often the end-ings of words are somewhat muted.*

# A Branch Without a Tree

### Zigrid Vidners

The big ship was moving. Moving ever farther away from the Baltic coast and our native country Latvia. Around us were only the darkening waters of the Baltic Sea and evening was coming. The darkness was even in our souls, for we were leaving behind all that we had ever loved and owned: our country, our home, our family and friends. It was August 1944, and my Mother, my twelve year old brother Jānītis and I, a seventeen year old girl, were on this ship, full of Latvian refugees, fleeing the Russians and going to Germany and an unknown future.

World War II was still raging all over Europe. The Germans had suffered great losses at the Russian Front and their armies had been constantly withdrawing. The Russians followed on their heels and were again invading our country for the second time. Remembering what life was like under Russian Communist rule during their first occupation of our country only four years before, many Latvians had made the hard choice to leave their native land and go to war-torn Germany rather than fall into the hands of the Russians.

I shall never forget that day of June 17, 1940 when the terrible and shocking news first reached us that the Russian armies had crossed our border and were advancing into our country with tanks and soldiers and all! A dark shadow fell over the land; we all felt it. It was as if an evil bird had flown over our skies and contaminated them. I was only fourteen then, a smallish girl with brown hair and blue-gray eyes, spending the summer on our farm working in the fields, but I felt it to the depth of my being. The dark premonition of what would follow was there.

Our family had moved from the capital Rīga to the countryside only a year before, in February 1939, when my father retired from the Latvian National Army. He had served it for twenty years, always dreaming of farming some day on grandfather's farm that he had helped to buy. It became our permanent home from then on. We children had spent our summers there from an early age, and Father thought that his time to farm had come at last. Things did not work out in his favor though, because unexpected changes soon followed—one after another.

Evil came upon us that summer of 1940, and a whole year of events followed that turned all our thinking and understanding upside down. The Russians lied to us from the very first. In October 1939, they had already forced our government to let them use our ports for establishing their military bases. There was no way our small country could stand up against this ultimatum. The Russians said that nothing would change in our internal affairs and even a document of mutual help and friendship was signed, but all that was rendered invalid on June 17, 1940, when their troops entered Latvia, ignoring all previous provisions. Our government was deposed in a degrading way and a puppet government was installed. Within a few weeks, elections were hastily arranged with only the Communist candidates on the ballot. No other choices were available.

During the following year many prominent people disappeared, and even regular people vanished without a trace on their way to work, not existing anymore in any registers. How could this be—a person suddenly not being there? Not anywhere? The distraught family members searched, but were met by the same cold, impersonal answer everywhere. There was no such person!

Sudden ransacking of homes happened in the middle of night—the Communist agents looking to find something that might incriminate those who lived there! Arrests, interrogations, imprisonments took place often after such events. People lived in fear, for nobody knew who might be next.

I had just finished my first year in high school, living with my Aunt Irma and her family in the small town Valmiera and was about to return to the farm for the summer, when even more dreadful things happened. The communists had been in our country exactly a year, when on the night of June 13 to 14 in 1941, thousands of innocent people were roused out of their beds in the middle of the night and taken away in armored trucks. Even the old and sick and mothers with babies were taken at gunpoint, with only a few minutes given to prepare, then taken away to stations where rows of cattle cars were waiting to deport them to the slave camps of Siberia!

When relatives or friends heard of this, they rushed to the stations bringing food or clothing or even a note saying good-bye, but nothing was allowed; not even a cup of water to drink to those who waited in

the crowded cars for their departure on this pitiful journey. The guards of the trains saw to it that the instructions were followed without mercy.

It was even more heart wrenching to hear afterwards that men had been torn away from their families and sent to even worse conditions to gulags up north beyond the Arctic Circle to work in coal mines. Hardly anybody returned from there.

The Germans arrived only two weeks later, in the beginning of July 1941, forcing the Russians to flee. It was a period of great chaos. The communists were fleeing, but still tried to take revenge where they could. My Father and many other men went into the forests to hide during this vulnerable time. They also watched the movement of the Russians fleeing, and tried to prevent any harm to civilians. The communications were poor, especially in the countryside where we lived. Nobody knew what was really happening—who was in charge or what would come next. This I can tell only from my childish perspective. Other people's experiences might be vastly different according to their circumstances.

After the Russian armies had left, the main prison of the capital Rīga was opened, exposing the barbarically tortured bodies in the prison yard. There were people who looked for their loved ones and what they saw were hands with pulled-off nails, faces with punched-out eyes, cut-out tongues and burned bodies. How could anyone do something like that?

The memory of that first Soviet occupation from June 1940 till July 1941 is written within us with horror that we do not want to ever experience again. The Germans marched into Rīga, and thank God they came when they did, or many of us would not be here today. Documents were found at the local establishments, showing that the next deportations would have taken place only three weeks later. Our family's names were on those lists also along with others, because anybody holding a position or owning anything of worth was instantly named an "Enemy of the State". We too were considered to be amongst these unwanted individuals who needed to be eradicated, because, firstly, Father had been an officer in the Latvian army, secondly, we owned the farm and thirdly, we had "exploited the working class people"! In regular language, this last charge meant just that they had been employed and paid for their work, so they could make their living. Those were all punishable things now.

What an irony! Our lifelong enemies the Germans, who had enslaved our peoples in the past for some 700 years, saved us now from a Russian demise by coming when they did! By doing that, they had given our family and another 200,000 Latvians a chance to escape by evacuating us.

When the Germans came during WWII, occupying our country in the beginning of July 1941, they came with their own purposes, of course, but even so, their coming saved many Latvian lives by freeing us from the evil things that the Russians still wanted to do to our people.

What the German future plans were, we did not know then. Many in the world still do not understand our position as a small country. For us it meant choosing between two evils at the time, and the Russian evil we had just tasted!

Many Latvian men, having lost loved ones who had been killed or deported by the Russians, wanted to go and help the Germans to fight the Russians from the very start. The Germans, however, were very wary about Latvians carrying weapons at first, but a police force was needed to keep order during the changing times in Latvia. In view of that, special "Peacekeeping" units were formed of these volunteers. First they served locally but soon, as this program expanded, they were sent to keep order in the conquered areas in Russia also, where they were soon drawn into fighting the war, though often unprepared for it. Young boys had joined right from the school bench, wanting to help their country, but were killed in their first combat. What did they know of fighting the war? But they had to go where the Germans sent them.

Later the Peacekeepers were renamed the "Police Battalions" and soon grew in numbers, for the need was great. The Germans, fighting on two fronts—the east and the west—were short of manpower, and the Latvians proved to be good fighters. Yes, they fought valiantly, believing that they did it to protect their nation from the Russians and to gain a renewed freedom for Latvia. At times the Germans let them keep thinking that to keep the Latvians in their army.

This, however, was not what the Germans wanted, and they forbade any nationalistic movements or institutions. That was made very clear as the leading commanders arrived from Germany. No such dreams! They only had to obey! Disillusioned by this, the numbers of volunteers waned.

Yet after the cold winter of 1942/1943, when the Germans had suffered great losses at the Eastern front, they started to draft Latvian men into their army whether they wanted to be there or not. They were made to sign a paper saying that they joined of their free will, thus circumventing the Geneva Convention, which forbade mobilization in occupied countries. The Latvian establishment, such as was allowed by the Germans, put forward arguments about the treatment of the Latvian recruits, especially about sending unprepared young recruits to the front. In the end, however, the Latvians had to give in, for the Germans mostly ignored their requests and things could be worse in the long run if they refused. If the draftees declined, they could be considered "enemies of the regime", and that might mean a journey to the concentration camp.

A Latvian Legion was formed of these draftees in the beginning of 1943 and continued by adding sections of the Police Battallions as circumstances were changing all the time. These units consisted of Latvian

soldiers, led by senior Latvian officers from the former Latvian army but under German command. They did not fight other Allies, only Russians. They wanted to protect their own Latvian people from ever letting the Communists rule in Latvia again. Nobody could foresee then that the final border for the Germans would be the River Elbe in Germany, and that they would have to move with them all the way there with the German army through Poland and East Germany, where many more Latvian soldiers would lose their lives.

All this was a very complicated period. It is still hard to present it in a few simple sentences, but I hope that the reader will have at least some notion of the times we had to live through and the burden the Latvian men had to carry. It was sometimes very difficult for Latvian officers, heading the units of the Latvian Legion, to be under the German commanders who often competed or where in conflict with each other, were haughty toward Latvian soldiers, and wasted many lives due to rash military decision-making. More information can be obtained from the many history books written about this.

My 19-year-old brother, Ilgvars was drafted in the fall of 1943, and sent to an instructor's school in Austria. My Father was called up into the German army in the beginning of 1944, when things were desperate and tough fighting went on just outside the Latvian border in the east. Many died there, and he barely got out, having lost everything. His unit was in shambles because of the shortage in ammunition and fighting men. He stopped by our farm just for one night as his unit came back from the front, moving along a road close to where we lived. He told us of the dreadful situation they had been in, with the Russian partisans all around them in the forest quagmire, shooting at them.

Those were frightening days for the rest of us living on the farm also—for Mother, my brother Jānīts and me, as well as our grandparents, who were in their seventies and eighties. They had been farmers and had worked hard all their lives to just make their living. My Father's wish to farm was never fulfilled, for the communists confiscated the land and property in 1940. The Germans gave it back, but then they drafted him into their army and he never got to see it again. My heart still aches for him because of this.

Though we had tried hard to believe to the very last that things might still turn around, it did not happen. In the summer of 1944, the Russians advanced rapidly and had already taken over part of our country. We, on the farm, carried on with our regular work that could not be left undone. It was the season of hay-making and that meant a lot of hard manual work, getting it into the barns for the animal's winter feed. As I forked the heaps of hay high up in the barn, I kept praying and pretending that the Russians would not overtake us! It just could not be!

But the heavy artillery "booms" came closer and closer with every day. My Father called from Rīga in the middle of August that he was being sent to Germany to form and train new units there. He wanted to see Mother!

When Mother went to Rīga to see him off, she found that her entire family from her home town Valmiera was there also, on their way to Germany. The front lines had been too close to where they lived; they could not risk being overrun.

For us on the farm too, the day to leave came as a shock, much sooner than we had thought. Mother and I had hardly got home from the station after she had seen Dad off, when suddenly the phone rang.

"Get ready to leave!" Our friend from the community center yelled in the tube! "The Russian tanks have broken through at Ērgļi and are rolling our way! The train on which you just returned from Rīga, has been shot through from one end to the other only a few stops down the line! Pack! Get out! Go to the forest!" she shouted, her voice trembling.

Shock! Panic! Despite warnings, we were not prepared—as Dad had warned us to be!

Luckily another call came a little later, again from our friend, saying that the Russian tanks had been destroyed by German units and the army was pushed back to Ērgļi! But that was still only 20 kilometers from us!

"Thank God!" Mother cried out. "Tomorrow! Tomorrow we pack and go to Germany as Dad wanted us to!" Strength and determination was in her voice.

That gave us one day to prepare and another to get out of the area on the last train to Rīga, because orders had been given that there would be no more trains for civilians on this line.

Oh, the pain, to leave everything we loved and to walk away from it! To pack, knowing that you will never be here again! To never touch these things… I was totally out of my head and could not be a help to Mother. She had pulled herself together and did the packing with great determination and the help of a refugee woman from Ukraine, who was staying on our farm with her family at the time.

It was even more heart wrenching, leaving old Grandma, Grandpa and Grandpa's younger brother Uncle August behind, for they backed out of taking such a journey. They felt they could not leave the farm and the animals—their whole life's work.

Uncle August, too, thought that this was where he needed to be. This was where his work was; this was where he belonged.

Now only the three of us were leaving the country: Mother, my brother and I. When Mother anguished about leaving the old people behind, Grandma told her sternly,

"You have to go! You are young and have children; you still have a

life to live! Don't worry about us, we will manage. Remember what your husband said when he left here!"

Yes, that was exactly what Dad had said: "Don't stay with the Russians! Under no circumstances stay with the Russians! They will not let you stay here anyway...You will end up in Siberia or worse..."

## To Germany

Our tearful journey began. We left our home on August 22nd and just managed to get on the last train going to Rīga. Three days later, on August 25, 1944 we boarded the German ship at the Port of Rīga, anchored on the bank of our largest river, the Daugava. There was the President's Castle and the Old Town with its familiar church spires before our eyes, reminding us what we would be losing, while silently, painfully saying goodbye to all that had been.

It was a heart-wrenching time for those whose loved ones stood down below on the bank and tried to shout up their last messages, which the wind tossed away. It was as hard for those who were leaving as those who stayed.

It had taken most of the day to embark. In the late afternoon everything was ready, and the ship slowly moved away from the coast. The dark slice of water between the ship and the embankment was like a knife cutting us off from all that was dear to us. The crowd of relatives and friends stood on the bank shouting to us in the wind, "Come back! Come back! We will wait for you!"

Some ran along the embankment waving, not being able to let go. A crowd of us, standing on the deck waved back, then stood silently, fearing to look into each other's eyes, as the waters of the Daugava took us away from everything. I can still feel the strong, cool wind blowing in my face as I stood there looking back...

It took several hours for the ship to move across the Bay of the Baltic Sea and to skirt the Horn of Kolka. The evening dusk already covered everything, when we came out to the open sea near the west coast of Latvia. A blue mist wrapped the coastline, and that was the last we saw of it.

"Oh God!" That was all I could say.

The Latvian coastline had disappeared from our sight a while ago. The big ship kept moving across the dark waters, taking us farther and farther away from our home and our beloved country. Tears and last goodbyes had wrenched the hearts of those who left and those who stayed. Now it was all over. It was no use looking back; we were empty and silent. There was only the ship and the now, nothing else.

Gradually, people began to relax after the stressful day of departing

from all they had loved and owned. There was nothing more to be done at present. By now everybody had found some sheltered spot on one of the decks and settled down to eat, for we had not eaten since the early morning. Now it was long past suppertime, and darkness was invading everything. Lights were not allowed, so we would not be spotted by the enemy. We sat on the floor huddled close to our belongings and ate whatever each had brought along. The ship slid silently through the night, and everything seemed peaceful. After eating, I wanted to go and look for my friend *Edīte* (Edith) for I knew that she and her family were on this ship also. Edīte and I had known each other since grade-school days and she was my best friend.

I found her on the deck below. Women with small children were somewhere lower down, where they had more comfort. When Edīte and I came up to the upper deck, the sky had cleared and it had become lighter. We even saw the stars coming out. That seemed to be a good sign and it made us feel better. The guiding stars… Perhaps the future would not be too bad after all.

The evening was quiet as we took a walk around the deck. We could hear the ship's engines working deep down below. Farther and farther into the night we sailed. On the deck people stood around in small groups, talking in low voices, sharing their experiences of the last few days and telling of the loved ones they had to leave behind.

At the very front of the ship, we came upon a group of older people, sitting on a heap of bulky ropes and singing.

*"Volga, Volga..."* their beautiful deep voices melted in harmony, singing this well-known Russian song about their large river, sounding so mellow and sad.

But why Russian? And especially at this time when we were fleeing from them for our lives? Perhaps they were people who had fled the country once before already during the First World War and were remembering that? Many had fled to Russia then, but that was before the Communists had taken over.

As we stopped to listen and looked on, it was almost like watching a movie set, their black bodies silhouetted against the somewhat lighter background of the sea. It looked so romantic!

But then, suddenly, everything fell apart. The ship's sirens screamed, and people ran! Just moments later, several planes swooped over us, flying low and shooting. Everybody scrambled for shelter. The ship's artillery shot back at the enemy, red sparks flying in the dark. They were Russian planes that had flown over and were back shooting again in the space of a few minutes. Sparks flew in the air again, but then they were gone, and it was quiet once more. Luckily, no one was injured.

We listened for a while, terrified, wondering if they would come

back again bringing even more planes, because now they knew where we were. Luckily it did not happen. No one, however, wanted to sing anymore. It was late, perhaps after midnight, and the air was also getting cooler. The time had come to get some rest. People quieted down and went back to their places of shelter. There were no beds, of course, so we just lay down on the floor, leaning against our belongings, hoping to get some sleep. What tomorrow would bring, we did not know. It was all in God's hands.

It was a gray morning on August 26, 1944, when we docked at the Gottenhafen harbor near Danzig. We were on German soil now and glad to have arrived here safely. Later we heard that ships, full of refugees and soldiers, had been torpedoed and gone down, some even just outside the harbor. Thank God! We had made it safely.

The disembarking started, and it took quite some time. We were told to take our belongings to the side of the train tracks adjoining the wharf, from where a special train would take us farther on. Where that would be, we did not know.

When my Mother put in the application for the evacuation in Rīga, she had been asked for an address where she would like to go. We did not know anybody in Germany, but then she remembered the name of the place her brother had been given by his boss, a higher German officer, whom he worked for as a chauffeur. The officer had given his hometown address to him, saying that if any of his family needed to flee, that would be a safer area region for them. It was north of Hamburg in a quiet, mostly farming region, with no war industry present. Now we were here in Germany, and our destination would be Husum, Schleswig-Holstein. It was good to know that we would at least be heading west.

The disembarking had ended quite a while ago. It was late afternoon. The sun was shining through the passing clouds, but we still waited at the empty railway tracks. There was nowhere to sit but on the pavement by the piles of our belongings that stood in heaps all along the track lines. Some children slept on top of the bundles. A few of the old people snoozed too, sitting on the ground and leaning against the bags next to them. The grown-ups stood or walked around, visibly eager to get going. A port was a vulnerable place where to linger; it might get bombed.

Evening was coming, but still no train. The harbor square was empty by now. Whoever had worked there had gone home. Only a couple of sailors still stood by the thick concrete posts at the water's edge, biding their time, and a few gulls flew around them in hopes of some food. One of the sailors had an accordion and started playing.

"Fly, little gull, fly far away and tell my beloved..." It tugged at my heart and perhaps others' too, for we had often sung this song in Latvia. It sounded unbearably sad in our present situation as we saw the pink evening sky become paler and grayer with every moment and here we were without a home or shelter... Blue shrouds of mist rose from the waters, and it was getting cooler. The sailors too had gone by now, but we still waited.

It was almost dark when the train finally came. At least it was an empty train, and we had plenty of room to sit. It did not take us long to settle down; then the whistles sounded and our journey began. We sat in the dark, swaying with the rhythm of the train, as it carried us through the night across the dark, strange land. Only after midnight did I remember that this was my eighteenth birthday. In my wildest dreams I could not have imagined it like this: being on a train in a foreign country, racing through the night without one speck of light! My thoughts still kept milling around in disbelief. How could this happen? But it was no use looking back. That life had been cut off.

After the long and tiring day at the harbor, we had finally dozed off, when suddenly we were jerked from our sleep. The wheels squealed against the tracks, and shuddering, the train stopped. We wondered what had happened. Was there an air raid? Had the tracks been bombed? While we still wondered, a guard came by and shouted,

"Everybody out! Go and find your luggage! This is Stargard!"

"But we thought that we would be taken to Stettin!" some argued and we were surprised, too.

"No, no! This is Stargard, a screening camp where you will be deloused!" The guard explained.

"Deloused!" "Deloused?" People looked at each other in confusion. This was unbelievable! We were not a band of barbarians who had crawled out of the bushes! These were mainly highly educated people, professionals, educators, business owners and people who had been in high positions! But it did not seem to matter; it was just the first degradation of many to follow. We later heard that it had been a very ugly and highly embarrassing experience for everyone.

We were lucky, because being dependents of an army officer—my father having been drafted into the German army—we could continue on our journey without staying there.

Mother and Jānīts got off the train and went to look for our luggage that had been piled high in some open cars farther down the line, but I stayed with our things in the compartment. It was still dark outside, and people were worried about how they would find their belongings. That was all that they owned now, but everything had been just simply thrown

into the open cars. A couple of men stood on top of the cars handing the bundles down, while others received them and put them on the pavement.

It was a mess. People milled around in the dark, trying to identify their things. Many suitcases looked the same, so nametags had to be found, but gradually everything got sorted out. Edīte and her family had to stay here, so we had to say goodbye. Their destination had been Stettin, where one of her relatives lived.

In the meantime, mother had made inquiries and found out, that to get to Husum, we first had to go to Hamburg. Now we had to wait for our train that would be arriving in a couple of hours. It was getting toward morning. The darkness was gradually becoming grayer. It was also quite cool. We stood on the empty platform next to our belongings, shivering and yawning. We had not slept or eaten much since we began our journey. Each of us had three pieces of luggage to carry, two by hand and one on the back. We knew it would not be easy to handle all that on a regular train.

That proved to be so true when the train finally arrived, already packed almost to capacity. People, however, were helpful. It was wartime, and they were used to these kinds of conditions by now. Somehow they managed to hand our belongings one to another through the window and the door. Somebody reached out and helped Jānīts to crawl in through the window. Mother had just gotten in through the door, but I was still standing on the steps.

*"Einsteigen! Einsteigen!"* (get on board!) The guard called outside and the whistles sounded, but I had nowhere to go. The whistles sounded again.

"Close the doors! Close the doors!" the guardsman shouted.

I was in a panic. What if I had to fall back? How would I ever find them? I did not have any money on me, either! With my last strength, I found a tiny spot for half of my right foot on the next step and tried to bounce up. A strong shove against my back suddenly pushed me up as the doors slammed shut with a bang behind me. More whistles sounded outside and we started moving.

From the sudden jerk, my backpack had been pushed up on top of my head. I was standing on one foot, but at least I was in. The situation was awful, but there was nothing else left but to bear it. After a little while my foot started to go numb, but then, little by little, I finally managed to squeeze my other foot to the floor, too. The swaying train shuffled people even closer together, and by turning this way and that, more room was created. We were still packed like sardines, but at least after a while I could stand normally. What a relief!

We reached Hamburg in the late morning, and as the train took us through this vast city to the station, we saw what devasta-

tion there was: just ruins and ruins and nothing else as far as the eye could see. Parts of the torn walls of five and six-story buildings, which had been apartment houses, stuck up above the rubble with gaping holes where the windows had been. Not one complete house was standing! It was unbelievable that there could be such devastation, and yet people still lived there somewhere. It was a dreadful, sinking feeling to see it. Now the sun had come out, and it almost seemed like a mockery that it still shone as if nothing had happened. But it had happened! We were so glad that we would be going farther away from here.

Later we heard of the many Latvian people who had chosen not to go too far into Germany, but had stayed in the eastern regions in hopes that they might be able to return home soon. This did not materialize, and because of it, they had to flee from the Russians again and again, losing everything–even their family members, especially the old and the very young. While moving along the packed roads, the Russians had shot at them from the low flying planes. There were stories full of horror, and it had been even worse for those who did not manage to escape the Russians. They had been plundered, raped and shot by the Russian soldiers, sometimes just for fun. We were really lucky to have had made the choice we had.

In Hamburg, my brother and I stayed with our belongings in the huge station hall that was like a big barn with nothing inside but a few wooden benches along the walls. Mother had just gotten back from inquiring about our trip north to Husum when suddenly the sounds of sirens split the air.

*"Flieger Alarm! Flieger Alarm!"* (Air raid!) People shouted and dashed toward the shelter that was well marked, and we did, too. This was the first time that we were in a place like this and we sat there numbed. My heart was pounding. What else will happen? Will our lives end here? We sat in the darkened room underground listening to what might be happening above. Several heavy "booms" sounded quite close, then some a little more distant, but then nothing. We still waited anxiously, but Jānīts was impatient to see what had happened and cautiously crawled out. He came back soon.

"There has been a hit!" he said "There is a big hole on the tracks just outside the station!"

The alarm had not been cancelled, so we still waited together with others. Jānīts sneaked out several times and came back with news.

"They are working on the damaged tracks. There are bulldozers and other machinery! It looked like they had everything ready for this kind of a repair. They are working really fast!"

Only half an hour had passed, when he came back with news: "The job is finished! The tracks are where they were! Amazing!"

Finally the siren sounded again, signaling us that we could come out, and everybody breathed easier. Understandably, we felt pretty shaken after such an incident.

Mother had found out that we had to take a train to Flensburg, a town close to the Danish borders, but it would also stop at Husum, the small town at the edge of the North Sea, on the west coast, which was our destination. Again we had to wait, for the trains did not run too often, but finally, in the afternoon, we were on our way.

This was a much more comfortable journey, for it originated in Hamburg, so there were plenty of seats available. The day was nice, the sun was still shining, but the recent experience still echoed within us. Riding on, we watched the surroundings with great interest. As we traveled northward, the land flattened out more and more and became sparse in vegetation. Only a tree or a shrub grew here or there, or a small clump of trees in this greenish-brown expanse of fields that stretched out to the horizon. Low, earthen walls divided the fields into larger and smaller sections, seemingly to keep the cows or sheep from straying from one field into another.

Occasionally, there was a village, half hidden in the trees. The farmhouses had heavy, reed-covered roofs, hanging low above the small windows. It was a lonely and harsh land as compared to Latvia's pleasant and changing scenery of green fields and forests, with its ups and downs, its rivers and lakes. This strange land looked so bare and unfriendly. And so it was. We soon experienced it when we met its people.

It was late in the afternoon when we arrived at Husum, but the sun was still shining. As we entered the station, we saw a big pile of belongings in the middle of the front hall, and a couple of small children running around it playing. While we stood there, wondering what to do next, we suddenly realized that the children spoke Latvian! That was a surprise!

"What are you doing here?" we asked in Latvian.

"Oh, we arrived here in the morning. Our mother and other Latvian people are next door in the dining room," one of the little ones said.

We entered the dining hall, and what a surprise! Mother's entire family, our relatives from Valmiera, sat there at the tables!

There was mother's oldest sister, my Aunt Irma and Uncle Kārlis, with whom I had lived the last three winters while attending high school in Valmiera, and their three children (my cousins): Ruta, Edvins and Ingrīda. There was Mother's younger sister, Aunt Elzī, with her four-year-old daughter Ilze, and Omī, our dear grandmother on mother's side. There was also mother's older brother, Uncle Heinī, and Austra with four-year-old Vitauts and their little daughter Silvija, barely a month old.

This was almost all of mothers' family, except for her younger brother, Uncle Ali, who had to stay at his post as a chauffeur to the German Gebietskomisar in Valmiera, Latvia.

This really was amazing, because they all had left Latvia two weeks before us, but they had had to stay at the screening camp. Now we were all here and glad to see each other. It gave us more courage seeing so many of our extended family here together. I was especially glad to see my cousin Ruta. We had become good friends while I lived with her family in Valmiera.

"You can get some warm soup without any coupons here in the station." Aunt Austra announced. "You most likely are hungry!"

"That is good news!" Mother said. "We have not had anything warm since we left Latvia!"

It certainly was good to have some warm food. Now we had time to exchange stories about our experiences while traveling the long way from Latvia to this place. The other two families here were also from Valmiera and had been with our relatives all along the way. They had all kept together, helping each other with their luggage and the small children.

A while later two ladies arrived.

"We are from the German Red Cross," They introduced themselves. "We will look after you and get you located."

Now we could leave the station. Picking up our belongings, we walked in a long line along the side of the road to the nearby town. The ladies took us to what was the local Craftsman's Guild Hall, which was quite spacious with a shiny hardwood floor and sacks of straw lined up all around it for sleeping. This would be our first home base in the foreign land. We were told that we would stay here until we all got "sorted out" where we would be sent, according to the work we could do. Since all the able-bodied men were at war, working hands were needed.

We chose our sleeping pads, putting our belongings close by. Then it was time to get some rest, for the darkness was upon us already, and we had not slept properly since we left Latvia. I was sure that thoughts about the uncertain future were on many minds, but it was even harder for those with small children. They were crying and whining, not being able to settle down in the unusual circumstances, but gradually everybody quieted down. Occasionally the sound of crunching straw could be heard as people turned over on their bedding, not being able to go to sleep. A few heavy sighs could be heard in the dark; then finally there was silence.

The next morning my cousin *Ruta* (Ruth) and I went to explore the town. Walking along the narrow, cobbled streets, lined by the small, one or two-story houses with steep roofs and small windows, they appeared to us bare and stark. They stood right next to the pave-

ment, with no front gardens, no trees or shrubs and no adornment! All was very neat, but the word "harsh" came to mind again. As we walked around more, we found that most of the narrow streets ran into the big cobblestone market square in the middle of town. A red brick church stood at one end of the square, its tall spire reaching through the surrounding large trees. Other buildings around the square were bigger too, containing some shops and cafes, as it usually is in a town center.

Near the church, we came across the monument of the poet and writer Theodor Storm, a native son of this region, who had described it in his works with deep love and sensitivity and had become famous for his writings. I remembered having been introduced to him and his works at our German language class at high school. The teacher had often made dictations out of his writings and made us learn his poem about Husum, called *"Die graue Stadt am Meer"* meaning "The Gray City by the Sea". I had thought then that it was a beautiful poem. How amazing that now I was here to see this place with my own eyes and to experience it!

We walked the streets of this small, gray-looking town, but it did not move us the way it had moved the poet, because our youth and our precious memories were tied to another place in another land. Walking along one of the side-streets away from the marketplace, we found ourselves at the harbor, which nestled inside the bay. Small ships and fishing boats stood tied up here at the small wharf and also in places farther away by the water's edge. The gulls flew around crying and looking for food; the dark waters washed against the harbor walls. This was the North Sea. The wind blew into our faces cool and moist, carrying the salty smell of the sea. There were a few more buildings farther along the edge of the bay, but in the distance was the gray horizon of the open sea.

## To Vioel *(pronounced – Fioel)*

The following day we learned what had been decided about our future; the assignments were made without any say from us, of course. They had to place us somewhere, and our family was scheduled to go to the small village of Viol, fourteen kilometers from Husum. Aunt Irma and her family had to go in the same direction, to another village even farther on, so the next day we were on the train on our way to our destinations. We were told that we would be met at the station, and we were.

Since our family was supposed to live at the bakery, the baker had come to meet us, and we all walked the considerable distance from the station to the village, carrying our heavy belongings. He did not offer to help carry any of it. The bakery was on the main street, a nice red brick building right in the middle of the village. The baker took us around the back, which was as much as we expected, but our spirits sank when he

proceeded to lead us upstairs along a steep, narrow staircase to a small
room in the attic and pronounced that this was where we would live. It
probably had been a storeroom, for the walls and the ceiling were just
raw boards with big cracks in them, through which you could see the
roof. Besides the three iron bedsteads, there was only an old wardrobe,
a small table and one chair. This new circumstance hit us harshly, but
what could we say? We were refugees and had to take what was given to
us—or so we assumed.

Without any ceremony the baker turned to mother and told her:
"You will have to work in the bakery and also help with the household
tasks. The boy will have to clean the pans, carry the baked goods to the
customers, and do whatever odd jobs there are."

"And you," he turned to me, "will be working for the farmer on the
other side of the street. I shall take you there later and introduce you to
your employers the Carstensen's." He left without saying one more word.
His coldness made us feel at point zero.

Since I had never worked for other people, I felt very uneasy, but followed the baker anyway when he came later in the afternoon.

The farmhouse looked like many others we had seen from the train,
with a heavy thatched roof that lay low over the small windows. There
must have been a reason why they were built this way, and it did not take
me long to learn that it was because of the constant wind and clouds that
brought rain from the nearby North Sea.

When we crossed the road to the Carstensen's, a large, heavyset
woman opened the door. Her slightly graying blond hair was parted
in the middle and combed smoothly back from her wide, fair-skinned
face and rolled in a small bun at the back. As I greeted her, her cold,
light blue eyes looked me over dispassionately, without a trace of
any kind of a welcome, giving me a feeling that it was really not her
wish to have me in her house. The farmer stood by tall and lean with
a wrinkly, weather-beaten face and a pipe in his mouth that he did
not take out even when he talked. He just pushed it to the corner of
his mouth if he was going to say something. His eyes were like big
balls in his round, skinny face, and there was hardly any hair left on
his head. Still, his attitude was kinder than that of the lady's. He said
something to me, but I did not understand him, although I spoke German very well by then.

Apparently they spoke a dialect called *"Plattdeutsch"* in this northern region, and that was something between German, English and Danish. It sounded to me like someone trying to speak with a hot potato in
his mouth. The farmer's wife talked to me in regular German, so I could
understand her, but she did not say much.

The Carstensen's had two children: the ten-year-old Anne-Grete,

dressed in a white cardigan with blue eyes and blond braided hair and the seven-year-old Andreas, also blond with blue eyes. They squeezed through in front of their parents eyeing me with curiosity. To me they seemed to be rather spoiled. After the introductions, the lady of the house told me condescendingly that I would not have to do anything this evening, but that I should be there at six o'clock the next morning. The cold eyes brushed over me again, which made me shiver inside. To soften the mood, the farmer said something that sounded friendlier and gave a laugh, but again I did not understand him.

I came out on the street feeling as if I had been beaten up. Those unwelcoming eyes were still boring into my back. I stood on the pavement taking in my present situation. I would now be a servant, the same as my ancestors once had been in ancient times when they had been servants of the German landlords. Initially, they had come with the Crusaders, had conquered, and then made the local people their servants—even slaves. They were called "the gray barons", and they knew how to squeeze the last out of those who had to serve them, for they needed a lot of money to support their aristocratic lifestyles. To be fair, there were some barons or their clergy who were more compassionate. Seeing how smart some of the Latvian farmer's children were, they helped them to get the education they deserved.

I knew there would be a lot of hard work ahead of me, but it was not work that I was afraid of. No, I had worked very hard every summer on our family farm in Latvia. During the last summers I had even done a lot of man's work, because my father and my oldest brother had been drafted into the German army to help fight the Russians. The work was not the point. The point was that I would be a servant to the Germans, our age-old enemies. That was the thought that caused pain.

It was a restless night for me, almost falling asleep, then again waking suddenly, sitting up with a pounding heart, listening to someone crying inside of me,

"I won't go! I won't!" My whole being was resisting what I knew that I would have to do.

Lying awake in my bed, I felt the cool air blowing on my face, coming through the cracks in the walls. It was cold. We were already in September. How would we live here through the winter, I thought, since there was no heating up here?

The shrill sound of the alarm clock woke us. I must have finally fallen into a deeper sleep. For a moment I could not grasp where I was. Then mother switched on the light. A bare light bulb hung from the rough ceiling. It was pitch dark outside, but we quickly got out of our beds and dressed silently. We had to do what we had to do. Our new life was beginning.

It was September 5, 1944. Only a month ago I had been cutting the golden rye in my father's fields.

"How is it possible that I am here," I asked myself as I climbed down the narrow stairs.

Outside, the darkness was just beginning to wane a little. A few stars and a moon shone above, but dark smoke-like clouds raced past them, at times covering them completely, then again letting them shine through. It was such a dramatic scene as you might see in a film—a horror film—forecasting doom. The black treetops surrounding the buildings swayed and moaned in the wind, matching my inner being completely.

I stood on my side of the empty street watching the galloping clouds, my legs refusing to take me across to that strange, dark house with the moaning trees. I was only eighteen, it might be understandable that I was scared.

"I will not go!" someone inside of me screamed again. But a gust of wind threw its callous, damp breath into my face, tore at my clothing and laughed,

"You'll go! Sure, you will go!" It was the wind of the strange, unfriendly land.

Never in my life had it been so hard to force myself do something as it was now, but I knew that I had to do it. I had to go, and of course, I would. There was no other way. What else could I do? Saving our lives was not enough, now we had to survive. I had to remember that I was not alone, I had a family. The daily bread had to be earned. I had never had to do it by working for somebody else, and perhaps that was why it was so hard. It felt like degradation even though I knew that there was no shame in doing any kind of work and that it was my duty to go. Gritting my teeth, I said to myself sternly, "No more debating or messing around with feelings!" I had to go and I went.

All this first period after leaving home was like living in another dimension. I did what I had to do, but everything inside of me felt dead. A wall was around me, and inside it everything was silent. Was that how a tree felt when it was cut from its roots, because the flow of the life-giving fluid had stopped?

We received some letters from Dad. He was living in a forest in a tent in very cramped conditions and it was raining a lot. They were supposed to train new units of soldiers, but there were no arms or even sufficient clothing for the young men, and winter was coming. Mother urged me to write to him, but I could not do even that. What would I say to him now in my present state of mind?

But life had to go on. I worked at the farmer's from six o'clock in the morning till nine at night, seven days a week. Only every third Sunday I

would get off. Gradually I learned to understand these people and their habits, their views on life. I learned also what it meant to be in servitude to another and how it felt when you were less than zero in the eyes of those above you. The Germans knew how to get as much out of you as they possibly could, for the list of my tasks was endless. As soon as one job had been completed, the next one was right on the line without a minute to waste. Even if there were just a few minutes left before a mealtime, they had to be used to accomplish one more job, to clean or polish one more thing.

The German women were very fastidious, methodical and stingy, at least in this region. In every house was the "best room" which might be the equivalent to a parlor in America in the old days. This room was used only for having the traditional Sunday afternoon coffee, for celebrating somebody's birthday, or when visitors came. Everything in there had to be kept at the utmost level of sparkle, and nobody, not even the lady of the house, entered it without taking off her shoes. This was her pride and honor, on show for other people's eyes. Every Saturday, without exception, all the windows of the whole house had to be washed and everything re-polished and re-shined. That was the order of things, and that was how it had to be done—by me of course.

Besides working in the house, I also had to help milk the cows. The farmer and I would put the milk cans and the pails in the back of a high two-wheeled cart pulled by a horse, and drive outside the village to where the cows were grazing in one of the walled sections of the field, called the *"kobels"*. The milking was done right there in the field, by hand, of course, but it was not always so easy to catch the cows. The farmer could handle them better, for they were more used to him, but sometimes it took quite a while to get hold of a naughtier one. That could easily make you mad. There were times when a cow would jump the wall and then you had to go and look for the gate in the adjoining kobel to get her back. That certainly was a pain in the neck, but that was how it was.

Some days, when the farmer was engaged elsewhere, I went milking with Kristine. She had worked for the Carstensen's for some years now and knew the job inside out. She had even gained a certain status in her working career, if one could call it that. It was an interesting order of things here, as I came to understand.

There was this thing called the *"dienst"* which means "service", and a service it was, almost something like being in the army. The tradition was that at the age of fourteen, the young daughters of farmers were sent to another farmer's wife in service. This meant to live there and to be a servant, learning from the bottom up to do all the things she would need to know for her designated future as a good wife to a farmer and a mother of his children. This would continue until they were grown up

and ready to marry. They were not supposed to have any other career, so it was better that they did not have too much schooling, or too much free time either, or they might start getting ideas of their own.

This seemed to me very strange and also cruel, but now I understood better the attitude and the cold looks of the farmer's wife, because I was somebody who had not been in the "dienst", so was not really qualified to pick up her dirt, scrub her floors or polish her furniture. I wondered how her daughter, dainty Anne-Grete would do when her time came to go into the service. At home she did not have to lift a finger even for herself. Her mother and I had to do that. I even had to clean and polish her and her brother's shoes, but that again was a built-in requirement for being a "dienst" person. Perhaps Anne-Grete would be spared. She was quite pretty with her blond braids and the blue eyes which were very similar to her mother's. She was often at my side asking all kinds of questions and wanting to be friends with me. That, however, was not to her mother's liking, who called her away if our conversation lasted more than a couple of minutes. It might slow me down in my work, and that just would not do. Perhaps she also did not want her daughter to associate with me—a servant and a foreigner, at that. It seemed that the old traditions in this northern country were strictly maintained.

The autumn days were becoming shorter, darker and wetter. The gray clouds moved from the sea across the brownish flatlands, layer upon layer, for there was nothing to hinder them. Time and again they turned into rain, coming down and sweeping the ground. This kind of land here up north was called *"Heide"* or *"Heideland"*.

Many of the earthen-walled kobels, which divided the land, were reinforced with two rows of barbed wires on top, so the animals would not jump across. But some of them did anyway and sometimes ended up with torn bellies.

A lot of sheep were raised in this region also, and they managed to get through the barbed wires easier, because they crawled through the space between them. Since these sheep had very thick coats, often big tufts of torn wool were left hanging on the wires. It was beautiful wool with long fibers, and we later learned that women from the village went and picked them off the wires and knitted warm sweaters without even spinning it. They would just keep stretching the wool to a desired thickness and then begin knitting by running some ordinary thread from a spool alongside, which would help to hold it together. I also tried it later on, and what a warm and soft sweater it was! The naturally white sweaters, vests and knee-socks were very popular, and were worn by young as well as old because they had plenty of sheep here, and it was economical, too.

Lately I worked with Kristine more and was glad about that. She was friendly toward me, and I could understand her speech better than the farmer's, although she too sometimes forgot herself, dropping back into the dialect which I could not quite handle yet. Kristine had finished her service some time ago. Now she was preparing her dowry and waiting to be married. Her fiancé, named Thomas, was a smallish, skinny man who was working for another farmer.

Kristine was a fairly large girl, as were many of these northern women. She had clear blue eyes and her face had a clean, fresh complexion, perhaps from being outside so much in the cool moist air. Her bushy, blondish hair was parted in the middle, pulled back from her face smoothly and twisted in a bun at her nape. She had to behave and dress with the appropriate decorum now, since she was waiting to be married. According to the local standards, she was not a young girl anymore, even though she was just past twenty. That meant no fluffy or loose hair! I thought that she really fitted the model of that perfect wife, mother and farmer's wife to be.

Kristine lived on the farm, in the cottage next to the main house and shared it with old *"Oma"*, Mrs. Carstensen's mother, whom she also looked after. Kristine took me in there once for a few minutes to show what she had for her dowry. With pride in her eyes she showed me the things she had made and acquired, and the small rooms looked cozy and spotlessly clean.

I saw here a person who did not need to run around the world to find her happiness and contentment. It was right here in the little house which would be theirs when she and Thomas married. It had all been calmly planned out, and there were no qualms about the future. Her life was simple, but Kristine was happy.

Since she was so knowledgeable about all farm work, I liked working with her and very much appreciated her advice on everything. Our good relationship also helped to lift my spirits somewhat.

This was the season when fewer cows needed milking, so we did not go to the fields with the cart anymore. Now Kristine and I went there on bicycles which were used here a lot in everyday life. We hung the cans and pails on the handlebars and off we went. Our footwear were wooden clogs, worn by just about everybody here, because they were handy and easy to obtain. Other shoes were almost impossible to come by, and you needed special permits to get those, if you could find any at all.

I was not quite used to the clogs because they do not bend, making it especially hard to ride a bicycle. They kept falling off my feet, and made me have to stop again and again. It also did not help that, while riding, the cans swung this way and that, making it harder to keep my balance— but gradually I learned to get used to these things.

Then one day the farmer decided that I could go and milk the eight cows by myself because he needed Kristine for other things. I did not like the prospect of doing it alone, but there was nothing else to do but to obey, so I set out on my way. The sky had been overcast all day, and it looked like it might rain. A strong wind blew, flapping my clothes around me. It was hard to balance the bike, and I had to get off several times. It blew here almost constantly, bringing along the endless gray clouds from the North Sea.

I had a hard time catching the cows this time, because they did not know me as well as Kristine and the farmer. The last one I chased until I was almost in tears. It was the last straw when she jumped the wall into the next section. I had to walk around and look for the gate. It turned out to be secured with a rope, which was tight from the moisture and hard to undo with bare fingers. I was really mad when I finally got the cow out of there and then, in addition, she did not stand still while I was milking her. What a day! It was the hardest one I had had so far. To finish off, it started to rain on my way back, and it was already getting dark when I got to the farm. I was soaking wet, but nobody cared, of course. Right away new orders were given for the next job. Talk about being a slave! My premonitions had been right.

Mother and my brother were not doing too well at the bakery, either. It turned out that the baker expected mother to knead large amounts of dough by hand, which is very heavy work, and she just could not do it. Because of her previous illness of tuberculosis, she had had a very serious operation, which left her with only one working lung and unable to do heavy work. As for Jānīts, he was only twelve years old and needed to go to school.

There were also other things which Mother should not have had to do, considering that she was the wife of a higher officer in the German army. It would be all right to help with the household chores, but she should not be made to clean and polish shoes for the whole family every morning. And whatever traditions these people had, she should not have to carry out their potties in the mornings. Such degradation was unbelievable. Perhaps it was done in the olden times for the barons, but not now, and they were no barons, just ordinary people.

Mother went to the local doctor, who verified her medical status and certified that she was unable to do heavy work and should not have been put in such a position in the first place because of her history with tuberculosis.

That put an end to my family's time in the bakery business, and it was just as well that it did, for we did not have to live in the attic anymore. Jānīts got registered and started to go to the local school. The governing

official of the village found us another place to live. It was in the house of an old German lady who lived there alone. Since it was wartime, the government had the right to confiscate rooms which were not being used. We would pay rent for it, of course, but now we had a large bedroom with proper beds and furniture and a small adjoining living room with a stove. What a blessing, because the days and nights got colder and colder. The old lady was quite nice, though we did not see much of her.

One more thing to get used to was sleeping in a cold bedroom, for the Germans preferred to sleep in the cold, even in wintertime. The feather beds were warm to sleep in, but what if your nose and ears were freezing? Then you had to crawl under the covers, but there was no air, and you got too hot. You were sweating under the covers, but could not put out your arms for fear of catching a cold. That was a tough thing to learn. We also had to be very careful how we used our fuel in the other room, for the coal was allocated in very small amounts. We could heat the room only a short time in the evenings, but it was still better than at the baker's, and we were very thankful for that.

Mother now had to think of a new way to earn a living because my wages were very low. We were supposed to receive part of our Dad's pay, but everything was in a chaotic state, so we did not know what we would get and when. We still had money we had brought with us, but who knew how long we would have to make it last? The value of the German mark was constantly diminishing, but there was not much that you could buy in the stores, anyway. Everything was on coupons or rationed, and the rations were becoming smaller and smaller. In any case, we would need some money.

Now the time had come to put to use the good advice our Ukrainian refugee woman had given Mother, when she had helped her with packing on the last day before our leaving home: "Take your portable sewing machine rather than much food and clothing," she had said. "That will provide bread for you when you'll have none!" and God bless her for those words!

Mother was a very good seamstress, even though she had just learned it by herself. Now she asked the butcher's wife, with whom she had become more acquainted, if she perhaps needed to have some mending or altering done, for new clothes were hard to come by these days. The butcher's wife was delighted. Mother did some work for her and as payment got some meat products "on the side". This seemed to be a very good arrangement, and news about Mother's skills quickly spread all through the village.

She was also very skillful in making old parent's clothes into children's clothing, which was a lifesaver for mothers with growing children. Her fame spread like wildfire after she found an old "ski-hat", made a

pattern from it, and created a new one for Jānīts and his friend. It even had a visor like it should. These types of hats, very much like the ones the soldiers wore, were very popular and also very much needed now that the cold weather was here. Jānīts wore his new hat to school, and now every boy in the village wanted one, because you could not buy them anywhere.

Mother now had her hands full, making them from the materials provided by the customers. She also constructed some slippers from the leftover scraps, and that again was a much needed item for grownups as well as for children. She could now spend her days in other people's warm houses sewing, and that would leave us enough coal for heating our little room in the evenings when we were all at home. As payment, Mother received some of the foodstuffs the farmers produced and that helped us immensely.

Jānīts was settling in his school well, even picking up the local dialect quickly, while playing and running around with his new friends. Sometimes he was out till dark and came in full of the fresh cool air and his cheeks rosy. Mother would urge him to get to his homework then.

My first free Sunday had come! What a blessing! The sun was out after the long row of gray and gloomy days. It was almost unbelievable that the sun was really still there! The morning was so beautiful, and I felt like I had come out of a prison. The first thought that entered my mind was to go to the forest! Trees had always given me joy and a new strength. I guess I felt about forests like other people felt about church. I just had to go there! I knew by now that there was a large shallow valley on the north side of the village and beyond it was a sizable patch of forest. That was where I would go.

I started out that way, but the road soon ended, and there were just kobels and more kobels with the earthen walls and even barbed wire on top of them. The ground sloped down slightly, then farther away, on the other side of the valley, it rose again. The forest did not seem to be that far. It was still morning, so I should be able to make it, I thought.

But the journey turned out to be much harder than I had envisioned. The problem was that I had to cross the countless kobels. I was not even halfway on my journey when my arms and legs were in bloody scratches from climbing the walls and crawling through the barbed wire. I came upon some gates and some opened easily, while others I had to climb over. I began to feel bitter that so many obstacles were in my way.

"Have I not deserved this little bit of happiness?" I asked myself. But in spite of the hardships, I was not ready to give up.

Finally the kobels ended, but to my chagrin, there was another new obstacle in front of me. A small stream! It was not too deep or wide but deep enough not to be waded across. I walked a little in one direction, then in the other, but there was no bridge and nothing that would help me in getting across. No rocks, no planks—nothing. I was looking at the forest, which seemed quite close now, and yet, I could not get to it. Tears rose up in my eyes as I stood there. Why was this joy kept from me? Why was life treating me so badly when so much had been taken away already? There had to be a passage across the stream somewhere, surely?

I walked quite a way alongside the stream and finally found what I had been looking for. The stream was narrower and shallower, and several larger rocks stuck out of the water, so I could finally get across. It was easier to walk on this side, for there were no more kobels, thank God! But the forest was still farther away than it had looked. I gazed at it as I walked, but I did not seem to be getting closer to it. Like a mirage in the desert! But I needed the forest so badly!

Finally I did arrive, and it was wonderful. The branches of golden leaves reached out above and around me in greeting, telling me that I was welcome. I entered it like stepping into a sacred place, even though it was not the forest of my beloved country that I missed so much. These were some kind of beech trees, which did not grow in my homeland, but a peace and deep happiness came into my troubled heart with the first steps I took in the forest. Looking up through the crisscrossing branches of the treetops, I could see the clear, blue sky, which you rarely see in this part of the world. Surely, it was a blessing that I had a day like this.

Walking further on, I saw also some fir trees. Such joy filled my heart.

"I made it... I made it..." was all I could say in my heart. It was like I had met some trusted old friends from home.

Somebody had once said that one did not need much to be happy, and now I knew why. As I looked up again, I saw a white bird high up in the blue sky. It shone and gleamed in the sun and was so beautiful.

"The white bird of peace!" I thought, "God himself is sending me a message!"

But then I saw more and more of the white birds coming. Coming in formations!

"No, they were not birds at all! These were birds carrying death, and this was their path to the large cities of Germany in the south!"

I knew that, and yet my deep happiness did not depart. It was within me, and nothing else mattered. I looked at the planes in the blue sky and could not understand. I asked myself: "How can I be happy at a time like this?" Yet my happiness did not seem to have anything to do with what was happening here. It was like a touch of eternity, an unexpected

comfort from heaven above.

I did not understand this and do not fully understand it even now. It has remained as one of the great mystical moments of my life. I remembered then that I had encountered something like that a few years before when a message reached me from somewhere and I had a notion that perhaps God was talking to me through this message. It was about life and death and choosing between them. I did not understand why this message was sent to me, but I never forgot it. But perhaps it does not need to be understood. It is enough to just know that there can be happiness like that. As I walked on in the forest, all the negative things seemed to fall away from me. There was only this overwhelming sense of happiness and nothing else.

I walked and walked under the golden canopies, with the red and gold leaves thick under my feet and the broken branches lying on the ground this way and that. As I waded through them, I thought how they, too, were broken off their trees the same as I was broken off the tree of my nation. But they accepted what had to be, and I knew that I also had to learn to accept what had to be. I came across an old tree stump, overgrown with green moss, but at its side, a new sprightly shoot had come up. A new, little tree! There would be a new life, a new living! That thought made me so glad. It was a promise.

I don't even remember anymore how I got home. I only know that I felt so enriched by what I had experienced that nothing else mattered— neither the hard journey, or the scratches and bruises. No, it had been worthwhile to make this journey. I had been to my forest and had found what I went for. It was a journey I never forgot.

On my next free Sunday we all went by train to Husum to visit our relatives. Aunt Irma with her family had apparently not stayed at the village they had been taken to, but had gone back the same day. Aunt Irma was not as humble as we had been. She was not going to live in some attic and work on a farm! She had never lived on a farm and that kind of work was alien to her, as well as to Uncle Kārlis, who had worked at a bank. Very simple, "Take me back, I am not staying here!" she had said, and that was that.

The officials in Husum had allocated them a basement room in a dentist's house not far from the station. Actually it was not even a room, but an area extended from the space under the stairs. The five of them were really squeezed together for sleeping, but in the open area under the stairs they could cook and wash, so it would have to do for now. Their room was actually just one large bed on the floor with bundles piled up alongside the walls, but at least they were in town.

We learned that the rest of our relatives had been sent to another

village farther away, but they were all close together there, and the other families they had traveled with were in the vicinity, too.

Apparently more Latvian people had arrived in Husum by now. My cousins Ruta and Edvins said that they went to the Craftsman's Hall (the first stop in town for the refugees) every day to check if there was anybody they knew amongst the new arrivals. More people seemed to be located here in town now. I guess they were wiser than we had been, but who knows?

Since it was fall, the Latvian parents were anxious about getting their children to school. Ruta said that two teenage Latvian girls had already been accepted at the Husum Gymnasium, a name for a high school here, and that she was going to try to get in there, too. Right away my hopes were raised also, but first I would need to get a certificate to release me from the farm work. My Mother was an energetic person and promised to try and get it for me, for I did need to finish my last year of high school. This right away made the future look brighter.

It was the end of October already. The days were dark and dreary. At the farm the cows were kept in the stable now, and we did not have to go out to the kobels anymore. At least that was easier, but now other things were happening. The slaughtering time had started in the village. This again was a special tradition here, when the farmers slaughtered the animals designated to provide meat for the winter and the coming year.

Since there was no refrigeration, other methods had to be used for preserving the meat. A lot of activity went on in all the farmer's kitchens at this time: braising and cooking the meat, then putting it in jars and sterilizing it—or else putting it in cans, which somebody sealed with a special machine. Some of the meat was made into sausages, which the butcher prepared to order. Of course, there was also a lot of washing of jars and utensils, a lot of cleaning up. I was glad when Sunday came, because then the heavy activities stopped and it was quieter, but for me it was still a working day.

This time, however, my boss was at a loss about what she could have me do. The breakfast was finished; the dishes had been washed and put away. There was a Sunday feeling around the house. Then, what a bright idea! She took a small knife out of the drawer and led me outside the kitchen door into the cobblestoned backyard that took up the space between the L-shaped house and the stable.

The morning outside was cold and foggy. The shrubs, around the house looked droopy and shriveled up. Everything was dying. I wondered what it was she wanted me to do. Then she pointed to the clumps

of grass that had come up between the stones and gave me the knife. So that was the job—to pluck and scrape out this grass! Satisfied that she had found a job for me, she went back into the house and closed the door, but I gave a sigh, stooped down and started working.

The church bells began to ring, somber and slow. The church was just up the road from here. Since the farm was on the corner of the main road and the side street, the people, passing by on their way to church, gave me curious looks, perhaps wondering what on earth I was doing there, stooped down in the middle of the yard on a Sunday morning. As I worked, a fine mist started to come down and soon turned into thick, steady rain. I thought that perhaps somebody would come and call me in, but nobody did. Most likely they had forgotten all about me. It was a sad situation. My hands were red and getting numb from the cold and the handling of the muddy grass. The rain began to soak through my clothing. I did not have any rainwear. I really felt like a Cinderella, and my head sank down lower and lower over the gray stones. Indeed, they were better friends to me than these people, I thought. The raindrops rolled through my hair and down my face, falling into the small ditches between the stones where the grass had been.

Aunt Irma once said that you could bury a lot in one small grave. Yes, you could. Even in a small ditch between the stones.

In the evening, when I got home, I was still shivering from cold, and Mother made me some hot tea, but next morning I woke with my head aching and my body burning with fever. There was no way I could go to work. Mother went over to tell the farmers of my sickness, and a whole week passed until I recovered from this episode. But in the meantime something good happened. A letter came, stating that I was given permission to go to school, if I wanted to!

If I wanted to? Oh, how I wanted to! I was so glad that I would not have to go to the farmer's anymore. Mother went over to the Carstensen's to tell them the news and to get my wages and ration cards. It turned out that my wages were a mere pittance, which the farmer's wife admitted, but not without adding that, "...of course, she could not do what the other "dienst" girls would have done!" That did hurt. How much more could one have done? I did not even want to think about it, and was overjoyed that I did not have to see them anymore.

"Your remaining rations, left over for the month, were also weighed out to a gram!" Mother said.

That was really something! They still had plenty of all kinds of foodstuffs, but I suppose that was what the big farmers in Germany had to do to retain their wealth. And so ended my career of being a "dienst girl "at the Carstensen's!

The winter was approaching, and a new problem came up. Our bedroom was cold and damp without any kind of heating, and the feather beds were now moist inside and out, for there was no way to air and dry them. It was dangerous, for Mother's health especially, to be in this kind of a climate, so she went to see the village official again. He was understanding and found us another place, this time in a carpenter's house. The carpenter was away at war at the present, but his wife was quite pleasant.

She had two rooms in the back of the house adjoining the carpenter's shop that were not in use. A separate entrance led from the back yard into the first, larger room that was actually a washroom with a cement floor, containing a stove and a big built-in pot for heating the water. At the back of it was a small, narrow room where, perhaps, some helper had previously lived. The carpenter's wife opened the door so we could look in there. A small, pillar-shaped iron stove was in the corner on the left, behind the door. A little farther, a single bed stood by the left wall, leaving a space just big enough to turn around between the stove and the foot of the bed. At the other end of it was a small dresser, and at the end wall stood a wardrobe and a small table in the far corner by the window. A skinny, old-fashioned sofa stood opposite the bed at the right-hand wall. Two chairs by the table completed the decor of this room, and it would have been all right for one, but there were three of us! We would really have to squeeze together, for this would have to be both our bedroom and our living room for the winter—but at least we would be warmer here. It would have been good, if we could also have heated the other room, for there was another old sofa as well as a large dining table with some chairs in there, but our fuel ration would not reach that far. It would be nice in the summer, though, and we decided to stay.

As we explored the place, we found that another door from the larger room led into the carpenter's shop, and farther beyond it was a passage with some stalls where animals may have been kept at some time. But now we would be keeping our coal there. It did not take us long to get situated since we did not have much. Mother would sleep in the bed, and I took the little sofa, even though it was too short for me to stretch out on. Between these two, the gap was just wide enough to squeeze in three chairs, one next to the other, where Jānīts would have to sleep. The room was small. You could not put one more thing in it, but what we did not need immediately we could store in the other room. And we would have to dismantle Jānīt's bed every morning to be able to move around.

In a way it was good that the room and also the stove were so small, because we could keep a low fire going even through the night by burning only a couple of coal briquettes. A small ring on top of the stove allowed us to do the cooking there, which was sufficient for our mea-

ger diet. Mother continued to do sewing for the farmer's wives in their homes, or sometimes at home at our small table. We finally felt settled.

Mother had gone to Husum and arranged about my schooling as well as rented me a room, for it would be difficult to make the journey by train every day. Now I was a final year student at the famous *Theodor Storm Gymnasium*. My German was good, thanks to our Miss Roller at our high school in Latvia, whose intensive teaching methods we had so resisted at first—but they had worked and served me well now.

The girls in my class, most of them blond and blue-eyed, were nice and quite forthcoming with friendliness. I could follow all subjects well, except it was harder with trigonometry. Our previous school year had been cut short, and now I was starting late. It was already November. Nobody was forcing me; I did what I could. They probably thought that this might be only a temporary situation, which it was, since none of us knew what the future would be. At least I had a chance to learn something and be in a different environment.

Now I had to get used to the new regime. As the teacher came into the classroom, we all had to rise to our feet, which we had done in the Latvian schools, too, but now we also had to raise the right arm and say, *"Heil Hitler!"*, to which the teacher replied, *"Heil Hitler!"*, and then we could be seated. Whatever I, or anybody else, felt about this did not come into it. This was the way it had to be, if one did not want to cause complications, which would certainly have serious consequences. Large posters were on the walls everywhere, showing a shadowy figure with a finger on the lips and a text that said, "Pst! The enemy is listening in!" It reminded me of the Russian Communist regime, which we had tasted for one year in Latvia. They did not fear so much that someone would listen in; it was rather that they themselves wanted to listen in to wherever they hoped to find their enemies. Anybody could be "It"—the same as now! Nobody wanted to be caught and labeled an enemy.

Quite often the classes were interrupted by the air-raid alarms. All the bells in the school would ring then, and we had to run downstairs to the shelters. By now there were five of us Latvian girls here at the school, and two of them were quite mischievous.

"Why go into the shelter?" they said. "Let's rather go to the park!" The large Castle Park was right next to the school, so why not? And off we ran into the park, where stately trees grew around the large patch of grass. Who would see us, or do anything to us here? Being in a crowd, our youthful exuberance was flowing over and making us reckless.

It was a sunny day for a change, with the first crispness of winter in the air, and on such days the air-raids could most likely be expected. Then we saw them. Like white birds in formations they appeared above

the tree tops. The air buzzed from the sound of the many engines. We knew what they were, but it was all so exciting! The planes looked beautiful, shining in the sun, and we even walked out on to the grass to view them better, when suddenly we were yanked back under the trees. Some recuperating German soldiers from the nearby military hospital had been walking in the park and had seen us doing this.

"Are you crazy, girls?" they shouted. "What are you doing? Is there not enough suffering yet?" they admonished us, showing their injured arms and legs, wrapped in white plaster and bandages.

Yes indeed, we knew that and had to admit that it had been a silly thing to do. Mostly these planes were on their way to the large towns of Germany: Hamburg, Bremen, Hanover and even farther down south, but bombs had fallen in the vicinity of Husum also for some reason or another. I guess we had not experienced them ourselves and did not have a real fear of them yet.

For better understanding, perhaps I should explain here that we young people just knew two main facts at the time: that the Russians had been very bad to our nation, and that the Germans had saved us from them. We did not know then about the bad things the Germans had done, or what their future plans were, (except we knew about the *Gestapo*, and that the Allies were trying to bring down Hitler and his establishment). We just wanted the war to end, and then all the problems would be solved. Understandably, it was very naive thinking.

For my school days, Mother had rented me a room in the outskirts of Husum. It was in a house belonging to a widow, who took in students to supplement her income. I was supposed to have a room of my own, but when I arrived there, another girl was living in it already. She was a German girl named Elke.

"You don't mind, do you?" The landlady Frau Shutz asked me concerning Elke's presence as she introduced us. Her tone implied already that there could be no argument about this, so she did not even wait for an answer while I just stood there looking at her. Frau Shutz could be in her sixties, I thought, and with her darker skin, she looked more like a southerner. She appeared very neat in her black dress, with her black hair smoothly pulled back and rolled into a bun, the way most women wore their hair here. But with her dark eyes and long pointed nose, she reminded me of a bird, perhaps a crow, for she too walked with her upper body and head stretched forward.

Apparently Elke was the daughter of an acquaintance, whom Frau Shutz had taken in while the girl went to school. Elke seemed to be nice, so I did not voice any objections. As we got acquainted we got on well, and she was good company to me at this time, when I was still so much

out of everything. Being younger, (I think she was fourteen or fifteen), she was as simple and natural as a child, which gave me a sense of normalcy that I had not felt for a long time.

The small, two-story house where I now lived was very neat and clean. Our quarters were upstairs in one of the bedrooms. The room was rather small, but comfortable enough, and I did not really need much. The frilly curtains at the window and the nice wallpaper and bedcovers made the room feel cozy and warm. Frau Shutz tried to be kind, but I noticed from the start that she had a very irritating habit. Each time she did something for you, she would add a self-gratifying comment.

*"Das war doch so lieb von mir, nie?"* Which means: "That was so good of me, was it not?", or "so kind, or loving, or nice of me", ending with the long stretched out word *"Nie?"*, which sent shivers through my spine and meant "is that not so?" Then the answer had to be, *"Naturlich, Frau Shutz! Danke sehr, Frau Shutz!!"* (Of course! Thank you very much!) Even though you had thanked her already in the first place! It made her kindness seem insincere and selfish. I wondered how she could ask that? I hated this kind of putting oneself forward, but I suppose she had a need for this kind of an acknowledgment.

But Elke was all right and our relationship even began to turn into a nice little friendship. Since every evening the electricity in our town was switched off for a certain period of time to save energy, we used a lot of that time talking to each other. Sometimes the blackout lasted an hour or more. The windows had to be specially blinded, so the room was in complete darkness. During those times Elke told me of her family, and I told her about mine, but most of all we liked to sing. Elke was teaching me German songs, and there was one I liked especially, but it was a sad song which made me want to cry. Maybe it would have been good for me to cry, because there was still so much sadness in me from losing my home and country. This song talked about someone dying and asking the other person not to cry, but just to remember... I still know that song.

We would sing until the light came on again and then got back to our school work. This continued for a little while, but then something happened that changed everything again. I had an accident falling from the parallel bars, at the gym class at school, and my knee got hurt badly. I had always loved gymnastics and went into it with enthusiasm, but I suppose, my young wrists had been weakened by the heavy work that I had done on our farm during the last summer. As I swung my body back and forth, I felt that my wrists lacked the strength and stability I had had before. A warning thought ran through my mind, a sudden doubt, and I did not manage to make the final swing back high enough to make a clear jump. My left knee got caught on the one end of the bar and I came down

heavily on my right knee. It hurt very badly and I felt crushed physically and mentally.

I was rushed to the hospital and x-rayed, but nothing seemed to be broken, so I was sent home even though something felt terribly wrong inside the knee; I could not walk. It was very swollen, hot and pulsating with pain, but no other care was suggested—just rest. I felt terrible about the whole thing, but after trying to recuperate for a week in Husum, I had to admit: it was clear that I would not be able to return to school any time soon. It was not worth burdening Frau Schutz, so I was taken home to Viol. I was very sorry to leave school, which had started so well, but there was nothing I could do but to stay off my feet and hope that it would heal soon, so I could go back to Husum and school.

It was already December. The days were dark and depressing. Back at the village, the large trees surrounding the houses stood bare, black and lonely, swaying in the wind back and forth, back and forth. I lay on the small sofa with my leg elevated and watched them through our window. That was all I could see. The days now seemed so long, since I spent most of them alone, and the harsh North Sea winds kept blowing all day and all night. I thought of Theodor Storm, and how he had loved this place, his beloved Heideland, because this was where he had lived and loved, and that gave him a totally different view of it.

Not being able to walk or do anything, I started to read his works and felt the deep love he had had for this land. It was the unique love of your homeland, which some Latvian poets, too, had depicted so beautifully in their writings, during periods of exile in previous times. Each blade of grass, each little stone, was so precious because they lay on the path to the place where those poets once had lived. I understood it so well, and it made me miss my homeland even more.

I thought back to the time when we left our home and our country, and my heart still ached for it terribly, but there had been no other way. We had to leave. Now the Russians were in our land and in our homes. But one day the war would be over, and then we would go home. There must come a day when there will be order in the world again, and then all this will be like a nightmare, which we will be able to put behind us. That was what I tried to hold on to during those sad and painful days.

I thought a lot about Dad these days. Dear, dear Dad, where was he now? His letters came very irregularly and some later ones came before the first ones, but he had written one to me personally, and that meant a lot to me. He wrote that they were going to move, and then again they didn't, so we never knew where he was and if our letters reached him.

"The weather is terrible here and there is no winter clothing..." he wrote, so we worried how he was coping. I had to think about that during my long, lonesome hours while lying on my sofa and nursing my leg. Mother went to the farmer's in the mornings to do the sewing; Jānīts left for school. They put a couple of briquettes in the little stove and left a few more on the side so I would not freeze and could make some hot tea at lunchtime, but it still got cold. I wrapped my feet in a shawl and put my winter coat on top, yet my feet were always cold, while the knee felt hot and pulsated with pain. It swelled up if I walked just a little bit. I had to stay quiet so that maybe one day it would be better.

To pass the time and have something to do, I started to write. I had to put somewhere all that was happening inside of me. All that sadness and pain! I had to find a place for it. A letter came from Aunt Elzī. She said that little Ilze and Vit, both four years old now, loved to hear stories, but there were no Latvian story books to read, so she had to make the stories up. Then I thought, perhaps I too could write a story for them? And so I began:

"Once upon a time there lived a little girl called Māra....."

I wrote it as a children's story, but it turned into my own story. There was the joy of living at the father's house and then the pain, the low down pain of being chased out of that house. And afterward there was the loneliness of being in the strange land, and the degradations while living there. Then there was the finding of comfort through memories; a new strength and hope budding again. Finally—the realization of the dream, returning to the father's house, having grown tall and beautiful in wisdom of heart. I believed that was how it would really be.

One of Mother's clients, who had heard of my misfortune, had given her a small box of watercolors for me that one of her grown up children had left behind. It was a great joy to me. I had always loved to draw, especially people and faces, and my teachers at high school had been very encouraging. They had said that I should definitely pursue art as a career. But Dad had said, "My dear, that's a beggars' bread! Choose a proper career to earn your living and then you can draw or paint all you want in your spare time." He was right, of course.

Aunt Elzī had gone through the Academy of Art and had enjoyed it immensely, but then nothing more came of it. I had decided to obey Dad, but then the war came, and all the dreams and plans were crushed anyway.

Since Christmas was nearing, I decided to make a present for Mother. Out of some thick paper I constructed a large envelope, like a purse, in which she could keep Dad's letters. As it was, there was nothing I could buy for her. I sewed the edges with colored thread and added colored cords for a tie. I also painted a nice big rose on the cover, hoping she

would like it. We waited for Dad, for he had said that he would try to get a few days off and come to visit us, but he still had not come. Perhaps he would come for Christmas.

The dark winter days were here. It was freezing outside. Then came the snow, and the children, of course, loved it. Jānīts and his friends were out until dark having fun. He came in with his fingers red and stiff from the cold. He actually did not have any proper winter clothing. At the age of twelve, he had outgrown everything, but that did not worry him. He was running around in his grey wool school uniform from Latvia. The sleeves and pants were getting too short, but he was happy enough. He had a lot of friends, and by now he was talking away in German, even using the dialect the same way as they did.

Sometimes he got home late when it was already dark, and then Mother would scold him. Since she worked, they did not see much of each other, and now it happened that each time they did meet, she scolded him. So he started to stay out even later. Mother felt bad about reprimanding him, and yet the burden of responsibility was on her shoulders, since Dad was not here to guide him. But Jānīts said to me, "What does it matter when I come in? I get scolded anyway!" True enough, I had to admit. A good thing was that his grades at school were good. Lately, however, he had adopted an irritating habit of hugging and kissing me when he came inside in the evenings. He just would not leave me alone! I could not understand it and fought him off. We did not do that in our family! But later I thought, perhaps the boy did need some loving from someone, for he had not had much of it during his childhood years. There had been Mama's illness when he was just five years old, and then came all the other changes within our family life: moving to live on a farm and then the war. And now Mother had enough on her shoulders. Her loving was more material than emotional, but it had to do for now.

Here in Viol, we also had the blackout times in the evenings to save energy. Since nothing else could be done in the dark, we would sing. One of us would begin, and the others would soon join in. We knew a whole lot of songs, which we could sing in harmony. My friend Edīte and I had learned them at school in the choir, and when she and her sister came to our farm during the summer vacation, we often sang together while working. In time, Mother and Jānīts learned them, too. Singing our songs now took us back to those beautiful summer days in our own country and helped to lift our spirits, even as we sat in our small dark room in this foreign land.

We did not always feel like singing, but it was easier to do it in the dark because then we could pretend, at least for a short while, that the bad things did not exist—that it was summer and we were at home.

With the return of light came the awakening, of course—the returning to reality—the war, the winter, and us in a strange land with an unknown future. No Dad, no Ilgvar... but life had to go on. Mother made supper, frying potatoes with onions on our little stove and pouring hot tea into our mugs. The evening had passed. We fixed Jānīts' bed. It was time to sleep.

I did not sleep well those nights. My leg still hurt quite badly, and the short sofa was not very comfortable. We had no medications, no pain pills. While awake, I sometimes heard Mother give a heavy sigh in her sleep, but perhaps she was not sleeping, either. She carried a heavy burden on her heart, having her husband and son in danger, and being the only provider for the three of us. But she did not complain or talk about it. Perhaps we were both awake. Only Jānīts slept a healthy child's sleep on his hard chairs.

Christmas was almost here. On the day of Christmas Eve, I hobbled around trying to spruce up our little room to make it more festive. Jānīts had found a small fir tree in a grove not far away from the village and had brought it home. We fastened it inside a jar and put it on our small table by the window. I made a few decorations out of paper and colored threads. The butcher's wife, who had been friendly with Mother, had given her five small candles with candle holders to put on our tree. That was very kind of her, because candles were very necessary. In Europe it was a tradition to put candles on the tree and light them on Christmas Eve. Christmas would not be Christmas without them, and there were no candles at the village store.

The tree was ready. Mother came home earlier that night and brought a few goodies with her, which had been given to her. We waited for Dad, hoping that he might still arrive on the last train, but he did not come. With heavy hearts, we sat down to celebrate our Christmas Eve. It was the hour of darkness again, but this evening we had the small candles giving us their gentle light. At times they flickered, filling the small room with the scent of melting wax, the smell of Christmas. We sat in silence for a while, each with our own emotions inside of us. It was not something you could talk about. This was our first Christmas in exile. But Christ was born this night, and the heavenly host was with him. We needed light, and the Light came to us. We knew that God would take care of us, whatever the future might bring. Mother began to sing "Silent Night", our most beloved Christmas song, and Jānīts and I joined her in harmony, our voices rising with an inner assurance as we sang along. The wonderful words wrapped us in their warmth, and everything was right and good again, for "...Christ the Savior is born, Christ the Savior is born!"

Christmas day dawned sunny, but cold. The snow on the road out-

side had frozen in lumps and grooves. Mother had gotten a wooden walking cane for me from somebody, so I ventured outside for the first time since my accident. In the afternoon Jānīts and I took a walk to the station. Perhaps it was too far for my first walk, for the station was quite a way out of the village, but it felt so good to be out in the fresh air. We still hoped that Dad might come, but only strangers stepped out of the train, and with heavy hearts we walked back.

My leg throbbed and hurt like crazy by the time we got home, but we went to the station several times more in the coming days, hoping that Dad would come, but he didn't. What had happened? We had not received any letters these past two weeks, either. Had he become ill, living in those terrible conditions?

Jānīts and I had finally given up going to the station to look for Dad, when suddenly on the day of New Year's Eve, around noon, he was here! I was reading in the back room when I heard the outside door close and then voices in the other room. I opened the door, and there he was, standing inside the door in his uniform, still full of the winter cold. What a wonderful surprise after we had given up all hope to see him! Hobbling, I ran to him and hugged and hugged him so hard.

"Dear, dear Dad, you came! I am so glad!" We were all overjoyed.

Now there was so much to talk about, as one can imagine.

"Where? What? And how?" back and forth, for how much can you say in letters? And some of those letters had not even been received. We listened to Dad's stories about the front and his living there, about his soldiers bringing him a piglet for Christmas, so they could all eat and celebrate. But most of all we looked at his dear face and rejoiced in him being with us.

"I am afraid that I can only spend this one night with you," he then said sadly, "I will have to leave in the morning." That was bad news, but then he explained: "I was only able to get a three day pass, and it is a long way back to my base. The train services are irregular too, and I must be sure to get back in time. I had asked for a leave at Christmas, but nobody was given one. Then after Christmas, I received the letter with news about Zigi's accident and obtained a leave on account of that." We so wished he could have stayed longer, but were grateful that we got to see him at all.

Dad was very concerned about my oldest brother, Ilgvar. He had tried to inquire about him through various channels, but there was nothing since that tragic day when the Russians cut off Ilgvar's unit at *Jelgava* six months ago. Where was he? And was he still alive or not? But while there was no news, we could at least hope that he was alive.

"There have been rumors lately that perhaps the older officers would be discharged and allowed to get back to their families because of the lack of supplies," Dad told us on a more cheerful note. "There is no ar-

mament, so it is impossible to do any kind of a serious training with the young recruits." He paused, but then continued in a low voice, "The men are digging trenches instead, in the rain and mud and now even in the snow and cold. The situation is very bad, because they do not have any winter clothing. They are stationed at several places in the vicinity of *Torn*. Some live in tents and have to sleep on bare ground without coats or blankets at zero temperatures. They get sick but there is no transportation to get them to a hospital or any other such place. Also the food supply is bad and erratic, because nothing is cooked on the spot but it is all brought in. The Germans do not care.

And can you imagine this? People live in tents in a forest in this cold weather, but the Germans forbid them to cut any trees! Not even to pick up and use dead branches from the ground!"

The war was drawing to an end. Everybody knew that but did not dare to say it. The fighting went on. How much longer? How many more lives needed to be sacrificed? It was not even our war, but it was not possible to get out of it, either. Hitler was still saying, "The victory is ours! It will be ours!"

Victory or not, we were so glad to hear that maybe Dad would be able to return to us soon.

The hours moved on. Eight, nine, ten... We sat on the edges of our beds in a close little circle talking. When the midnight hour neared, Dad handed Mother a bottle of wine to warm up for our New Year's toast. We drank it and kissed and hugged each other, wishing happiness. The year 1945 had arrived, and we hoped that, perhaps, it would bring peace to the world and something better for us, too. We visited till well after midnight, but then Jānīts was getting sleepy, and we decided that it was time to go to bed, for Dad had another long journey ahead of him the next day.

Morning came, and Dad would soon have to leave. Mother packed some food and clothing for him–whatever he might be able to use from what we had. Then we all walked to the station. Mother was going to go with Dad as far as Husum, so they would have a little more time together. Jānīts and I stayed on the platform waving as the train moved out, hoping that we would soon see Dad again. We did not know then that we would never ever see him again. Years later I thought, if it had not been for my accident, perhaps we would not have seen him at all.

It was the winter of 1945. Soon after the New Year, quite a few refugee wagons drove into our village; they were all from the eastern regions of Europe. They had left their homes when the Russians were approaching, for they had heard enough about what happened to those who stayed. The homes were robbed and vandalized by the Russian soldiers, women and girls raped, men degraded and even shot just because

it was fun to see others suffer. They had seemed to delight in smashing everything in sight. Wherever they went, they left devastation behind them as if saying, "If I can't have it, you must not have it either!" And it was done with a special pleasure.

More new inhabitants arrived at our house after the beginning of the year also. They too were refugees from one of the eastern regions. The family consisted of a tall skinny woman and her four children. Judging by their clothing, they seemed to be country folk. They had been given rooms in the attic, which we did not even know about. A staircase led up there through a door next to our entrance. These people were friendly toward us and often stopped to chat, especially with Mother.

"My husband also is in the war, but I do not know where he is and have not had any news from him for a long time," the woman said.

Many women in Germany were in that situation now. Since things were not going well at the front, and the armies were withdrawing so quickly, it was harder for the mail to find them. From what we heard, not all who were in the army wanted to fight for Hitler, but when the orders came, they had to go.

There were refugee wagons now sometimes standing on the main street for several days in the cold winter weather, until they could be placed somewhere. Rooms were not so easy to find because these hard northerners were very reluctant to let anybody in their homes, even though they had rooms standing empty, and even though the refugees were their own people, not foreigners, like we were. Their cherished "best rooms" were, of course, guarded especially and you could not blame them too much for that. Although they were used just for family celebrations, it was an old established tradition in this place.

We knew all about such celebrations by now. A lot of baking was done in preparation, and the tins and pans with prepared baking items were taken to the bakery for baking as was the custom. The relatives came from the neighboring villages on Sunday afternoons, riding in their high carriages, the men dressed in dark suits, the women big and heavy with hats on their heads and big shawls around their shoulders. The children were dressed in their white pullovers and cardigans and the white knee-socks knitted from the wool of their own sheep.

As we lived here longer, we too picked up some of the local habits which seemed good and worthwhile. The German women were great knitters, and I learned to like it also. They knitted mostly in white only. They did not use any dyes since they were hard to come by, but the white sweaters, done in their many intricate stitches, were beautiful. Since I still could not do too much walking, it was a great pastime for me. We also learned to do the baking the way that they did. It was a custom to bake something every weekend for Sunday. That was a must, and people thought up the

most unbelievable recipes from whatever they had in the house. Would anybody have thought of baking a potato cake or rice pastries? But we did.

The overall understanding was that everybody was short of everything, for nothing could be bought without coupons, but on Saturdays, everybody had found something and baked anyway, taking their pans to the bakery. We followed the pattern and did it too. We had found that you could get skim milk at the local dairy for free and without coupons. The Germans did not seem to have much use for it, but we brought home a full bucket, let it go sour, and then made curd out of it by heating the sour milk slowly, then adding some fresh milk until the curd would draw together and become solid. Then we would just pour it into a cheese-cloth and let it drain. You could eat it with bread, or make pancakes, or bake as scones, or buns or breads. In times like these, people learned to make do with whatever they could find.

Our biggest problem now in wintertime was how to keep warm, for the fuel was in short supply, but the weather outside was getting colder and colder. Sometimes Jānīts brought home some piece of fallen wood that he had found in the nearby patch of trees, but trees in this area were scarce. Our coal was kept in the area of the stables at the other end of the house. We had to go through a long, dark passage, and I was scared to go there in the evenings because sometimes there were rats sitting on the posts, big like cats, their eyes gleaming in the dark. It was so horrible that I ran back without the coal. Jānīts teased me about me being scared, but he did not like to go there much, either.

Gradually time moved toward spring in this year of 1945, our first one in this country, but the war was still raging on between the Germans and the Allies and moving ever closer to us. Nevertheless, as the snow melted, the earth dried and new shoots of grass sprouted everywhere, a new hope rose in us too for brighter days ahead.

"How about going to Husum to visit Aunt Irma and her family," Jānīts said one sunny Sunday morning "We have not seen them for quite a while!"

We thought that was a good idea and got underway. We found them still living in the basement of the dentist's house, but they had made it as comfortable as they could. It was good to see them and visit with them, but since there was only one train going back to Viol in the afternoon, we did not have too much time to spend with them.

As we boarded the train again after our short but pleasant visit, quite a few German soldiers got on also. I sat at the window enjoying my ride and looking out at the passing fields and up at the clear, blue sky. After a while I noticed a white bird flying high up there.

"How high that seagull is flying!" I thought to myself, always loving

to watch the nature around me. "How beautiful!"

But the next moment, before I could even grasp what was happening, I was yanked off my seat and thrown to the floor.

*"Tieffliegers! Tieffliegers!* (Strafers). Get down to the floor!" screamed the soldiers. All hell seemed to suddenly break loose. People shoved and shouted and fell to the floor, the soldiers falling over them. The train shook, rumbled on for a little, then gave a big shudder and stopped.

"What happened? What happened?" people shouted, questioning each other, while getting on their feet and trying to look through the windows. "Keep back!" The soldiers shouted and blocked their way until some of the soldiers cautiously alighted and surveyed the surroundings, making sure that there was no danger. Then the others got off the train also. The engine still puffed, and a thin stream of smoke still came from the smokestack. As we could see now, our train was bullet-ridden from one end to the other, going at the level of the windows, and the engine was covered with holes. It was quite amazing that nobody was hurt or even wounded, thanks to the soldiers who knew what to do.

It appeared that the train's engine was totally disabled. We sat in the grass on the embankment, not knowing what to do and waited. What would happen now? How would we get home? People talked excitedly, discussing the situation. Some had been through this already at some other place and related their stories. After quite a long time another engine came and rescued us, but the experience had shaken us quite a bit. It was so good to be back at our village again. After this the train service between Husum and Viol was closed for civilians altogether.

However bad this had been for us, it really was nothing compared to the much more devastating circumstances of other refugees, who had to flee west from the eastern regions again and again while the Russians advanced, shooting at the fleeing people on the open roads. People living in the big cities suffered from the burning and falling buildings, or died in the fire when the Allied bombs were dropped on them. We later heard that whole streets had been wiped off the face of the earth. No, we should not complain at all.

We wished very much for better days to come, but they did not happen. Rather the opposite was true. The war was coming ever closer, making itself felt even in this rather remote place. Every evening as I prepared for bed, fear mounted in my heart, for I knew that soon I would hear the droning sounds of the many engines in the sky as the planes would come from England, formation after formation, flying over us with their loads of bombs to drop on the big cities somewhere down south. We had already seen the ruins of Hamburg. It seemed that

no more damage could be done there, for hardly a house was standing in that huge city, but there were more cities farther south.

The planes usually started to come around ten o'clock at night. More and more of them came, leaving behind the horrible feeling that soon many innocent people would die. Sometimes the bombs now fell in our vicinity also, perhaps by design, or perhaps when anti-aircraft artillery provoked them. We were glad, though, that we did not live in any large city, or it would be much worse.

Letters from Dad had been erratic, since he had moved several times, but the last news was that he was in northern Germany at the command post in Stettin now. There still was no news of my brother Ilgvar, whose unit was cut off last July when the Russians suddenly broke through the front line in the southern part of Latvia. We worried about both of them; the times were so chaotic. Hopefully the war would soon be over, and then they would be with us again.

Things, however, changed for the worse, and more bombs were dropped on our area too. Perhaps it was because more army units were situated here now. It was even scarier, because the raids mostly happened at night. The whole house shook from the blasts; the doors and windows rattled and sprang open. It was as if everything would fall on our heads the next moment and bury us. I sat up in bed trembling and listening to the escalating noise which made me want to scream and to run outside into the fields! To flee, to hide somewhere, anywhere! I wrapped a blanket around myself, ready to do that, but Jānīts just lifted his head and said quite unconcerned, "What are you fussing about? They are not going to bomb us!" and turned over and went back to sleep. The healthy sleep of a child!

I lay back down on my pillow again and thought about the soldiers in the field who had this going on around them all the time. How did they deal with it and survive? And many did not survive, of course, but panicking would not help, either. We just had to trust that God would see us through this.

Many army units were withdrawing now from the north and walked right by us. Most likely they were coming from Denmark, for the large *Flensburg-Hamburg* highway was only a small distance outside our village. One day a whole unit of soldiers turned into our village for a few days rest and was given permission to settle in our backyard, on the large grassy patch at the back of our house. They had their own kitchen with them and also some artillery. All this was very disconcerting, even though the soldiers tried to reassure us. They said that nothing bad was happening, but the tension amongst people was growing. What was happening? Was Germany finished? Nobody knew.

Another night, a strange noise again roused us from our beds. As we ran outside, we saw what looked like a small lighted Christmas tree up in the sky, which was the enemy's way of illuminating the whole village from above. We saw planes circling around the church spire, and red sparks flew in the air as they shot at one another, while everything was as light as daytime. It was a frightening sight. Could they also see that our backyard was full of war machinery? Would they be shooting at us also? That was even scarier, although the soldiers tried to pass it off as nothing. The war was literally in our backyard now, and nobody had any concrete answers to any of our questions.

The main thing we wished for was that the war would end and no more people would get killed. And when there would be peace and order in the world again, we would go home and live in our land together with our loved ones. This was the thought we held on to.

Spring was well on its way now. The trees burst out in new leaves, the first blossoms bloomed, but there was a sadness in me that was hard to conquer. All this made me think even more vividly about the last spring when we were still at home. My leg was finally getting better. I could manage to walk pretty well without the cane, but I could not get to school anymore, for there were no trains, and I would have missed too much, anyway. I wandered around the fields outside the village and watched the new growth, but it all evoked memories, which tore at my heart. Upon returning home, I started to write to unburden myself, and some poems emerged. The words flowed without thinking. The writing helped, because my feelings needed to be channeled somewhere.

Although I was only eighteen years old, I thought a lot about life, our living and the meaning of it. A book I had borrowed from the library and was reading also dealt with these problems, and it affected me deeply. It was written by a Norwegian writer, *T. Gulbransen*. There were sayings in it I still remember today, but the one which has haunted me almost all my life, was: "…the only sure thing we know is that we shall die." It sounded so unbearably sad that all our living was just dying? I had to think of that often.

Then suddenly one day, the war was over! It was May 8, 1945. In the beginning it was almost unbelievable, because in our vicinity nothing particular happened. But Germany had capitulated. Hitler was dead. There would be no more fighting! Yet the communists were still in our country! They were still in our land and in all of Eastern Europe! There had been a rumor that perhaps the Allies will now go against the Russians and chase them back to their boundaries, but it did not happen. Nobody wanted to subject themselves to more fighting and more danger.

That was understandable, but why were the Russians allowed to stay there, when other nations went back to their previous borders?

Did they not know, or did they not want to know that the Communists were even more evil than the Nazis? That they had already committed millions and millions of people to the slave camps in the arctic regions of Russia, where many of them were dying all the time? Did they not consider that all of Eastern Europe would now be subjected to bear the burdens of the repressive Soviet regime, and many more millions of people would be imprisoned, deported and killed? Perhaps there would not have been the Cold War and the atomic weapons race afterward, if the Russians had been made to withdraw within their own boundaries like everybody else? But that was the way it was, and we did not even know at the time that a deal had already been made in Yalta in February 1945 by Roosevelt, Churchill and Stalin, behind our backs. Being ignorant, we still believed that something would change.

The German soldiers started to come home from wherever they had been, happy that they would be back with their loved ones and able to live normal lives. Germany was totally destroyed, but at least they were alive! They would work and build it up again.

Streams and streams of soldiers now came out of Denmark along the highway from Flensburg, the city on the Danish border. Amongst them were some wounded, still wearing bandages, but their faces were happy. They were going home! The war was over! It looked like they were not even sorry that they had lost. The main thing was that they did not have to fight anymore. In truth, many had known for some time that this was the only way this war could end, but while Hitler and his cronies were still sending out their propaganda about their imminent victory, nobody dared to say anything to the contrary for fear of falling into the hands of the Gestapo. Now nobody would have to fear them anymore. It would be a new life!

Since the Flensburg highway was not far from our village, my brother Jānīts went there every day and sat at the roadside watching if he could spot any soldiers with the small badge of the Latvian red-white-red colors on their sleeve. If he did, he went out to greet them, inviting them to our place for a meal and some rest, if they wanted to. We did not have much, but we were willing to share with them what we had. Who knows, maybe somebody would give something to our Dad if he was in need? We had not had any news from him lately, but thought that it was only a matter of time till he would be with us.

One day Jānīts brought home a very nice, dark-haired young soldier called Valdemārs, who stayed with us for a few days to rest.

"I am so glad to find someone I can talk to in Latvian," he said.

"Somehow I ended up in a German unit and have not heard any Latvian spoken for a long time."

We talked, and he taught us a beautiful song about a brown-eyed girl, far away back home. Perhaps he had one back there waiting for him? It was a sad song. As we said good-bye, I hoped that he would find her. I still have this song in his handwriting. God speed, Valdemār! But it was not only Valdemār that I felt sad for, but the tragedy of all the many young men who would come out of the war, but their girls, their wives and families would be on the other side, which now belonged to the Russians.

A few days later Jānīts brought home another soldier. He was small in stature, but what he lacked in height, he doubly had in spirit. He was a bit older, perhaps in his thirties or even forties, and had a wife and four children at home in Latvia, but he was such a dynamic personality! He stayed with us a whole week, for now it was warm, and he could sleep in the front room on the big sofa. We loved having him, because he had so many interesting stories to tell about his times in Russia with the German units, and he told them with relish and humor, his small eyes twinkling and even closing in laughter. He had studied the Baltic and Slavic languages and that was how he was placed in a German unit, so he could translate everything for them.

He also told about an incident that had made him deeply unhappy at the time.

"I had volunteered to join a special unit in the German forces at the very beginning of the occupation, anxious to help rid our country of the communists who had killed and deported so many of our people. To my great disappointment, I was refused because of my insufficient height. Only later I discovered that this unit had been formed for shooting the Jews and thanked God that I escaped that." So sometimes in life, the bad can turn out to be good.

More Latvian refugees arrived in our area. Several families had been settled in the neighboring village, and one Latvian lady with her teenage son had been placed in our village too. We found out that they were Mrs. Zaķis and her son Ronald, a shy but handsome and very courteous young boy. We soon got acquainted with them, and they instantly responded to our friendship, for they had no other family or friends. One could tell instantly that they came from a higher class of society of Rīga. Mrs. Zaķis' dresses were made of unusual fabrics, simply but elegantly styled, and Ronald wore a nice shirt and a tie even in the hottest summer weather. They both were always impeccably groomed. We had never belonged to those circles, but when Mother invited them to visit us, we found that we all felt very comfortable with each other right from the start.

I suppose our life in the military environment had groomed us at least to some degree toward higher standards of behavior, for my parents, together with other army officers, had often been to important receptions and even to the President's Ball. That, of course, did not matter anymore, but perhaps it gave us a greater compatibility with our new acquaintances. I was especially glad for Mother that now she would have someone to share her thoughts with, for she did not share them with me. Maybe she did not want to cause me pain talking about Dad, knowing how much I loved and missed him.

Mrs. Zaķis was about the same age as Mother, perhaps in her early forties. She was a beautiful woman with very blue eyes and naturally blond, very simply styled, wavy hair. A few aging lines were beginning to show in her fair, intelligent face that conveyed a kind and sensitive personality. There was only one drawback with her, and it was very sad to see that her slim body was handicapped from polio. She walked heavily limping to one side resting on a cane—and if possible, on her dear son's arm.

As we met with them more often, it was so interesting to watch this mother-and-son relationship. Ronald, though only fifteen years old, knew so well how to help his mother and did it with great patience and empathy. You could see that he had been doing it for some time and knew each movement or gesture of hers. I don't know when she contracted the illness, but her husband had divorced her and married somebody else, which must have been another hard knock in her life.

She must have gone through a lot, and now she was a refugee in a foreign land with no help but her young son, yet her stature and her attitude never conveyed the tragedies she had gone through. As I looked at her face and into her blue eyes, I could see only kindness, patience and often even humor. I loved to talk with her and to be in her company. Even her voice was soft, and a certain kind of inner light emanated from her, which drew my respect and admiration. She was a lady, yet she never insinuated in any way that she was any better than anybody else. That really lifted her in my eyes.

And Ronald, the good-looking, shy Ronald—so much like his mother, with his blond hair, deep blue eyes with long dark lashes—and always so polite and correct! There was only one problem with him; he occasionally stuttered, especially if he felt uneasy or excited about something. I could see how embarrassed he was when that happened; he blushed dark red and lowered his eyes. Poor Ronald! He had not had a regular childhood, and now he did not have his youth, either. He had grown up with "boundaries". Perhaps at times they were even chains, though he never showed it. For the time being, he was living his mother's life, but it could not be any other way, since mother and son could not do

without each other.

Our Mother tried to help them in every way she could and often invited them to come to visit and share a meal. They seemed to like that very much, for they did not have anybody else. Mrs. Zaķis and Mother were soon on a first-name basis, and we were glad to have her and Ronald as part of our family.

The days got warmer. Summer was coming. Since life around us had begun to normalize, we waited for changes to happen for us also. Surely, all the nations would go back to their previous borders now! We just had to wait for the news when we could go home. We also waited for Dad. Any day now he should arrive, as did all those who had stayed alive. But time passed, and he didn't, nor was there any more news from him. These, however, were still chaotic days. The last news was from the region of Stettin and Rostock, and that was also where the Front was when the war ended.

There was no more news from my friend Edīte either, who had stayed with some relatives near Stettin and who had communicated with me all the time. In her last letter she'd written that she was engaged to a nice young Latvian soldier. But perhaps the letters were just somewhere still on the way. We had to be patient.

It was the third week in June, the time when in Latvia we used to celebrate our Midsummer Fest—John's Day *(Jaņu Diena)* and *Līgo Night*, with bonfires and much singing and feasting. Now we could only remember it, and yet we wanted to mark it at least in some way. We invited Mrs. Zaķis and her son to come and join us in the celebration of this event, for my brother's name was Jānis, the same as our Dad's, only in Latvia, most children were called in the endearing or diminutive form of the name, hence the name "Jānītis". This was a festivity honoring all men called Jānis, for in the ancient Latvian beliefs John was the son of God, riding around the country during the shortest night of the year and bringing blessings to people who stayed awake and welcomed him.

It was good that we could use our large front room now because no heating was necessary at this time, and there was space enough at the bigger table and chairs to entertain our guests. To decorate the room in the traditional way, Jānīts brought some branches of birch and oak from somewhere. I picked grasses and wild-flowers out by the fields and put them in jars all around the room to create the feeling of summer indoors. We had prepared food and even baked a cake. Now it started to look and feel like a celebration. Whatever was missing, we could dig out of our memories and pretend that it was like it once was. To make it even more festive, I dressed up in my national costume that Mother had made for my grade school graduation. It was a beautiful thing consisting of an

embroidered white linen blouse, a red and black plaid long skirt with a bodice of the same fabric, and a patterned hand-woven belt to wrap around my waist. To top it off, I had made a circlet of white daisies to wear on my head.

When everything was done, Jānīts and I were quite excited. We stood in the open doorway waiting for our guests, enjoying the beautiful afternoon. It was nice that our entrance faced the back of the house which opened to the grassy open yard. Nothing was planted in it, but trees and shrubs growing on the other side of the fence; they leaned over providing nice green surroundings for us. A side street passed the open section of our yard, leading out of the village. It went past the neighboring houses and soon ended in the open fields.

The air was full of the scents of grasses and green leaves as it always is at the beginning of summer, when everything grows and blooms. The golden afternoon sun lay over everything and shone into our large front room which now even looked cozy. Everything seemed so nice for once that I almost wanted to sing as I did in the old days back home.

As we stood in the door, we saw a small group of soldiers walking up the side road. A unit of wounded soldiers was stationed in our village. Perhaps some of them had come out for a walk. As they passed by, they looked our way with a certain curiosity. It must have been my national costume which had roused their interest. They walked up to us smiling and inquired what this was all about. We told them shortly about our special Midsummer fest, but just then our guests arrived, so we went inside and they left.

Now the celebration could begin. Of course, it was nothing like it used to be at home in Latvia, where bonfires burned and the people feasted and sang all through the night till the morning sun rose. No, it was nothing like that, but we could remember those days together with our friends and feast on what we had, being grateful that we were alive and could do even this.

A few days later, as I walked along the main street, a German soldier greeted me. I was puzzled at first, for I did not know anybody here. But then I recognized that it was one of the soldiers from the group who had passed our house on that festive night. I remembered him being the tallest in the crowd, and he was also the one who asked the most questions.

"I think we have already met," he said smiling, noticing my puzzlement, and then I remembered. "Do you mind if I walk along with you for a bit?" he asked. "We have been sent here to recuperate, but it is so boring with nothing to do."

"That may be so," I answered, "but at least you are not in danger anymore."

"That is true, that is true," he agreed quickly, then stopped, facing me and introduced himself formally:

"Paul Fibig, Lieutenant from Westfalen." He bowed and clicked his heels as he said that, then asked for my name. I told him, and we kept walking till we reached our house. Mother had just come out by the door that stood open now in the summertime. The Lieutenant introduced himself to her also very courteously, and she, wanting to be kind toward a soldier, asked him to come in for a cup of coffee. He accepted graciously, walked in and sat down on the sofa, taking off his cap and putting it on the seat next to him.

After the coffee was made, Mother sat with him talking about the war and also telling him about our Dad. I sat with them listening at first, then walked around the room, tidying this and that and did not join in the conversation. I did not feel comfortable to leave the room though, for after all, I had brought him so he was my guest. The Lieutenant sat on the sofa, sipping his coffee and smoking, but I noticed time and again, when I glanced at them to show that I was not ignoring them, that his eyes were following me. I found it a bit disconcerting, but what was it to me? I thought, "Let him watch if he wants to!"

After this he came by now and then, and Mother liked talking to him. She spoke perfect German and understood how a soldier might feel lonely and may want to talk to somebody. I joined these talks only minimally so as not to appear rude. One time, however, as he was about to depart, he asked: "Would you like to take a little walk outside?"

Well, I thought, why not?

"Yes, I suppose I could," I answered. Life was pretty lonely here for me too. I put on my off-white summer coat, tied a flowery scarf around my neck and off we went.

It was an overcast, breezy day, as it often was in this region. We walked along the main street talking, he being very polite and attentive. He asked a lot of questions, stopping each time facing me so as to look at me while I gave the answers. Of course, it might have been just the mere fact that he was tall and I was short. That way he could hear better what I said, but it was quite a stance the way he stood there, resting his body somewhat back on his left leg, holding a thin stick in his hands (such as the British officers carried) and gazing down at me through half-closed lids with those big brown eyes. While listening, he half-smiled, with one corner of his mouth pulled up, occasionally tapping his long, shiny boots with the stick.

"Was he trying to impress me?" I thought. "Me, a young, naive girl?" Yes, I was naive, but I was not stupid. I did not like this arrogant

posturing, and it made me want to draw back. He looked haughty, and he could be. Being good-looking and tall, he could afford such an arrogant stance, and the uniform helped too, of course—but otherwise he was very charming.

We walked as far as the station and then slowly came back. The evening was nearing, and the street was almost empty. We talked about all kinds of things. He was quite knowledgeable, and it was interesting to listen to him. He also tried to guess where I was from.

"You know, I can spot anybody by just hearing their accent," he bragged, calling out several regions of eastern Germany (obviously assuming that I was a German), but I just shook my head. Now he was really puzzled, but I still did not tell him. He did not really need to know.

While we were still on the main street, I suddenly saw our young friend Ronald walking toward us. As he saw us, he looked so taken aback that he lowered his eyes and blushed dark red. Then he looked up, greeted me quickly and rushed by. The next time Ronald was at our house, he reprimanded me, "And you, Zigrid, are g-g-going with a German?" he said stuttering with reproach in his young voice and his face serious.

"Oh Ronald! What do you mean 'going with a German'" I laughed it off. "We were just passing the time of day, since there is not much to do here."

I went out a few more times with the Lieutenant, but it was nothing serious. We just walked along the main street, enjoying talking together, and that was it. One day though he jokingly said something, which I did not even comprehend at first, but thinking about it later, the light dawned on me, and then I knew that this friendship had to end. I was not a child anymore, and yet I was. I did not have time anymore to go walking. There were things I needed to do. He soon understood and did not come to ask me anymore.

It was a sunny afternoon a few weeks later, when I took a walk down our side street where it opened up into the fields. There I almost came upon a couple laying in the grass in a small incline. It was "my" Lieutenant with a woman in a flowery dress. Good, I thought. He had found what he had been looking for! I quietly backtracked, so he did not even know that I had seen them.

He did come by once more, however, and told us that they would be leaving the next day. He had come to say goodbye and had brought me a photograph. On the back of it was a poem he had written, saying that no way would be too hard for him to come and find me again. His signature read: "In love and in reverence, Paul Fibig." Reverence?

I did feel a bit moved by this. I guess there had been some little attraction after all, but there certainly was no thought of love. It had just been a pleasant interlude, since we both had felt at a loss. But perhaps

his attentions had just boosted my girlish pride, making me feel special, seeing the village girls eying me enviously as they passed us by on the street. But that was all finished now.

"Good-bye, Lieutenant! Good luck!" I was sure that we would never see each other again and we didn't. I felt a little sad after that and wrote a reply poem to him in German, but never showed it to anyone. It did not really matter. It was just a memory stored away.

The hot July days came. Our landlady's husband came home and so did many others, but there was no sign of our Dad. We had our first fears that something had gone wrong somewhere, for he should have been here by now. Mother tried contacting various people who might have some information, but the only thing she heard was that the Russian Front in the last days of the war had been where he was. What had happened? Would anybody ever be able to tell us?

Mother went to Husum to the Red Cross office to inquire. The news was that a lot of soldiers were still in prisoner of war camps, and everything was very much in chaos. It would take time to sort things out. We would have to be patient. The Red Cross registries were not yet complete. Also, our Latvian newspaper carried a lot of advertisements of people searching for family members, relatives and friends, who had been separated by the activities of war.

The month of August arrived and with it my nineteenth birthday. We decided to mark it with a little celebration, since last year on my eighteenth birthday, we had been on the train racing across Germany after the ship had just brought us from Latvia.

I invited my cousin Ruta from Husum. She said she would come and also bring her boyfriend, a young Latvian man she had recently met. That sounded nice, and I looked forward to seeing them. On that day, they both arrived on the afternoon train, and she introduced us to Žanis, a good looking young man with strong features, dark hair and big blue-grey eyes. I could see that Ruta was quite smitten with him.

I had already set the table with the cake I had baked, and everything looked nice and festive. Soon Mrs Zaķis and her son arrived also, and the celebration could begin.

As we sat around the table, Ruta told us of the latest happenings in Husum.

"An old army base called the *Fliegerhorst* has been opened for housing the refugees now," she said excitedly. "It is just outside the town, near the airport. There are so many foreigners in Husum and they need to be placed somewhere. Of course, those are just wooden barracks at the camp, but people are glad to move there to be out of the German houses. The camp is filling up fast and there is much excitement about it.

We have applied to get in there also, as soon as possible, because now in summertime our under-the-stairs dwelling gets very hot."

"It would really be like a ghetto," I said, "but I think that people will like to be together with others of their own nationality and culture."

"The Lithuanians live there also," Ruta added, "but they are very much like us."

"I am sure the Germans will also like to have their homes to themselves once again." Mrs. Zaķis interjected.

While we sat at the table visiting, there was a sudden knock on the door. The mailman had brought a telegram for me!

"Who on earth could send me a telegram?" I wondered.

I opened it quickly and read the message. It was from Viktor! I was stunned! That was a surprise! How had he found me? Viktor, my brother Ilgvar and I had been friends in our childhood days when we used to spend summers at our grandfather's farm. He had been the neighbor's boy, just across the small river, which separated our properties. We had had some nice times together, for there were no other children in the vicinity. But after that, we did not see each other for several years. When we met again, I was fifteen, and he was already nineteen.

After this, we met on and off, and I sensed that he was nurturing romantic feelings toward me. I did not feel the same way, and there we ran into difficulties. Still, he kept pursuing me. Now I had not seen him or communicated with him for almost three years, since I had walked out on him in anger the last time we met. He had a habit of getting me cornered into situations where I did not want to be, and that infuriated me. I thought I had left it all behind me when we left Latvia, but here he was again, wishing me a happy birthday! I crunched the telegram in my hand and shoved it into my pocket, angry that he was following me even here. Still, I did not want to spoil our party and returned to the table.

Later, when our other guests had left, Ruta, Žanis and I decided to go for a little walk. The evening was so nice and mellow; it would be a shame to sit indoors. It had already been planned ahead that Ruta and Žanis would stay the night with us, for Ruta could sleep with Mother and Žanis on the sofa in the front room. Now they did not need to hurry back to catch the train and we could visit longer.

We walked up the alley toward the church at the top of the hill where the road ended. A nice old cemetery was right next to it. Flowers, shrubs and trees made it a very pleasant place with their various colors and scents. As we walked along the paths slowly, Žanis talked, but time and again my thoughts wandered off. Viktor's telegram had brought back painful memories of leaving our home and country, and losing my first love. He had to go back to the war after the heavy illness, contracted at the front. I thought I had laid it all to rest—at least to some degree—but

it was still there and hurting.

I also thought about the happenings of this last year, and how we were at a dead end now, not knowing what our future would be. That made me sad.

But then I pulled myself together. That was no way to think on a birthday! And what was I grumbling about, anyway? I was still alive, and the day was beautiful! Was this not enough reason to rejoice? A beautiful white rose reached its perfect bloom toward me, breathing its wonderful fragrance into my face. What more could one want?

A year had passed since we had left Latvia on that gray and sad August day in 1944. It now seemed a lifetime ago. Everything had changed in our lives. Nothing was left of the life we had before. Yet, that past life was still within me. At night I dreamed of blossoming meadows, of birch groves and of bird songs that I knew. As I woke in the dark, I thought that perhaps I was still at home, and all this other was just a dream, but then I felt the edge of my narrow sofa and heard Johnny's breathing right next to me, sleeping on the chairs. The first gray of the morning was just appearing in the window. Then I knew, as many times before, that my dream was just a dream, not the reality I wished for with all my heart.

"What will happen to us?" I often thought as I roamed about in the meadows and gazed at the forest on the other side of the valley. I usually found solace in nature, but not now. I could only think of the bitter truth that all the nations came home after the big war, but we had nowhere to go. The enemy was still in our land, and nobody cared that it was so. That was painful to bear. Perhaps I was on my own too much with my sad thoughts. I could not let go, and there was no one to talk to here or to share my feelings with.

Then I remembered how Ruta talked so enthusiastically about the camp at Fliegerhorst when she was here at my birthday party. She had said that the social life there was booming. Since there was not much else to do, activity groups were formed. There were sports and dancing in the big social hall. Of course, the young people would be excited about that. It gave them an opportunity to meet and also to have some fun, which they had not had for a long time. She had said there would be a dance there the following Saturday and she invited me to come.

I thought about it and decided to go. I needed to be with other young people. First I went to Ruta's family and visited with them. Then in the early evening, Ruta and I walked to the Fliegerhorst where her boyfriend Žanis met us. He had brought along a friend, a tall, lanky, pleasant-looking young man, named Mārtiņš. Žanis introduced us to him, and we talked for a bit together. Apparently they both lived in Kiel, a larger town

on the east coast of the peninsula and they had come to the Fliegerhorst to take part in a volleyball match against a Lithuanian team. The match was now over, and they were ready to stay for the dance.

Music was already floating through the open windows of the dance hall. There were all the new and popular tunes that we liked, and the big hall was filling with people. We too walked in. The musicians had settled on the small stage at one end of the room, and more and more couples started to swirl around the dance floor. Ruta and Žanis soon disappeared amongst the dancers, and Mārtin and I were left alone.

He seemed to be a quiet person, a bit shy, but so was I. We felt a bit awkward at first, but as we began to dance, we soon became quite comfortable with each other. We exchanged a few words, and as I looked up at him, I saw that he had big, dark gray eyes with long lashes, and there was something boyish in his face, which was very disarming. I smiled.

"What are you smiling about?" he asked.

I just shook my head and did not say anything. He squeezed me closer to himself, and we just kept on dancing. We stayed together all evening, since neither of us wanted to be with anybody else. On and off we caught a glimpse of Ruta and Žanis, but then they melted into the crowd again.

Time was moving toward morning, and then suddenly the dance was over. People quickly dispersed, finding their quarters amongst the dark barracks. Mārtin and I went outside, too, in the just graying morning light, and met Ruta and Žanis. Ruta did not want to go home yet, since Žanis had found a place for them, where they could stay till the morning. He had also made arrangements with one of the musicians, whom he knew well, that Mārtin and I could stay in his room. It was occupied by several young men, but apparently they had some empty space there.

I did not really have a choice. I could not go back to Ruta's parents, for I did not want to spoil her plans. And where else could I go now at nighttime? So Mārtin and I just followed the accordion player who was a nice fellow and led us to his room. It really was no big deal. During wartime people had gotten used to living and sleeping in all kinds of situations and nobody made any big fuss about it.

The streets of the camp were empty, and the wooden barracks lay dark and quiet in the very early morning light as we walked to the place where we would be staying. It was a large room with six two-story bunk beds, a couple of wardrobes, a small table and a few chairs. These were bachelor's quarters that was very obvious, and nobody here probably owned very much more than the clothes on their backs—since most of them were discharged soldiers. It turned out that there was only one bed free, an upper bunk with a blanket and a pillow on it. That would have to do for the short while till the morning.

There was nothing else to do but to settle down the best we could, Mārtin by the wall and I on the outside in the curve of his tall body. That was the only way we could sleep, for the bed was narrow. It was all quiet in the semi-dark room. I could only see the somewhat lighter rectangle of the window across the room, for there were no drapes. After all, the camp was no luxury hotel, but a poor refugee's shelter.

As we settled down, Mārtin put his arm over me and that was all right, since he had nowhere else to put it. I was not scared of him. What could happen here, in somebody else's room with so many other people around? After a little while though his hand started to slide lightly over my body, but each time I gently put it back where it belonged. There was no big fight here, no abuse. Mārtin was a decent guy, I had sensed that all evening while we danced, otherwise I would not be sleeping here. Finally we both had drifted into sleep. When we got up, the accordionist looked at us, smiling a bit sheepishly, but did not say anything. And why should he?

Then it was time to part. Mārtin looked at me with those big, gray eyes as I reached out my hand to say good-bye.

"Till next time!" he said.

"Yes, till next time!"

Mārtin and Žanis had to get back to Kiel. I had to get home, too, but the next train would be only in the afternoon. Then Ruta suggested that I try to hitch a ride from someone going down the highway. I had never done that, but thought perhaps I could give it a try.

She came with me to where the highway led out of town and we both waited, but since it was Sunday, there was not much traffic. Then a man came by on a bicycle, stopped and offered to take me. Only fourteen kilometers, that was not too much, and I agreed.

We had gone some distance, when the man said that perhaps we should rest a little. Of course. Why not? It was not so easy to carry another grownup on a bike. He turned into a small side road; we got off and sat down in the shade of some shrubs. He took an apple out of his bag and offered me half. We sat there resting and everything seemed normal.

But then, suddenly, he was coming at me. I did not even understand at first what was happening. I was such an innocent lamb!

"You know!" he said, pushing me back on to the ground, obviously surprised at me pulling away. Did he really think that I had planned this? And I did not even know what "this" was, I only sensed danger coming.

His face was angry now as he tried to grab me with force. I knew then that I really was in danger and started to scream, pushing him away, but he was stronger. Then I remembered a Girl-Scout trick. To protect yourself from an attacker, you make a "fork" out of your pointer and

your small finger and push them into your attacker's eyes. I did that and it worked. He jumped up, got on his bike and was gone.

After he left, I sat there trembling, only then realizing what might have happened. How naive I was! I wanted to cry, but could not even do that. The tears were stuck deep into my throat. My chest felt so heavy that I could hardly breathe. I was so ashamed that I had allowed myself to get into such a situation. I felt as if I had rolled through mud. It was so awful to have an experience like this, especially after the nice evening with Mārtin. For I really liked him, and I thought he liked me, too. Was this a punishment for sleeping with him? But nothing bad had happened!

I wanted to get out of there but then noticed that my coat was smudged with some mud from the nearby ditch where the man had pushed me down and I tried to wriggle away. It had to be cleaned up. I could not go home like that.

Though still feeling shaky, I cleaned up my coat as best as I could by rubbing it with my hanky and my scarf, then laid it out in the sun to dry a bit. My thoughts kept whirling around. How could this happen? Why did I enter into such foolishness?

When my coat had dried somewhat, I got up and set on my way, hoping that Vioel would not be too far away and I would be able to make it. I walked along the roadside. The gray pebbles of the unpaved road crunched under my feet; the sound cutting through me, reminding me of what had just happened. A car sped by, but I did not even look at it.

"Never, never will I trust a stranger again," I vowed! Then I thought again, "Did this happen because I had slept with Mārtin? Did we have to pay for everything that was nice in our lives? Like that time when I went to see Ilmār at the hospital last spring, then missed the train and was stranded in a strange place at night and a cold one at that, with nowhere to go... Yes, those too had been bitter tears...

When I got home, Mother had a guest, another lady who had recently arrived at our village. She was busy entertaining her, so everything worked out all right. I went into the back room and stayed there quietly, avoiding any questioning. As I think back, though, my Mother did not question me much about anything. Perhaps she was always too preoccupied with her own thoughts, and I guess she trusted that I would know what I should do or not do, and mostly that was so. Except today... It would have been so good to lay my head on Mother's chest and be comforted now, but I was used to not having it.

In the coming days I spent a lot of time in the cemetery by the church, walking and thinking. Somehow I had to regain my inner peace. The incident at the roadside had shaken me more than I first thought. I had to get over it, put it behind me, but it was not so easy. I never told anyone about it.

I was still reading the book by the Norwegian writer, and it raised a lot of deep questions within me. What was this life that we were living? Why did the evil in people so often overshadow the good? How should we live a good life? What was it that we needed to do?

The leaves of the trees in the cemetery had started to fall. I watched them fluttering down slowly, then laying themselves quietly on the hard ground. They told me that there might be some joys, but that hurt never really ends. There was one kind of hurt and then another, it just had to be accepted. I gazed into the blue sky, searching for more answers, but it stretched out there, clear and uncaring. Then I remembered reading a saying in Gulbransen's book: *"Life breaks our pride but we understand life best when it is broken.."*

I did not know if I fully understood the meaning of those words, but they touched me deeply. That something in me had to be broken…That thought made me sad. And yet, the book said that you had to go on, and strive forward and upward, always upward, even though the pain is still within you.

## To Camp Winnert and Camp Hockensbuhl

It was only a few days later that news came, which put an end to my painful deliberations and also brought an end to our fairly tranquil life here in Vioel. An International Refugee Organization apparently wanted to gather the refugees into special camps, so the Aid Workers could look after us better. Was it so? Or was it rather so we would not be in other people's way? I suppose I had become cynical.

The change happened very quickly. It was good that we did not have much to pack. Two days later, on September 6, 1945 we left Vioel. We had spent a year here almost exactly. An army truck came to pick us up, as well as the other Latvians living in the vicinity, and took us to some camp. We did not even know where we were, for there were no maps to see the location, but we heard that it was not too far from Husum. I would have preferred to go to the Fliegerhorst instead, but apparently that was already full. There was talk that schools would be organized there, and I felt sorry that I would not have the opportunity to finish my last year of high school, which I had missed because of our leaving the country.

Nevertheless, we were taken to a camp called *"Winnert."* Nobody asked us if we wanted to go or not. It was already arranged, and we were just part of a crowd that had to be placed somewhere. An empty square, surrounded by gray wooden barracks, awaited us. No other houses could be seen from here. Perhaps some army units had been stationed here or perhaps some worker's corps, which the Germans had formed in order to help with the war effort. Some trees could be seen farther on. Perhaps

some "regular" people lived there. We were not in that category any-more. We were "irregular". We did not fit anywhere. We were the "left over people", which nobody knew what to do with. "The refuse of the world"! Somewhere, somehow we still had our pride, but it was at a very low point at this stage! We were literally mowed down by the events of the world.

We had become DP's, as we were called now, short for "Displaced Persons". We were people who came from nowhere, for there was no country called Latvia anymore. It had been given away as a gift to the biggest butcher in the world, and we were left with nowhere to go. It seemed that it would have been good for the big and the mighty, if they could cross us out of their registers altogether, but here we were, and they had to do something with us.

Those were very bitter and degrading thoughts, but I understood that it was necessary to learn to live with this reality. After all, somebody was at least making the effort to look after us. Perhaps it would not be so bad. Low clouds dragged along the gray sky, and the wind blew sharply across the bare field, carrying the torn leaves from the trees, the same way destiny carried our torn lives around. The gray wooden barracks sat around the square looking uninviting; our new home.

We were allotted a small room in one of the barracks with a window facing the back of it. That was nice, because it was more secluded, but we could not help seeing the cracks between the boards in the wall and the floor. How would we live here in wintertime? Two bunk beds stood at the side walls opposite each other with a window in between them on the back wall and a table and a couple of chairs in front of it all. There was also a narrow ply board wardrobe and a small round iron stove with the chimney, extending through the roof as we had had in Vioel. Families with small children were given larger rooms, and single people or cou-ples without children had to share the largest rooms. They divided them by hanging up blankets on ropes to retain at least a minimum of privacy.

Now everybody washed and scrubbed, trying to make their new dwellings more acceptable. However meager and bare, they had to be made into homes. It is an inborn necessity for the Latvian people to have some beauty around them even in the poorest of accommodations. When everything was clean and the beds made, one could put a few wildflow-ers in a cup on the table. A treasured book, a photograph of a loved one, or any small treasure which gladdened the heart would be used as a decoration. A postcard, or a page from a calendar, pinned to the wall, right away made the room look more homelike. One did not need very much, really. We were used to doing with little by now and knew how to improvise with what we had. It was all right.

A totally different life began here at the camp. We had never lived in

such a crowded situation before. There were at least a couple of hundred of us Latvians here. We were informed that we would get one hot meal a day from the communal kitchen and some hot water in the mornings and evenings. Rations for the rest of the meals would be handed out once a week.

Standing in lines was now one of the main activities, at least for one member of each family. In the mornings, people stood in a line by the communal kitchen in order to get the hot water for their morning coffee or tea. Mothers stood in a line for milk for their children. At noontime there were lines for fetching the midday meal, whatever it happened to be, usually some soup or a one-dish concoction. People stood there with their bowls or saucepans, or whatever container anybody had to hold the appropriate amount of food for their family. The former soldiers, usually single men without families, stood there with their army food vessels in hand, shivering in the harsh autumn wind, not having any warm clothing. In the evenings there was again the standing in line for the hot water.

Once a week, usually on Friday mornings, was the time to stand in lines again for our weekly rations: half a loaf of bread per person, a little margarine (about 3 Tbs.), a small lump of fish conserves, usually pilchards (about 4 Tbs) and a small glob of jam (about 2 Tbs). That was it. It had to do for the week.

Even so, life at the camp began with gusto. This was something we had never experienced before. After getting our little rooms organized, there was not much to do, so energetic people began to organize schooling for the children and various activities for the grown-ups. People needed something worthwhile to do, and regardless of how hopeless things looked now, it would depend on us to hold on to the heritage we had brought with us. Soon there was a choir, a drama group, sports and other activities. Now, when we did not have to worry about our daily bread, there was plenty of time for those things. Some also worked for the camp establishment: in the office, in the kitchen and other necessary positions.

At first it felt a bit strange to be in a Latvian environment again after such a long time and to hear Latvian spoken all around us. It was nice to be amongst our own people, but soon also the negative side of this living together began to appear, such as envy, jealousy, gossip and the like.

Germany in those days was divided into areas of authority. There was the British Zone in the north, then the American Zone farther south, the French in the west and the Russian Zone in the east. Since we were in the British Zone, our camp commanders were either British or Canadian officers, working for the United Nations Refugee Relief Association or UNRRA. The everyday life of the camp, however, was managed by a Latvian commandant with his helpers, who coordinated everything with

the military establishment.

Gradually we became used to the new situation, and life settled into a certain routine. Yes, one could live like this, but for how long? That was a question many asked. What of the future? It was even more uncertain than it had been before. Mother was still looking for Dad and Ilgvar, for there was still no news from either of them. A Red Cross office was in Husum, so Mother went there every few weeks to inquire. Finally, results! Apparently Ilgvars was in a prisoner of war camp in Neuengamm where the German Waffen SS officers were kept, and the news from there was grim. Somebody who had been there warned Mother:

"Go and get your son out of there as soon as possible! People are dying there of starvation every day!" Now Mother used all her energies to get him out of there, and she succeeded since he was not a German and had been drafted by the German army in an occupied country.

He had to go through two other camps, however, before he could get officially released. He ended up in a camp in Zedelgheim, Belgium, where a lot of the other former Latvian legionnaires were sent. Apparently, things were bad there also: starvation, the winter cold and in addition, abuse by the Belgian guards—but we only got to know about that later. The main thing was that Ilgvars was alive. We just had to be patient until he could be with us again.

After my birthday in August, when I received the telegram from Viktor, I put it aside and did not think about it anymore. I did not love him and he knew that, yet he had kept after me. I did not like it, but he was part of the life I had had back home, and I could not quite discard that.

In October I received another surprise letter from him, when Mother brought it back from the Husum Red Cross, where she had gone again in search of Dad. Viktor wrote: "I am living in Luebeck now and have known of your whereabouts for some time already, but knowing how you feel about me, I have been reluctant to bother you. Finally I decided to write anyway. So here I am."

Actually I had suspected that one day it would happen, knowing how persistent he could be. But with that my old resistance was rekindled. No, I really did not want him to bother me! I put the letter away and that was that.

As the activities at the camp developed, I was right away roped into the drama group. A lady who lived in our barrack had written a play and thought that I would be a perfect candidate for the role of her main character. The director, who also lived in our barrack, thought so too. But then my problems started. He was trying to get too friendly with me, always crossing my path somewhere, which made me very unhappy. He

had his own wife and a small son. Why did he do this?

Luckily, other exciting news came, which changed everything. A Latvian high school was being formed in a new camp just on the other side of Husum! Since there were quite a number of young people living in the surrounding camps, a high school was necessary. It would also have boarding accommodations, so the students could stay there during the week, and on weekends the UNRRA drivers would take them back to the camps to be with their families. On Sunday evenings they would be brought back to school.

That sounded great, and I signed up right away. This also gave me a good reason to withdraw from the drama group and so get out of the uncomfortable situation with the director. The instruction at school would be starting soon, so there was no time to waste. I moved to Hockensbuhl at the beginning of November and was pleased to see that it was a totally different situation from Winnert.

What a change! The two-story red brick buildings were solid and clean with central heating and washrooms. This was a real luxury after living in the cramped quarters before. The rooms were large, clean and bright with big windows and good lighting. The camp itself was not too large, only some six or seven buildings with asphalt walkways and an irregular patch of grass with a few trees in the middle of the compound. It was on the very outskirts of Husum.

It apparently had been a military school, and it looked like it had been built fairly recently. The camp was only just opening, and the people who now moved in seemed to be of a more privileged class—the higher educated ones like teachers, artists and other knowledgeable persons. But of course! They would be needed here for teaching the school! Since the higher educated people had been the ones the Communists had wanted to eradicate most, they were the ones who had fled, so now we had several professors as our high school teachers. Life should be good here.

And so it was! The first and most important thing was that the food here was better, at least for us students. Every afternoon, each of us received half a loaf of fresh, fluffy white bread, such as we had not eaten for ages. Spread with some margarine and a little sugar sprinkled on it, it tasted like a cake. In the first few days we absolutely gobbled it up.

We also started to receive Red Cross food parcels once a month. I think they must have come from America, for there were some foodstuffs that we had never seen or tasted before. There was powdered Nescafe coffee, sweet condensed milk and egg powder. We soon found that by mixing these three together, we could make chocolate! And who did not want chocolate? We had not even seen any for a long, long time. There were also some coffee beans and some cigarettes, which were very

useful for exchanging for something that money could not buy. Money could hardly buy anything in the stores anymore these days, for they were empty, and the money, the Deutschmark, was practically worthless.

As it turned out, there were six of us girls staying at the boarding accommodation, sharing one large room. Two bunk beds stood at the opposite side walls with wardrobes next to them, and they were quickly occupied by the four younger girls. Tatjāna, the youngest, was sixteen, and her sister Irina a year older, but they quarreled a lot.

"I am not going to sleep with you, that's for sure!" Tatjāna exclaimed talking to her sister.

"Well, I don't want to sleep with you either! Don't even think of it!" Irīna retorted, taking her stuff across the room to the other set of bunk beds.

"I'll stay here with Ausma!" she said.

Biruta, the same age as Irina, was the daughter of a famous Latvian artist, a cartoonist. She came from the same camp as the sisters, and bunked in the lower bed with Tatjana. I liked Biruta. She was a pretty girl with blond hair and hazel eyes, serious and sensible, but with a good sarcastic sense of humor. The last of the foursome from Aarensfeld was Ausma, who was eighteen years old. She was a country girl, it could be seen right away. She was heavier and had thick light brown hair that she wore in braids around her head. We all liked her because she was simple and kind and always in good humor, even though she was handicapped and limped with one leg shorter than the other. She was always the pacifier if any arguments arose in our small family, and it was good to see her smile with her round cheeks shining like rosy apples. On the whole, we all got on quite well together and even had our laughs and fun.

One more bunk bed stood to the right of the door which led out to the hallway, so I decided to take the upper bed of that one, because then I could use the top of my wardrobe as a nightstand, or even a desk where I could put my books. This was very handy, for I did my writing and studying right up there in my bunk, where I was more comfortable and also more secluded. No one was sleeping in the lower bed, so I had the whole thing to myself. This was some luxurious living! Not like in Winnert where the floorboards gave way when you walked over them.

One more single bed stood in the left-hand corner of the room by one of the windows, and that was already occupied by the sixth girl when we arrived. She was older, and it appeared that she had a different status than we did. In the beginning it was a bit of a mystery because her parents lived in the camp. So why was she here?

Her name was Vizma and she did not really quite fit into this situation, for she must have been two or three years older than I, and I was nineteen. She should have already made it through high school in Lat-

via, but here she was. Obviously, she wanted to get a high school diploma, which she had not, for some reason, obtained yet. Perhaps she had dropped out?

Vizma was a pretty girl with blond, bushy, naturally curly hair and big blue eyes in her fair-complexioned face. Her full lips knew how to give a charming smile, and she smiled often. Her whole attitude and behavior was that of a person who had done some living already. Compared with her, the rest of us were mere children, inexperienced and naive.

It even seemed to me that I had already seen Vizma somewhere. Was she not one of those girls who came to my friend Julia's house one Easter in Latvia, when I was visiting there? She came with Julia's brother and two other soldiers with two more girls in a "horse taxi", all in a quite happy state. It was during the wartime when I was at high school. The young men were part of the police force in the German army, soon after the Occupation, and were on leave, bringing the three girls with them. Julia's mother had prepared a nice table with festive foods, and they drank, feasted and lived it up all night. We girls did not go in there, just peeped in occasionally. The next morning the room was in shambles. Perhaps it had not been Vizma, but I thought to myself that she could have been one of them.

As the classes started, it turned out that there were only three of us girls in the senior class of the high school: Vizma, I and another girl called Sandra, who lived here in the camp with her aunt's family. When they had fled Latvia, her own parents had planned to join them later, but had never made it out of Latvia.

Our classroom was in a smaller building, and it had only two desks in it. Vizma and Sandra sat in the front; I took the back seat. Our home teacher, Mr Kalnājs was a very pleasant, quiet, middle-aged man who taught chemistry. All other subjects were each taught by a different teacher, and we thought—we'd better study hard, for we did not know how long we would be here.

Vizma had a rather hard time with her studies, and it seemed that she did not have any real interest in them either, although she tried not to show it. I was also amazed how often she claimed that certain information had "slipped her mind", when it looked more like she had never even had it. Was she trying to jump over some period of learning, which she had never done before? Later she told me, "You know, actually it was my parents who persuaded me to get back into school and get the diploma. Also the principal of the school, a good friend of my parents, talked me into it."

He had even let her understand that one did not even have to know everything so thoroughly; the main thing was to get the diploma, and this was the opportunity to do it. The idea was not bad, and who will

scrutinize everything so closely now in these changing times? So Vizma just kind of played at being a student, but otherwise she was a pleasant girl.

Sandra was nice too, though a little more remote and she did not live with us. She had black shoulder-length hair and her big brown eyes in her pale, square face always looked serious—only her pointed nose gave it more of a cheerful lift. She was a very eager student but very nervous. Perhaps it was because of the tragedies in her young life, of being separated from her parents, whom she might never see again. Then there was also the other tragedy—that of losing full use of her radius finger through an unsuccessful surgery. She loved music and had dreamed of becoming a concert pianist. Now that finger was stiff and straight. Her dream was finished, and her thin lips were usually clipped tightly together. She rarely smiled.

As I had suspected, Viktor was not going to let me off so easily. In November, I received another letter. He was scolding me, saying he could not understand why I had not answered his letters! Again the same persistence and refusal to take my silence as an answer for not wanting to communicate with him! And even accusing me of being haughty!

"I know your mother does not like me, because I don't come from a good enough family for you!" he said.

Now that was not true at all! My family was not in the habit of judging people like that. It was very unfair, so I could not leave it at that and just had to respond. Yes, my Mother did caution me early on not to continue a relationship which I had no mind to fulfill.

"Don't play with fire!" she would say. "A person's feelings are sacred." Apparently she had once been in a situation like that where she had been burned.

But I was not playing. Viktor knew how it was with me, that I did not love him, so I did not have to worry on that account. But I did not want him to have wrong thoughts about my family and wrote him to straighten it out. Now I am thinking that perhaps he deliberately provoked me into this! Yes, he was very happy about my letter and answered me right away.

To pacify me, he said that he was not asking me to love him, only to share a small part of my life with him because he worshiped me. Now that kind of talk again was too far-fetched and made me feel uncomfortable. I was who I was, but no object for worshiping!

"I still live in Luebeck," he wrote. "A couple of famous Latvian musicians live below me. When they practice, it gives me great joy to listen to them, but I feel rather lonely here, although I am occasionally invited

to their small parties. I am homesick and worry about my old mother how she is faring back in Latvia under the Communist regime."

He related what had happened to him since I last saw him in that summer of 1943 when we parted. I was very angry at him and vowed to myself never to see him again, but here we were, communicating again! He had already been drafted into the German army in that summer of 1943 and was stationed in Rīga at that time.

"Later I served in an ambulance unit and life was very hectic. I saw a lot. In the summer of 1944 we fought in Vidzeme, the central part of Latvia, and then in Kurzeme, as far west as the Baltic coast, where we stayed till the end of the year. On January 8, 1945 we were shipped to Germany, to Gottenhafen, then to Koniz. There we worked for quite a while and a lot of blood flowed. Then we withdrew to Neustettin, where we experienced many Russian air-raids. Again we had to withdraw, and in many places the Russians were there already. Some from our unit fell prisoners of war there. I and some others were lucky enough to finally get out and get to Luebeck. What I inherited from all this, is a love for medicine, and I want to become a doctor."

"I know, a doctor does not have a personal life," he added, "but I do not have one anyway..." That much from Viktor.

The studies at school were quite intensive because we did not know how long we would be able to carry on this way. The transport was provided as promised, and we were taken back to our camps to be with our families for the weekends. On Sundays we were brought back to camp Hockensbuhl for another week of schooling. The only problem was that we never knew when the transport would come. Sometimes we spent the whole Saturday waiting, and the truck arrived only in the evening. Then it was hardly worth while going. The camps were not too far from Husum, but there was no other way to get there. We were totally dependent on UNRRA arrangements, but of course, it was good of them to take us at all.

We were carried back and forth in the open-back covered army trucks. In the winter it was cold, and we did not have any really warm clothing. We sat closely together on the bare boards shivering, but it was nice to see our families even for that short period of time. Sometimes we were taken to other camps also, if some special events were taking place there, like a concert, a play or a dance. I loved to dance, and sometimes we danced for most of the night. It was good that people in the camps were very active in producing a cultural life. They put their hearts into something they liked and gave joy to others at the same time. It gave them a feeling that they still did something worthwhile.

After such outings, we rode home singing, sometimes pressed

together like sardines in the back of the truck. It did not matter then whether it snowed or rained. We were happy, because we had been in our own culture; we had been "home". The good old songs were sung, songs which everybody knew, mostly folk songs and others close to our hearts. We also sang the ones which had been so popular during the wartime, the love songs the soldiers sent home to their girls. They were still in our hearts. The most popular was a song about the girl in the blue scarf going to meet her sweetheart. Then there was the nostalgic song of someone shedding flowers into the river as a greeting to his or her love. All that! Oh God! It was all before our eyes. No darkness could overtake us, if we had our songs! Wrapped in one beautiful dream, we swayed with it as the songs carried us back to the land we all loved so much.

But sometimes all this remembering got too much for me, and I had to stop singing as tears choked up my throat. They rolled down my cheeks silently, as I realized that none of those things we sang about were true anymore. There were no forests, no blossoming meadows, no love or romantic summertime, only the dark night in which we moved from nowhere to nowhere. And yet, life had to go on.

Occasionally some social events took place also at our small camp of Hockensbuhl. There would be a concert or a literary evening, sometimes followed by a dance. At one such gathering I met a pleasant young man called Ralf. As we danced several dances in succession and talked, we rather got to like each other. He looked a bit older, perhaps in his late twenties, or even thirty. Later, we sometimes went for a walk together, or he stopped at our boarding room window to say "hi!" and chat a bit when passing by. At first I felt a bit attracted to Ralf, but as I saw more of him, I found that we really had nothing in common and I grew more reluctant to go out with him. No, I did not really want anyone in my life right then.

Quite a few of our high school students came from the Fliegerhorst camp also, including my cousin Ruta. They had to walk the considerable distance all across town every day, for the Fliegerhorst was on the outskirts of town on the opposite side, but since they all came in a crowd, it was not so bad. They always had some fun going on as it usually is in a crowd of students, and they too liked to stop at our window, for we had some attractive girls in our room.

Ruta and I had been close friends throughout all my high school years, when I lived with her family, but now as we grew older and did not have the opportunity to be together as much, our personalities did not match as well anymore. She liked fun and being in a crowd, I preferred more solitude. Even so, I rather missed our companionship, for I did not connect with people easily.

Christmas was nearing again, and everybody prepared for it in some way. We students were on our Christmas break, so I was back at Winnert. Mother had managed to get some extra food from the black marketers, and a small Christmas tree with candles stood on our small table. But somehow this year, the feeling of Christmas did not come to me. I did not feel at home anywhere, neither in Hockensbuhl, nor here in Winnert, but of course, it was good to see my family. Mother had befriended the two neighbors who lived in the rooms adjoining our small hallway, and I was glad about that. Also Mrs Zaķis with Ronald lived in the same barrack, and they could visit often.

The big celebration at the camp Winnert was going to be on New Year's Eve. First there would be a play, in which I too had been initially chosen to play. I was so glad that I had been able to get out of it, for I did not care for the play, or the person who would have been my partner in it. But most of all, I had detested the director making passes at me. He pursued me wherever I went. It was so embarrassing, and the worst thing was that I did not know what to do about it. I could not tell Mother, nor could I tell him to "get lost!", for he was a prominent person in the camp, and I was raised to respect my elders.

Because of him I sometimes almost did not want to come home on weekends anymore, for he always had a way of finding me when nobody else was around. He would try to touch me or kiss me, which I abhorred, and I tried to evade him the best I could. If anybody happened to come into the room, he just pretended that we had been talking and left. Everything looked very natural from the outside, so how could I complain? It was awful. Life suddenly seemed dirty, and it made me very unhappy. How could he do this? And why did he not leave me alone?

Now I was afraid to go to the New Year's Eve Ball, because I knew he would be there, but since everybody was going, even the kids, it would be very odd for me to stay at home. And why should I? I loved dancing, and if I had a good partner, I could dance all night till the morning.

That evening the hall was packed. The play was over, and starring two middle-aged, old looking lovers, it was not the rage of the evening. Now the dance was in full swing, for everybody wanted to celebrate tonight. My family was here also.

The director had already asked me to dance with him several times. Why on earth did he not dance with his wife? But she too was having a good time with her neighbor's brother who had moved here recently from somewhere. He was tall and handsome, no wonder she was attracted. Who could understand these grown-ups? I believed that a husband and a wife should be together.

During a break, I ran into Mrs. Zaķis son, Ronald. I had not seen him much lately. He was sixteen now, but was still just as shy as before,

going red in his face as soon as I looked into his eyes. Yes, he did have beautiful eyes, deep blue with long lashes.

"Ronald, why do you not dance?" I asked him as the music started again.

"Who will da-a-ance with me? I don't kno-ow how," he answered stuttering, but I could see that he would very much like to.

"I will!" I said. "You want to? I'll show you how!"

"I do, I do! But I will be ste-e-epping on your toes!" he said anxiously.

"Never mind, let's go!"

Ronald was even embarrassed to put his arm around me and again blushed dark red as I took his hand and put it around my waist.

"It's all right, Ronald. Everything is fine!" he looked back at me and gave a weak smile.

It was rather rough going in the beginning, but gradually we adjusted to each other and it went better. Ronald was so happy, and that made me glad. I knew how lonesome he must be sometimes, living with his sick mother and looking after her, even though they seemed to be good companions. But I saw how much he would have liked to be part of the young crowd, only he did not know how. He had never been free like other children.

We milled around amongst the dancers, and Ronald was smiling. Time and again he glanced at me, as if asking if he was doing all right, and I squeezed his hand and said,

"Good, Ronald!  Very good!"

But the director stood at the side, watching us with a haughty smile on his face, sometimes even half-smirking about Ronald's efforts. I was glad Ronald did not see that, and we both danced on ever merrier. We stayed together also during the breaks, for we were old friends. That way Ronald was happy and I was saved.

When it was almost midnight, the lights in the hall dimmed. The choir director, Mr. Albering said a few words and wished everybody the good fortune to celebrate the next New Year back in our own country. Then he invited us to all join in singing the Latvian National Anthem. We stood and sang, but then it suddenly got too much for me. I did not want to dance or celebrate anymore. What was there to celebrate? Whom were we fooling? I told Ronald that I wanted to go home, so we went and got our coats. Ronald, being the well-mannered young boy that he was, offered to see me home, and we walked out into the dark of the night.

Outside it was cold and clear with a myriad of stars in the sky. Only the black roofs of the barracks loomed around the square marking our surroundings. We stopped in the middle of the field, gazing at the wonderful glow of the stars and then heard the church bells floating across

the quiet fields from the neighboring village churches. The New Year had come. It was 1946!

The air was frosty, the ground crackling under our feet, but it was good to be just standing there in silence on this special night enjoying it. But then some third person slid out of the darkness and came to stand beside us.

"Are you going home already?" that unknown somebody asked, and I could not mistake that voice. The clean, beautiful moment was ruined. I quickly said goodbye to both and hurried home.

The next day however, the director found me when I was alone in our room. I had deliberately not gone anywhere, so I would not meet him. Now he asked me,

"What has happened to you, and why are you so huffy?" I was mad at him for following me around and had answered him in only short syllables. What could I say?

"Please go to hell?" I could not say that. It just would not be fitting. But it also was not fitting what he was doing to me. Luckily, Mother came in and he left.

I wanted to get away from Winnert, so I would not have to say anything to anybody, but the truck would not be here till the evening, so I had to wait. I was glad when in the afternoon our neighbor asked Mother, my brother and me to come and visit with them. She was a small young woman with a little son. Her two brothers, former soldiers, shared the room with her, since they were considered a family by the officials at the camp. They were nice, simple people from the poorer region of Latvia. The young woman's husband had been lost in the war, or at least he had not returned yet, the same as our Dad. We sat together singing our dear old folk songs and that put everything back into the right perspective again.

We had exchanged letters with Viktor for a while now, and however strange it was in our situation, he was now my only friend with whom I could talk and share my unhappiness because there was nobody else. He was always so reassuring, even though I did not tell him the reason of my unhappiness and my struggle against the attentions of this married man. Life suddenly seemed so ugly. I needed some comfort, and he gave it to me. But then, in the beginning of January, again a telegram came from him!

"Do you happen to have any vacancies at your boarding school? Perhaps I could join you?" Oh, Lord! I did not want that!

Luckily, very soon after, a letter arrived explaining the situation. He had been renting a room in a private house, but now he, too, had to move into a refugee camp, so he had thought that maybe he could move to

Hockensbuhl and also finish his last year of high school. He had started high school late because of family circumstances when he worked and attended school in the evenings. Now, however, news was circulating that a Baltic University would be opened at Pineberg near Hamburg, for there was no shortage of professors who could teach.

"In view of this," he wrote "I changed my mind and shall instead try to get in the University even though I do not have a high school diploma. Since I have been a soldier and moved around so much in all kinds of circumstances, I could have lost it along the way. At this time I don't think it is so important. Now I think, if I could manage to get through the exams, I would try to get into the medical school."

Well, that would be good for him and good for me too because he would not come. Great!

As for me, this was a strange period in my life, and I thought about it a lot, questioning myself. Even though all kinds of activities took place, and I joined in some of them, I always felt that somehow mentally I stayed apart, not being able to meld with others completely. Or was I perhaps standing in the middle of it all, letting everything slide by me, without being moved myself? Why was I like that? I suppose deep down I did not really want to be part of the crowd.

I don't know if it was because of this, but sadness often filled me, and then it was like my joy was ebbing from me, seeping away in little streams like spring waters do. Perhaps it was because I did not have anybody close enough with whom I could share my thoughts. But then, had it not always been like that for me, even since my younger days? I did not even know how to share my thoughts.

During the last years in Latvia, when I lived with my aunt and uncle's family during the school year, my closest friend had been my cousin Ruta, but now she lived at the Fliegerhorst and had her own host of friends. I saw her quite often, since they all came to our school, but we seldom met alone. And even so, it would not have helped. She and her friends skimmed the top, savoring their youth, but I was always digging, digging to find a meaning for this life we lived. The boarding school girls were just mere children, except Vizma, but she had a different perspective on life than I did, so there was no solution there, either.

To deal with my troubled feelings, I often walked to the sea, which was not far off. There were no more buildings beyond our camp; only marshy fields that stretched as far as the high earthen wall, built to protect the lowlands from the sea. The wind whipped the coarse grass as I walked down the lonely path across the field. It matched my mood perfectly. Perhaps I too wanted to hit at something to get rid of what was paining me. I knew the wind would be even sharper up on the wall,

but I climbed it anyway. When I got to the top, it tore at my hair and my clothing, but I stood there and let it beat me. The salty sea air hit my face with its damp coldness, but it felt good. It soothed the burning pain inside of me.

I watched the dark waters throw themselves with fury against the wall again and again, dashing the water high in the air, the white foam smashing against the rocks, but of course, they did not get anywhere. They could not break down the wall. Seeing it, I thought,

"They are as helpless as I am, letting my thoughts beat against the injustices which have been done to my country. Always, always these bitter thoughts. Why do I have them?"

I saw the heavy gray clouds move across the waters. On and on they went...Was not my life, too, passing by like these clouds—my young days just moving on without me being able to really live them? But there was nothing I could do about it. I had to stand still and wait. How long? This state of hopelessness and uncertainty was hard to bear. It was like I was living two lives. The everyday life was not too bad right now; I loved school, but the other, the other hurt so much.

The winter was with us, and the sharp wind, coming from the sea, brought rain and sometimes also snow. At night it howled, whistled and wailed around the corners of our building, sounding as if the sea had climbed over the wall and was all around us. But, thank God, we were inside where it was warm. These houses were strongly built and had central heating, which was not the case in most German houses. We were lucky to have it, but I had to think of my family at Winnert, living in the flimsy wooden barrack, with only the small iron stove for heating and not much fuel, either. The wind chilled those rooms so quickly that in the morning, water was frozen in a cup if you left it there overnight.

Our classrooms were not so well heated, either. The fuel had to be conserved, so we sat at our desks in our overcoats. Even so, after a while we began to shiver and were glad when we could get back to our living quarters. After eating and a little break, we would start on our home-work, each in our own corner, some sitting at the table, some sitting or lying on their beds. There was hardly a word exchanged until bedtime.

One evening we had a surprise visitor. It was a German fellow, a black marketer, offering to sell us a harmonica. That got us excited, because accordion and harmonica music was very popular in Germany. It made you feel relaxed and happy. None of us knew how to play it though.

"I'll show you, "he said. "It's easy!"

It was a type of instrument—something between a harmonica and

an accordion. The man played us a tune and showed us how it was done. Now we were even more excited.

"Wouldn't it be nice if we had our own music!" One of the girls exclaimed, for we had nothing, not even a radio! We began to talk about it more seriously.

"Could we?" "Should we?" we asked ourselves.

"What do you want for it?" Irina asked.

"I want 450 grams of coffee beans," he replied, and we were really tempted now.

We each had some beans, which we had received in our Red Cross packages, but nobody had enough to buy the harmonica separately. We would have to pool the beans and buy it together! Yes! Let us see! We took the beans out of our cupboards and poured them on the table. It was not quite the amount the man wanted, but he said it would do, and the harmonica was ours.

We knew our mothers would not be too pleased when they heard of us wasting the coffee beans, for which you could get some meat or some other food by exchanging. But we wanted our music, and now we had it!

We began the learning exercises, and that was the worst part of it! Each of us wanted to learn to play, so we would take turns, but of course, the sounds which came out of it were sheer torture for the others. When one player finished, the next one started. Our supervisor, Miss Gūtman, who had a room next to ours, came in one day and screamed,

"I can't take it anymore! Can you, please, give a little rest to that music box?" We all knew that she was a highly strung spinster, but did understand that we had to cool it for a bit, because our nerves were somewhat frayed, too, from all this, and the homework had to be done also.

There was another headache we created for our supervisor. It was smoking, and Vizma was the one who started it.

"Let's have one!" she said to me one day when the younger girls were not there. I did not even understand right away what she was saying.

"Have what?" I asked.

"Have a cigarette!" she said. "You smoke, don't you?"

"Well, I have tried it a few times; you know… just to try out what it feels like, but I have never smoked regularly." I answered.

Vizma looked at me thoughtfully. She probably had smoked before, but did not feel comfortable smoking alone, so asked me to join her.

Well, we had the cigarettes, which came in our monthly packages, but usually they were used to exchange for something that was needed. But surely it would not matter much if I had one! So we lit up, and the next day again. But then one such time, the supervisor came in unexpectedly and stopped in the door aghast.

"Now what is this?" she exclaimed, but Vizma was not perturbed at

all. I think she must have prepared herself for this, because it was inevitable that one day it would come to light.

"Miss Gūtman," she said as she got up quietly from her chair and amicably walked towards her. "We are all grown up people here, are we not? So what's the problem here?"

And Miss Gūtman did not know what to say, because she herself smoked, and we knew it. So she just admonished us not to do it when the younger girls were there. And that was it. Vizma had played her card right.

"See, what can be done, if one has enough courage!" I thought to myself.

And later, when we were studying Latin for the exams and sat in Miss Gūtman's room where she gave us special coaching (since she was also our Latin teacher)—all three of us smoked, blue smoke twirling up to the ceiling. Those were the days, however, when almost everybody smoked, perhaps trying to nurse their dashed hopes or smoldering heartaches.

To relax, we girls, and sometimes also boys, went to Husum to a cinema, where some good German films were shown. Theo Lingen, Marika Roeck, Sarah Leander! They lifted us out of our present existence into some happier times. We loved the songs and learned them all by heart.

When some traveling Latvian group of artists came to give a concert or put on a play in Husum, we went to see them too. The only problem for me then was to evade my enemy—the director—for people from the camps were brought to see the shows also. Sometimes I was lucky, sometimes not, but at least it was not as bad as in Winnert.

My favorite pastime, while resting from school work, was to lie in my bunk and let my thoughts wander back to what had been. One day, I began to write it down and found that it gave me great comfort. I wrote about my first working summer on our grandparent's farm, when I was only twelve and had my first "crush" on a young man who worked for us that summer. I wrote also about my last spring in Latvia, which was so special for me. I thought of my young love and the loss of it. It seemed so long ago now. The writing helped to live through my bitter times, filling them instead with something clean and beautiful. Was I escaping life? Perhaps I was.

Compared to the life we lived at home in Latvia, this to me was not a real life, nor was this a real joy. Even though there were dances and activities, it was more like fleeing and hiding from the bitter truth that there was no home, no country and no future. We were a branch, torn off a tree, lying there and lingering but not really living. Our roots had been

cut. And yet, people around me lived. Not everybody took it as hard as I did. In a way, it was my own fault.

Then one day, news came that my older brother, Ilgvars, had returned from the prisoner of war camp. He was already with my Mother and Johnny at Winnert! I was so excited that I could hardly wait for the Saturday when I would get home. We had not seen him for three years, and now it seemed like he had come from another world. And he did come from another world, the one from which many did not return. He was the same, yet not the same, when I saw him. His face was full and round, like a blown-up balloon, which made him look like a stranger. Later it returned to normal, but he said that this was from the starvation at the prisoner of war camp at "Zedelgheim", Belgium.

"Many died from the cold and starvation there," he told us. "They had survived the war itself, yet they had to die like this, because somebody somewhere had decided to keep us as prisoners of war for six more months." He stopped, perhaps thinking back at that time.

"What an injustice!" I saw that he was quite perturbed recalling that.

"I know," I joined in. "Because our Latvian men never fought the western Allies, they only fought the Russians to protect our country and nation from their dreadful abuse! They knew what would happen if the Russians would establish their regime in our country again."

"Right! Going together with the Germans at that time, was the only possible way to do it. And for that we were so cruelly punished!" Ilgvars continued.

"Yes, but nobody seem to understand it, or perhaps rather chose not to understand who we were, or what we are about." I finished.

When Ilgvars and I were children, we used to be very good friends, but during our growing up years, we each lived in a different place and did not see much of each other anymore. Ilgvars went off to an agricultural high school, which was also a boarding school. Dad wanted him to learn agriculture, so he would be able to take over our farm when the time came. Since they were required to do practical work in the summer, he came home to our farm only for short visits.

I thought it was a good thing that there were a lot of career-oriented high schools in Latvia. The students followed the required high school curriculum, but already were taking subjects preparing them for the future. For instance, there were commerce high schools, technical high schools, music high schools etc., and this was how they were prepared for a job even without going to university.

Now Ilgvars was here, and we had a lot of reacquainting to do. Each of us had gone through a lot. When I came home for the weekends, Ilgvars and I walked along the quiet country roads, talking. The neighbors had seen us and reported to Mother:

"Ah, we finally caught her! She never used to go with anybody, but now she has a boyfriend!"

To their chagrin, Mother told them that he was my brother. What a shame! No reason to gossip! Ilgvars told me that he had been in the western part of Latvia almost to the last days before the capitulation and often behind enemy lines, since he had been in communications. It was hard to imagine. Such danger!

"Have you any news about Edīte?" he asked.

Edīte was my best friend and, his first young love. Now I told him: "Edīte and I exchanged letters all the time until the war ended. We even planned to, perhaps, go together and train to be nurses. We wanted to help in some way; wanted to go somewhere and be in the middle of the big life that was happening. Nothing came of it, of course, because of my hurt knee, and perhaps they were just youthful dreams. Only God knows where Edīte is now. I believe she is on the other side, because no more letters have come since the capitulation, and everything happened so fast in those days. Our Dad had been in the same area too, and there is no news from him, either." We both felt very sad about that.

Time gradually moved toward spring. At the camp rumors started to circulate that we would be moved to another place, and indeed, they turned out to be true. All the camps from this region would be moved to a larger camp near Flensburg, a town on the Danish border. The thought behind it, supposedly, was that then they would be able to take better care of us. Whether it would be so or not, we would have to see. Most likely it would be cheaper and more convenient for those who were doing it, but if they had not given our country away to the Russians, we could have taken care of ourselves. That, of course did not come into it.

This caused a big uproar at school. The studies had to be intensified, so we could finish the school year before the move, because it might not be possible to reorganize everything so quickly after arrival at the new place. Now we had to study, study and study! The teachers gave us extra tutoring and extra hours, especially the three of us who should be graduating this year. In the evenings we went to Miss Gūtman's room to cram Latin.

As if that was not enough, only a couple of weeks before our graduation date, our director Mr. Ritmanis came up with the idea that we should be given exams in all the subjects we had already completed in the previous years. That meant exams in geography, in natural science and even in arithmetic and geometry! We were very upset about this and mad as hell at him. We protested that there was too much work already, but he did not give in.

"What's the matter?" he would say. "Why are you so excited? You

know all that already!"

Yes, but when you have been away from it for some years, you may not recall everything so well! Knowing a subject is not the same as passing an exam, and we did not want to have our grades brought down by getting low grades on exams we were unprepared for. We told him it seemed so unfair, but he just laughed it off.

We did get through somehow, but it was a very stressful time. It was the hardest for Vizma. At times she was totally lost and asked me for answers again and again. I tried to help some, but I had my own work to do as well. The younger girls had gone to their families back at the camps, for they did not have to take any exams. Vizma and I were now on our own in the large room. We studied and smoked and were not even afraid of Miss Gūtman. In fact, she sometimes came in and joined us.

Quite unawares, springtime had arrived. The sun shone, the larks lifted their jubilant songs high up in the sky above the greenish-grey meadows along the coastline. I sometimes walked to the sea to cool my head from studying. One such time I met Ralf, the young man I had been friendly with for a while, walking there with another girl. He looked somewhat embarrassed for a moment, but it was all right with me. I did not care.

Then the exams started: one or two each day and finally it was all over! We had made it, and even Vizma had squeezed through somehow, or perhaps she got pulled through, as had been promised. Who will check, and who will know? These were such times.

I walked again to the sea along the lonely path through the coarse grasses of the meadow. I should have felt happy for what had been accomplished. I should have felt joyful and free, but instead there was just another kind of sadness in me. An important era of my life had ended. Never again would I be a schoolgirl. I climbed the wall and looked out to the sea. Never again... What will the future bring, I wondered. But there were no answers. The sea brought its dark, white-capped waves to the shore and stretched out as far as the eyes could see. No answers.

Tomorrow would be our graduation day, and the whole camp was getting ready for it. I had to give the farewell speech from us, the graduates. I had written it, but the words still milled around in my head. It was strange that now, when we would be parting, suddenly our teachers whom we had sometimes even feared, suddenly seemed like lovable close friends. They had really tried to give their best to us for our future.

On graduation day the large room was decorated with greens. On the table in front of the room was a vase of flowers and a candelabrum with lighted candles. Behind it were our Latvian flag and also the British flag. The guests of honor sat in the first row of chairs behind the table together with the teachers. There was the camp's commandant with the people from UNRRA. After the principal's speech, our home teacher spoke, congratu-

lating us and issuing the diplomas. These were real works of art, made by Vizma's father, who was an artist. He had made the three of them by hand, using ink and watercolor, depicting three national symbols: the oak-leaves for strength, a beautiful girl's head-dress for virtue and the ancient music instrument "kokle" – for singing, which was an integral part of Latvian people. We also each received as a gift one of his paintings of this land's desolate coastline to remember this time of our lives.

Then it was my turn to speak, and as I did, many had tears in their eyes, for the words came out of my heart. More speeches with good wishes came later as we sat at the tables, feasting on what had been provided. Then we relaxed and started singing our dear old folk songs, for Latvians never celebrate anything without singing. The British officers liked our songs, too. Some of them even tried to sing along, especially the most popular one which they had heard before on other occasions.

"Blow the wind, carry my boat, take me back to the Kurzeme coast..." Yes, that was the song we needed to sing, to hold on to each other and to the thought that one day we would be back there. We still believed it.

And then it was over.

"Good-bye, school! Good-bye, Hockensbuhl! Good-bye, sea!"

## To Camp Antwerp, Flensburg

Back in Winnert the packing had begun. Not that there was so much to pack, but we did not want to break any of our meager household items during the journey. On May 4, 1946 we said good-bye to this place also. The army trucks came in a long row and carried us out of the camp, leaving it bare and empty as it had been before. The locals would probably be glad not to see any more foreigners around here and understandably so.

After several hours ride, the trucks turned in through a wide gate. Above it was a name "Camp Antwerp". It was a gate made of barbed wires! A camp surrounded with barbed wires! Will we be living in a prison, like our soldiers had been in Belgium? I hoped not! Those soldiers had been told that they would be taken to be released, but had been taken to a camp surrounded by barbed wires, where they had to stay for another six months, during which time many more died from cold and starvation! No, they could not do that to us!

Beyond the gates, rows of gray wooden barracks lined the wide central street which led through the camp, a number of side streets expanding the compound even bigger. This would be our new home where we would live, some thousand people together, all Latvians.

Again barracks and rooms were allocated, according to how many people were in a family and what it consisted of. The families with children were given the larger rooms, which was understandable. Uncle

Heinī got one such room for his family because they were five adults and three children. All through their journey since leaving Latvia, Heinī and his wife with their two small children had incorporated in their family Omī and Aunt Elzī with her small daughter Ilze, for there was nobody else to look after them. Aunt Elzī's husband Alfrēds Krimuldēns had also been drafted into the German army and had not returned. Since he had been in the region of Danzig, which the Russians had surrounded and cut off, it was very likely that he had been captured and made a prisoner of war. Heinī's family had also "adopted" a lone soldier for some reason, and now the eight of them lived in the one room. Uncle Kārl and Aunt Irma with their three children also had gotten a larger room and were quite comfortable.

Our family, being almost all grown-ups, did not get any breaks. We got a small room again in a barrack on one of the side streets. In fact, it was even smaller than the one at Winnert, and we could barely turn around if the four of us were there at the same time. A bunk bed stood at each of the side walls with the window in between and a table in front of it. This time there was no room for chairs at the sides of the table, except two at the free end. When we were eating, two of us had to sit on the beds. Two narrow wardrobes stood by the opposite walls closer to the door, as well as a small, round iron stove with a chimney pipe going through the ceiling. Well, we had been in a similar situation before. The only difference was that before I had mostly lived at the boarding school, but now I would be here all the time and Ilgvars was here too. If we would all be at home, most of us would have to sit or lay on our beds, but that also was nothing new.

The camp was situated in the very outskirts of Flensburg in an area called "Sharnhorst", perhaps a mile or more from the city center. There was no sea to walk to anymore, but a beautiful large, old cemetery was close by. It was more like a park with many trees and blossoming shrubs, and a small stream flowed through it with an arched, Chinese-style bridge. Right now everything was blooming, and it was a real delight to walk there. Birds sang in the trees, the different scents of the flowers floated in the air. It was like a paradise, only it was not, because it brought back memories of other springs back in our own country. Thinking about that made you want to sit down on some old bench and howl like a dog. Yet, what would that help? We had to live, and it would be better to not think too much about our losses.

But we had to think again and again of what had been done to us; that all of Eastern Europe was left in the hands of the Russians, facing a fate worse than death. Did not anybody know what the Russians did? The small countries had not been considered or consulted and that

really hurt. Our destiny had been sealed, but this injustice still burned in the hearts of those who had hoped in the fairness of the big powers.

Now we heard that the Russian agents went soliciting in the refugee camps, coaxing the people to return to their countries, promising good treatment, housing and a job. They wanted to get back those who had fled. Most likely they wanted more people for their slave camps to do their work, but they also wanted revenge toward those who had escaped or fought against them. The people knew better and did not respond to their invitations.

It was very sad that one nice young man from our camp, a former soldier, did go back, for he had an old, sick mother and he was the only son. He promised he would write and let us know how things would go. And he did write that he had been given all that had been promised. To convince others to return also, he even made a speech on the radio several times, praising the Russian establishment and saying that all was well, but after that there was silence. Nobody ever heard from him again. He had done the dirty work for them and was not needed anymore.

It turned out that the Russian agents had also been soliciting in the prisoner of war camps and had even tried to take people by force. Luckily, the commandants had been alerted about this and the Russians were stopped.

There was, however, worse news about our soldiers who had managed to get to Sweden at the end of the war to save their lives, knowing full well that it would be a death sentence at the hands of the Russians if they were captured. But the Swedish government handed them over to the Russians anyway, even after the soldiers had gone on a hunger strike, some committed suicide and the whole country was outraged! By allowing the Russians to come and take them, even drag them to their ship, some 158 men were sent to certain death. How would one not mourn them? But there was nothing that could be done about that anymore.

It was good that not all people were as pessimistic as I. In fact, there were a lot of very energetic people in the camp, and all kinds of activities were started right away again. Some were carried over from the previous camps, like the choir, the drama group, various crafts groups and workshops, where people shared their knowledge with others. There were also language classes, for everybody knew that they might need them in the future, especially English. Also the schools would have to be planned for the children again: the grade school and also the high school.

The scouting activities had already been initiated at camp Hockensbuhl, and I had joined the senior Girl-Guides there. Here in Antwerp were even more young people and children, who were just ready for these kinds of activities—so many joined. It was a great program for them in

the summertime, giving them something positive to do. Soon the scouting activities were in full swing in all categories, beginning with Brownies and ending with new leaders. School was out for the summer, so we all had plenty of time for scouting and went into it with great enthusiasm.

To learn how to be better people! How little we had thought about it before, perhaps not at all! Now we talked about it in our small groups, learning the good principles of scouting. Maybe for the younger girls it was too serious, but I liked it. I had always wanted to understand this life that we were living.

After some intensive instruction, we older girls were ready to give our solemn oath. It was a warm evening in June when we walked together with our leaders to the nearby forest to do this very special thing. It was a beautiful dark fir forest. A fire was built in a small clearing and there we gave our promise. It was a very meaningful moment, and in our young hearts we really wanted to be those beautiful, worthwhile people. The trees stood dark and silent around us; only the stars high above the tree tops witnessed our sacred moment. Afterward we sat around the camp fire in silence, watching it burn down slowly, thinking over what we had promised. As the logs gradually began to fall apart, red sparks in little spurts shot up, vanishing in the dark, then the light slowly grew dimmer. In the end only a little heap of gleaming coals were left, and we took that gleam with us in our hearts as we left. Perhaps someday we would be able to bring some light to where it was needed.

After this, the first big job for us older guides was to host the famous Zuika's men's choir, which would be visiting our camp and giving a concert. We felt greatly honored and did this with joy. We set the tables, served their food and took them out for a walk in our lovely "cemetery-park". The concert was in the afternoon; and their beautiful singing gladdened the hearts of all of us who had filled the hall to capacity, as well as those who stood outside the windows, since there was not enough room inside. People would not stop applauding, and the men sang more and more additional songs. A spirit of special warmth flowed between the public and the singers. We experienced deeply that we were still one nation, one people under the sun. Not each on our own, scattered and fearful, but one nation, gaining strength from our songs, giving each other comfort and hope for the future.

Later, after the men had finished their evening meal and were still sitting at the tables, they sang a song for us girls only, as a thank you for looking after them. It was getting to be dusk in the room as they sang, and we, still with aprons around our waists, stood inside the door listening to them. The sounds rose softly, so softly,

"Roses, roses..." One had to stop breathing, listening to this. It was so beautiful that it made us cry. When they finished softly again, resolv-

ing into absolute silence, there was no more room for words.

It was hard to combine the facts that these were the "rough soldiers" who had walked through the dangers of the war not so long ago and yet could sing with so much beautiful feeling. Not just their voices were making these sounds, but their very souls. The choir was created at the prisoner of war camp at Zedelgheim in Belgium by the energetic musician Robert Zuika, to keep the men from giving in and giving up. I am sure it helped them, as it helped us now, and we saw them off with our heartfelt thanks.

Toward the end of June, news came that a folk dancing course would be held in Luebeck for Girl-Guide and Boy-Scout leaders, and even though I was not a leader yet, I was appointed to go and attend it. Why not? I was glad to go; folklore had always been close to my heart.

There were about twenty of us who had come for this course, and it was a wonderful experience for all of us, and me especially, because this was my first time being in a gathering like this. It had been arranged that we could stay at a boarding school on the outskirts of Luebeck, for the school was out for the summer. Our leader was fantastic, and we fell in love with him instantly. He was a tall, lean, middle-aged man, a scout master who must have had a background in dance, for he walked as if he had no weight at all. Not heel to toe like we all walked, but toe to heel instead. He made us practice it too, and what a difference it made. Instead of walking, we were gliding!

The Latvian folk dances are rather simple, mostly done in polka or small running steps. They are more like playful visiting with each other rather than exaggerated movements and steps. Often they are accompanied by singing, so playful interaction is very important. I had never done it like this, and was overwhelmed by the beauty of this kind of dancing. Our leader not only taught us the dancing, but also led us into the very spirit of our age-old national culture. I suppose, we had never realized what a treasure it was. Only one week, but we learned such a lot to take back with us to our various camps in Germany where we lived. This would be a treasure to share with others when we got back.

It so happened that the last day of our instruction coincided with the Summer Solstice, the great Midsummer Fest, which was usually celebrated in Latvia by lighting bonfires and singing and dancing all night. Because of this, we were free to spend the last afternoon getting ready for it. We made crowns of oak leaves for the boys and wildflower circlets for us girls to wear on our heads that evening; we sang our special Līgo songs while doing it. Later we sat around the campfire and sang, but soon, one after another, we became quiet and sat just watching the flames till the morning. There was a lot to think about. We did not re-

ally want to celebrate. It weighed on us heavily that we were in a foreign land, for our own land was lost. But what we had experienced this week seemed to give us a new strength, a notion that there was something good in this world after all. Even if that good could be only within ourselves, we could cherish it and cultivate it like a growing plant.

When I returned to the camp, I was asked to become a leader of the Brownies, even though I had not had any instruction in that field. I feared that I couldn't do it, but at our first meeting the little girls surrounded me like little birds, each wanting to get closer. So how could I refuse? Yes, I would try to give them my best. And gradually my confidence grew as we all learned together: they, to be good brownies and I—a good leader.

A lot of young people were at our camp now, as well as some former soldiers who had not been confirmed, because the Germans had drafted into their army even seventeen-year-olds. The Latvians were mostly Lutherans, and in this denomination, their confirmation usually took place around the age of eighteen, after finishing high school. It was like a threshold to adulthood and a very special day for the young people, the family and even the whole community. The parents now thought that this was a good time to have the confirmation ceremony, for who knows, where we would be the next year? Our situation here was fairly stable right now, and there was a nice big church in Flensburg. We also had a minister at the camp, Mr. Pavasars, the same one who had been my teacher of religion at my high school in Valmiera, back in Latvia, and also at Hockensbuhl. I knew him and his wife well, for she was our girl-guide leader here. Once it was decided to hold the confirmation, Mother wanted Ilgvar and me to also use this opportunity to get confirmed.

The confirmation instruction started. We knew a lot already from our religion classes at school, but now there was much more. It was one thing to memorize what we had to, but what did all that mean? What was required of us? Will we be able to fulfill what we promise? These were serious things. About the eternal life, what was it? How to believe if you don't know what it is?

"Someday you will understand," the minister said.

And what about the dead? How will they be able to rise?

"Indeed they will," was his answer, but he did not elaborate, since we did not have much time to go into depth with everything. Perhaps he did not know, either. Perhaps these were things for which there were no human answers, so the confusion remained. It seemed enough that we knew the ritual and the sacraments for now.

The other preparations went full speed ahead, too. Fabric had to be found for the girls' white dresses; the men needed dark suits. Plans had to be made for what to exchange through the black market to get

more food for the celebrations, for the weekly food rations were getting smaller and smaller. Also the Red Cross parcels came to us with some items already removed. Who was doing that?

Now and then a shipment of used clothing or shoes arrived at the camp, but those, too, were already picked over, and the best was gone. Again, who did this? When and where? Later we heard that a lot of that stuff was sold in the black market. Things sold to German farmers for food which again could be exchanged at the camp for coffee or cigarettes, which could be sold again to the farmers for food and so on and on. Some people got rich, but then again, the average person could not have survived without getting something extra from the black market, since the money was worthless.

We were lucky that Mother had found a new way to make some new "currency" for us. By exhibiting some of her intricately ornamented leather work, which she had brought with her from Latvia as personal items, she had attracted the attention of the British officers at our camp.

"Do you think you could make something like that for our wives at home?" they asked Mother as they looked at the leather handbag she had made with the fine patterns worked in the cover of it.

"I would gladly do that," Mother had replied, "but I do not have any leather or tools to work with!"

"We can provide the materials and the tools needed for this work," they said. "No problem! You just let us know what you need!"

The payment would be in cigarettes, which did not cost much to the officers, but would buy things for us on the black market. The deal was made, and that helped a lot toward what we needed for the confirmation celebration.

The big day came. It was July 7, 1946. We were glad that the day was sunny and nice; only the wind blew strongly, chasing the white clouds across the sky. Those of us who were to be confirmed were taken to the church in the same old army trucks as always. When we arrived, the beautifully decorated church was already full of people, and at the sounds of the organ, the minister led us in. We walked in pairs behind him. The girls went first, all in long white dresses; only Sandra, my former classmate from Hockensbuhl was dressed in black—in mourning for her lost parents, and another girl, wearing a national costume that somebody had lent her for this occasion—for she also did not have her parents. Behind the girls came the young men in dark suits, some thirty of us altogether.

We sang the first hymn, "A Mighty Fortress is Our God", and the organ boomed along with the words. The following service was all like a dream for me: we, kneeling at the altar, then taking the holy sacrament for the first time. My heart trembled inside of me. I was all emotion.

Then the minister blessed each of us by putting his hands on our heads and saying some words of Jesus.

"I am the way, the truth and the life..." the minister said as he blessed me, and tears rolled down my cheeks. I was moved by these words, but also sorrow filled my heart that this could not be in the church in our own country. But then it was all over. There was no time for crying. I wiped my tears, and we walked out of the church accompanied by the jubilant sounds of the organ. As we came outside into the sunshine, rows of people stood there on both sides of the pathway with flowers in their hands waiting to congratulate us.

Where did they get all those flowers when there were none to be had anywhere? I ended up with my arms full of roses and was glad that so many of my family members were still around me here. But some of the former soldiers did not have anybody of their own to greet them, so we gave them some of our flowers, and the ladies committee from the camp saw to it that they had a celebration, too.

Back at the camp, one more table had been squeezed into our narrow room right up to the door, so that at least our closest relatives could share in our celebration, but then nobody could get in or out anymore. Mother had managed to get some extra food for the table, and the celebration could begin. In the middle of it, a telegram came from Viktor again, and he had also sent me a gift, a nice pendant with a black stone in a silver setting which I, however, could not bring myself to wear (except for a few times). More flowers arrived from my "secret admirers" at the camp, more congratulations and cards with meaningful words, but my heart belonged to no one.

Viktor still kept writing to me, and I answered. Somehow it was easier to talk with him than with anybody else, because I knew that he was listening with his heart. He wrote that since March he had lived in Hamburg, where, after successfully passing the exams, he was admitted to the medical faculty at the newly opened Baltic University in Pineberg. He was very happy about it, of course, and urged me, too, to apply soon. The living quarters were in a camp near the university, but the drawback was that the food was even more meager there than in other camps, and apparently more students were contracting tuberculosis because of it. That for me was a rather frightening factor, since Mother had already had this disease. I did want to go to the university to prepare for some kind of a future, but there was time enough before fall.

The warm summer evenings at the camp were pleasant. Since the small rooms became hot in the summer weather, more people were outside, standing around in the doorways, and chatting or promenading along the main street. For us, the young people, the favorite

place to congregate was near the big hall in the middle of the camp. Somebody would go inside and start playing the piano. The sounds coming through the open windows would coax some to go inside and listen, then more would go in; a couple might start dancing, and before long the hall would be full of dancers. Others would stand outside the windows, urging them on or teasing until the darkness thickened around them, and it all had to end.

Amongst the young people there were also quite a few former soldiers who did not know how to dance, for their young days had been so cruelly interrupted. They just stood outside the windows watching, or sat at the sides in the hall. My brother, Ilgvar, was one of them.

"Come inside," I said to him, "I will teach you." It was already dusk, and the hall was in half darkness, so no one would see if he made mistakes, but he was not comfortable doing that.

"Let's go to the sports field behind the barracks instead," he said. "Nobody will be there at this time." So we went and danced around the basketball court, learning the steps until it got dark and the stars came out.

A few days later, he told me that other young former soldiers wanted to learn to dance too, and one of them had already gone to town to arrange for some dancing lessons at a studio, but they needed twenty people for the group. He urged me to come too and be his partner, for there were fewer girls than men. Well, why not? It would be nice to learn to dance better, because I knew only what I had picked up at school dances. So the lessons started with great enthusiasm, and how nice it was to feel how much more fluent and graceful the movements became, when you did the steps properly. We were delighted.

## Scouting

Then, however, an announcement came that there would be a training camp for the new Girl-Guide and Scout leaders in Greven, and I was selected to go. I really needed that training, and it would be great to take part in such a gathering, for the scouting movement seemed to give us a new substance for our living—a new hope for the future. Now I had to choose, to finish one more week of dance lessons or go to the camp. The camp won. I could have dance lessons anytime, but there might not be many more camps like this.

It was decided that our Girl-Guide leader, Mrs. Pavasars, and I would go together. So on August 6, 1946, we both got on our way. First we had to take a train to Hamburg, but traveling in those days was very cumbersome. The train stopped in many places, seemingly for no reason at all, and we just had to sit and wait. It took us six hours to get to Hamburg instead of two or three. Mrs. Pavasars had arranged for us to over-

night at the Baltic University camp. She knew a man and his wife from camp Hockensbuhl who now taught at the University. It was my former English teacher from high school and her husband. They were very kind and took us in when we arrived. It also gave me the opportunity to talk to them about my coming here to study. They too urged me to put in my application as soon as possible.

This was the camp where Viktor now lived. I had written to him about this, and in the evening went on my way to see him. How will it be, I wondered, as I walked along the sparsely lit streets of the camp. It had been three years since we last met, and I had walked away in anger at that time for what he had done. He had again cornered me into a situation I did not want to be in, and I did not like to be manipulated. He did try to see me one more time at our farm a year later, in the summer of 1944, but then I took off before he arrived. The next day my brother Jānīts gave me a message from Viktor that he would wait for me that evening on the bridge of the small river which ran between our parent's properties, but I did not go, vowing to never see him again.

But he found me. He always found me and knew all about me. Did he really love me so much, or was it because he could not have me? He found me in Viol and "cornered" me into answering his letters after I had decided not to do so. Lately we had communicated quite often and perhaps grown closer than we had ever been before. But we had always done it better in letters than in person—at least on my part. I had to admit that talking to him had helped me. Was I using him? Perhaps I was, but then, he had said many times that it would make him very happy if he could help me in any way at all. In his letters he never forgot to mention how much I meant to him, but also right away apologized for saying it, fearing that it would make me want to "escape" again.

But no, I would not escape. In fact I was going to see him of my free will now. I had grown up. And yet, as I walked this evening to his place, there were mixed feelings within me. I knew he loved me, but I hoped he would not try to touch me. I did not want that. Finally I was at his door, and he was waiting there. We went into his room, where just one small light was on the table. He apparently had been writing, and nobody else was there. This was a student's room, divided into four cubicles by hanging blankets, in each an iron bedstead, a small table and a chair. At least that was all I could see in the darkish room.

He took both my hands in his and held them, looking at me and saying again and again, "Zigi, Zigi, Zigi…"

We did not stay there for long but went outside. The evening was warm and kind of sultry. We walked along the quiet street talking, the shrubs and trees emerging from the dark. This seemed to be an extensive place with many barracks. He told me again how happy he was about

getting into medical school, and I too was happy for him. He also urged me to get in my application papers soon.

"Why don't you send your documents to me," he said, "and I shall see that everything is arranged properly."

We did not talk about ourselves, and I was glad that we didn't. I did not stay long, for it was rather late already, and I did not want to inconvenience our hosts. Then we shook hands again and said good-bye, not knowing yet that this would be the last time we met.

The next morning, Mrs. Pavasars and I continued our journey. It was a long way to go, and we had to change trains several times. If I remember correctly, we went from Hamburg to Bremen, then to Osnabruck and to Muenster. They were all in ruins, and it was dreadful to see all the devastation. Finally another train took us to Greven. It was already early evening when we arrived there and found the Latvian camp. Mrs. Pavasars stayed with another leader who lived at the D.P. camp in Greven, but I walked to our designated camp site a little farther out in the countryside.

It happened to be in a beautiful place, a field covered with blooming heather, dotted by clumps and rows of birch trees. A larger fir forest surrounded the whole area. What a perfect setting! Two large tents had been erected at one side of the field, but no one was there yet. The sun was just setting over the tree tops, and its last rays painted the heather red. It was so beautiful and I was glad that I could celebrate this sunset hour all by myself! Just a little farther, down the slope of the field, was the River Emse, carrying in its waters the changing reflections of the evening sky.

I left my things in one of the tents, then took a towel and went down to the river to have a wash. The cool water was so refreshing after the long journey. When I got back, two more girls had arrived, and we introduced ourselves. From the other side of the field, where the Boy-Scout's campsite was situated behind a clump of birches, came the sounds of an accordion being played. Somewhere from farther away in the countryside, a threshing machine sounded.

We spent a wonderful week in Greven even though it was rush-rush all the time. There was quite a number of us, the young leaders, and the older ones were there to guide us. A lot had to be accomplished. Some activities, we girls and young men had separately, others we had together.

Our days started early, soon after sun-up. First exercising outside in the fresh morning air, then running to the river to wash. Quickly back to breakfast! Eating, tidying everything away, then rushing to the morning prayer and raising of the flag. The leaders already stood in a line at the flag post. There was the chief scout leader, Professor Dunsdorf, called

"Vecais", "the Oldie" behind his back. His small stature belied a very intelligent man with a sharp mind and sarcastic humor. We all sort of feared him when he came for inspections. He saw everything, even the smallest discrepancy! There was also Mrs. Laufer, the chief girl-guide leader and other well-known leaders in scouting. After the raising of the flag and a prayer, we began our busy day with all kinds of assignments and problems to solve, with sometimes a lecture in between.

The things we had to do! How about being sent into the forest bare-foot, with no tools but a neckerchief, a knife and one match to build an overnight camp, make a fire, bake bread with a little flour provided, bring water from the river, no vessel provided! All that had to be done in a limited time, when the chiefs would come for breakfast. That was fun! We scurried and worked, figured how to do things, made decisions and carried them out, which always took some innovations. On these projects we usually went in mixed groups, so we got to know each other and built a good camaraderie. Another time we would have to take care of an in-jured person, put him in splints and transport him across the river. Each assignment was well planned and taught us something.

In the midst of all that, we also had to come up with ideas about what to contribute for the evening entertainment. No special time for it was given. The theme was announced each morning, and it was a real scramble to come up with something, but it was always done just in time. It really needed a lot of invention, since we did not have any props, but perhaps because of it, everything came out even more interesting.

The best times were after everything was done, just to sit around the campfire and sing, celebrating our togetherness as guides, scouts, and also as children of one nation, even though banished from our land. We knew many songs and sang them until the last logs finished burning.

Rumors came to us from some veteran campers that there was an unwritten tradition during the camp life to test how alert and watchful the other side was, meaning, guides versus scouts. It meant trying to do something unexpected to the other side to shame them, to show that they had not been watchful enough. Our opportunity came quite unexpect-edly. One late afternoon I saw the scout's guard walk into the tent for a few minutes, and I stole their guard dog, even though only a stuffed one, which was tied up at the boundary of their camp! After I brought the dog to our side, we spied on the other camp to see what would hap-pen. Very soon a lot happened! The scouts were frantic, when they saw the dog missing and wanted to get it back. Of course, they knew that we were the culprits. And we knew that our tents would be searched as soon as it got dark, when we would be at the campfire. So where should we hide the dog?

"Why not hide it in the stack of logs near the campfire?" I suggested. That was halfway between both camps, and so we did that. While we sat at the campfire, we could sense something happening in our tents a little distance behind us, but we did not worry, for the little dog was sitting right there in everybody's view with his nose even sticking out, if anybody had thought of looking there. That was a hectic night, and we only half slept, fearing that the tent might come down over us in revenge. It did not happen though, and the next day we returned the little dog. We had proved our point and won!

The last night at the camp came sooner than we would have liked. I had to be out on a watch starting right after midnight, but I was glad to be there. Everything was so quiet and beautiful. Bright moonlight flooded the field, wrapping its silvery shrouds around the birches. The forest loomed black and mysterious against the night sky. I thought about the time we had spent here. A new world had opened to me, and I felt deeply enriched in a way I had never felt possible. How could people, who did not even know each other personally, feel so close? The same thoughts? The same ideals? A new kind of unity.

Our time here had come to an end. The next morning we packed. There was not too much to pack really, since we were still the poor refugee kids with only a minimum of possessions and clothing, yet we felt rich at this moment. I was sorry to leave this lovely place, so much like our own beloved country. I picked a few branches of heather for remembrance and stuck them in my breast pocket as we left.

Then we were all at the small station, saying our goodbyes before each going our own way again. The train came in already full, and we had to squeeze together to capacity. Some men even got up on the roof, some rode on the bumpers, which was reckless, but nobody cared. We were so full of high spirits, and it was just a short distance. At Muenster we all parted, and I continued my journey alone, for my leader had decided to stay on and visit a bit longer. Again I had to change trains several times, but even that did not matter this time. The exuberance of spirit inside me remained throughout all the long journey, and even walking along the-tree lined road from the Flensburg station to the camp, I still hummed one of the happy scouts songs: "A scout - he is a wholesome man... he's not like flimsy tissue paper" *(jo skauts - tas esot - tāds varens vīrs, tas nav vis kāds - tāds zīdpapīrs...)*

Back at the camp in Flensburg, life seemed static after the busy days at the training camp. It took some adjusting and rethinking everything. There were plans for the future to teach folk dancing to the guides and scouts, to work with the brownies, but that would start later in the fall.

It was the end of August, and my birthday was nearing. As always,

that for me was a time when I liked to take stock of what there was and what was not. I would be twenty. What would the next year bring? I had sent my application papers for the University to Viktor as he had advised me. Would I be able to go? Somehow my hopes were low because of the bad food situation there. In our camp, too, it had deteriorated very rapidly lately. It was a poor scenario. Could I risk moving there, knowing my family history? Here at least Mother could sometimes get extra food from the black marketers by exchanging it for the cigarettes she had earned, but there it would not be possible.

Actually, I didn't know how my Mother felt these days. Not knowing what had happened to Dad must have been hard for her, but she never talked about it, and I did not ask—did not even think of asking. These days we each lived in a world of our own and did not have much communication, except for the ordinary everyday things. It was strange. It was the very opposite of the togetherness we had enjoyed during our childhood when Dad was there. I guess all the past happenings and the circumstances in which we lived, had something to do with it. Perhaps each of us tried to hide our own individual pain...

My birthday dawned gray and dreary, and I did not expect anything of it, either. Mother sat at the table sewing as I climbed down from my top bunk, which was my living and sleeping quarters these days, for there was nowhere else to be in this narrow room. She did remember to wish me a happy birthday and said that maybe later she would make some pancakes. The boys were out as usual—Jānīts being together with his crowd of Boy-Scouts; Ilgvar, having befriended some of the former soldiers, spent time with them playing cards or doing whatever they did. After completing the dance lessons, he often went out in the evenings to some local places to dance. I was very much on my own and felt that way especially this morning. I guess I did want this day to be special in some way, but it seemed like nobody cared. I felt a turmoil, a protest rising within me—all those hidden, unhappy feelings that did not know where to go.

I decided to go to town. At least, it would be something different. A light sprinkle was starting as I set out, but I felt defiant and went anyway, even though I did not have an umbrella. The long walk would be good for me, to get rid of these negative energies within me. Feelings of resentment and hopelessness were overtaking me again. Everything seemed so pointless and sad.

"Why do we continue to do anything at all, if we cannot live normal lives like other people do?" I argued with myself. Bitterness against fate churned inside of me, and the constant struggle to keep on top of things was wearing me down.

Once in town, I wandered through the streets aimlessly. There really was nothing to do or to see here. No display windows or shops to look

at. The rain continued to drizzle. Everything looked empty and forsaken. No people around either. Then I noticed a line of them standing outside a cinema and decided to join them. Perhaps it will cheer me up if I see a show. Since I did not have a life of my own, at least I could watch how other people lived. I took my place at the end of the line. The fine rain came down more steadily now. I pressed myself closer to the brick wall for shelter. My hair was already soaked through and stuck to my head; the raindrops ran down my face like tears. Was I crying? No, just gritting my teeth tighter, trying to swallow the bitterness that kept welling up in me, when I thought that at the camp we hardly had anything to swallow at all these days. For two weeks we had not had any bread. Instead we had been handed out something like hard dog biscuits, which were almost impossible to chew, because the gums would bleed.

I was glad when we finally could go in and sit in the dark warmth of the cinema. The show started, and a beautiful ballroom came into view where magnificently dressed ladies danced with their uniformed, aristocratic-looking partners under the sparkling chandeliers. People talked, laughed, swayed with the enticing rhythms of the music. I saw it, but at the same time my thoughts went in circles. Something cataclysmic was going on inside of me... anger and sorrow and shame for the state we were in, and which we were helpless to change. I felt like a beggar picking up crumbs under somebody's table. No, this was not the relief I had been looking for.

When I walked home, the rain had stopped. It was late afternoon by now, and here and there, in the little houses the lights were on. People lived there. They were at home. That again brought up in me the deep feeling of loss.

"Will we ever be at home anywhere again?" I thought. "What did a home mean to one? Not a castle. No, it was much more than that. It was a place where one belonged." And we did not belong anywhere.

As I walked, I gradually calmed down. What was the use of hitting my head against the wall? The anger was spent. The shame remained and also the sadness. Passing by a garden wall, a scent of roses reached me, again reminding me of the loss of my own garden and home.

"Would I now always be only looking in from the outside?" I asked myself.

When I got home, Mother was still sewing. She was so absorbed in what she was doing that she hardly saw my coming in and most likely the pancakes were forgotten also. And so it was. Soon after she folded away the sewing and said that she would go to see some lady in one of the other barracks. I did not say anything, just looked at her with a question in my eyes, but she did not even look at me. The door closed behind her, and she was gone. I climbed up into my bunk and pulled the blanket

over my head. It was not even worth crying. My twentieth birthday was over. Outside it rained again.

It rained for three days, but then the morning dawned sunny and bright again, and I thanked God that the rains and the tears belonged to yesterday. It had been a bitter time, but I wanted to try to believe and to hope again. I decided to walk to the nearby forest. It really was a beautiful day! The sky looked so high and blue, and autumn was in the air, even though it was only the end of August. The birds would be leaving soon, I thought, but we would stay, for we had nowhere to go. Two years since we had left our home, but we were no closer to anything.

Sadness wrapped around me again. No, I did not want to cry. Somehow I just felt weak and a bit lightheaded today and strangely, there was not much strength in my legs. The bright sunlight hurt my eyes, and a slight dizziness overcame me as I looked up into the deep blue sky. What was happening? Then I remembered that we had not had any bread for almost three weeks. That was it. We did not even have our little bit of daily bread anymore... I would not go any farther. I sat down under a tree and stayed there for a long time. It felt so good to be there, so close to the earth, with the sun warming my body and a silvery, mist between my eyes and what was out there.

Here and there in the trees I could see a golden or red leaf. Yes, autumn was coming, and then all the golden and red leaves would go. A strange and sad thought came into my mind, that perhaps I too would be gone by then if this continued. My heart felt so heavy. The silvery mist looked like white smoke from an unseen fire, in which my past and future days were burning up.

I don't know how I got home that day, but there I was. The next day we again began receiving bread, the body recovered, and life returned more to normal again.

The trees outside the camp had turned yellow and red. The autumn had come. Schools were starting, as well as all kinds of other activities. A choir was formed and all four of us from our family joined. That was so good; it lifted the spirits as song always does. I was also asked to take part in a play—one of our much loved classics—and I agreed. The director was the same one as in Winnert, whom I disliked, but I had learned how to evade his advances. Perhaps he, too, had finally understood that this romance would not be going anywhere, and now we could communicate normally.

I also started to teach the Scouts and Girl-Guides the folk dances I had learned at the training camp, and everybody enjoyed it very much. It helped the teenagers to get together and have their fun in a very positive way. My work with the brownies turned out to be very rewarding too,

and I gained more confidence as we went along.

Then one day I was asked if I could help out at the kindergarten for a bit, and I, though reluctantly, agreed. I had thought that I would be just a helper, but as it turned out when I got there, nobody else was there, and I had to be in charge! That was pretty devastating. What do I do? I had no training in this whatsoever!

When I entered the classroom, I felt like I was in a zoo. Every child seemed to want to show off! Were they seeking attention? Some were on the table, some under it, some standing on their heads, some fighting about a book or a toy. How do I get some order here? Never mind about teaching anything!

Calling out to them did not do anything. Nobody listened, except some of the very young ones, who stood at the side, looking at all the goings-on with their scared little eyes. I felt sorry for them, and then and there decided to handle this from a totally different point of view — from the point of personal prestige. Perhaps it sounds silly in application to small children, but it worked. Each person, however small, wants to be something bigger and better, something more worthwhile. I think it is in all of us, to strive for something better.

First, I got hold of a couple of the biggest boys (and the naughtiest too!)! I did not scold them, but told them that I very much needed their help in getting the younger ones in some order, because being older, they would of course know how to do this better! I told them what I thought we should do, and they went ahead, took charge, and very soon I had an orderly classroom!

There was just one child who still refused to integrate into the over-all order, and that was young Ilona. She was a pretty little girl with curly blond hair, but sometimes it had not been even combed, and her little face had not been washed. She refused to sit down and just stood by the wall, obviously full of defiance, and if there was an opportunity, she pinched or hit somebody who passed by. Then I heard that her mother was one who liked to live it up with men and was not taking proper care of her little girl. I was sorry for little Ilona. Her young heart was hurting. To try to get her involved somehow and to lift her spirits, I invited her to be my special helper.

"Ilona," I said, "I really need somebody who would help me with distributing the papers and pencils and to tidy everything away after the classes have ended."

Ilona responded and soon I could not have wished for a better and more obedient child, always anxious to please. Occasionally there was even a smile on her little face, when I praised her for a job well done. That made me very happy.

Since I did not have any knowledge of teaching, I could only rely

on my natural responses to how things were. I felt that, if it is explained to children first, why they must do or not do a certain thing, their own integrity will teach them to choose the right direction. That would give them and also me satisfaction and pride that they had done something good, without any ordering, but by their own will.

Again, we had to start by being orderly. In the beginning, they all crowded around me with their papers, wanting me to look at them, each trying to get closer to me, which made it impossible for me to help them. Then I asked them to go back to their places, and I would tell them something special.

"Do you want to hear how things are done in a real school where the big children go? Would you like to do what they do also?" I asked.

"Yesss!" was the excited, unanimous answer.

I went on to tell them how it was done, and from then on the children stayed in their seats, proudly lifting their hands and waiting for me to come to them to help or to view their work. We had developed a good working system and I was glad.

S orry to say, my teaching career did not last too long, for another offer came along which I could not resist. In the beginning of October, news came that there would be another folk dancing course for the young scout and guide leaders, because there seemed to be a great interest  in this activity amongst the young people at the camps. I, of course, loved it and would not miss it for the world. This was something that bound us to the past of our nation, to the old ethnic traditions, almost the same as singing.

It would take place somewhere south of Osnabruck, in a place called Wolterdingen. The leadership of our girl-scout organization wanted me to go, and I was more than willing to do it. The course would take two weeks, and we would camp in a forest. That sounded fantastic!

I packed my backpack again. I don't even remember where I got it. Perhaps my brother Ilgvar brought it when he came back from the war. The soldiers called it "the monkey", because the cover of it was made of a hairy cow's hide. For traveling like this, it was very useful and easy to carry. Besides, it could also serve as a pillow. The days were getting cooler. I packed my warmer clothing, whatever I could find, for the choice was not great. We would be living in tents and be there till the end of October. In Europe that is a time when winter is already on the way.

Again I was going together with our leader, Mrs. Pavasars. We started out early in the morning to catch the first train to Hamburg. It was still dark outside and a bit foggy, as it often is in the fall. The streets were quiet. Not a soul anywhere. As we walked under the big trees in an alley, the night dew fell on us in big drops making plopping sounds on the

pavement. Our steps sounded hollow in the empty street and yet, to me these sounds had a joyful ring. I was going to a camp again, to that special world where life was so different! It will be good to have this change. At least for a little while we would be able to forget the realities of life; that we lived in a cage, subsisting on other people's mercy.

The train was already in place when we got to the station. Since this was the starting point, we had no problem finding seats. We sat in the darkness and waited. When we finally moved out of the station, a thick, white fog covered everything outside. Nothing could be seen through the windows, and soon the gentle sway of the train lulled us to sleep.

The train service was still far from normal. Stops were made in places for no apparent reason, and we had to sit and wait. Sometimes more cars were added, the train maneuvering back and forth until we could move again. It took us six hours to get to Hamburg again, which otherwise would have taken two or three. At least the fog had lifted, and after a little while, the sun even came out.

As we arrived in Hamburg and the train made its way through the city, our joy in seeing the sun soon evaporated. It was difficult to view the ruins, and they reached as far as the eye could see. Half walls, half houses with empty, gaping holes where the windows had been. We did not see one undamaged house where people could actually live, only piles of bricks and rubble. How many people burned to death, when these houses were falling? How many got buried? This was where those bombers came when they flew over us in Vioel. One could cry about what people did to other people, if one started to think about it.

But this was not the time for it. We were on our way again, changing trains in Bremen, then Osnabruck and finally to Wolterdingen until we were stopped again. This time it was in the middle of a forest. The engine just left us sitting there. We guessed it was needed somewhere else more urgently, so there was nothing else to do but to wait. An hour or two? It seemed a very long time, but by now we had learned patience. I was glad I had brought along my knitting this time.

At last it was Wolterdingen, a small station in the middle of a forest, but as we got off the train, quite a few more of our people alighted. We recognized them by their uniforms. And there, to welcome us and to take us to the camp were the local young scouts and guides as well as some of the leaders we knew from the previous camp in Greven.

We were led straight into the forest, which welcomed us, spreading its green arms around us. It was so great to feel the soft moss under our feet and green branches occasionally touching our heads as we walked along the narrow track. This was a forest so much like the ones we used to have in Latvia. Old fir trees mingled in places with birches, with some smaller trees in between here and there. And this was where we would

live! Could anything be better?

When we got to the camp, some had already put up their tents, and others were still doing it. One could see that these people were knowledgeable and not doing it for the first time. A lot of activity went on everywhere, for the evening was near, and we had to get settled.

Not everybody was part of the folk dancing group. There were other instructional courses as well, but again, there were about twenty of us who wanted to dance. The names for the occupants of the various tents had to be taken from the animal world, and the girls in our tent named us "the Squirrels". Some of the young men of our folk dancing group named themselves "the Owls". I don't remember how it happened, but they soon "adopted" me as one of them, because my last name was Sparrow.

"You are a bird," they said, "What are you doing with those squirrels? You ought to be with us!"

Right from the start a special friendship developed between myself and the "Owls", perhaps just sensing our common views about things. Of course, I did not move in with them, but we were partnering all the time as I danced with each one of them in turn. There was Ēriks, Aivars, Kaz and young Fredī, all very nice boys, or perhaps I should say young men, for they all had been soldiers in the war. Even Fredī had been called up as an artillery helper at the age of seventeen. Perhaps this was one reason for our camaraderie. Because I had grown up in a military environment, I felt a certain kinship with soldiers. Also, we all fiercely loved our country and felt the loss of it deeply. Now we all searched for the good and the beautiful in life, even though our future looked bleak.

Sorry to say, our instructor was not the one we'd had the previous time in Luebeck who was so inspiring. This man was older, and his instructions were not always so clear, but he had brought quite a lot of material with him that we could copy from, music as well as instructions. So whenever we had a little break, we would use it for copying more stuff to take home with us. The main thing was that we could dance, even though our dance floor was just a more spacious clearing between the majestic firs. The moss soon got worn away under our feet, and sometimes a protruding root made us trip, but that was nothing compared to the joy we experienced.

As time went on, I danced more and more with Ērik, because somehow he always happened to be at my side. We were very lucky that the good weather held, and we had sunshine almost every day, even though the mornings were frosty. As we ran to our morning exercises, frozen leaves crunched under our feet, and our breath came out in white puffs in the cold air. After this, though, new life came into our bodies, and we were ready for the new day.

One evening it started to rain, and some people had to move their

tents in the middle of the night because water began to seep into them. Even that had to be taken in stride, for a scout did not dare to complain or be grouchy.

At the end of each day, we had the campfire evenings again, sitting under the big firs with our faces turned to the flickering flames, watching the sparks fly high and then disappear into the night sky. Again we sang our songs, first the bracing songs of the scouts, then the patriotic songs so dear to our hearts, but at the end, they were always the sad orphan songs of the children far away from their home. One song we liked especially. Its chorus had words, which were so true for us, saying that: "Those who are far from their country, come to love it more fiercely; for them, always the most beautiful song will be the one they sing about their native land. They will carry it in their hearts wherever they go…"

And so it was and is even after these many years. The song about my country is always the most precious, the most beautiful, wherever I am. These songs at the campfires always tied our people together like nothing else could, and we wanted to become better, more noble people, so God would have mercy on us and let us go back to our Latvia someday.

After the last coals in the fire had finished glowing, we walked back to our tents in the dark, but above, beyond the treetops, the sky was full of stars. I remembered it written somewhere that "the darker the night, the brighter the stars." Was it so with us now that in these times of despair and hopelessness, when we so much wanted to find something good? As we looked up to the sky, the stars looked back at us kindly. Was it a promise? A hope? We wanted to believe that it was.

When our camping time ended, my friends, the Owls, invited me to go back with them to their camp Hallendorf for another day or so. I thought about it and agreed. There was no hurry for me to get home, so why not? We had to go to Hannover first and then change trains. As it turned out it was a long, long ride. At first we talked, joked and sang, then got sleepy and snoozed. It had been a long day, and we had not slept much the night before.

Hallendorf was not an attractive place. The gray barracks stood around an empty, graveled square. The sky was overcast and gray also, and the wind swept dry sand around the corners of the buildings.

In the evening, we sat by candlelight in my new friends' room, and it was dark and cozy, for they had made a fire in the small iron stove. We talked, still reminiscing about the happenings at the camp, then we sang. Since they had all gone through the war, the good old soldier's songs came up again, like the one, "… good-bye now, my white birch grove…" or "… and do not cry, if I don't return…" which made me want to cry, for my Dad did not return, as well as so many others.

In the dim light I could see the narrow, two-story bunk beds, like they were in all the camps. Above each on the wall was some small symbol of Latvia. It was a constant reminder of what had happened, a pain that could not be quenched, for so many had stayed in the killing fields. These boys at least, had come out alive, and they were grateful for it. They did not ask much of life right now, only to exist.

One of their roommates who joined our little party was an artist. He showed me some of his works, small watercolor paintings, mainly depicting country scenes of Latvia. I liked them very much, so he gave me one depicting some old farm buildings with birch trees, which I liked particularly. I have treasured it all these years, and it still hangs on my wall even now. He also offered to sketch my portrait, and since the "Owls" applauded the idea, I just had to sit and pose. All that happened with a lot of joking and teasing, and we spent a fun evening together.

My friends had arranged for me to stay the night with a family they knew at the camp, so it all worked out well. The next morning, I got ready to leave, and the boys took me to the station. Sadness was in their faces, as we said our goodbyes. How close people can get in just a few days! It felt as if we had known each other forever, even though we knew very little about each other's past or who we were. It was very strange, yet beautiful.

Finally—the last good-byes through the train window, and the boys calling out,

"Write to us! Write! Perhaps we will meet again!"

But perhaps not. We did not know where life would take us. Ērik was the one who waved the longest. He seemed to be a nice, sincere person and I liked him.

The train took on speed. I looked through the window at the gray scenery, but my thoughts wandered around that what had been. It was no use thinking about what would be, but at least we had today. I would go home and try to pass on some of the goodness and skills I had received at the camp. We did not have a homeland, but we were still a nation. We had to hold on to the treasures we were entrusted with and teach others, too. I thought of the brave scout's songs we had sung at the camp, full of challenge and assurance, which made us feel so much on top of the world. At that time we really felt that everything was possible. There was light, there was warmth in our hearts. Would we be able to hold on?

The train kept racing through the gray and brownish fields, which became grayer still when it started to rain heavily. At times we stopped and waited, stopped and waited again, sometimes for quite a long time. By then I had ceased wondering why it was happening and instead tried

to snooze, leaning on my monkey bag. Time moved so slowly!

When we arrived in Hamburg, it was already evening, and to my dismay, I found that the next train to Flensburg would only be the following morning. Oh my! It meant spending all night in the station, but that too was nothing new in those days. People were used to waiting during the war years. The train would come when it would come and leave when it would leave.

The barn-like station hall was huge and bare, with a high ceiling and a cement floor. High up at the one end was a large clock, counting the minutes, so at least I would be able to watch it for my departure time, for I didn't have a watch, and had never had one. Only a few wooden benches stood by the walls, and they were already taken. The rest of the people sat on the floor, singly or in small clusters, surrounded by their belongings. I too settled myself on the floor by the end wall.

At first we could still watch the people crossing the big hall, arriving or leaving on some of the late trains, but then everything became quiet. Those remaining in the hall, tried to settle down for the night the best they could, me included. I tried to snooze on my monkey bag, which at least gave a softer surface for my face. I dozed and woke, each time looking at the clock, but it had only moved five minutes, or sometimes ten. Slowly, so slowly the time was moving, but finally the morning came. It was gray and cold. It felt good to be walking to the train, which would offer more comfort.

It took another half a day to get to Flensburg, then another couple of kilometers to walk to the camp on the outskirts. I had not had anything to eat or drink since I left the boys the previous morning, for there was nothing to be had. Still, I did not worry about that. I was fine.

Then finally home, bed and oblivion...

Viktor still wrote, urging me to get ready to come to Pineberg. But then I would have to live at the same camp as he did. How would that be possible? Knowing how persistent he could be, I might have great difficulty in dealing with him. Perhaps we could learn to be just friends? But then I considered the food situation, which had not changed. If anything, it was even worse now. It was understandable, because the poor students had no means of getting anything extra from the black marketers.

At the same time, news began to circulate at the camp that England was now offering to take young and able women from the refugee camps in Germany to go and work in the hospitals there. I was not interested, for I had no wish to part with my family, but my brother Ilgvar kept urging me every day,

"Think what an opportunity this is for you, to get out of our starving

Germany! Things are not going to get better here for a long time yet. You then would be able to help us here, too ! And you are the only one who qualifies for this!" In the end, I did hand in my application, feeling that I had to do this for my family.

It still would not mean that I had to go, if I wanted to change my mind. Then something quite unexpected happened! Going through the medical examination, dark patches were found on my lungs, and of course, my application was denied! What now? Tuberculosis was already in our family. Mother had had it in her thirties, and at that time some small patches were found on my lungs too, although I was not ill. Because of her previous illness, Mother was now getting some extra rations, and now she offered them to me, so I could recover. All this really lowered my spirits. How could I think about going to the University now, if my health was so bad? Perhaps it was not meant to be for me?

Then one day, another surprise. A letter from Viktor, but with a different address! He wrote that he had to leave Pineberg for reasons he could not tell me in a letter. That sounded very ominous. He said he had handed in my application papers to the University, but was very sorry that he had not been able to bring the whole thing to a conclusion. Apparently he was now somewhere in the Southern Alps in a small village and that perhaps he may have to get married?

What it all meant, I never got to know, even though he wrote me several more letters—he still did not tell me what had happened. I was very surprised about the marriage news. Could that have something to do with his leaving Pineberg? But really, it did not matter one way or another to me. If he had found somebody, I was glad for him, and decided it was best not to write to him anymore, so he could leave the past behind altogether. I wished him the best, but perhaps it was just as well to make a final break now. I never saw him again, nor wrote to him, even though he had later written to my Mother asking for my address in England. I had told her not to give it to him and she didn't. Years later, I sometimes wondered what had happened to him, especially when his birthday came around, which was in the same month as mine. After all, we had been friends for quite a long time.

The weary, gray days of autumn came with rain and more rain. The ground was soaked and the puddles between the barracks got bigger and bigger. It was hard to get through and around them in our inadequate footwear. Everything we had brought with us was getting worn out, but new things were not available anywhere. Also, our weekly food rations had shrunk unbelievably. They might suffice for two days but not for a week! Even the little bread we received was made of corn or some strange additives and it broke up into crumbs when cut. It was good

that we had gotten from somewhere the salty powder of dried ground peas to scatter on the bread or crumbs. Together with the black coffee (which was not even a relative to coffee) it was something that would at least satisfy for a while.

From the communal kitchen we received only some bulky root vegetables like turnips or kohlrabi. One day they were in a watery soup, the next day they were cut in larger pieces with some sauce, in which you could barely find a sliver of meat. I sometimes could not force myself to eat it. Instead, I would crawl into my bunk and sleep.

New life came into me when I started to write a Christmas show for the guides and scouts. I had an idea to show the ancient Christmas traditions on a Latvian farm; to show how they prepared for and celebrated Christmas in the olden days. Everything would be done using our Latvian folk songs, called *dainas*, either in reciting or singing them. Then later, during the celebrations when the visitors came, there would also be folk dancing and reenacting of the old traditions. That way I would teach the scouts and guides the old customs, and at the same time give enjoyment to others. This helped me to forget the dreariness of everyday life and lifted me into a different realm.

Often at night I lay there with my eyes open, thinking about it all – about the beauty and wisdom that flowed from the words of the *dainas*. They were just short four-line rhythmical verses, made up by simple everyday people centuries ago, telling so clearly how our ancestors lived and what they believed in. The nobility of even the most everyday things, the love and even reverence towards everything and everyone! Where did it all come from? And these characteristics were established even before they were introduced to Christianity!

The Crusaders and the German invaders made them their slaves, and life was very hard for them, yet they preserved their God-given beliefs and virtues. I have often wondered about this. It seemed that they already knew the Christian values before they even heard about them! Their beliefs were very much along the same lines. They believed in one God who was very close to them and even sometimes walked and talked with them, as they worked. Was that where they got this nobility and courage? Did the hardships teach them to see what was really important, so that they could 'put their sorrow under a rock and walk over it singing', as the *dainas* said?

We sang too, and we too were orphan children, like they used to be, but we did not have our land—that beloved earth under our feet—from which to gain our strength, nor the rock under which to put our sorrows. We did not have anything and yet, we sang, and the song united us and lifted us up beyond our sea of sorrows. I know that not everybody took

it as tragically as I did, but that was the way I was, and I could only give what I had.

Again the rain pelted the roof right above my head as I sat in my top bunk writing, but it did not matter now. I had my beautiful dream. We started rehearsals for the show involving the Girl-Guides, the Boy-Scouts and even the Brownies. I wanted to involve as many as possible, and everybody was very excited. There would be a family of three generations in the presentation: the guests, young boys and girls from the neighboring farms, would come dressed up as the old tradition required. Later they would take off their masks and make themselves known, ending it all by them pairing off and dancing. Songs and dances had to be learned and practiced; the whole show needed to be put together.

It was good that a month earlier we had put on the play in which I played one of the main parts and it had gone well. My artist Aunt Elzī had painted the decorations for it, and since one of the scenes had taken place inside a farmhouse, the same decorations were exactly what we needed for our show, too—so it worked out perfectly.

Christmas was nearing, and Mother was busy working at her leatherwork projects. Our British commandants had shown her work to other officers as well, and more orders came in. She made handbags, wallets, albums and book covers and all kinds of smaller things. The payment was still in cigarettes—the best thing for trading with the black marketers. For the British it was dirt cheap, of course, for they did not lack for cigarettes, but it satisfied both sides equally.

Christmas Eve came. It had been announced in the camp that a Christmas Eve service would take place in the big hall late in the afternoon, and now people came streaming in. A large Christmas tree stood near the stage inside the hall with small white candles on it, as was the custom in Europe—lighting them on Christmas Eve. The large building was soon packed with people. Everybody seemed to have a need to come and did not even mind standing, for there were not enough chairs for everyone. Children, with their little arms around their parent's necks, looked at the Christmas tree with wonder in their little eyes. They did not know that we were in a strange land and that there was pain in their parent's hearts. People came to hear the good news of the birth of Christ, to receive new strength and comfort for their souls. Many cried as the service began, overcome by emotions. This was our second Christmas in exile, and we all missed our country and those we had to leave behind.

Each family had also decorated their room with some little greenery and a candle or two in celebration of Christmas. However small, they helped to create a little warmth and the feeling of this sacred night.

Our show was scheduled for the third day of Christmas, which was December 27th. Everything was ready. I did not worry, but the night before the show, I could not go to sleep. My thoughts would not stop working, keeping me sleepless and alert all night.

In the morning, still being awake, I got out of my bed early, took the large saucepan and went to the communal kitchen to get some boiling water for the morning coffee. During the last days, it had snowed a little and melted a little. The main road through the camp was now bumpy and uneven as the slush had become hard during the frosty night. It was not fully light yet, and only a few people were out at this early hour, walking along the road with their heads drawn into the collars of their coats and hands deep in their pockets.

I got my water and started to come back, taking care to walk very carefully on the icy road. But even so, the ground suddenly slipped from under me, and I found myself falling in a sitting position, still holding the saucepan in front of me. It would have been better if I had let it go, but now, as it hit the ground, the lid flew off and the scalding water splashed back into my face and onto my gloved hands. I screamed, dropping the saucepan and grabbing my face with my hands. How lucky for me that someone was out on that road and took me over to the medical office right away, where a nurse took care of me. She sent for the doctor instantly, and since the doctor lived in the same barrack, she arrived within moments—but I slid away into unconsciousness as they pulled off my wet gloves.

When I came to, Mother was there, looking at me with a worried face. Mine was burning, and as I glimpsed a reflection of myself in the metal lampshade, I saw that it was all covered with something white. After the first aid was given, I was helped to get home, where Ilgvar allowed me to use his lower bunk, so I would not have to climb.

"But my show that should take place tonight!" That was the foremost thought on my mind. I could have cried, but my face was stiff under the thick cover, and I could barely open my mouth to talk. How lucky that my eyes had shut just in time and were not hurt! Oh, God! I suddenly felt so weak.

The news about my accident spread through the camp quickly. Our senior Girl-Guide leader came and comforted me, saying that she would take care of everything concerning our performance, and we would do it whenever I was ready. That took a load off my mind, and I could finally close my eyes and sleep.

My face was a mask that got tighter with every day, but the doctor said that was good, because it was a sign that underneath it was healing. I lay on my bed and waited. Every so often somebody came

to see me. A soft knock on the door, then it slowly opened. Perhaps whoever came was afraid of what he or she would see. They were friends,
scouts and guides and acquaintances from the camp. I suppose I did look
awful with my white face and I could not talk much because the plaster
around my mouth was stiff and hard. I thanked God again that my eyes
were all right.

Gradually the plaster began to peel off, and after a week it was almost
gone. Only a tiny spot was left on my nose, which I could camouflage with
some make-up. That was really a miracle. Our show could go on now.

On the night of our performance, my boys and girls were all so
nervous. Like children, they crushed around me seeking comfort. I, on
the contrary, felt amazingly peaceful and serene, as if nothing was happening at all. The curtains opened, and the show began. I was so relaxed
that I almost forgot that I was the first to speak. But everything went fine,
and the applause would not stop when the show ended. The hall again
was packed, for this was something that everybody could understand and
enjoy, even the children.

Then it was all over, and I could breathe a sigh of relief. The chairs
were put to the sides, and the musicians took place on the stage, so the
evening could continue with dancing and fun. I had dreamed how nice
it would be if we could start this part of the evening the old fashioned
way by all linking hands and walking around the hall singing some well-
known folksong, then at an appropriate time stopping and taking partners, whoever was near, and continuing in some simple and well known
folk dances. After that the regular dancing could proceed. But I did not
want to impose my wishes on other people who might not feel as strongly
as I did about these things.

So everything started as usual on such occasions, and soon the big
hall was full of cheerful dancers. I also danced a few dances but then had
enough. My job was done, and I was not really needed here anymore. I
also realized how very tired I was after all this. I put on my coat and went
outside. The muted sounds of music still flowed from behind the lighted
windows as I walked away into the clear, cold night. Coming out on the
wide, empty main road, I stopped and looked up at the myriad of shining
stars so far away. And suddenly I, too, felt far away from everything and
everyone. This gaiety, that I had just left, did not have anything to do
with me. My joy was in a distant land beyond the sea.

This was a deep and cold winter, such as had not been seen for
a long time. The year 1947 had arrived frozen in ice. The root
vegetables, which had been stored in ditches in the ground, as was often
done, had frozen this year from the severe cold. They tasted too sweet
and ugly, but that was all we had now for food. The more energetic people

made rounds to the farms trying to exchange something, but there was not much left to exchange, and also the closest farms had nothing more to sell. Things were bad. We did receive some Red Cross parcels occasionally, but all the best things had already been removed.

Then one day, a surprise call came from the medical office for me to have another examination! I wondered why, because I had already given up the thought of going to England, but I went anyway. Since I was not given any results, I was no wiser about any of this and did not know what to think. No news had come from the University either, even though Viktor had told me that he had handed in my papers.

The days passed by, gray and dull. Deep snow was now everywhere, and it was also very cold. Without warm enough clothing or footwear, it was not possible to go anywhere. The only thing left was to wait for spring.

That came slowly, but at last the icicles around the roofs of the barracks began to melt and drip. This was already our third spring in exile. It was March, and as usual, it brought back the memories of the last spring at home. There was so much to remember, and I started to write again. That helped to fill those empty days, even though it renewed my sense of loss.

Then one day, news came that changed everything again. The message was that I could go to England! It was incredible. To England! Did I want to go? No, I didn't! I didn't want to leave my family, my friends, my work with the Brownies, the Guides and the Scouts. How could I go and leave it all? How could I go away alone into the unknown world? And yet I knew that I had to for the sake of my family, and also for myself. For how long could we sustain our health in these conditions? Besides, nothing better was expected in the foreseeable future.

Perhaps I would be able to make some kind of a living for myself? England was the first country offering to take refugees out of the starving Germany. At the interview, I was told that we, the applicants, would have to work in hospitals, but if our language skills were good enough, after a few months we could start training to be nurses, if we wanted to. That sounded good. I might like to do that. It would be a challenge, but I would have a career.

In any case, we, the women who applied for this program, would have to sign a contract that we would work only the government-appointed jobs for the next three years. That seemed fair enough. If we would work, we would have food and a roof above our heads. Those were the two most important things. Hopefully we would earn enough to give help to our families also. In the night however, I could not sleep, thinking about it, and my heart was heavy. I really did not want to go, and yet I knew I had to.

# Good-bye, Germany!

The departure time was near. There was not too much time to contemplate, and even though still unsure, I began to put my things together. There was not much to sort, though, but I had a few things precious to me that I wanted to take.

The last days came, and many stopped by to say their good-byes. A stream of people came all day long. My Brownies, my sweet little birds, brought me a nice little woven basket, made by one's grandfather. It was not as if the people at the camp sat around doing nothing. A lot of beautiful things were created practically out of nothing. The guides and scouts came, as well as the leaders. During this year we had established great relationships. Other friends and acquaintances came too. I never knew I had so many friends. Some brought small gifts for remembrance, whatever they had. Nobody had much these days, but they gave to show their love and appreciation. The guides brought me a pair of dolls, a boy and a girl, dressed in national costumes to remind me of our dancing together. They certainly would be a joy to me in the new place, for I knew how precious anything like that could be when you were far away from home.

Others brought small poetry books, issued in Germany by Latvian publishers. These were mostly on bad paper, but we all wanted them and read them. It was our language that we treasured. Many of them were illustrated by our best artists, a treasure in itself. That was food for our souls, and people bought them whenever it was possible.

Receiving these gifts and sensing the love of all these people, I suddenly felt so rich. I did not think I had done much, nor that it had been so meaningful, but it looked like it had been worthwhile after all. Now there was a new hope in me that perhaps I would be able to do something worthwhile in the future, too. My English was fairly acceptable, for I had been learning it at school since I was ten years old. The main thing was to have a chance to use my abilities, to make something of my life.

People came all day, and even late into the evening, to say good bye. They stood around in our narrow room and looked at me with sad eyes. There were also a few young men I had got to know, holding my hand for a long time and looking into my eyes.

"You will write, won't you?" they said. What could I say? My heart did not belong to anyone. It was not my time for love yet. I knew that more had to happen before then. There was also Ralf, the young man whom I had met in Hockensbuhl, who also lived at this camp and had visited me occasionally. I teased him and laughed with him, but that was all.

There was one person whom I would miss especially. That was our

Senior Guides' leader Mrs. Kalnājs, the wife of our former home teacher at Hockensbuhl high school. She was a very intelligent and dynamic person, and I liked her for that. We vowed to write to each other.

It turned out that there were about twenty of us going to England from our camp, and on the very last evening before our leaving, the management had prepared a surprise farewell party for us. We were the first from our camp to embark on this kind of a journey, and it seemed that the whole camp came. The choir sang a few songs, then we all sang together. The hall was full of people who had come to give us a send-off. All that was very moving and uplifting, but at the same time also sad, for we did not know what would await us in the new land, or when we would again hear our Latvian language or our songs after being dispersed to the various parts of England.

The last morning came. Mother and my brothers walked with me along the main road to the gate at the other end. There we would be picked up and taken to the station by one of the UNRRA vehicles. It wouldn't be a limousine, not even a bus, but the usual army open-back truck, of course!

The morning was foggy. The mist lay heavily over the black roofs of the barracks as we walked by.

"Good-bye, old roofs! I won't see you anymore!" I said to myself as we passed by.

It was all the same to them, of course, but it was not all the same to me. I would not be here anymore. We had been at camp "Antwerp" almost a year. A year of living and that is always precious! Now one chapter of my life again was ending. What would the next one be like?

When we arrived at the gate, quite a few people had gathered by the administration building: the ones who were leaving and the ones to see them off. Some were sniffling and wiping away tears, others gazed away into the distance, where fog lay low over the gray buildings, perhaps so as not to show their feelings. Still others looked with sad eyes into the faces of their loved ones, as if probing them for something that was yet unsaid, or trying to absorb the features, so as to remember them for all time. Many of us would probably never see each other again. Time would sever the present ties, and make the memories fade. What was important today would not be important tomorrow or the day after.

Goodbyes and more goodbyes... Wishing well and reminding to write and not to forget. Then the big truck came through the gate, turned around, and with the wheels crunching, stopped before us. This was it. The last hugs and kisses, tears wetting cheeks as one after the other we climbed into the truck that would take us to the Flensburg train station—our first step in our unknown journey. There was not enough room for everybody to sit on the wooden boards, so we, my friend Sandra and

I, being the youngest, stood at the back by the opening and could still wave. The driver got into his seat and slammed the door.

"Ready? Okay!" The truck started to move.

It was strange. When I got up early in the morning, getting ready for the journey, my heart had pounded so heavily and fearfully, but now all that had vanished. I felt as if I was not really there, as if I was not part of what was happening but suspended somewhere in mid-air. The past again was cut off, and the future not yet there, just as that time when we were on the ship leaving our homeland Latvia.

To my surprise, I suddenly felt free as a bird in the sky and full of joy. All the doubts and the sadness had disappeared. It would be a new life! There would be hope! I had no tears, even though everyone around me was crying. Only when the truck began to go faster, and the crowd of those staying behind got smaller and smaller, did it hit me that those were my family and friends standing there in the fog waving, and that this was goodbye, perhaps forever. Something hot welled up into my throat, choking my breath, and I covered my trembling lips with the back of my hand to keep from crying also.

Then a turn in the street cut everything off from our sight, and the break was complete. I gritted my teeth and swallowed back the tears looking down at the small pebbles jumping up from under the wheels, as the truck moved faster and took us away from what had been.

"It will be all right! God will see us through!" I told myself. Only one tear sat in the corner of my eye for a long time.

Soon we were at the Flensburg station, where the train was already waiting, and we could get in. It would take us to Hamburg and then farther on to the port of departure. We were glad that it was warm and cozy inside the train, for it was still early spring, when everything was full of cold and dampness. It was almost midday when we finally left Flensburg. We left it wrapped in the thick, white fog, like the one which in time would cover the memories of the days we had spent there.

We reached Hamburg at about four in the afternoon. The ruins were still around everywhere. When would someone be able to clear all this away and rebuild it? Right now, however, we had other things on our minds. We had to think how we would build our own lives now. Another train took us to Bremen and from there, yet another one to the port of Cuxhafen. The short spring day was turning to dusk as we left Bremen. The last part of our journey to the port, we raced through darkness and rain.

It was eight o'clock in the evening when we arrived at Cuxhafen. We were very tired after the long journey, but the place we were taken to spend the night was cold and uninviting, like a big barn. That made our

spirits drop to zero. If it was like this now, what would come later? We wished to get away from there soon and were promised that we would leave first thing in the morning.

More refugee women had come from other parts of Germany, and now there were quite a lot of us here, perhaps around hundred. After spending a bad night in the barn—or it might have been an empty warehouse—we still did not get anywhere in the morning. It was already noontime, when we were finally taken to the wharf and could board the ship.

The ship was impressive, big and white, with wide black bands around the chimneys. On the side of it was the proud name "Empire Halladale", whatever that stood for. It looked like we were expected and could board right away. Everything was gleaming and shining here. I had never been in so luxurious a place, or on such a big ship. There were comfortable salons, beautiful dining rooms, mirrors, chandeliers and lacquered floors. The white-uniformed stewards walked around quietly, gliding like shadows. Something like this had only been seen in films.

There were a few restricted places though, where a sign said: "For guests only". That hurt a little. It said that we were not guests but were here by mercy only. Also, our sleeping quarters were somewhere deep down in the ship in a large area with compartments. Everything was nice though—clean, white and warm. It was all right. What more could we wish for? We should not be oversensitive.

While we were busy down below, settling into our sleeping quarters, we had not noticed that the ship had started to move. When we got back on the deck, we saw that the coast was already in the distance. I stood at the railings and looked back for a long time. There lay the unhappy coast. Will the next one be happier? Only God knows.

# To England

*Part Two*

It was March 22, 1947. Around us was the North Sea, smooth and gray like lead. The big British ship *"Empire Halladale"* had just left the German port of Cuxhafen, and was heading out to the sea. A hundred or so refugee women from the Baltic States, including me, stood at the railings watching the receding coastline as the ship slowly navigated through the bay. Big and small pieces of soiled ice floated on the gray water crowding around the ship like a band of dirty beggars. White gulls circled around the ship crying. Did they cry a farewell to us, the refugees from the displaced person's camps of Germany, now on our way to England to work and start a new life there?

Seeing the gulls made me think of the time two and a half years ago when we had just arrived in Germany at the port of Gottenhafen. The Germans had evacuated us from our homeland, Latvia, where the Russians were again invading our country. The war was still on. What a dark time that had been! Then too, the gulls had flown around as we sat at the empty harbor yard next to the railway tracks, waiting to be taken west, farther away from the danger that the Russians could bring us.

Now we were in transit again. We were like those gulls, like torn off leaves, carried by the wind. This was not a pleasure cruise for us, just as the previous one had not been, but at least we did not have to sleep on the floor on the bare decks as before. This was a British ship, a nice ship, and we hoped for a better future.

Time moved on. We had left the bay a long time ago, had explored the ship and had a nice meal. The evening had come again. The ship swayed up and down, cutting the cold waters of the North Sea. Down

below, the ship's engines worked hard, taking us over to our new land. I lay in my soft, white, second-story bunk, deep inside the ship's belly.

"Dear God, do not let the new country be too harsh on us," I prayed. "Let it not disillusion us too much... and please allow us to return to our own country one day! Oh, God! Oh, God of mercy... Our only hope and helper..." The muffled droning of the engines, the swaying.... Up and down, up and down.... Everything around so white... then nothing more. Just sleep.

The new morning arrived windy and cool. It was March 25, 1947. Our large ship fought the waves, going up and down as if climbing over mountains. Apparently this was a zone where the waters of two different currents either flowed together or crossed each other, and that was why the going was so rough. Some people could not stand the vigorous movement, especially after the good breakfast we had had, and disappeared down below. I too went down a little later. It seemed that the impact of the up and down movement was felt even stronger down there. Walking along the hallway, I kept bumping from one wall into another.

There were four of us from our camp "Antwerp" in Flensburg, northern Germany who had kept together since the beginning of our journey. The two "older ladies", Mrs. Avots and Mrs. Bērziņš, were perhaps in their forties or early fifties. My former classmate Sandra, from the Hockensbuhl high school and I were both twenty. We were all glad to be together, sharing the same sleeping quarters and being able to support each other if there was a need. Our older companions were having a harder time with seasickness and stayed in their bunks, but Sandra and I went back to the deck a little later.

"Walk fast, it will counteract the sickening movement!" one of the sailors called out to us as we went up the stairs to the top deck.

Wow! The wind was strong! It tore at our hair and clothing, throwing into our faces gusts of very fine sprays of moisture, but we just put our heads down against the wind and, holding close together with locked arms, marched forward. After a little while the situation did not seem too bad. It was even beautiful. Our lungs were full of the fresh invigorating air, our faces alive from the gusts of wind pelting them again and again. Huge clusters of clouds rose up from the horizon, and the restless waters flew up high toward them, as if wanting to join them.

Now and then the clouds parted and the sun even came out, playing on the waters and making them sparkle as if sprinkled with diamonds. The whitecaps kept rising out of the deep, and the strong wind picked up the foam from their crests, carrying it back in white sprays. It was wonderful! They looked like wild horses running with their white manes floating behind them until they fell again, joining the gray waters! I had

never seen anything like it before. The gulls followed the ship, flying around it and then again diving down to the churning water.

"Let's hold on and watch!" I shouted to Sandra through the gusting wind, when we were at the front of the ship. The view here was most dramatic.

"Look, look how the nose of the ship lifts itself up! We're going to heaven!" I cried, but as soon as I had said it, the ship started to go down, down, sliding steeply into the foaming waves as if it was going to disappear in them.

"Hold tight, for goodness sakes!" Sandra screamed at me.

"I'm holding, I'm holding!" I shouted back, enjoying this even though I got goose bumps all over me as I watched it.

We spent a long time on the deck as, mile by mile, we were taken forward and nearer to our new life. Toward evening, it became quieter and the ship's movement was smoother. People had recovered from their sickness and, after a good dinner, we sat in the large salon playing cards and listening to a concert provided by our own talented ladies. Out came arias from operas and operettas; some sang along. Somebody else played the piano beautifully. Chopin, Grieg, Beethoven. At the end of the evening, we all sang a simple Latvian folksong together—a lullaby to get us ready for sleep, and then we went down to our bunks.

When we awoke the next morning and went up to the deck, we were surprised to see that we were already in the River Thames in England! Excited, we viewed our new surroundings, but our first look was disappointing. What we saw were just ugly gray buildings with tall factory chimneys. The drone of the engines down below became lower, then stopped altogether. Chains clanking, a big anchor went down into the water and we stopped.

"What happened? Why are we stopping here?" We looked at each other in dismay.

"We have to wait here for the customs inspectors to arrive before we can go into the port," one of the officers explained. That was disappointing.

Waiting restlessly, the uncertainties of the unknown future lay heavily on our hearts. Finally, shortly before noon, the inspectors arrived and started to check our documents. We stood on the deck in line, and everything went so slowly. We were counted again and again.

"Like a flock of sheep sent to a slaughter," Sandra whispered to me.

At the end of the inspections, a tag was pinned to each of us with a name and a number.

"Are we prisoners too?" she whispered again.

It was very degrading, but of course, there was nothing we could do

or say. This was their country. The official's faces were cold and dispassionate. We were just things—goods to be delivered.

It was about three o'clock in the afternoon when we were finally pulled into the harbor by tugboats, and the big ship slowly aligned its side to the wharf. We drank tea standing on the deck and watched how the other passengers alighted and were welcomed by their loved ones.

"Oh darling, how lovely to see you home again!" we heard.

"Sweetheart, how I missed you!"

Nobody was waiting for us. We alone were the ones who waited nervously, wondering what our future would be. Since nothing else happened, we went back to our quarters and waited there for most of the afternoon. Then at last the disembarking command came. It was already five o'clock.

When we finally got off the ship, a heavy shower pelted us as we ran across the street to the large building where we had been directed to go. There we had to walk through a narrow barrier with officials again checking our papers, viewing and observing us with their cold eyes, as if evaluating a herd of cows to be put on the market! I felt a shrinking inside of me. I was getting smaller and smaller by the moment. At last we were through and could get into the five buses provided for us. As we left the place, we saw a sign written with large letters: *The Port of London Authority*.

## To London

L ondon itself was quite a distance away, but that was where the buses would take us. We looked through the windows with great interest. At intervals, we saw small clusters of houses, usually crowding around some factory. The first things that drew our attention, were the strangely divided chimneys, which looked like cigarette butts sticking out of the roofs.

There were also the two-story brick houses that were built all in one row like a wall with small paned windows. Later we learned that they were "the terrace houses", the simplest living quarters for the factory workers, and they were everywhere in the old parts of the industrialized towns.

Between these small communities was open countryside with fields and meadows, where the first green of spring was appearing. Here and there we saw large lone trees in the middle of fields or meadows. In places, rows of low growing-hedges separated the land into larger and smaller areas. This reminded me of the earthen walls that divided the land in the same way in Schleswig-Holstein where we had lived in Germany.

In many places we saw high mounds of black tailings, or coal, or whatever it was.

"Do you think they have mines here?" Sandra asked.

"I don't know," I said. "But look at all the factories! I wonder what they make there?"

Again and again we saw the massive gray buildings with the tall chimneys towering above them. It almost seemed that there was nothing else but these. The horizon was wrapped in a grayish mist, and only the tall chimneys emerged out of it like pale blue columns, completing the semi-circle view in front of us.

We traveled for what seemed a long time. Then gradually the distances between the scattered housing developments became smaller. Occasionally we saw barracks, surrounded by barbed wire.

"That must have been a prisoner of war camp," I said, "and look, those low shack-like buildings must be the temporary buildings in place of the bombed ones!" We also saw big holes in the ground occasionally, presumably made by the bombs during the war. Some were already becoming overgrown; others were full of all kinds of junk, used as garbage dumps.

The rain had stopped. Gradually the dark blue-gray clouds sank lower, leaving the sky above clear. A soft, pinkish light emanated from behind the dark clouds, making their edges glow like mountain tops covered with snow.

We were entering the outskirts of London and moving more and more towards the city center. Colorful billboards and signs shouted at us from all sides, but the daylight was fading rapidly. Soon only a bluish twilight was around us. The first lights came on, throwing their reflections into the wet streets. Evening was coming.

There were no more gaps between the buildings, which became bigger and bigger, like walls on each side. People, cars and buses moved by in both directions. We looked to the right and to the left, trying not to miss anything. In places, we saw the remains of some buildings that had been destroyed by bombs, but it made me think that these bombed ones were far fewer than those that were left standing in the bombed cities in Germany.

As I looked up, the sky looked so calm and peaceful. It was pale blue with a touch of violet blush as it usually was in springtime. Such peace up there, but down here—people rushing home from work, two-story red and yellow buses slowly winding their way through the busy streets! Billboards flashed their colored lights, painting fascinating designs on the wet pavements all around them.

It was already dark when we reached our destination. We had traveled for almost two hours, although it seemed much longer. The buses stopped on a wide street in front of a big gray brick building that extended for several blocks. It felt strange when we were led down the steps

into something that looked like a half-basement.

"What is this building, I wonder" I said anxiously to Sandra, but then we came into a huge hall. It gave us a fearful, mystical feeling. Tall, arched windows were covered with black drapes, perhaps left over from the wartime blackouts. The high ceiling contained a large round painting, which we couldn't see well because of the low lighting. Apparently this had been a cloister and this particular room, had perhaps been even a church, but I could only guess.

As soon as we arrived, we were asked to go to the tables to have a meal, and we were really hungry by this time. Afterwards, we were led upstairs to our sleeping quarters—large, long rooms with rows of beds. Perhaps, during the war, this place had been used as a hospital for the wounded? We felt better here, for it was warmer. After choosing our beds and putting down our hand luggage, we were summoned to hasten downstairs to a smaller room, where we were met by our Latvian ambassador, Mr. Kārlis Zariņš. He was a very pleasant elderly gentleman with white hair and black-rimmed glasses. A couple of other embassy workers were with him.

He greeted us on our arrival to this country, and gave some general pointers about this land. It helped to raise our spirits a little bit.

"Above all," he said, "keep together and do not lose touch with each other! It will not be easy, and you will have to be strong. Don't forget who you are. You are the ambassadors of our nation. People will judge our whole nation by who you are and what you do."

We sang a few folk songs together, then he invited us to sing the well-known Latvian lullaby *"Aijā žūžū..."* That was usually sung when putting children to bed, for it was time to say "goodnight" and to part. This had been another very long and tiring day.

It felt so good to stretch out in the clean, white beds after the long journey. The lights went out, talking ceased. Everything was quiet. No drapes covered the high windows in this room, and one little star looked at me through one of them as I settled down to sleep. Did it bring me greetings from my loved ones from far across the sea? But then this one star became two, then three... A whole tree of stars glistened in the dark, quiet room. The darkness itself started to move. In silent steps came the monks and the nuns, those who had once inhabited these walls. Their life stories flowed from the walls like a silvery mist, combining with the soft velvety darkness. And the stars shone so brightly, so beautiful... a whole tree of silvery stars... then nothing, as I fell asleep.

As I awoke the next morning, I could not remember right away where I was. The high ceiling, the tall, arched windows, a clear soft morning light. Where was I? How did I get here? My eyes rested against the high ceiling. The trip... No, not the ship... The long journey yester-

day across this strange land... The Ambassador... We were in London. Yes, London, and today it would be decided what would happen to us—where we would live and what our future would be. Perhaps the rest of our lives would depend on that.

Right after breakfast the sorting began. Several official-looking ladies arrived from the government's Welfare Department, and we were offered choices of a number of cities where we might go. The four of us from the camp "Antwerp" in Flensburg still wanted to stay together and discussed what we should do.

"London is so big! We'd better not stay here, we might get lost!" said Mrs. Bērziņš who did not know much English.

"Yes, and it is the capital. Who knows, somebody might start to bomb it again!" added Mrs. Avots and the same thought had just crossed my mind also.

How absurd! These kinds of thoughts in our heads, even two years after the war! In the end, we decided to go to Birmingham, the large industrial town in the center of England. We were told that it was the second largest city after London. A few other girls from our camp decided to go to that area also. Perhaps we would be able to meet sometimes? At least we learned that all our luggage had arrived safely and nothing was lost. That was a great relief!

After the midday meal we met again with the lady officials and were issued some money, two pounds each. It made me feel sad.

"Here we are, like beggars..." I thought. "But we will work and earn our own money. Nobody must ever call us beggars!"

Outside it was a beautiful spring day. The sun shone, the buds in the trees and shrubs were swollen, the birds sang. In the afternoon the local Latvian pastor Mr. Slokenbergs came and offered to take us out and show us a little bit of London. The big city buzzed around us. Again there were a lot of people, traffic and colors; everything was so different from what we had seen in the past years in war-torn Germany.

Mr. Slokenbergs even took us for a ride in the underground, which was a new experience for us all. Escalators, leading several levels underground, tunnels, the warm air, like a wind blowing through them, the fast trains! There they came, and there they again went, the lighted windows flitting past! It was a good way to get somewhere quickly, instead of crawling at the slow pace of the buses, which had to make their way through the traffic and people-clogged streets, yet you did not see anything of the vicinity going underground. You missed seeing the people, the streets and all that was in them.

When we got back, the sun was already setting, but the evening was so nice and mellow. A bird's song, long drawn out and moving suddenly came from the bushes near the entrance of our building. A nightingale

here in the middle of London? I stopped for a moment and would have loved to linger and listen some more, but the others went into the building, and I did not want to lose them.

After returning, the pastor held a short service for us in the chapel. He was a good speaker. He said that faith could conquer even death... And that we were travelers, always going nearer and nearer to our homeland. Those were good words, words which we wanted to hear. Even though we had come to this foreign land, we had not given up our dream of going home one day. Yet, was that what he meant?

"Something could always change!" I said to myself. "We will go back! It cannot be any other way!"

I believed that our whole existence now was to still be there for our country. But perhaps the pastor was not talking about the homeland on this earth, but our eternal homeland? That thought did not enter my mind at the time.

Then we prayed and sang. And suddenly tears began to flow, hot and sorrowful. Tears, which I had held back for a long time; tears for all that was lost. Even my family was far away now. Would I ever see them again? And I—alone in the world now... It would have been good to cry and really get it off my heart. But the order of the day called for us to go and have some supper; except when we got there, nothing was on the table. The others had eaten and gone, everything was tidied away. There wasn't even anybody around whom we could ask. Bitterness welled up in me for such carelessness. Not because of that bit of food, but in the way that we were treated.

After that we gathered in another room. There was talking and singing, but I did not want to sing anymore. A rock was lying on my heart. I knew there would be much disillusionment ahead of us, and we would just have to learn to take it. I'd better make peace with myself. Tomorrow we would start our new life.

## To Birmingham

Early the next morning, we were on our way to Euston station, from where the train would take us to Birmingham. As we left London, we saw through the window the suburbs, flitting by with long rows of red brick buildings. Since we were higher up than they, we could see their narrow back-yards with clothes-lines and some miserable looking shacks.

Soon we were out in the countryside. The first green was emerging after the long, cold winter. This had been an unusually cold one in all of Europe. We saw some animals out in the pastures: cows and sheep, nibbling away at the new grass. Small patches of woods grew here and there on the low undulating hills. An occasional farmhouse came into view,

half hidden in the bare trees. Large, lone oak trees stood here and there on the slopes or in the middle of the fields, black and bare. Small streams and ponds, surrounded by bushes, dotted the landscape. Farther away, a village or a small township on a hill could be seen, with the church spire protruding through the roofs and trees. We did not talk much on the way, each being preoccupied with our own thoughts. Perhaps they all ran along the same lines. Where would we end up? Would we be able to manage? What would our future be?

It took us almost three hours to get to Birmingham. There we were met by some ladies from the Welfare Department again. Their job was to get us to our designated places. About fifteen of us had come in this direction, but now we were divided into smaller groups. Most left for other surrounding communities in the area, just the four of us stayed in the city of Birmingham. Our chaperone was a very nice lady, named Mrs. Linzy, and she really was a lady. She was small and slim, neatly dressed in a gray suit, and was very kind to us. She calmed our fears when we found out that some of our luggage was missing.

"Perhaps it is because your luggage was carried in a separate car. It will be found and delivered to you, don't worry!" She said.

Sandra and I were the ones who communicated with Mrs. Linzy the most, because we were the ones who spoke English better than our companions.

At the station, we all got into Mrs. Linzy's comfortable car and began our journey through Birmingham. The city center looked nice with the big old buildings, but they all looked dirty, blackened by soot.

"That is because we use so much coal in this country," explained Mrs. Linzy. "Year after year the smoke settles on the buildings, making them black. It really would be time to wash them down!"

Washing houses? That was something new!

As we drove along the main streets, we saw a lot of shops with colorful displays in their windows. We had not seen anything like that since the Russians had occupied our country for the first time in 1940, and had emptied our shops. A year later the Germans arrived and emptied them even more, shipping whatever they could to Germany, but the shops there were still empty when we left it a few days ago!

Driving along New Street, we came to Victoria Square. It really was not a square, but rather a big plaza on slightly elevated ground, where a number of streets ran into this big opening. Several important looking municipal buildings stood at the right side of it as well as the Museum of Art. There was also a library at the back of the plaza and a music academy on the left side. In the middle of it stood the striking old, colonnaded Town Hall, built after the pattern of the Greek Parthenon, and a little lower in front of it was the statue of Queen Victoria. Sitting on a high

pedestal amidst a nice bed of flowers, she could watch the cars whizzing by and around her.

The city center itself was not very big, only three main intersecting streets: New Street, Corporation Street and Steelhouse Lane. An array of small streets was between them, where most of the business was done. In time the city had grown, of course, and had expanded far out to all sides. After passing Victoria Square, we turned onto Broadway, which was a newer street leading us out toward the suburbs.

"Your workplace will be here in the city center at the General Hospital," Mrs. Linzy told us. "We will go there later. But first, I want to take you to where you will be staying."

We, of course, were most interested in that, and she continued,

"It turned out that there were no more vacant rooms left in the domestic housing adjacent to the hospital, so the hospital's administration will be renting lodgings for you at the Salvation Army House. It is just a short distance away from here on Ladywood Road," she said. "I shall take you there first. You will have a nice large room there to share together."

We looked at each other, and our spirits sank. We had hoped so much that after the crowded living in the camps, we would each have even the tiniest room of our own. That dream was now shattered and made us sad, but nothing could be done about it. We would have to take what was given to us.

After driving some distance along the wide Broadway, we turned into a narrower side street where we saw the same red brick wall houses that we had seen on our way to London.

"These are called 'terrace houses'," Mrs. Linzy explained, sensing our curiosity.

Now we could see them close by. They were built like one long brick wall without any breaks between them, except after every two houses a tunnel passage led into the back where each house had a narrow strip of a garden with a shed for keeping the coal and a place to put garbage. The houses were small with narrow windows, except for a larger one next to the entrance door that led straight from the street into the living room. Being so close to the city center, these were the living quarters of the working class people; they had been here from times before, encircling the city and then extending outward.

A high, solid brick wall along the left side of the street ended at an open gate, and Mrs. Linzy drove through it, stopping in front of a large white house. We had arrived. Two big columns graced the wide steps leading up to the front porch. As we entered, I noticed that there was an extensive garden with trees adjoining the side of the house, and was glad to see that.

Mrs. Linzy went inside and after a few moments returned with a middle-aged woman at her side in the dark blue Salvation Army uniform, a letter "S" on the dark red collar.

"Come in, come in!" She beckoned to us and we obeyed, following her along the poorly lit hallway with its black and white checkerboard tiled floor. From somewhere came concealed laughter, then a scream, and unseen steps could be heard disappearing elsewhere in the house. Strange!

We were led into a large sitting room, furnished with big overstuffed sofas and chairs and a big fireplace at the side wall. More officers had gathered in there to greet us, and it was all rather formal. The ladies showed stiff faces and so did we, not knowing how to take this. I sensed that they were not too happy about having us here and watched us with probing eyes, perhaps trying to figure out who and what sort of people we were. To break the awkwardness, one of them said,

"This is the sitting room. You can come and sit in here in your free time, for this room is heated." It sounded good, except the stuffy, unventilated air in the room conveyed that the room was not used much, and the fluffy sofas were probably full of dust and not very inviting.

"I shall take you to your room," One of the officers said, and we followed her.

Going along the hallway, we heard the smothered laughter again, and two bushy-haired heads appeared for a moment, hiding around the corner.

"What was going on here?" We wondered. "Was this a mental institution or what?"

Later we learned that these were young girls who had got onto a slippery path. Some were pregnant and had been rejected by their parents, for in those days it was still a shame for the family to have a disgraced daughter. So this place was their salvation. Here they were taken in and helped; here they were taught how to lead a better life. It probably was not easy to teach someone who had never been taught, or someone who refused to take advice. All this made us a bit scared, but we kept following the officer up to the room on the second floor.

"Well, here it is!" the officer said as she opened the door and we stepped inside.

It was a nice room, large and long with the end wall opening to the garden with three big connecting windows. I liked that we could see the greenery outside; it gave the room a cheerful look, and the windows let in plenty of light. I suppose it could be called a dormitory, for there were six iron frame beds in the room, three on each side, with a nightstand and chair next to each bed. Two wardrobes and two chests of drawers stood by the end wall near the door, and there was also a wash basin.

Well, that was enough, for we did not have too many worldly goods.

"Take any beds you like," the officer said. "The two spare ones will be used by two English girls who will also work at the hospital."

We took the beds closer to the windows to be together. It looked like there would not be too much difference between living at the camp or here, but at least the room was bigger and brighter. What could poor non-citizens ask for? At least the four of us would be together here to share our daily sorrows, and there was no doubt in our minds that we would have many of those.

While we still looked helplessly around, not knowing what to say or how to feel, a tiny, elderly woman came in. She was also in the dark blue Salvation Army uniform, but in contrast to the other officially clad ladies, she smiled at us, her small, bluish-gray eyes twinkling behind her glasses even a little mischievously. Her wavy, slightly graying dark hair, though combed back into a little ball at the back of her head, fluffed out a bit around her small, narrow face, and gave it a kinder look.

"I am the Major," she introduced herself, "and you will be my children now! I shall look after you, and you can come and tell me all your problems. I will help you all I can," she said.

That was good to hear, but looking at this tiny woman, this sounded almost comical. What could she do for us? Yet she seemed to be genuinely kind, and that lifted our spirits somewhat. Then we went downstairs again where Mrs. Linzy waited for us. We got into her car again and drove to our new work place, so she could introduce us there also.

We drove back to town as far as Victoria Plaza, then turned left on to Steelhouse Lane, the third largest street besides New Street and Corporation Street (these three constructed the old city center of Birmingham, as I have mentioned). Steelhouse Lane contained mainly office buildings and ran in a straight line to the other side of the city center. About halfway through, on the right hand side, was another large plaza with some landscaping and a large church in the middle. Farther down on the left we saw another railway station, after which the street went somewhat downhill.

Then it came into our view! The General Hospital! It was almost at the end of Steelhouse Lane, looking more like a castle than a hospital, with its large and small towers and the various wings extending to all sides. A high red brick wall took up a whole block, enclosing the huge imposing red brick building. A big gate, with a built-in guardhouse, separated the spacious front area of the hospital from the street. As we entered the gate, we could see some ambulances parked by one of the entrances on the right side. We could not help noticing that the buildings here too looked blackened by soot and age. This would be the place where we would work now.

We were impressed seeing the inside of the hospital—so spacious, light and well planned. Three wide stairways, one at each end of the long, wide main hallway and one stairway in the middle next to the lift, led up to the other floors. On the ground floor were mainly the administrative offices, but at the far end of it the outpatient department branched off to an additional wing.

I must explain here that in England the first level in a building is always called the ground floor and only above that is the first, the second and successive floors. The various wards for patients were on the first and second floors, branching off the main hallways in separate wings, sectioned off by large glass-partitioned doors. Through them, we could glimpse a huge long room with a row of beds on each side and nurses moving about. Very impressive indeed!

First, Mrs Linzy introduced us to Sister Griffiths, the supervisor of the female domestic staff. She had spent most of her working life at this hospital. Now, as a reward, she had been given this easier job in the administration. She wore the blue uniform of a Ward Sister, with white, stiffened cuffs, collar and apron, and a white starched cap on her black, slightly graying hair.

"I too am a foreigner. I come from Wales," she said smiling as she shook our hands and greeted us. Her dark eyes were observing but looked at us kindly.

From then on Sister Griffiths was like a "house mother" to the four of us. We could go to her if we had any problems, or if there was something we did not understand, and she would take care of it. First, she took us to our appropriate work-places and introduced us to the ward Sisters. I would be working on ward 15/16, on the second (third) floor, which was the Ear, Nose and Throat ward. Sandra would work in the Women's ward on the same floor. Mrs. Avots' work-place would be in the Pediatric ward, but Mrs. Bērziņš would be in the kitchen, where she could manage with less English.

The hospital was huge, and we were fearful of getting lost at first.

"You will have somebody, who is familiar with everything work alongside you the first week." Sister Griffiths told us.

That was a calming thought. Then we were each given a list recounting our timetables and our duties, and that list was very long.

It was already evening when we left the hospital. We were worn out from the long journey and the many new impacts, and more than happy when Mrs. Linzy took us back to our new dwelling place or as the British would say, to our lodgings. At last we could lie down on our beds and close our eyes. It had been a very long day, and tomorrow we would start working.

"Get up! Get up!" Mrs. Avots' subdued voice called us in the dark at

the first sound of the alarm clock at six in the morning.

Oh, how I wanted to sleep just a little bit longer! Yesterday had been so exhausting. But the lights went on, and there was no time to lose. Quickly we washed our faces, got dressed and made our beds. At six thirty we were ready. Taking our overcoats, we silently went down the stairs so as not to waken anybody. Some tea and toast had been put out for us in the dining room, for it was unimaginable for any English person to start their day without a cup of tea. When we went outside a little before seven and walked to the bus, it was barely light. But it felt good to be out in the fresh morning air and get fully awake. Two English girls, who also worked at the hospital, walked with us to show us the way to the bus stop.

"It's not far," they said, "only about a ten minute walk."

We were surprised to see them wearing high-heeled shoes but no stockings in this cool March weather, even though they had thick shawls wrapped around their necks! That seemed so odd. As we stood at the bus stop waiting, they shivered and at times rubbed their legs one against the other.

"Why did you not put on your stockings?" I asked.

"Ah! Stockings are very dear! And they are on coupons," one of them explained, revealing an Irish accent.

It was rather strange to find out that even almost three years after the war, many things were still rationed in England!

Both girls smoked, blowing big puffs of smoke in the cool morning air. When we pointed to those, they said that they were very "dear" too, meaning costly. It looked like they would rather do without stockings than the cigarettes. Well, that was their choice, of course. We would have asked more, but the girls, speaking with their Irish accent, were difficult to understand. It was embarrassing to ask them to repeat something again and again, so we just let it be.

Our own language skills were not so great, either. Sandra and I had learned English at school since we were ten years old but to do well in conversation, we needed much more practice. Our older ladies had learned it only in the classes at the refugee camp in Germany, and we had to help them out, but since we would each be working in a different place, they would just have to try to get by.

When we arrived at the hospital near seven-thirty, Sister Griffiths awaited us, giving us green, button-front uniform dresses to change into, and then the work day could begin. The first job, cleaning the floors, was the hardest. They were hardwood floors, which needed to be swept with a broom and then waxed and polished every morning. No machines of any kind were available, so everything had to be done by hand and within a certain time span, as specified in the list.

Sweeping, of course, was no problem, but there were the beds, the lockers, the chairs and end tables by each bed, which had to be moved and replaced. Later I saw how the Irish girls did it. They did not take it as seriously, but just pushed the broom one way, then another, looking around, stopping and chatting with patients. What of it if a bit of dust was left here or there? They were friendly girls or women, but they had been here long enough to learn how to get by taking it easier and not breaking their backs because of a bit of work! I could not do it that way. If I did something, it had to be done right. My Aunt Irma had taught me that while I lived with her during my high-school years. Of course, doing it right took more time and energy.

My ward consisted of two large rooms with ten beds in each: one ward was for women, the other for men, with bathrooms at the end of each one. A spacious hallway, angled in a zig-zag fashion, separated the two, so they could not look into each other's room.

The center part of the hallway was a walk through for nurses going to the nurses' home. Three small rooms opened off the hall space between them. One of these was for private patients or the very seriously ill; the second was the ambulance room where the dressings and some procedures were done, and the third one was the Sister's office. All these floors also had to be waxed and polished every morning, since every drop of any fluid spilled on the floors, would leave white marks.

The waxing and polishing were the hardest. To do that, I had to spread some medium soft wax with a wooden spatula onto a piece of old woolen blanket and then work it into the floor using the long-handled "bumper". This, I would say, was a very primitive tool, consisting of a big rectangular wooden block, about a foot long by a half foot thick with a big piece of lead fastened on top. A long handle was attached to it with a special hinge that allowed it to be swung back and forth in long sweeps. Every so often the wax had to be replenished to the cloth, so it was quite time consuming.

The last step was to make it all shine with a clean piece of woolen blanket and the heavy bumper, going back and forth, back and forth and one more time back and forth, until the floor was shining like a mirror. I must say, there was satisfaction to see it so nice, but it was very hard work, especially in the beginning, when our starved bodies did not have so much strength. The first few evenings, after having worked like this, I did not even feel my arms anymore. As I fell on my bed in the evenings, wanting to rest, there was just something very heavy and very hurting on each side of me. Since we were new in the country, we did not have any medications either to kill the pain. We just had to get used to the hard work. That was all.

Although my ward was for the ear, nose and throat patients, where

each Monday morning a number of tonsillectomies were performed on mostly children and younger people, we also had a certain number of cancer patients. These were mainly people from out of town who needed the radiation treatments but could not travel back and forth each day; therefore they stayed at the hospital while the treatments lasted. Seeing these patients made me feel so thankful that I was healthy and could work, no matter how hard the work was. In gratefulness, I wanted to work even harder and do the job the very best I could. When the patients saw me doing it, they asked:

"Why are you working so hard? The other girls, who come here on your days off, never work like that!"

I just smiled back at them and replied:

"Because I can!" This seemed to leave them a bit puzzled.

Sandra worked in a women's ward that had mainly gynecology patients. She had the long room with twenty beds in it, and her routine was similar to mine. Mrs. Avots had been assigned to the children's department, which was in a new wing at the back of the hospital. To get there, she had to walk through a long, temporary passage-way. Mostly she had the same routine as we did, only in a more relaxed atmosphere. She liked it because she loved children. I did not know our older ladies well before our journey to England, but Sandra knew them both, since they had lived in the same barrack at the refugee camp in Germany.

A question may be raised as to why Sandra and I still called Mrs. Avots and Mrs. Bērziņš by their last names, since we lived and worked together. In Latvia, it was courteous to address all adults in this way to show reverence and respect. Only relatives and very close friends would be called by their first name.

Mrs. Avots could have been about my Mother's age, only a little taller and heavier. She had dark hair and kind, brown eyes. As I got to know her better, I found her to be a very warm and loving person. Since my Mother was far away in Germany, eventually she became my "second mother" as our relationship developed over time. I was amazed about her. She had lost both her own children. Her little twelve-year-old girl had died of meningitis. Her son had been drafted into the German army and did not return. Her husband, also an army man, had died of a brain tumor only a short time before she left Latvia. So much tragedy, yet she never complained, only carried her loved ones in her heart and was good to others.

Mrs. Avots, now called Pauline by the hospital staff, fitted into the children's ward perfectly. Seeing the person Mrs. Avots was, the Ward Sister was very nice and accommodating, and right away a good relationship was established between them. Mrs. Avots loved cleanliness and order, and pretty soon the difference was unmistakable; everything

sparkled and the Sister was delighted. This was a totally different job from what some of the Irish girls did, who went over everything rather superficially, and nobody complained too much either, because up 'til now they were the only ones who did the dirty work.

Only later did we learn that the Irish were very poor people, and being Catholics, had big families that they could not sustain. So the older girls were sent to England to earn money to supplement the family's income, but many of them were poorly educated and could only do the menial jobs. There were, however, also quite a few with better educations, who had become nurses, or were studying to be nurses and were doing a good job.

Mrs. Bērziņš, now called by her first name Irma, was the oldest, perhaps around fifty or a little more. Her two young granddaughters had been my brownies at the refugee camp. She too was a comfortable person to be with. A bit heavy, with graying, naturally-wavy hair and light blue eyes, she appeared to be the more helpless. Perhaps it was because she was used to being taken care of by her son and his family, when they all lived together in one room at the camp. She worked in the kitchen now and was satisfied, because she had always liked cooking. Her biggest problem was the language, or the lack of it. Even though she had taken classes at the camp, the words just would not stick. When we all discussed our day's experiences, she bemoaned her lack of language skills, saying that the best way she could talk was with her fingers. But gradually she too made some headway.

Our working day was so full that it would not be possible to squeeze one more thing into it. The whole day's activities were timed minute by minute. The floors had to be polished by nine o'clock, for the doctors would come on their rounds soon, and the wards would have to be tidied before that. It gave me an hour and a half to do all those rooms. Then it was time for our own breakfast at the domestic's dining room upstairs, near the kitchen. That was a time when we could see each other for a few minutes while eating, but there was no time to linger. While we were upstairs, our next job was to pick up the groceries that the Sister had ordered, and bring them back to the ward. Sometimes it took me longer to finish the floors, and that meant—no time for breakfast.

Back at the ward, a trolley full of dirty breakfast dishes would wait for me, and they, of course, were also done by hand. Other cleaning jobs were stacked one on top of the other all through the day. The main jobs were washing the dishes and cleaning the floors, and there were always more floors to do. There was also the whole open area between the two wards, the kitchen and two bathrooms and two toilet rooms at the opposite ends of each ward to clean. These floors were made of fine, multicolored, polished stone, which had to be scrubbed with a brush and

then rinsed off, kneeling on the floor, one little patch after another. This was usually done in the early afternoon, while the wards were quieter, and there was less traffic in the hallways. It took me the whole week to get through all the areas, which needed to be scrubbed and cleaned, and after that, the whole thing had to be repeated again week after week.

That was not all, though. There were also other smaller cleaning jobs, like cleaning shelves cupboards and the stove, which had to be done in between the big jobs, following the schedules each day. Monday had to have this, this and this done; Tuesday that, that and that, and so forth. There were no chairs in the kitchen to sit on, and even if there had been, there was no time to sit or even think of aching body parts. The regimen was tough, but we had to keep up with it and we did.

This situation was rather similar to what I had experienced working for the farmers in Germany, and physically this was even harder, but this time we had hope that someday a better future would be ahead of us. Our wages were very low, only three pounds a week, but then our food and lodging was included, so we did not have to worry about those.

We had our breakfast, dinner and supper at the hospital, and the meals were good. Admittedly, we came from a worse food situation, and for us any food was a blessing, but it was really painful to see how some of the rougher girls handled the food if it was not to their liking. Since meat was still rationed, we sometimes had rabbit stew for dinner that they disliked. There were two of the girls who threw their plates all over the table, cussing and swearing. Perhaps some of them came from rough circumstances; or maybe it was more of a show in front of us. But we had to think of the many thousands of people, still in the refugee camps in Germany who were half-starving. These girls, however, did not know any of that, but not everyone behaved that way.

It was equally painful, and even more so, to see all the good food that was left over in the containers after the meals had been served on the wards, to be just dumped into the trash bin. It made me want to scream and cry, but that was the procedure. Apparently somebody made use of the food feeding it to pigs. We, the former refugees, all bewailed the wasted food, but of course, there was nothing we could do.

The dinner on the wards was served at midday, and that was the time when we, the domestic workers, had our meals too, upstairs in the staff dining room. When we got back, all the dinner things had to be washed and tidied away, and then we had our break time. It was from two till four, and we could surely use it. It was so good to have a "breather" after the hectic morning activities, but perhaps this is not the best word to use for our afternoon break. In this situation, breathing quite often was not the easiest thing to do. The other girls all smoked, and the sitting room, where we would spend our breaks, would be blue with smoke.

They chatted and laughed loudly, so there was not much peace either. The good thing was that they were not there always. The older ladies would put up their feet and close their eyes for a bit, or we would try to write letters. The evenings were too short for doing that, and we were too tired by then.

Our teatime was also included in our rest time, and after going up to the dining room and coming down, there was not much time left for resting anymore; but even that time was precious.

At four o'clock we went back to our wards to wash up the patient's tea things. After that were a few smaller jobs and then again sweeping all the floors with the broom. Finally, washing the patient's supper dishes and finishing at six-thirty, if the nurses managed to bring in all the dishes in time. That was it!

It was so great to get out into the fresh spring air after the long day, for the hospital's windows could not be opened. Mrs. Bērziņš already waited for us at the gate. During these first weeks, we were let off work at the same time, so we could all go home together and not get lost, for what would Mrs. Bērziņš do if she lost her way, not knowing any English?

We also had great difficulty delivering our fares on the bus during the first days, for we could not understand what the conductor said. No wonder! He spoke "brum", the local dialect, with an Irish accent! Since there were quite a few coal mines and many factories in the vicinity of Birmingham, it was called "the black country" and they spoke "brum" or "brummie", a very disjointed and ugly sounding English.

"Thopens heipny!" the conductor said when we asked what the fare was.

"What did he say?" we looked at each other, totally confused.

"Thopens heipny!" he repeated, getting impatient.

We would open our palms with the coins we had and let him take what he needed. It was so embarrassing, but one day, a man sitting next to me explained: "Tapens," he said it differently again, but that, apparently, was because this man was English but the conductor had been Irish. Anyway: "Tapens is two pennies, heipny, half-a-penny!" and he showed me the coins. "And this is a threpny bit," he showed another multi-edged copper coin. That is three pennies. There is one even smaller coin. Look at this! It is a quarter of a penny. It's called a farthing."

By the time he had explained all that, it was time for us to get off, and I thanked him kindly.

Sometimes we went into some store for a few minutes just to look, for we did not have enough money to buy anything. The fruit on the counter smelled and looked so enticing. Luscious grapes, pears and oranges! We had not seen or eaten fresh fruit since we left Latvia three years ago, but it had to wait. Quite a lot of things would have to wait, for

our first thought was to save what we could to send food packages to our loved ones in Germany.

Passing the Snow Hill railway station on our way home, we saw a woman standing near the entrance, selling flowers. A large basket stood next to her with bunches of pussy willows, daffodils, irises, tulips and narcissus and even some lilac! In a smaller basket nested colorful anemones and small bunches of violets. We just had to stop and look! The colors and fragrances of the flowers were so delightful. We had not seen any flowers like that for a long, long time. We could not buy them, of course, but wanted to know how much they might cost and asked the woman. She answered, but again we could not understand what she said. We asked again, but received the same answer. It sounded like another language and it was. It was "brum", the dialect they spoke in Birmingham and its surroundings.

We stepped aside but still stood there trying to figure out what she had said.

"Bob a bunch o' daffs, ahf a crown the tulips..." her voice rang out almost non-stop as she held out her hand with a bunch of daffodils. "E'ya! Tsaik 'em, only a bob a bunch!" (meaning "here you are! Take them, only a shilling a bunch!)

What did she say?

The woman started to give us dirty looks, so we moved on, the fresh smell of the flowers following us. Some day we will buy some, we promised ourselves silently. I would have loved to have just one white narcissus right now! Just one white flower, but I gave a sigh and walked on.

Within a short time we, the Latvians, had become a sensation at the hospital. People we came in contact with wondered who we were, for we did not work and behave like the usual domestic workers. The greatest surprise for them was that we worked harder than was absolutely necessary. They could not understand why we would. Wherever we cleaned, everything sparkled, and that brought us joy. A job well done was a reward in itself. We felt that if we could not prove ourselves at any higher capacity right now, we could at least prove ourselves in the job we were doing at the present. And we praised the heavens that our bodies were able to do it.

In England the head of the hospital and of the nursing staff was the Matron. It was her custom to make rounds through all the wards in the late afternoon, when they were the quietest. She walked along the hallways in her simple dark blue dress, accented with a white lace collar and a white, lace-trimmed cap on her graying hair. Etiquette was very important. The Sister, being the head of the ward, instantly joined her as she entered through the glass doors and chaperoned her around the ward,

giving comments about the patients they passed. The Matron would listen, then bowed her head royally toward the particular patient. Occasionally she would say a few words, or ask someone a question, give a smile, or just lift her hand in acknowledgment and move on. She did not stay long, but her eyes saw everything, and beware, if some corner of a sheet or blanket hung lower than the other, or anything was not as the regimen required! And, of course, she could not miss seeing the shiny floors.

Everybody was in shock when the Matron stopped at the open kitchen door to talk to me.

"I have never seen these floors as shiny as this! Thank you!" she said, and added: "I would like to see you as a nurse in the ward as soon as you are more acquainted with the language!"

"Yes, Matron! Thank you, Matron!" I was almost speechless for this honor.

I had actually thought of perhaps going into nursing later on, but when I found out what the training entailed and how little pay the nurses got, I had to change my mind. They got only half of the small amount of money that I did, so how could I help my family then? I also found in time that I was not emotionally suited for hospital work.

It was interesting though to observe and learn how things worked and the hierarchy that went with it. The nursing program here in England was perhaps different than anywhere else in the world, but the training was very thorough and the discipline unforgiving, at least here at this hospital. This was a teaching hospital, and the nurses worked and studied at the same time. Their housing, food, uniforms and their training was paid for, as long as they followed the course and observed the regulations.

They started with three months of primary instruction, going into the wards only once a week to get acquainted with the routines. At this time, they wore yellow, short-sleeved uniform dresses with white collars, white starched aprons and caps, and were called "the lambs". I thought it was good that in the English hospitals one knew exactly who was who on the staff by just looking at their uniforms.

After the preliminary training, when the nurses entered the wards, they were "juniors" and wore finely striped, white and medium-blue short-sleeved dresses with white collars, caps and aprons. They also had to wear black stockings and black, low-heeled shoes. The hair could be worn shoulder length. If it was longer, it had to be put up under the cap. At this stage, the nurses stayed on the particular ward for three months, learning everything that pertained to the activities and treatments of that ward. They learned to give injections and to do the simpler medical procedures, mostly doing the more menial work, like making the beds, distributing food, helping the patients to wash, attending to bedpans etc.

Additionally, they had to attend lectures in their free time and pass exams before moving on to the next ward.

As the nurses progressed in their training, they took on more and more medical responsibilities, working three months on each ward again, learning all they needed to know. After passing certain exams, they became seniors, and everybody could tell that from seeing their medium blue, short-sleeved dresses. After more training, and doing more and more serious work, they got their navy blue belts, and later still they were awarded their silver belt buckles, which meant that they were fullfledged staff nurses, able to stand in for the Sisters. Finally, they would become Sisters and Ward Sisters, if they chose to do so and if there were vacancies. The Sister's uniform was a navy blue long-sleeved dress with stiff white collar and cuffs, a belt with a buckle, and a white starched apron and cap. It took about four years for them to get there. During that time they had also made their rounds in the Women's, the Children's, and the Maternity Hospitals, as well as in the various operating theaters. While in training, the nurses and Ward Sisters could not be married and had to live in the hospital dormitories. Such was the order of the day, but I am sure things have changed a lot since 1947!

I thought the system was very good and thorough. Everybody on the staff knew at any time what was going on with every patient, and what they needed to do, for reports were given three times a day when the shifts changed—the main, extensive one being in the morning by the Ward Sister.

All this was very important to me also, since my activities were very much connected with all of them, and I wanted to do my best.

Once a week we did get a day off, but it was not necessarily on a Sunday. If I remember correctly, one or two evenings a week we could finish at five o'clock, but then we had to work through and did not get any rest time in the afternoon. This free time was very precious. It gave us the opportunity to catch up with anything else that we needed or wanted to do.

A surprise letter came to us Latvian women, one day. It was an invitation for us to take part in an English language class. An old, retired English professor was offering to teach us. That certainly was a welcome idea. We all needed improvement. Our kind Mrs. Linzy had organized it and had made arrangements for us to meet free of charge at the local YWCA. We then could have our classes and other activities together with other Latvians working in different hospitals.

It was also conveniently located downtown, where it was easy to find. As we gathered on the appointed evening for our English class, we were pleasantly surprised to see more Latvian women who had come

from other Birmingham hospitals.

The elderly Professor Strahan, who would be our teacher, was a real English gentleman in the best possible sense of the word. Rather small in stature, with slightly bent shoulders and not very much soft gray hair left on his head, he was dressed in an impeccable gray suit, shirt and tie. His clear, light blue eyes glistened behind the small gold-rimmed glasses, and his face was smooth like a baby's, with hardly a wrinkle as he greeted each of us kindly by shaking everyone's hand. He asked for our names and tried to repeat them, which caused quite a bit of laughter.

We did not know why he had taken on this job, but it seemed that he was genuinely interested in us. One could see right away that this was a highly educated man with a much wider world view than most people. He already knew something about Latvia while many did not even know that there had been such a state.

Mr. Strahan talked to us slowly, pronouncing words very clearly, explaining everything with humor. We found that we could teach him something too. He called our capital Rīga, "Raiga"! But in Latvian "a" is an "a" and "i" is an "i"! Therefore it is pronounced as "Riiga" with a long "ī". Right away a good relationship was established in the class, and quite a lot of laughter was raised when some of us did not pronounce the English words correctly. He also talked to us, the younger ones. Would we perhaps want to go to the University some day? But how could we? We were alone with no backing by parents or anybody. Where would we get the money? Our pay barely stretched to cover our basic needs, and besides, we were bound by a government contract to work in the hospitals for three years.

His conversation made me remember that if I had stayed in Germany, I would now be in Pineberg at the Baltic University, near Hamburg. The papers of my acceptance had come through soon after I had left for England. At the time, however, I had been the only one in our family who qualified to go to England, so I did what I had to do, to be able to help my family to get through these hard times. It was no use looking back now.

Thinking about it made me a bit sad, but actually there was no reason to grumble. I had food and shelter, I could earn my living. After the lean years in the refugee camps, that was a lot, and I was grateful. Only those who have been in such a situation would understand that.

After Mr. Strahan got more acquainted with us, he began to invite us, a few at a time, to his home for tea, to introduce us to this age old English tradition of drinking tea the way they did. Actually, it was a whole ritual. First of all the tea making itself! A very precise procedure had to be followed! First put on the kettle to boil the water. Then warm the teapot, by pouring hot water in it, letting it sit for a minute or two, then swilling it around and dumping it. Next, measure the tea: one tea-

spoon for each cup, plus one for the pot! Now pour the boiling water over the tea leaves, slowly drenching them, stir and cover the pot. Let it sit and brew for three minutes, and then it is ready to serve!

At the hospital we got our tea already mixed with milk, so we did not know any better.

"But no, no, no!" said Mr. Strahan. "That is not the way to drink tea! First—the cups! Preferably china! Second, milk and some sugar, if preferred, and only then is the tea poured on it!"

Ah! That had an altogether different taste! We were learning. The teatime in England was usually around four o'clock. If company was expected, it was served with small, dainty sandwiches. Thin slices of bread, a quarter inch thick with the crusts removed, were cut into squares and spread with butter, cream cheese or pate with fresh cucumber slices on top. For the sweet tooth, a fruit cake or biscuits (cookies) might be served.

Later we learned quite a lot about these customary mealtimes. The term "dinner" usually pertained to the Sunday dinner, at least for the working people, and it was served at about one or two o'clock on Sunday afternoon, and would invariably be roast beef, potatoes, green cabbage leaves just boiled in water, gravy and Yorkshire pudding. We had it at the hospital every Sunday, and the beef was sliced very thinly, because it was so tough that it was hard to chew it even then.

Then there was the "afternoon tea" which I described, and "high tea", the last being the meal after work and may consist of a lamb chop or sausage with beans in the evening. Coffee time was usually around eleven in the morning, and that was made by almost burning the coffee grounds in a small amount of water, then dumping boiling milk on it. At least that was how it was made at the hospital in the ward kitchen, but it tasted good, especially with a lot of sugar. Oops! Sugar was rationed! So much for the weird English habits as far as I knew them!

Time gradually moved into spring. The evenings were warmer and the light lingered longer. Budding and blossoming was going on everywhere. Walking downhill from the bus stop on my way home from work, a white cherry tree leaning over the high wall scattered white petals all over me! What a delight! Everything looked so peaceful in the golden evening sun, but beauty always brings sadness into me. Perhaps it is the knowledge that one day it will be gone. The connection between living and the dying; it is always with me. Thoughts about it never completely leave me. Looking down at the peaceful scene of the golden evening sun on the rooftops, I saw three tall chimneys amongst them, sending thin golden streams of smoke up into the sky, and I wondered if my young life would also trickle away like that? Will the big life I had dreamed of never happen to me?

I was not grumbling. Everything was all right at work, yet something seemed to be missing in this life. The Sister and nurses were kind to me. I did my work gladly, but the sadness remained. Then I thought of God, how He had looked after us all these years. He had let me escape from the Russians only two weeks from being deported to Siberia. I must never forget that in whatever conditions I am in now, I need to look to Him, to give me strength to overcome these negative thoughts.

Sister Griffiths, our supervisor, was very caring toward us and tried to understand our needs.

"I arranged for the four of you to have your free day at the same time during the first period of your working at the hospital," she said. "That will give you a chance to be together and to be able to help each other."

That was very nice and considerate of her. Rushing to work in the mornings and then through the busy days, we hardly saw each other, and in the evenings there was only enough time to get washed, to rinse out some small pieces of clothing, and then go to bed. No time or energy was left for much of anything else, for we worked six days a week.

Our day off was the time when we would make packages to send to Germany. We had already bought some coffee beans, cigarettes and chocolate. Those were the things which could be most easily exchanged for food. We had also saved up our sugar, margarine and cookies, which were handed out to us at the hospital as our rations. Since our meals at the hospital were sufficient, it was no hardship to save these extra foods. Perhaps one or two more small things could be stuck into the corners of the box, but that was all we could afford. Our three pounds a week did not reach very far. Maybe later we would be able to save up for some clothes or shoes, but for now it would have to do.

Still feeling like strangers here, we very much looked forward to receiving letters from Germany. Our thoughts were often with our friends and families there. After all, it had been our home, even though for just a short time. Everything was familiar there and seemed even dear to us now. Here we were like a small island of our nation, like a cut-off piece of ice in the sea. Would we survive?

Yes, we will! Of course, we will! Our "old ladies" learned English, their noses buried in books during our free time. Mrs. Avots wrote long lists of Latvian words, which she wanted to have translated to English, and Sandra and I helped her all we could. Mrs. Bērziņš, the oldest one of us, had the hardest time learning English. Half sitting up in her bed, she held the book in front of her, the spectacles way down on her nose, and every so often, she would let the book fall down on her lap, gasp, lift up her arms and let them drop in despair,

"I can't!" she would cry out and again "I can't!"

"Give it time!" we would encourage her. "You are doing just fine!"

We comforted her good heartedly, all having a good laugh together. A few words did stick, and that would have to do for now. We shared stories and had fun telling about our various happenings and miss-happenings at work. Occasionally we said something wrong or misunderstood what was said, creating funny situations.

Just the day before, as I had walked through the ward, a patient had said something to me which I did not understand.

"What did she say?" I asked another patient.

"Oh, never you mind, luv!! She was just pullin' yer leg!" the other woman said in her "brummie" way of talking.

"What? What is wrong with my leg?" I was even more perturbed and kept checking my legs for runs in my stockings or anything. By now all the women were laughing, while I became more and more embarrassed.

"No, no! Nuthin's wrong with yer legs, luv! She was just teasin' ya! Poor girl! You shouldn't be doin' that to her, Nancy!" the other woman reprimanded the first, and went on to explain that it was just some funny saying she had used. The only thing I learned from that was that "pulling your leg" meant teasing you.

I also had a great difficulty understanding my Staff Nurse, a hefty Irish girl with bushy red hair and freckles all over her round face. She was friendly and jolly, but when she started rolling those words as if her mouth was full of marbles and very fast at that, I could not understand anything. I would ask her once, twice and sometimes three times, but could not make out what she was saying, but that would only tickle her. Then some other nurse would come along and say it in English.

"But that's what I said!" the Staff Nurse would laugh, her reddish-brown eyes sparkling with mirth.

"It was not!" I argued and we all laughed together. I understood then that she had done it purposefully just to tease me.

Of course, it would just happen in the kitchen in a more private situation and when the Sister was not there, otherwise she would not have dared.

It was interesting to observe the hierarchy at the hospital. At the very top was the Matron with her helpers. Then there were the Sisters, the "captains" of the wards who oversaw and were responsible for everything on the ward. Everyone "jumped" when the Sister appeared. She chaperoned the doctors when they came on their rounds to see their patients. The doctors came alone or together with students and interns. The Sister knew by heart what was going on with each patient, the tests and results they had had, and whether they ate and slept as they should. She also saw every smallest discrepancy or deviation from the rules, and her orders rang like gunshots if she saw a nurse stopping even for a second

needlessly.

"Nurse, what are you doing?" and again: "Nurse, don't you have anything to do? There are instruments to be cleaned and sterilized! And there is a basket of laundry in the hallway to be put away!"

The nurses were not allowed to sit down while they were on duty. The Sisters made out working schedules for the following week and there were morning, afternoon, night and split shifts, each shift containing nurses from various levels, so they all got the appropriate time of training.

I thought it was a very effective way to get trained, not only for the career, but also for character, because these were all young girls, still doing their growing up. The discipline was good for them. After their shifts, they would put their dark blue capes around their shoulders and walk away through the glass winter garden hall that connected the hospital with the nurses' home, where each had their own small room.

Another peculiar thing was that, while on duty, the nurses were not permitted to call one another by their first name. It was "Nurse Hill", "Nurse Smith" or whatever. Also, the answers to the Sisters had to be "yes, Sister", "no, Sister". Perhaps it was good that everybody knew their place. Order gave stability. But also between the nurses of various levels in training, there was a certain etiquette that had to be observed. The seniority was very important, and also away from their work, the older nurses were not supposed to fraternize with the younger ones.

Unknowingly, I had overstepped this rule one day, and it was quite embarrassing. All the nurses were very kind to me, and sometimes we exchanged a few words while they were drinking their coffee in the kitchen at their allotted time. Somehow we had come to talk about art, and one of the nurses told that a friend of hers was attending the college of Arts and Crafts in the evenings. Then I confessed that I too liked art and loved to draw portraits. Later on, one of the young nurses asked me:

"Could you draw my portrait? I would love you to do that!"

"Why not? Let's see what we can do!" I said. She had a nice face, and I was quite excited about drawing her. We arranged that I would come to her room in the nurses' home on a day when our free times coincided, and that was what I did.

The drawing came out good and was almost finished; it only needed a few more touches. We arranged another meeting, but the next day she told me that we could not do it.

"The Home Sister, walking along the hallway in the nurses' home, saw you in your green working uniform enter my room. I received a reprimand from "above" that it was not fitting for the nurses to fraternize with domestic workers." That was the end of our drawing project.

"I am awfully sorry," the young nurse said, but it did not sweeten the

bitter pill of being put back into my proper place. After all, I was only a manual laborer here, even though my education was probably better than that of this young girl and many of them here. But that did not come into it, of course. There was no reason to get upset either. Nothing of that sort mattered anymore. "Had been" doctors and other highly educated professional Latvian men were sweeping floors and moving garbage at the English hospitals today. They should be the ones feeling hurt.

On the whole, there was still a rather strong class system in England. Being British alone, seemed to place one above everybody else. This we felt most distinctly from the attitudes of the less educated people, the so called "lower class" people. They had left school at sixteen, and the older ones even at fourteen, as the law had allowed it in those days. They had gone straight into factories to work and supplement the family's income, living at home and helping to raise the rest of the children. That was the custom of the day. For them, all foreigners were either Germans or Poles. Most likely they did not know any other, but in their eyes we were certainly objects to look down upon, because we were not British! In time though, as they got to know these "bludy for'ners" a bit better, some good friendships evolved.

It was interesting that with the more intelligent class of people it was quite the opposite. Even though many had not heard of Latvia, they were most anxious to know and find out why we were here and what had happened. The patients sometimes asked about that also, and I tried to explain in the shortest possible way, but the floors needed to be done, and I could not stop to talk for long. Anyway, I didn't think they would understand.

"When are you going back to Latvia for a vacation?" they would ask.

"I can't." I would reply, already starting to swing the bumper.

"Why not?"

"Tell you another time..." I would say and move on. There was not enough time for discussions of this kind. So they were left with puzzled faces, their understanding being that we were like the Irish girls, who came over here to earn some money and then went back home. No, it was not like that for us, but it had to keep. Time was moving on. The doctors would be coming soon.

As the days and weeks went by, I got more and more used to my life at the hospital. Mostly I was alone in the kitchen. The nurses came and went on their business. At times we exchanged a few words, but there was not much time for talking. In the beginning I sang a lot. Standing at the sink and washing the dishes, I would quietly hum some folk song to myself. It eased the heart. But the songs required concentra-

tion and the thinking slowed down the work, so I gave it up. I did it only when I was not rushed. But the pain of losing my home and my country was still there. Nothing could ease that.

I spent a lot of my time at the sink. Dishes and more dishes morning and evening and in between... At times I thought that one of these days I will take root here. My only contact with life outside was the view through the window in front of the sink. What I saw was a spread of gray roofs with a tall factory chimney standing in the middle of them. That was my scenery, framed like a picture by the two dark red, soot-blackened towers on each side of the window. In time the chimney became my friend, because it was always there. Only two trees were part of this picture that sometimes was sunny, other times gray, but for me, it still was only a picture. It was part of the entire world outside, where I could not be. My place was here at the sink, behind the hermetically sealed window, and this was where I would have to stay. Only by looking at the trees could I tell if it was the spring or summer. And when the leaves would turn yellow, I would know that it was autumn. When they would be all gone, I would know that it was winter time.

I stood here at the sink like the blackened chimney out there amidst the roofs, having accepted my destiny. I would have to stand here for three years while my young days trickled away, for that was the agreement with the government that had brought us here. My thoughts always stumbled on, seeking connections between what I saw and what happened within me.

"Were we not like that big chimney in our everyday lives?" I thought. "It gives out the smoke day in, day out, for that is its job, its daily work. Sometimes it puffs slowly, sometimes fast, giving out black plumes of smoke, sometimes spitefully, dejectedly, other times easily, with quiet joy." My thoughts kept rolling on:

"It would be good for us to think about this limited life sometimes, to think of our short time on this earth—but we don't. Immersed in the rush of days, we just hurry on and on. But then one day the chimney would not be smoking anymore. It would be still. And, if it does not smoke tomorrow and the day after—that would be the end. The chimney would never smoke again. And life would be over..."

Those were hard thoughts that went through my mind while I worked, but it was not always so bad. When sometimes my dark friend, as I called the chimney, stood quiet, then I knew it was Sunday. Then I saw only the thin, white streams of smoke coming out of the countless small chimneys of the houses. People were at home, enjoying their fireplaces, celebrating Sunday and drinking their tea, which, being English, they could not do without.

We were not required to do any extra cleaning jobs on Sundays, ex-

cept the everyday regular chores—the floors and the dishes. Everything moved at a more peaceful pace. To feel more like it was Sunday, I usually attached a white collar to my green uniform dress because at home we used to dress up on Sundays. When it was nearing ten o'clock in the morning, I would take off my apron and walk along the hallways down to the chapel, which was on the ground floor. It was not large, but the inside was pleasant, with yellowish marble walls, a small, simple altar and dark wooden pews. People came quietly and slipped into them. There were nurses, some Sisters, and also some doctors. We, the very lowest on the ladder, went too and sat down in the back pew, even though here the difference did not matter. Everybody who came in lowered themselves down on their knees on the low upholstered praying stools and bowed their heads on their hands for a few moments, as was the custom. We did the same.

The service was short, only fifteen minutes, for the people were needed back at the wards. Most of the hymns and the music were unfamiliar to us, but the sermons were good, and even a few words could do a lot. Coming out of the chapel, we felt unburdened and comforted, for we had been in a sacred place. We were grateful to the Lord that He had given us the opportunity to live and work and serve in this special way. I believed that perhaps in doing this, I could earn my way back home, if the Lord would grant it.

Sometimes the pastor lifted up some new thought that I had to think about all week. One Sunday he said:

"Your God is your home."

"Yes, I could agree with that. Perhaps any other home is not even needed?" I pondered later, for the term "home" meant so much to me in those days. Maybe it was not even right to wish for one, and yet it was such a deep-seated need.

The end of May was already here. We had spent two months in this country and were somewhat acquainted with everyday things. It was a beautiful, quiet Sunday evening, too nice to stay indoors after I got home from work. Picking up my writing things, I went down into the garden. It was quite large, spreading out from the side of the house for a good distance, being surrounded by the high red brick walls. There might have been some fruit trees farther at the other end, but I did not go there. I did not know if we were permitted to wander like that.

A huge linden tree grew a short distance from the garden side terrace. The tree must have been very old, for its branches grew low, even down to the grass. It was beautiful here and I loved this natural garden. The trees grew however they could in the uncut grass. It was a lovely place, so quiet and peaceful. I sat down under the big linden tree, mean-

ing to write some letters, but my hand would not lift to writing. I listened to the birds, still making their evening conversations in the trees above. The air was full of the earthy smells of the grasses and the moistness of the approaching evening... It was very much like it used to be at home on our farm... It was hard to think about home; even harder to talk about it. The heart hurt like an open wound, yet those thoughts were always there.

Somewhere in town the church clock sounded ten and I thought: "If I were at home, I would walk down to the river! The buttercups would be blooming and a soft, white mist would be rising from the meadows..." But the road there was cut off with a sharp knife, which cut into my heart day and night, never ceasing.

Still I did not want to think these sad thoughts on this nice evening, and suddenly a comforting thought entered my mind:

"I shall go back," I said to myself. "Even if I have to wait until I am old and sick. When there will be nothing to expect from life anymore, I will go back. Then nobody will be able to do more harm to me than they have already done. I shall go home to die and my death then will be sweet. Only to be there one more time..."

It was almost dark and getting cool. Time to go inside and to bed, for tomorrow would be another hard day. I wished that I would have something better to give back to this lovely evening than these sad thoughts, yet even so, I gave thanks to God for everything.

Another month had passed and moved us into summertime. The evenings were nice and mild, although the English weather could be quite unpredictable. It was a Saturday evening and another workday had ended. I walked up Steelhouse Lane to my bus stop. Actually, there was a whole row of bus stops right next to the nice big plaza with the massive St. Phillip's church with some large trees next to it. It was seven o'clock, and the trees looked so peaceful here with their branches golden in the early evening sun. The new grass spread out over the plaza like a rich velvety carpet. Here and there were flower beds. From somewhere came a sweet aroma like honeysuckle, even though none could be seen. The rays of the setting sun played around the square tower of St. Phillip's cathedral, which rose above the surrounding trees. Several pathways led through the green lawns to all sides, disappearing into the narrow old-town side streets.

As I waited, I looked at the church tower. A gentle, pale blue sky surrounded it with just one small puffy cloud in it. This peaceful scene was in such contrast to the busy traffic, flowing on the streets around the square, although it, too, was becoming slower at this late hour.

Then suddenly the bells of the old church began to ring. I had never heard such ringing of the bells. In a moment the streets and the buildings

were flooded with beautiful sounds, flowing and vibrating through the whole city. It was such wonderful music, and it played for a whole half hour. I was so overtaken by it, that I could not leave until it ended, letting my buses go by one after another.

During the war the church had been bombed, and it was not in use even now. But the bells gave out their victorious music nevertheless, resounding inside the empty, damaged walls where the rays of the sun flowed in through the broken windows, golden and meek. Everything was forgiven and evened out, for there was peace on earth.

Then I remembered that this was a Saturday evening. In Latvia we called it *svētvakars,* which meant the "sacred evening"; the time for people to prepare their bodies and souls for Sunday. I recalled the Saturday evenings back home on my grandfather's farm, where I spent summers during my growing-up years. I would stop on my way as I crossed the yard when I heard the sounds of the church bells floating across the fields from our closest church in *Madliena,* ten kilometers away. We did not go to church, but the sounds proclaimed that all work should be put aside now. And people did that. They went into the sauna, washed their bodies clean, put on  fresh clothes, and then it was "*svētvakars*" with its own special peacefulness. And Sunday was Sunday when nobody worked, except the most necessary chores. I loved to listen to those bells. I remember standing there, on the pathway, even holding my breath, to hear them better, for the sounds were faint.

Now I stood at this busy street in the strange city, where I now lived, and watched how the lights came on in the big Grand Hotel across the street. Through the large ground floor windows I could see the silhouettes of the waiters flitting by. It had to be the restaurant. There, perhaps, was the "high life" that the rich people lived. Because of the war, I had never even been in a restaurant yet.

That, however, was all right with me. I was not at all envious that I had to stand here and wait for my bus while across the street luxurious cars came and went. Well-dressed people stepped out of them and disappeared into the whirling hotel doors as the uniformed doorman bowed before them. They probably had a lot of money. I had very little of it, but to me belonged all the beautiful sounds of the bells playing and the golden evening sun shining on me. While they sat in their expensive cars, they probably did not even hear or see anything.

Was this not happiness? I had fallen in love with these home-coming evenings, when the day was done and the sun was going to rest. I thought then of the camp back in Germany and how the people were perhaps promenading along the main street in this evening hour. I sent them greetings, but it seemed that a whole eternity had passed since then.

Now I was here, in another world, in another life, trying to stand on

my own feet. Would I ever be able to make something better out of my life? I wondered. But I had been here too short a time to even contemplate anything like that. It was all right the way it was for the present.

That was my outward thinking. But there were occasions when I felt someone crying silently inside of me. Tears dripping like raindrops from a bare, lonely tree branch, falling into the very soul of me, forming a river, a secret stream, swelling and wanting out. A dam needed to be broken.

Then one day a letter came! It was from Mother. I stood in the middle of the treatment room leaning on my broom and read it, my eyes filling with tears.

"Oh, Dad! Dear Dad! Will I really never see you again?" I asked myself.

I stared into the shiny floor, but saw only my dear Dad's beloved face, as I saw it for the last time on January 1, 1945 when he visited us at the German village where we lived at that time. Now it was July 1947. He had been drafted into the German army in February, 1944 and sent to the Russian front, and then later to Germany in August of the same year to train new units.

The mailman had just brought me the letter, for all my letters were addressed to the hospital. We still feared the long arm of the communists. Mother wrote that after a long search, she had finally located two soldiers who had been together with Dad in his last hours, just one day before the capitulation. They had been in the area of Rostock, withdrawing rapidly. The Russians had been on their heels. Dad had been riding a horse, but somebody got wounded and Dad had given his horse to him. Walking quickly through the forest, sharp spasms had suddenly attacked his legs, and he had not been able to walk anymore. The others had wanted to carry him but he had refused, urging them to save themselves rather than be delayed because of him. He had stayed in the forest, sitting on a tree stump, saying that he would end his own life.

End his own life! How terrible and unjust! On the very last day of war! When he had visited us in Germany on that New Year's Eve of 1944, he had told us that he had been given just a three day leave, and his journey was long, so he could stay with us only less than a day, but perhaps he would return to us soon. The army apparently had plans to release the older officers. Since there were no weapons or ammunition for the new soldiers they had to train, there was no reason for them to be there. We really expected to see him soon, but he did not come. We waited so long and hoped. Mother crisscrossed Germany looking for someone who knew what had happened to him. What did she experience during that time? We never knew. Perhaps that was why she often was so

hard and closed up within herself. And now this, the unmistakable news that it was all finished for him!

"What happened to you, dear Dad? Where is your grave, if it is anywhere?" I asked as I broke down crying. I loved my Dad very much. There was a special bond between us...

Shadows began to cross my path and darken my life. One day, when I was on my knees scrubbing the multicolored stone floor in the hallway, it all suddenly went black. Next I just felt that somebody lifted me up and sat me on a chair. My hands and legs trembled. I could not understand what had happened? Was I ill?

I felt well and was grateful for what there was for me. Yet somewhere inside of me someone was whining like a thirsty, locked up dog. I did not want to hear it, but I did. In my thoughts, I continued questioning: "Why did I have to listen to it? Why did I constantly have to ask: why I was here and what was the purpose of all this? Why could I not live like everybody else did? Was my constant remembering of our loss the reason why I blacked out? Was my body fighting against this mental anguish?"

When I expressed some of these feelings to my friends, they just laughed and said that I was chasing clouds and living in another world-- that I should not be doing that! But I could not get away from the clouds; they followed me everywhere. It was summer outside, but I did not see it anymore. It seemed that darkness was gathering around me.

My Ward Sister was concerned about my passing out and arranged for me to be checked out by the doctors. It was found that I had enlarged tonsils. Could they have been the cause of my blacking out? She had me see our Chief Surgeon Mr. Moffett who was also the chief of our ward. He looked me in the eye and said,

"We'd better have them out! And soon! I'll have the nurse look at my schedule." He got up to leave, then turned around. "How old are you?" he asked.

"Twenty," I answered wondering what that had to do with it.

"You cannot sign your own release unless you are twenty-one. Do you have a family member who could sign for you?"

"No," I answered sadly.

"Then we'll have to wait. When will you be twenty-one?" he asked.

"In the end of August."

"Good we'll do it after that." he lifted his hand in farewell and left.

It was a Sunday in the middle of August, a time when back home we used to celebrate Memorial Day at the local cemetery in Madliena. I traveled back there in time and could see in my mind's eye the roads full of people, streaming toward it, carrying flowers. I heard the big

old fir tree whispering softly up on the hill in the cemetery, and saw a small crowd of people gathered around it. The minister, standing on a small pedestal under the tree, preached the word of God. The sun warmed the backs of the people who stood around listening to him, and the sweet aroma of phlox filled the air. It was a hardy flower that grew in many places here in the cemetery. And there, at the very edge of the

ZIGRID VIDNERS ON HER 21ST BIRTHDAY

crowd, stood my grandmother, shielding her eyes with the corner of her scarf and crying bitterly, for she did not know where her children and grandchildren were. There was no one to put a comforting hand on her thin and bent shoulder and I felt so sorry for her...

My thoughts always kept going back home to the place I loved so much. Perhaps I was trying to live two lives at the same time, and that was why it was so hard. I could not let go. I did not want to let go.

## My 21st Birthday

My twenty-first birthday came. The sun shone, and I welcomed it with all my being. Now I was an adult, although it seemed to me that I had been one for a long time already. Perhaps since I was eleven... when Mother got ill and our family life suddenly disintegrated...

But the day was beautiful, and I started it by praising the Lord for His gift of life to me. It was a working day for me, but I did not mind. When I returned from my lunch and came into the kitchen, I had a big surprise! There was a cake on the table and a twenty-first birthday card with a big key on it! The nurses and the Sister came in congratulating me

and even our young Doctor Gordon was amongst them. They all sang me a "Happy Birthday" and I was so overtaken by this loving gesture that I had tears in my eyes.

How did they know? I had not told anybody? Then I remembered that not long ago, when I had to go through the medical examination, all my information had been put in the files. The reports came back to the ward, and of course, all my data was there.

All this unexpected attention was really moving. Being surrounded by kind people, by friends I had not thought that I had! The young doctor even handed me a small package.

"A fountain pen! How nice! Thank you so much. It will certainly be useful for writing my letters!" I said.

Doctor Gordon was nice. He was on our ward a lot, since he was the intern for Mr. Moffett, the tall, bony surgeon who was the ear, nose and throat specialist. In the mornings I made coffee for Doctor Gordon, and while he was having it, standing around in the kitchen, we sometimes talked a bit. He was a little shy, and looked very boyish, but not at all high-minded or haughty. He was rather small, only a little taller than I, and also looked very young. Because of that, the nurses sometimes liked to tease him.

Once, after returning from my tea break, I found the kitchen door closed, and when I opened it, pandemonium was going on in there. The nurses were trying to get the young doctor into the chest-like wicker laundry basket, and he was fighting for his life. Everybody was red-faced, disheveled and a little ashamed about their rather childish game, when they saw me standing at the door. The poor young doctor felt especially uncomfortable, but so what! They were all young people and perhaps needed to let off steam while the Sister was off duty. Doctor Gordon spent quite a lot of time in the children's ward also and Mrs. Avots had given him a nickname "Piparinš" that means "the Little Peppercorn". Anyway, after eating the cake, I had one more surprise.

"Since this is your big day, you can have the rest of the afternoon off!" The Sister said smiling. "Just wash the dinner dishes and then you can go!"

"Oh thank you! That is kind of you!" I answered, hardly believing my ears.

What a delight—a whole half day all to myself! There could not have been a better Birthday present than that! What shall I do? How should I use these precious, golden hours? An idea came to my mind that I should go and have a photograph taken. After all, I shall never be twenty-one again! It would be a keepsake and I could send one to Mother. I was wearing a nice off-white, short-sleeved blouse, which I had made myself from some parachute silk that Mother had gotten somewhere while we

were at the refugee camp. I had even done some pulled thread embroidery on the top part of the blouse, and it looked very nice on me.

I did as I had planned and felt very happy about it. While I was still strolling leisurely amongst the city crowds, another idea came to my mind. I had recently heard one of the nurses tell that a friend of hers was attending some evening classes at the College of Arts and Crafts here in Birmingham, and she had even told me where it was.

"It is behind the City Hall, at the other end of Steelhouse Lane!" She had said.

"Why not go and at least look? Maybe even I could..." I did not even dare to think any further. But what a joy that would be! At least I could get some information.

I walked up to the Victoria Square. Adjoining the City Hall was the Art Museum, with an archway and a clock tower. I walked through the archway to the back of the Museum, and there it was: The Birmingham College of Arts and Crafts! It was a large, three-story, red brick building in Gothic style with tall, arched windows and numerous spiky towers as decorations, and it spread out in two directions on the corner of the two narrow streets.

I had found it! Now in summertime, everything here was quiet, but taking courage, I walked up the wide stairway anyway. The large doors, ornamented with all kinds of metal, opened heavily, but everything was quiet inside. The doors from the lobby stood open to the adjoining rooms, where I could see chairs stacked up high. Surely somebody should be here? My steps echoed on the hardwood floor as I walked along the hallway looking for some living soul, but nobody came. I was about to leave, when finally a woman came out of one of the side rooms and asked what I wanted.

"I would like to have some information about classes in the coming semester," I said.

"The information and the class schedules will be here in two weeks. Please come then," she said kindly. I thanked her and left, but my heart was so full of joy that I could hardly contain myself. Yes! Yes! I will come! Whether I would be admitted, I did not know, but at least I could hope!

September had come and almost gone. I was now a college student. Really! When I went to register on the fifteenth of September and was admitted, I was in seventh heaven. I registered for the portrait class, which was three evenings a week from seven to nine. The only problem now was to be able to get there in time because my work officially finished only a half an hour before the time when the class started. I begged the nurses to try to get the supper dishes in a bit earlier

on those nights, so I could wash them and get out in time. Sometimes it worked, sometimes not and that made me very nervous.

As soon as I was done, I picked up my things and ran with my drawing board under the arm. Actually it was not even a proper drawing board. I did not have money to buy one, but I found an old wooden draining board behind the cupboard and borrowed that, because it was not used. It was rather bulky, but the one side was smooth, so it would do. The school was not too far, some fifteen minutes' walk away, but the streets at that time were full of other people too, who were trying to get home. I weaved through them, excusing myself to the left and the right, to get ahead faster. Then up the circular stairs to the third floor, where our class was, and there I flopped. Luckily the class did not start so punctually. While the model got seated and the lighting adjusted, I could take a short breather and get ready to draw.

We sat at small desks in a semicircle around the model. The older and more advanced students, who painted, stood behind us at their easels. Then the work would begin. I did not know what it was that attracted me to draw people's faces, but I had done it since my childhood. I found it so exciting and uplifting to see what there was in each face. Was it the uniqueness, the special features, which God had given each of us to express our personalities?

The models were young, old or middle-aged, but each face had a story to tell. My job was to hear that particular story, and sometimes I did and other times I didn't. When it did not go well, I was down in the dumps, and it seemed that everything was lost. But then again, when I did well, I was in heaven. Nothing had ever given me a lift like this! I floated on the clouds!

Our teacher, Mr. Eggison, an old tall gentleman in a dark gray suit with white hair cut short around the top of his bald head, walked slowly between the desks, letting us get started. He stopped and talked with the painters, shared a little joke with them, then walked on, a hint of a smile on his face. His small, gold-rimmed glasses were pushed down to the middle of his nose, as he walked around, his hands clasped at his back. Now and then his tall, meager body would lean down to one student or another, pointing out something, then he walked on, observing everything. Later he would sit down for a little while with each student, giving his critique and telling what could be done better, but also never forgetting to say something good and encouraging.

It seemed that he had taken some notice of me already during one of the first sessions when I had managed to do pretty well. And, of course, he noticed right away that I was a foreigner and wanted to know where I came from? Now he always gave me a kind smile, and when he sat down beside me, he would turn toward me, look into my eyes over the top of

his glasses and say:

"And how are we doing today?"

"Fine, fine!" I would answer, and then he would start his critique.

When I got outside after the class, it was dark. I walked across the square to my bus stop. In the evenings the buses did not go so often, and sometimes it took quite a while waiting. I watched the wind chasing clouds above the black rooftops. For a moment I would see a little star in the dark sky, then it would disappear again. Fall was coming. It was cooler and sometimes it rained. It wasn't until I got on the bus that I would suddenly realize how tired I was. It had been a long day. But the school was the compensation for all I had to go through during my day at the hospital. That was the balance I needed so badly. Sometimes, while swinging the heavy bumper, black flashed before my eyes, but I did not dare to say anything for fear that I might not be allowed to go to school anymore. It will be all right. I shall manage.

The nice ladies from the Welfare Department, who took care of us on our arrival in Birmingham, had arranged a gathering for those of us who had come to England on this program, so that we could meet and get to know each other. More refugees from Europe had come —there were also some Lithuanians and Estonians amongst the fifty of us who had responded to the invitation. It was nice to learn that there were more Latvians working at another hospital in Yardley Green on the other side of town, and we soon made friends. After some refreshments, an invitation was extended for the girls to show their talents, so there was music and singing.

The Welfare ladies were already making plans for a Christmas gathering at an English ladies' club and asked: "Do you think that you could prepare some kind of a program about Latvia as entertainment for that occasion?" Mrs. Linzy asked.

That gave me an idea to form a folk dancing group! That way we could present some of our culture! Since this was another thing close to my heart, I went into it with great enthusiasm. It would have to be an all-girl's group, since there were no young Latvian men around, but even so, there were not enough of us Latvian girls. Then two Estonian girls volunteered to help us out, and we could start practicing. Luckily, with the help of our Mrs. Linzy, we were given permission to practice at the YWCA, so the problem of having a facility was solved.

"But what shall we do about our dress?" Sandra asked. "None of us have the national costumes!"

"I suppose, we will just have to make them," I said, "if only we could find the right kind of materials!"

We looked for the appropriate fabrics in the stores, but they were on

coupons too, and the selection was not great. I chose to make the national dress representing the region of Nīca, on the western coast of Latvia, and it was a beautiful outfit once made. I needed a special red color for my skirt but could not find it, so I decided to use a red hospital blanket. It was on the heavy side, being all wool, but I was slim and it would have to do. I would embroider it, as the traditional designs required, with green and yellow woolen yarns in up and down patterns creating colored stripes on the skirt. At the bottom, there would be a rope sewn into the hem to make it stand out. It would also have a gray woolen bodice, embroidered with black, and a white blouse, embroidered with red pattern. A lot of work was ahead of us. It was a very tall order we had taken on.

Sandra chose black for her skirt, which would have a red, embroidered panel at the bottom, representing Bārta, a region not far from Nīca. Mirdza chose navy blue, which was not hard to find, and it would have silver and gold ribbons attached to the bodice and to the bottom of the skirt near the hem. This would represent another region close by the other two, a region called Rucava. That way we would depict the national costumes of three different regions of Latvia. Mirdza was a newcomer to our little group. She was Mrs. Bērziņš' niece and shared our room at the Salvation Army where we all lived.

We looked high and low for some linen fabric for the blouses but could not find any, so we bought some white pillowcases and undid the seams. They were very hard to embroider on because we needed to count threads for the cross-stitch pattern, but the weave was uneven and too fine. But again, we would do the best we could with what we had and used every spare moment to do the embroidery.

I was also making the headdress, which for this particular national costume was a crown of red felt, embroidered with small pearls, silver ribbons and large crystal pearls on the top edge. It was difficult to find the large pearls, and I walked around antique shops, looking for old crystal necklaces that I could use. In the evenings, while embroidering, my eyes got so confused from looking at the red cloth that everything else looked green, but I had to get it done.

I was almost glad, when at the end of October I was scheduled for the surgery of my tonsils. I would be able to have some much needed rest. Usually it meant a week in the hospital and a couple of weeks convalescing. On the last day before the surgery, I was given a free afternoon to go home and get ready to come back in the evening. As I was leaving, our young doctor Gordon "gave me an eye", and said mischievously,

"Well, Zigi, I'll see you tonight in bed!" It embarrassed me terribly, and I did not know what to say, so I did not say anything.

It was good that I would be in my own ward, because the tonsil surgeries were performed here every week. The patients were mostly children and young people. They came in on Sunday evenings, went into surgery Monday mornings and were let go home on the following Saturday. The Operating Theater was right next door from our ward and I knew all the doctors, for they came into the kitchen for coffee. Mr. Moffett, the specialist, usually had his with the Sister in her office and so did Mr. Fullford, the orthopedic surgeon, who also used this operating room for his patients, but they never failed to greet me, too, when they came in. Mr. Moffett came in every morning to check how his patients were doing, the Sister accompanying him and giving reports.

Mr. Fullford was a large, jolly man with dark hair and a small dark mustache. He would walk into our ward during his break, still in his "greens", a white cap on his head, a face mask hanging down around his chin. He walked in with his big boots still on, and I knew that he had come for his coffee. I poured him a cup and he would walk into the sister's office, exchange a few jokes with her, and then come out again saying: "Well, I'd better go and take a leg or two off," giving a chuckle.

That gave me shivers. It sounded so awfully callous, but we knew Mr. Fullford. He was a very nice and kind man.

I had complete confidence in our nice nurses, and indeed, when I came back to the hospital in the late afternoon, a bed had been made up for me in the private side room and the nurses bustled around me joking and making me comfortable in every possible way. A little later, Doctor Gordon came in to pay his admission visit and was very nice. All the bravado was gone. He was again professional though a little shy, and avoided looking me in the eye—but it was fine.

Everything went well with my surgery, and the nurses looked after me, even spoiling me. At the end of the week I could go home, but since I did not have a home where somebody would look after me, I was sent to a convalescent home in the countryside not far from the city of Birmingham.

I was to go to the Windmill House at the small village of Weatheroak, and a taxi was to take me there. I might add here that the hospital made all the arrangements and I did not have to pay for any of this. It was part of the system. We drove through a valley with pastures and rolling hills on both sides, then turned off to the left, where large trees lined a narrow gravel covered road that took us up a low hill. This was a very pleasant place, the perfect setting for resting and recuperating. I could already see the large old country house ahead of us amongst more trees. It was built of gray stone and sat on top of the hill, spreading out to the sides, rising three stories high. It had several outcroppings in the roof, from which small windows looked to the outside.

The taxi edged slowly up the hill and stopped at the big oak doors in front of the house. We had arrived, and only a moment later a tall gray-haired gentleman opened the door and stretched out his hand to greet me.

"Come in, come in! We have been expecting you!" his voice was welcoming and warm as he led me into the large comfortable living room, where a fire burned cheerfully in the huge fireplace. It was a very cozy room with dark, heavy wooden beams at the ceiling and comfortable chairs, sofas and small tables with lamps in several places. I felt good in this place right away.

A young girl came, and the gentleman asked her to take me upstairs and show me my room on the second floor.

"Take your time!" He said! "Come when you are ready! We'll wait for you!"

The girl carried up my suitcase and then left me. I stood in the middle of the room and was surprised to see how large, bright and comfortable it was. Two beds were in it, though there was no other occupant. I washed my hands, tidied myself and then started back downstairs to get more acquainted with my hosts. On our way up, I had taken notice of quite a few stairways and turns in the hallway and hoped that I could find my way back to the living room, but I did it all right. I liked the place and the people. It would be lovely to spend two weeks here.

To my surprise, a few days later my friend Sandra arrived also!

"How is it that you came here too?" I asked.

"I had thyroid problems. I was sick and in bed several days." She answered.

I had not even known about it, since I had been in sickbed also. Now we were both together here, sharing the same room. What a life! We had never experienced anything like it before! In the mornings we were served breakfast in bed, as the protocol required. We could really feel like "ladies", sitting against the soft pillows and eating our porridge, a soft boiled egg and toast with orange marmalade. What more could there be? Oh, tea! But, of course! One could not be without one's tea, which was served in small individual teapots.

Later in the morning we took a walk outside. The air, damp and cool, brushed our faces. It was already November. Brown leaves lay on the road and crunched as we walked over them, while the wind brought new ones down all the time. There were not many of them left in the trees that swayed and moaned as if saying a painful goodbye to something. Was it the bygone summer they were bemoaning? As we walked slowly, we could smell the moist earth and the decaying leaves. The fresh air was invigorating, yet it was good to get back inside into the warmth after a little while. I still felt a bit weak in my knees after the surgery.

When we came in, a nice fire burned in the big rustic fireplace, spreading its warmth throughout the spacious lounge. We sank into the soft, comfortable armchairs for a rest, enjoying the peacefulness of the place. There were a few other young people staying here, but we did not see much of them. It was nice to just sit with a cup of hot tea and watch the yellow flames lap at the big logs. They twisted and turned as in a dance. Occasionally a log fell, sending a swarm of sparks up into the chimney, then again the flames kept on the gentle swaying.

I don't know why, but I always felt that I should fill my time by doing something. Was it still that far back vision about the day and the night that would come to me, too, one day, so I should use my days to the fullest? There was a feeling in me that I should pay back to life for my living. I had to accomplish this or that as a cost for what I had been given. Even now my embroidery sat in my lap, but I did not touch it. Perhaps it was not necessary after all. I felt so peaceful and content.

During the twilight hours, Sandra sometimes sat down at the piano and played for us, although she needed a lot of coaxing. She still felt very bad about her stiff finger, messed up in a bad surgery that ruined her dreams of becoming a concert pianist, but she played beautifully, especially Chopin, her favorite as well as mine.

Our host, Mr. Howard, who ran this establishment together with his wife and some helpers, was a very nice man. As we discovered, he was also a very knowledgeable man. In the late afternoons or evenings, when we were all in, sitting around the fire, he would lead us into all kinds of interesting discussions. One evening he touched the subject of art, which was so close to my heart. As I listened, I thought that perhaps I too could have some success in this field, if it were not the way it was; if I did not have to earn my daily bread, if I did not have to help my family. But I knew where my duty lay, and I would never forsake them, whatever the cost. My heart ached at the thought of loss, but I knew that this was a dream of mine which had no future. There was no point in even thinking about it.

The logs fell apart at that moment as if agreeing with my thoughts. As the red sparks flew into the dark chimney and disappeared, I knew that my dream also would be gone like that. With a heavy sigh, I picked up my sewing and climbed the stairs to my room. Only a few more days, and we would be going back to Birmingham and to our work at the hospital. There was no mercy, no escape.

The days were getting ever shorter. The ugly November fog appeared such as we had never seen before. The sky became yellowish-black and pressed down over everything. It was an out-of-this-world feeling. Everything seemed to be silent, as if frozen in time. When

it really thickened up, you could not see to go or drive anywhere. The roads were gone; the whole world was gone.

One afternoon, as I stood at my kitchen window, I could see the black skies coming down again over the rooftops. Even the upper part of the large factory chimney had disappeared, together with the smoke it exuded. Our Ward Sister came into the kitchen and said, "Pack up, dear, and go home while you still can! It is getting darker by the minute now. The nurses will take care of the supper dishes themselves."

I picked up my things quickly and hurried off. Long lines stood at the bus stops, and the sky looked as if the night was closing in on us.

"What will I do if I do not get home?" I thought anxiously, as I saw the fog already pressing down between the buildings, and the lines at the bus stops moving down slowly. Thank God, I made the bus in time to drive me home.

December came, and we were busy getting the packages ready, which we wanted to send to our loved ones, so they would receive them before Christmas. We sent the regular things and a few other small items that we could squeeze out of our meager pay, but it was a joyful task. Yes, we did not have much, but in comparison with the people at the camps, we were so rich. We had our health, our work, our living!

In the middle of December, our friends the Welfare Ladies had arranged the Christmas party they had promised us. It was for the foreign women workers from Europe, and it took place at some Lady's Club. The setting was nice. A huge lounge was decorated with palm trees and other plants, and of course, also with a Christmas tree! It seemed rather odd, for in our country we never had a Christmas tree out before Christmas Eve! The ladies, who had gathered to host us, were very nice and kind, and we could see that these were ladies of a higher status, not regular housewives. We did our folk dances, and our hosts liked them, as well as our national costumes that we had hurried to finish for this event. Even some newsmen had come, and the next morning a large picture of the three of us—the dancers in our national costumes—showed up on the front page of the Birmingham Mail. We were something new in this city, but I am sure that it was more an advertisement for the goodwill of these ladies and their club.

During the pause and refreshment time, many questions were asked about our refugee life in Germany.

"Why did you leave Latvia? What happened?"

"Yes, yes of course, it was wartime!"

People seemed genuinely interested, but how much did they really understand? If they had no knowledge of the whole background, then it was too complicated a story to be told in a few words. Besides, our language skills were still rather poor.

It was kind of the hostesses to do this for us, yet I could never for a moment forget who we were in relationship to them. Although we were proud of our nation and culture, for them we were probably only a peculiarity, an object for charity and perhaps a little compassion. But the charity bread is bitter, and my heart ached when we left. It just reminded me more sharply of who I was today. Most of us would have probably preferred not to have had this party, but maybe it was my own fault for being too sensitive.

## Our First Christmas in England

Christmas was nearing. The streets and stores were full of happy holiday shoppers. They milled around the counters of the department stores looking for the most desired gifts, being squeezed and shoved through the narrower spaces between the counters, trying to see what was displayed on them, but nobody seemed to mind. It all belonged to the spirit of Christmas. The crowds were especially thick during the lunch hour and the after work hours before closing, when those who worked in the city tried to get their shopping done. Those were the days when the stores were closed on Sundays and in the evenings. The shopping had to be done whenever one could. There were also not so many cars and no supermarkets, so shopping did not get done by carloads, but what you could pack in two carrier bags, picking up a few things at a time on your way home from work. The shops downtown mostly closed at 6 p.m. Only two of the largest department stores stayed open on Thursdays till 8 p.m. during this season.

A few vendors stood outside on the street corners trying to woo the passersby into buying their goods as well. There were toys, balloons, cheap jewelry, wrapping papers and other small items. They shouted repeatedly while holding out their goods:

"*E'ya!* Two fer a *tanner*! Anyone you like! *E'ya*, only a quid! Luvely dolls - only a *quid*!" Again the talk was in the common dialect, the "*E'ya*" meaning "here you are!" In the beginning we did not understand any of it until it was explained that a "*tanner*" is a six-pence, and two sixpences make one shilling or a "*bob*", and twenty shillings make one pound or a "*quid*". The British money system was complicated, for the monetary units were not in tens and hundreds as elsewhere in Europe.

By now it was all clear to us about the "*tanner*" and the "*quid*". There was also a silver coin of two shillings, and another larger one of two and a half shillings, called a "half a crown", or "*aaf-a-crown*" in the dialect. Besides these, there was paper money of ten shillings a pound and a five pound note.

There was another less frequently used denomination called a "*guinea*". I suppose it still remained from previous, more aristocratic times, and its worth was twenty-one shillings. Even though there was no monetary unit as such at this time, the term was still used in the more exclusive shops like Harrods and amongst the rich and mighty. It certainly had a more sophisticated ring to it, and if someone used it concerning their purchases, it denoted that this person was not the regular run of the mill shopper, but had taste and perhaps the wealth to buy the finer things in life in the better stores. Since I did not have the opportunity to even see any notes of higher denominations, there is no reason to talk about them.

This was a rather painful time for us who could only watch the happy holiday shoppers, for we had to make do with the three pounds a week that we had. And at this time especially, the realization that we had no real home or our own country, was harder to bear. For the first time I was so far away from my family, alone in a foreign land amongst strangers. This feeling of being separate was also magnified by the fact that there were no seasons here as there were in our Latvia, where each of them came with its own special beauty and change. At this time the whole country would be covered with snow.

Here it was almost always gray. The sunny days were few. Outside my hospital window was the same gray sky above the same gray rooftops—whatever the season! The clouds moved across the sky giving rain, then moved on. I did not get to see even one yellow leaf on "my" two trees in my window scenery. One day they just stood there silent and bare. The autumn had come and now it was winter. Christmas was nearing, and my heart was yearning for snow. How could it be that there was no snow? How could it be? But so much was different in this land, and this was only the beginning for us. We had not really seen much up until now, there was just work.

The day of Christmas Eve had come. We called it "Holy Eve" in Latvia, because for us Latvians, it was that Sacred Night when Christ was born. The pre-holiday excitement was felt here at the hospital also. I was working in the ward's kitchen as usual, when I heard voices and laughter outside the door. Sister must be off, I concluded, for she would not have allowed a commotion like this. As I heard more outbursts of laughter, I went to see what was happening. What I saw was—the nurses blowing up colored balloons in the hallway, and our dapper Irish Staff Nurse standing on a chair, trying to fasten a colored crepe paper garland to the ceiling lamp. So that was it! The nurses were kidding around while she was doing the job, and they were all having fun.

Dumbfounded at seeing all this, I stopped at the door. I could have

never imagined Christmas decorations like this! What would be happening here? A circus? All this cheap splendor was against everything I had ever understood about Christmas!

"How do you like our decorations, Zigi?" the Staff Nurse called out to me, seeing me standing there.

"Good," I said. "The decorations are good."

I turned around, holding back tears and went into the kitchen, closing the door behind me. Then I could not hold them back any longer. I had cupped my face and the tears rolled through my fingers, and a big lump sat in my throat. What kind of a place had I come to? What kind of a Christmas will this be? This cultural gap, more than any physical distance, made me feel farther away from all I had known and loved.

But work was waiting for me. I put my hands back into the dishwater and resumed the washing, but the tears would not cease. They rolled down my cheeks, falling into the dirty dishwater in the sink, and I felt as if I had just rolled in some dirt. I could have howled like a dog to get rid of this heavy burden that had mounted within me during these last days. But no, I could not afford to do that, even though nobody saw or heard me here. I wiped away the tears with my shoulder and let clean water run into the sink.

"No more crying when work has to be done!" I said to myself. "Soon it will be teatime! I better prepare the trolley for it, get out the dishes and put the kettle on to boil!" It really did not matter what I thought or felt. It was necessary to move on.

Since this was Christmas Eve, we got off work at four o'clock in the afternoon, for the next morning we would have to start work even earlier, at seven o'clock. Sandra and I came out of the hospital together. The sky had become lighter, and by the time we got off the bus, the sun had even come out for a little bit before setting. That right away made our hearts lighter. Before turning into our gate, we noticed a couple of tiny Christmas trees standing outside the door of the miniscule one-room shop across the street from our entrance way. We could not resist going to look at them. What if we?... We looked at each other. The same thought had crossed both of our minds. How could we have Christmas without a Christmas tree? But they cost five shillings! That was a lot of money for us, because each of us earned just three pounds a week and that was 60 shillings, but we hesitated just for a moment.

"We'll take it!" it came out of us joyfully almost in unison. We also bought six candles with holders and suddenly Christmas was ours! We rushed across the street and upstairs to our room. The last ray of the setting sun shone through the large window as if showing us where we should place our little tree. Here, on the small table by the window!

I found an empty glass jar and we fastened the little tree in it. It re-

ally was small, not even two feet long, but the fresh soft green branches smelled like a forest, and it seemed to emanate joy that we had chosen it and put it in the place of honor for tonight. I fastened on the candles and cut strands off some leftover silver and gold ribbons, which we had used for our national costumes. If I tied them in little bows, they would make nice decorations. That would be enough!

Now we could wait for our other friends to come home. We tidied and spruced up the room the best we could. Then they came, puffing and sighing, like older people do, from too much exertion. The first thing for them was to kick off their shoes and rest their legs.

"It was like a hell's kitchen today!" Mrs. Bērziņš told us, dropping down on a chair.

"So much food to prepare! For the patients, the workers and for the doctors' big Christmas dinner tomorrow! I did not even have time to remember that this was Christmas Eve..." she gave a big sigh.

But gradually everybody did quiet down. The day was done, and all that had to be put aside. It was not important anymore. After all, this was Christmas Eve, and we would celebrate it! It was dark outside by now. After resting a bit, we each sat down on our own bed in silence, setting our hearts ready for the Holy Night. I picked up the matches and began to light the candles. And suddenly it was like the heavens opened to me. Christ was born! The gift of heaven was given to us! With each candle I lit, I felt the wonderful message growing and spreading inside of me like a tree! Sandra turned out the ceiling lights and there it was—our gleaming little tree!

Christ was born! Born also for me, for us!—the cast off, the driven out, the left over people.... He was born for all of us! That was such an overwhelming, joyful thought, that suddenly all the sadness and heaviness was gone. Only joy and immense gratitude remained in my heart.

The burning candles spread their gentle light through the dark room, reflecting on the walls and touching every face with their warm glow. I sat back on my bed, which was the closest to the tree, and began to sing "Silent Night". Next to me on my night stand was the basket my Brownies had given me, and in it sat the two dolls in the national costumes, given to me by the Guides as a farewell gift on my leaving for England. Those were the ties to my country and to my loved ones. Tonight I sang for us all.

I heard sniffling and crying sounds coming from the other beds, but I just kept on singing joyfully. I had nothing to cry about, for I knew God was with me. Gradually the crying ceased and we sang a few more well-known Christmas songs. Then each of us began to search for something under our beds and, believe it or not, there were presents! Nothing much, of course! A nice smelling soap, a tube of hand-cream, some bath salts!

They were all useful things, but there was joy all around that we had thought of each other in this way.

"Thank you, thank you! *"Priecīgus Ziemsvētkus!"* (Merry Christmas) We hugged and wished each other a happy Christmas, grateful for our friendship and all that God had given us. It was getting late and time to get to bed, for we had to get up very early the next morning to get to work on time. We blew out the candles, and soon there was silence in the big room. Just one or two deep sighs in the dark and then everything was quiet.

We got up at five the next morning. It was Christmas Day and still dark outside when we started on our journey, because we knew that there would be no buses running on this day, and we would have to walk all the way to the hospital on foot. The streets were quiet and empty, not even a car in sight. Only the street lamps stood there in the barely emerging morning light, lonely and silent like faithful watchmen. We walked at a good pace and in good spirits, not minding that we had to work today. The glow of last night's candles was still with us, giving us a new strength and a special knowing. It was a great gift that we were able to work.

When we arrived at the hospital in the gray dusk of the morning, there was plenty to do. The Mayor of the City was expected to visit the hospital at nine o'clock, so everything had to be immaculately clean and shiny. Everybody chipped in this morning; the nurses and even the Sister helped to get this accomplished. The beds and lockers flew out of their places. The floors got freshly waxed and polished. Even the Sister took a turn at swinging the bumper. Meanwhile, the others dusted, shifted back the furniture, straightened the bedding and ran back and forth. Not a thing dared to be out of place when the highly esteemed guest arrived. Also the breakfast had to be served to the patients before that. Luckily we did not have many patients left in the ward, for most had been sent home for Christmas. Finally it was all done. Let them come!

And they did. Not exactly at nine o'clock, for there were twenty-four wards in the hospital, but they came soon after. The elderly Mayor in a black suit and a thick golden chain around his neck, looked very distinguished, walking along the hallway next to the Matron. She, as always, was keeping up her royal posture.

The nurses stood lined up in the hallway, the Sister being the first. As the guests arrived, she instantly took a place beside them, continuing into the ward and taking them around the beds. We could see the Sister telling them something and the guest nodding, smiling and looking around. They stopped at some beds, exchanging a few words with the patients and smiled, wishing them well. The same procedure was repeat-

ed in the other ward, and then they were gone. Everybody relaxed and breathed easier. Thank goodness, it was over! The Matron had eagle's eyes and the slightest impropriety would have been noticed. Nobody wanted to deal with that.

I thought it had been almost like a President's reception. It brought to my mind a similar event back home in Latvia, when I was twelve years old and was a patient at the Military Hospital in Rīga. It was at a time when our President Kārlis Ulmanis came to visit the hospital, because a new wing was being opened there. At the same time, he also walked through the rest of the hospital. It so happened that he stopped at the open door of my room talking to the Sister, then came in, shook my hand and asked whose daughter I was. It was so similar to what had happened here today. At the time it did not seem to be that special to me, but I suppose it was. Not everybody got to be so near the President.

But this was a different country and a different time. I went into the kitchen, but the festive feeling could be felt everywhere today. I did not have to do any of the extra jobs I usually did, and the nurses helped even with the regular things, so I could have some of the Christmas feeling too. It was good to see that others cared. I learned that there was a special tradition here at the hospital, that at Christmas the roles were reversed between the higher and the lower class workers. It was a "thank you" from the higher class people to the hard working "domestics" who had cared for them doing the menial but necessary work.

Another English tradition was that a large bunch of mistletoe was hung somewhere in the room, and whoever stood under it could be kissed. In our ward it was hung in the spacious hallway, right between the male and the female wards, and when our surgeon Mr. Moffett came to check on his patients, the Staff Nurse came into the kitchen, grabbed me by the arm and said:

"Come, Zigi, come! Mr. Moffett wants to see you!" a wide smile and a cheeky look in her eyes.

When we opened the door, I saw Mr. Moffett and a few others standing in the hallway near the mistletoe.

"Come, Mr. Moffett wants to kiss you!" she dragged me out laughing.

I could have died when I heard that! I ran back into the kitchen and shut the door. I was so embarrassed. No way would I go out there, Mr. Moffett or no Mr. Moffett! The episode had shaken me considerably. I was not ready for these kinds of jokes. In my upbringing a kiss was not a plaything; a kiss was a precious and very personal thing, but then of course, I grew up in a much more sheltered environment. I had a different view on these things.

On the whole, this Christmas Day turned out to be very pleasant

after the morning's work and rush was over. In the afternoon, the nurses did not even let me wash the teatime dishes, but sent me to go into the ward and visit with the patients. A young boy who had had an ear operation a few days ago sat at the small table doing a jigsaw puzzle. I sat down beside him on the leather couch and offered to help.

It was already getting to be dusk in the ward, when our young house doctor Dr. Gordon appeared in the wide doorway. He looked very smart in his black smocking and the whole attire. Then I remembered that the Doctors were having their big Christmas dinner that evening. He said he had come to check on his patients, but was looking straight at me. He came up and asked me smiling: "May I sit down with you for a moment? I want to see what you are doing here. I still have time left before the dinner."

What could I say? Of course, I let him sit, shifting a little so he would have room on the leather sofa next to me. Needless to say, I felt a bit uncomfortable about this. He had beautiful, dark gray eyes, which were as clear as a child's. A fresh clean smell came from him making me even more self-conscious and puzzled why he was sitting here so close to me. I quite liked him, but I would never show it, of course. We chatted a little, then the Staff Nurse came in, too, and stood behind us, watching our little scene. Suddenly she shouted out:

"Mistletoe!" holding a branch of it above our heads.

Before I took in what was happening, the young doctor had put his arm around my shoulders and was going to kiss me! The naughty Staff Nurse! I instantly dragged myself away, but doing so, my left hand touched the end of the cigarette that he was holding aside in his left hand. As I cried out, he saw what had happened and, of course, the kiss was ruined. He kept apologizing that he had burnt me and hurried to the treatment room to get a bandage. It was not too bad, but there was a big white blister on the inside of my wrist and it did hurt. He put on some ointment and bandaged my hand himself, looking at me with those big eyes and still apologizing.

But for the Staff Nurse this whole thing was a big joke!

"You should not be so bashful!" she said laughing. "Everybody is doing it!"

Now I understood that, most likely, this had been planned ahead. A conspiracy! How could I not see it coming? I was so naive.

It was evening at last and I could go home. By this time it was dark outside, and it was raining quite heavily. Unfortunately, with all the rush this morning, I had not brought my umbrella. There would be no buses this evening either, I knew that. I just had to start walking and I did, but the city center tonight looked quite eerie. The usually busy streets were silent, empty and dark! No people, no cars, not one! No extra lighting ei-

ther, for nobody lived in the city, just worked there. And this was Christmas Day, when everybody would be at home celebrating. It seemed like I had stepped into another world, mysterious and strange. Seeing the dark and empty streets, a thought suddenly went through my mind: "Tonight the town belongs to me!" I said to myself. It was quite an exhilarating thought! "I can even walk in the middle of the street. Of course, I can! The town is mine!"

As I walked on along the wide Broadway that led out of the city center to the suburbs, it started to rain even harder. I still walked along the middle of the road, hugging to myself the preposterous thought that even the road was all mine! It was so absurd that I felt like laughing. In cheerful spirits, with my collar turned up and my eyes squinted against the rain, I began to walk faster. My hair was wet through. The raindrops rolled down my forehead, my cheeks, and fell down on the street. As I followed them through my half-closed eyelids, I suddenly noticed that where they hit the black pavement of the street, a golden spark lit up like a sparkling diamond. Now I looked around and saw that the whole street was full of these sparkling gems, jumping up around me, lit by the street lights that were much brighter here on Broadway. They were under my feet, under my every step! How did I not see it before? Such beauty! Such riches!

I opened my eyes fully, looked ahead, and what did I see? Like magic, in front of me stood a whole row of golden gates, one behind the other! I felt as if I was walking into a fairyland and there, beyond the very last gate must be the golden city! I hastened my steps, now seeing only the golden gates. They sparkled and glowed, putting such joy into my heart. I knew that it was only an illusion of the street lights reflecting on the wet street, but I opened myself to this magic, full of overwhelming joy.

"To the golden city! Closer, closer, yet still far away!"

But then, suddenly, there were no more gates! What happened? Where was the golden city? The gates? I looked back, and there they all were, behind me. It made me think, and my parallel thinking mind caught right away on the next conclusion.

"Is it not so in life also? Do we not all strive to get to that golden city of ours? Toward our precious goals? To the place where we would be happy? And wise is the man who sees and enjoys his golden gates. They bring joy to our journey; those high moments that make life worth living. We stand in the light and light spreads all around us, reflecting in everything. Darkness does not have the power. It does not even have shadows.

We hasten, we hurry through our moments and days, through times of quiet happiness and small and large accomplishments, through work and play and earned times of relaxation—through the one gate and the

next and the next, to the last which glows the brightest. But suddenly they are all gone. None are left. What happened? Where did they go?

You look back. You slowly turn your head, and there they are, one behind the other, glowing as bright as ever. It is your whole beautiful life, even though there were painful times also, but it had never seemed beautiful enough. And then you notice that your hair is gray, and your hands are wrinkled and old. You have walked your life's journey, and the most beautiful was what you did not know until you saw it when you passed through the final gate."

"Will it be so with me also?" I asked myself.

The wide street ended. It branched out in various directions, disappearing amidst the dark buildings. I turned into one of them where only the darkness was around me. The festivities were over. Christmas had passed.

And so it was, but not altogether. A day or two afterward, the hospital gave a special Christmas dinner for their domestic staff. On the whole, it was nice and another new experience for us, the Latvian "maids". The doctors' dining room, where it was served, was decorated with balloons and colored streamers, the tables were festively decked with branches of holly and a Christmas "cracker" at each plate. The crackers were a must at English Christmas dinners, perhaps for the built-in socializing factor. The big, candy-like cracker gave a crackling noise when pulled at both ends, and inside the cylinder core was a small toy, a fancy party hat and a paper slip, forecasting one's fortune. These were all things that caused curiosity and could be shared with others. They certainly caused interaction, laughter and put everybody in a party spirit. Everybody, except us! To us it seemed like such a childish thing, and we did not wear those funny hats either.

"Why would people diminish themselves to silly clowns?" we asked. It was a culture we did not understand, but perhaps we had been raised to be too serious.

This dinner was special, because here the doctors and the Sisters were the ones who served us and that again was a tradition of showing appreciation for the work that had been done, because without that labor the whole system would not work. The doctors, wearing aprons and the funny hats on their heads, brought around food, at the same time chatting and cracking some jokes to create a happy atmosphere. The Irish girls loved it and even threw some rather daring comments back to the doctors, which they would not have dared at other times. But this was their time to have fun and everybody understood.

This was quite an experience, seeing the British culture at work, but there had already been another one at the end of November. The hospital had arranged a Christmas ball for the domestic staff at the Grand Hotel,

of all places! That was incredible! The "poshest" place in town for us!
But it was true. Sandra, Mirdza and I did not want to go. We felt like a
bad joke was being played on us, but Mrs. Avots reprimanded us: "You,
girls, sound like old women! You must go and have some fun! I am going
too!" she added. Then we finally agreed to go, though reluctantly. But
what to wear? None of us had anything much for dressing up. Since Mrs
Avots did not have any family back in the camps, she had saved some
money and bought a nice new dress. It was lovely! We all admired it. It
really made her look like the lady she was. I had a simple black dress,
made of some finer material by my friend's mother back in Rīga when I
was 16, but it still fitted me well.

The ballroom was beautiful, but all evening I could not rid myself of
a sense of deep discomfort. I felt that we did not belong here. Not in these
circumstances with the gleaming hardwood floors, the mirrors and the
crystal chandeliers! It was really shameful to bring us here! Tomorrow
we would be washing out toilets and scrubbing floors!

We could also invite guests, but did not know anybody to invite.
There were no young Latvian men around. A few older Latvian men
worked at some other hospitals, and Mrs. Avots had invited one of them
who was more her age. He was a beautiful dancer and they seemed to
make out very well. Amongst the domestic staff, there were not many
men, and they were all older. The very few young doctors, who were
supposed to dance with us, had brought their own girls. Who would want
to dance with domestics if they had a choice? The Irish girls did not care
if they had a male partner or not. They just got up and danced by themselves, happy enough. We had never seen anybody doing that. Mirdza,
Sandra and I just could not bring ourselves to do that, so we did not
dance. Refreshments were set up in the adjoining room, where we could
sit and watch the whole thing, sipping our punch and snacking on mince
pies. We were just biding the time until we could go home. Such was our
luxurious ball, but we were relieved when it was over.


Without drums or trumpets sounding, the year 1948 had arrived.
School started again, and I was so glad to be there. That was
food for my soul, an assurance that there was another kind of a life than
what I had at the hospital, even though I was grateful for that too, for how
else would I live?

My drawing was going well. Portraiture had always been something
I loved and could get excited about. Also, our teacher Mr. Eggison had
noticed my work. One day he asked,

"Have you considered continuing your studies at the Academy of
Art?"

He thought my work was promising. Sadly, I had to tell him then

that there was not the slightest hope of that.

"I have to work a government-appointed job for three years. That was the contract when they brought me here. And even if it were not so, where would I get the money? What would I live on?" I asked.

He looked at me with his kind eyes, smiled and gave an understanding sigh: "Yes, I understand. But you do not need to feel so hopeless. There can be solutions. Sometimes rich people sponsor needy but able students who are willing to work hard. I personally know the famous chocolate factory owner Mr. Cadbury who has done this in the past. I could show him what you have done, just keep on working!"

This elated me no end.

"Could something like that really happen? My greatest desire fulfilled? Could it? Oh God! I will work, I will work," I promised myself!

Then and there I decided that—to concentrate harder on my studies—I would give up writing so many letters to the many friends and acquaintances I had made during our scouting days in Germany. They were nice people, mostly young men who had been through the war and were now rather lonely. I wrote to them because I felt sorry for them, since they had no relatives. Now I was their sister or mother that they did not have, trying to keep up their spirits through this difficult transition time, giving them hope that one day they will find a happier place and circumstance. Maybe some of them hoped for something more from me, but my heart did not belong to anyone.

Yes, letter writing took a lot of time, and I did not have so much of it. I wanted to climb my mountain, but then I would have to leave other things aside. I would have to sacrifice my friendships, even though I valued them highly. But to be successful, an artist needed to be more selfish. Would I be able to do it, to take up this lonely road? I did not know.

I had a response soon enough from my closest friend Ērik, whom I had met at the scout leadership training camp in Germany a year and a half ago. We had been exchanging letters since our camping days in the autumn of 1946. Now he was very disappointed in me. Not just disappointed, but very bitter, even angry! As if I had promised him something and now had deceived him! I knew he had been fostering unreal dreams about him and me, which I had tried to discourage. He talked about his dream of marrying me someday and then both of us going back to Latvia and building a beautiful life there. How unrealistic could one be? Now the disillusionment came. But I could not help it. I had my dreams as well.

Those had been beautiful and unforgettable times, which we, the young people from the refugee camps, had spent together at the guide and scout leadership training camps in Germany in the summer of 1946. I think they were the happiest days in our otherwise hopeless and sad

lives, spent at the camps in dire poverty and deprivation. During those few weeks, we were lifted out of it into another world, where there was no evil. They were days filled with friendship and idealism, and we all heartily believed that our road would lead us back to our beloved country. We believed in strong and beautiful humankind. We learned to believe in ourselves and believed that we could be such people.

But then we had to part and go back to the places we had come from. I was here in England now. At the end of last year, the men had been allowed to come here also, to work in the coal mines and in agriculture. Ērik was in England now too, only farther north in another town. He wrote me many letters, lately talking even more of us getting married and building a life together in Latvia! But it won't ever be like that, Ērik! I never let you think that it would be! Perhaps it was just as well that we broke it off now.

I remembered my Mother's words, said long ago: "Don't play with fire, or somebody will get burnt!"

That meant not to play with other people's feelings. But how could one know when friendship will change into something more in someone else's heart? When the quiet flame of friendship will turn into a fire scare? Did it mean that we should not have friendships, so as not to create such traumas? I thought I had been very careful not to create situations like that, but there it was. I was sorry for Ērik, for he was very bitter. He felt deceived, but they had been his dreams, not mine. He had not asked for my thoughts.

Mother had said the same words to me about my friendship with Viktor back in Latvia, and for a long time I tried to evade him. I did not answer his letters, thinking that it would put him off. But he always found me. He let his friendship and quiet love flow toward me even though he knew I would not answer it. But perhaps he still hoped? After I came to England, Mother wrote me that some letters had come from him, but I told her not to forward them or give him my address. One should not play with fire.

I felt a bit sad, because of the bygone days, when Viktor tried to be good to me. I was sorry that he wasted his love on me, knowing how it was with me. But you cannot order love. I hoped that someday he would find someone else and perhaps he already had. I wished him well.

News! Dad was alive after all! My dear Dad was alive! Mother had not written to our grandparents in Latvia anymore, for fear that it might cause them problems with the Soviet establishment, but she had written to a friend who lived in the vicinity of our farm and would know what was happening there. Now she had received a reply from her, just a short note, stating that the grandparents still lived on the farm

and were alright. But the greatest surprise was the news that they were exchanging letters with our Dad!

"Where was he?" we wondered. "Had he been captured and was a prisoner of war, or was he living somewhere under an assumed name? Perhaps even living in another country?"

Puzzled by all this, Mother had written back, asking for more explanation, but an even shorter note had come back, containing the same message as before. Apparently her friend had written a longer letter before, explaining things, but it had never reached us. Most likely it had been confiscated by the Soviet government, for they discouraged and even punished people for communicating with people outside the Soviet Union. Mother understood then that it would be better not to write anymore, for she did not want to cause problems for her friend. But at least we knew that Dad was alive, and hope remained that maybe someday we would see him again.

It was February 18, 1948 when Mother received this letter. It wasn't until years later that I learned that Dad had died only three months later on May 8, 1948, at a prisoner of war camp in the Soviet Union. He had been condemned to ten years of hard labor, working in the stone mines in the Ural Mountains, for having served in the German army. Dad was not a strong man, and had survived just three years of the hard labor, having been captured on the last day before the capitulation of Germany. What a difference a day could make!

Years later I also learned that Grandpa had died only three weeks before Dad. What a sorrow that must have been for Grandma—her husband and her son dying within three weeks of each other!

As we learned much later, more bad things had happened. On March 25, 1949 another deportation had taken place in Latvia and some 45,000 people were arrested and taken to Siberia. This time they had been mostly farm people, because the Communists wanted to destroy the individual farms and instead create the collective farms called the "kolhoz". Dad's sister Elza lived on a neighboring farm not far from ours with her husband, his mother and two young daughters. They too had been taken away. Poor Grandma! She had lost both her children: my father Jānis and her daughter Elza—and all her grandchildren: my two brothers Ilgvars, Jānīts and me, and Elza's girls Zinta and Velta who were quite young at the time. She never saw any of us again. Only her youngest son Kārlis survived. He had been captured by the German military police while walking on the street in Rīga and taken to Germany to work, but he had later returned to Latvia and lived in Rīga. In later years, Grandma had lost one leg due to gangrene that had set in after she had frozen it outside in the freezing winter weather. Her son Kārlis had

taken her to Rīga, where she had died on October 18, 1957, at the age of eighty-eight.

Here in England, the seasons were moving toward spring again. The wind blew, bending the trees, and the rain washed over everything. Storms came and went. So also my thoughts swayed back and forth, digging into the past, for my work did not require much thinking, only physical strength. I looked back at all that had been and that had happened. Scenes came to my mind and again slid away. So many bridges were broken, bridges which had seemed strong. So many streams had carried away the happy days of my youth, and had made me seek new ways, new solutions. The former life was gone. The whole world in which I lived now was so different.

I could not help going back, though. I remembered that heart wrenching late August afternoon back home in Latvia, when I buried my diaries and other precious personal things on the hillside, knowing that the next day we would have to leave for ever. What is "forever"? Perhaps only our hearts hold the answer to that. It was so unbelievable that we should leave, yet it happened. It seemed so long ago now! Almost four years! But the memory of our leaving was with me still, every day, every moment. The pain never stopped.

Now I was in this big, old, smoky town, in a foreign land with strange customs. I had survived, but I was not the dreaming girl anymore. My hands were rough, and life had forced me to look straight into its eyes. Yes, I had matured, and yet there was still a child within me, seeking heaven to heal my soul. My heart was still in my native land, warming itself in the sun of the by-gone days, listening to the ancient song, not letting the smoke and the dust of this foreign land touch me.

It was a great surprise to us, the four Latvians at the hospital, that we would be having a vacation! It was early March and we had worked a year, so we were entitled to have a week off. What wonderful news, we thought! We would be able to catch up with the many small jobs which needed to be done. We could rest up, perhaps take a walk in a park or explore the city. But Sister Griffiths, our administrator, dashed our dreams telling us that we would be going to the seaside. "To the seaside! Why to the seaside?" we all exclaimed almost in unison.

"Because here in England it is customary for people to spend their vacations at the seaside." she said quietly. "You need the fresh sea air that will be good for your lungs! It will be healthy!"

Our protests fell on deaf ears. The arrangements had already been made for us, and all we had to do was to be on the train on a certain day. The destination would be a small resort town on the Welsh coast, called

Rhyl. There was nothing else for us to do but to obey. At least it was good that we could all go together at the same time and that the hospital took care of it all.

As we sat on the train and looked at the gray and dismal countryside, we wondered what we would do at the seaside in the cold March weather. It was often blustery, and it rained a lot. Would we even be able to go outside?

The small guest house, where the hospital had made the reservations for us, was nice and cozy. The lounge was warm and comfortable; the meals were good and were included in the whole package as it usually was in these guest houses. Everything was all right, but we felt a bit lost in this unusual situation. What would we do here, we wondered?

We went out for walks, at times even if it rained, and sat in the small glass-walled shelters along the promenade. The walls of the shelters facing the sea were open, so we could be protected from the rain and still breathe the fresh air. It was not a bad idea, especially in a country like this where it rained so much. We could see the waves crashing against the coast and receding over the sands. The sounds of the rough sea pounding the coastline made me remember my days at Camp Hockensbühl in Germany, where Sandra and I went to high school after the war. Our refugee camp was near the North Sea, and I used to go there often when my heart needed solitude.

Here in the shelters we could not sit for long, because it got too cold and we had to go back to the house. In the afternoon, tea was served in the lounge in front of the fire, and that tasted good after having been out in the cold.

When we had nothing else to do, we walked around the small town's shopping area, where the windows were full of souvenirs, but this was not the season for that. Very few people were around, and we did not need any souvenirs, nor did we have any money to spare for things like that. The sea air was invigorating, we had to admit, but we were glad when we could go back to Birmingham. We had planned to do some sewing and mending in our free time, but that remained undone. Well, never mind. It had been one more English experience.

When we returned, it was still early spring. The mornings were not dark anymore when we left for work, but it was cold, and there was frost on the grass in the garden. As we walked along the quiet street to the bus stop, sometimes the red disc of the rising sun greeted us. It looked almost unreal as it sat there in the middle of the blue morning mist just above the rooftops. It was a cold sun, but then I noticed high up in the pale blue sky, thin white clouds just turning softly pink. What a beautiful message for beginning a new day!

It was Easter. We had to work, of course. Somebody had to do it.

Right now was the spring break time at the college, but next week the term would start again. I was waiting for it anxiously, but I knew it would mean very long days without any rest and often with no time to eat. It would not be too good for my health, but I would have to manage. I had to hold on to my dream.

In the beginning of April, an announcement came from the hospital administration that they would start a new category of work which they had not had before. We, the Latvian girls, were given the first opportunity at filling these new positions. It was gratifying that our hard work had been appreciated. The Matron had said it several times during her evening visits to the wards that she had never seen everything so clean and sparkling in all her days. Now we had the chance of doing easier work, and that sounded wonderful.

In this job we would be nurse's aides, taking over things that anybody could do, like distributing drinks and meals, gathering up the dishes, doing some dusting, and arranging the flowers the visitors brought in, especially after surgeries. We would also help patients to wash, and help nurses to make beds, which were changed every afternoon. The nurses would have more time then to do the actual nursing. Our wages would be higher, as well, but then we would have to find our own places to live outside the hospital.

Sandra and I both applied for the new positions and were accepted. She had already thought of moving out, for her boyfriend—whom she had met way back in Hockensbuhl, Germany—was here in Birmingham now. They had found a room to rent in a house owned by some Pakistani people. I would have to start looking too. The new job would not start until May 1st, so I had a little time.

Mrs. Avots also had received a promotion. She had been asked to be the Matron's personal maid, or rather her housekeeper, for the Matron also lived on the hospital's premises, having her own apartment. We all thought that the Matron could not have chosen anyone better than Mrs. Avots. She was a person of integrity, liked cleanliness and order. She would be the perfect housekeeper for the Matron. She was also a lady, perhaps no less than the Matron was, only life had dealt her different cards.

The Matron was overjoyed. Pauline did things for her that nobody had done before. She kept her apartment spotless, looked after her clothes, cooked delicious meals, baked breads, cakes and cookies, and received her guests. In time she became friends not only with the Matron but also with her friends, and they often gave her tickets to the theater or concerts, knowing how she loved music.

"I am so happy!" Mrs Avots said. "I could not wish for anything

better in this situation! I have lighter duties and am practically my own boss. I also have my own room in the nurses' home now. What more could I wish for?"

Mrs. Bērziņš remained to work in the kitchen where she did not need to use as much language. She knew the ropes and the routines by now and felt comfortable with them. The only problem was that she had to be on her feet practically all the time, and being a bit heavier, that made it harder for her. It was nice, though, that her niece Mirdza worked there also, as well as two other Latvian women who had arrived later. That made all of them feel better, for they could talk together and communicate better with the English speaking staff.

Another new development was that the government had conceded that we could also get our family members out of Germany to join us, if we could find accommodations. That was wonderful news! To have our family together again! I would definitely search and search until I found something. Also, more young Latvian men had arrived in the vicinity of Birmingham, working in the coal mines near Walsall and Wolverhampton, not far from Birmingham. So things were changing all the time.

In the evenings I still went to school. If it happened to be the day when I worked until five, I could walk to school in a more leisurely manner. Going up Steelhouse Lane, only a block farther along, was the Snow Hill railway station. Quite a crowd usually milled around near the entrance. It was a popular meeting place for dates, and people stood around watching for whoever they were waiting for. The newspaper sellers stood next to their bundles of evening papers, shouting their sales pitch every other minute.

"*E ya-a*! 'Patch and Mail! Come and get it!" ("Patch" for "Dispatch")

I had to pass here every day. People were queuing at the bus stops a little farther up the road, trying to get home after work. Now, in the spring time, the streets seemed more crowded than in winter. But, of course, it was the time when particular excitement was in the air. Springtime, the joyful season was here! Everybody rushed somewhere, mostly in pairs. And on almost every corner stood a girl or a young man, looking around with anticipation in their eyes. I passed them by quietly, my drawing board under my arm, just letting my eyes slide past them. I did not have time or interest for things like dating right now.

On the right side of the street, opposite the bus stops, was the Grand Hotel. A doorman stood in front of it in his red uniform with golden buttons, and the revolving door behind him turned without stopping. The taxis kept coming, releasing their passengers, then leaving, making room for others. Across the street from it, in the St. Phillip's Church plaza, the first green was appearing in the trees, and the massive gray tower looked so dramatic against the yellow evening sky with its lavender col-

ored clouds. But then I noticed that the clock in the church tower showed twenty to seven and began to walk faster. This was the first class after Easter and I did not want to be late.

A bunch of people had just alighted from the bus right in front of the college. I made my way through them and up the stairs. A warm feeling enveloped me as I entered the now-familiar building. It was so good to know that I, too, had my place here. How strange it was. My Dad had said that art was a beggar's bread, and I had decided to follow his advice not to study art, even though my art teachers at school had noticed my abilities and had urged me on. No, I did not want to be a beggar! I wanted strong ground under my feet, so I would not have to wash other people's floors.

But that was then. The war had destroyed the previous hopes and dreams, and now I was washing other people's floors, and it was not so terrible after all. Now my art was not the beggar's bread, but the bread from heaven.

Another work week had ended. The evening was nearing, and somewhere in the distance the thunder still rolled, wrapped in a dark blue cloud, low over the rooftops. It had rained, but above the sky was clear.

I walked down the hill from my bus stop at the other end of my daily journey, joyful for the free day ahead, breathing in deeply the fresh spring air, fragrant and moist. It suddenly seemed much warmer. The trees were just opening their leaves and stood quiet and heavy, full of the heavenly dew. It made me remember another evening very much like this, exactly four years ago back home. Then too, I had stood on a hill, taking in the marvels of nature in spring. It was the last spring at home and that was so special for me, for I was in love and somebody loved me. I could not have been happier.

It was strange how things repeated themselves and yet in different ways. Again I stood on a hill, but not at my home in Latvia, but in the far away England. Now, after these years, it was just a dear golden memory of a dream once dreamed.

At times, it made me feel sad that I did not seem to be able, or was not even willing to connect with another person. There was no special love in my heart for anybody. Things were happening all around me, but I was like a rock in a stream; I just stood there letting the waters go by. Nothing could move me. I suppose, I was still numb within from the trauma of losing my country. It was with me day and night. I would feel a bit sorry for myself, but I could not help it.

During these sad times, when I dwelt deep within myself, I seemed to hear music coming to me from far away. Closer and closer it came as

I listened, pressing into my heart painfully, as if coming from another world. Were they the souls of those who had given their young lives for Latvia and were grieving their un-lived lives? Were they calling out, not to be forgotten? We, who were alive, had to live for them also! We had to love our country more fiercely, not just for us, but for them as well! We did not dare to lose hope that Latvia would be free one day again. Was it my Dad who sent me these thoughts? Many years later I learned that he had already been on his deathbed at this time, and his life had finished only two weeks later in a slave camp in the Soviet Union. I could not stop grieving for him and for the fate of our whole nation back there in Latvia, now once again having to live under Russian rule.

In 1948, more young Latvian men had been arriving in the vicinity of Birmingham. In Sutton Park, about half an hour's bus ride outside the city, was an agricultural hostel, actually very much like the camps in which we had lived in Germany, with their gray wooden barracks. Near Wolverhampton was another camp for men working in the coal mines, and there were older men working in the hospitals. Perhaps the British government had realized what a good and responsible workforce the Latvian people were, so why not bring more of them over to do the heavy work the locals did not want to do? And they were cheap too!

One day, those of us at the hospital received an invitation from the men of Sutton Park hostel to come and enjoy the concert by the famous Zuika Choir that they would be hosting. This was very exciting, since this Latvian men's choir was already well known amongst the Latvians in exile. Of course, we would go! Many others had responded to the invitation also, and people had come from far and wide to the concert that Sunday. It was so great to see so many of us Latvians together again. There were probably a hundred of us there.

The concert was wonderful, as we knew it would be—for we had heard it once before—when they sang at our refugee camp in Germany. The songs, as always, were moving and uplifting. They took us back to our country and made us so proud of it. And these were the Latvian men in their new suits and sun-browned faces, healthy and strong. Our hearts went out to them. They had survived the war, and now new hope was in their faces.

After the concert, people did not want to leave. Lingering, they savored this togetherness as the children of one mother, our mother Latvia. Latvians are not very forward people. A reserved attitude is part of our culture. This was our first meeting. People were mostly watching each other, the eyes roaming around, touching the faces, coming back to some, watching more closely. The older people were more eager to talk and ask questions, but we, the young girls, felt a bit shy. After all, they

were strangers, and yet they were not. The blue eyes carried the color of the Latvian skies and the blond hair was reminiscent of the ripe wheat fields of Latvia. They were our boys, our men, and they were very dear to us.

We did get to know some of the young men in time, and since there were more of us here now, it was decided to form a proper folk dancing group together with the coalminer men. There would surely be more socials from now on, and folk dancing was a nice entertainment that everybody liked to watch. Mrs. Marta Roze, a pianist who worked at the Yardley Green hospital, said she would like to also form a small choir, for Latvians have always loved singing. It looked like the social life in Birmingham would get much more active from now on. I was willing to teach the folk dancing again. It would take even more of my time and energy, but folk dancing was another of my passions

## Mother is coming!

I had written to my Mother about the new job and had also told her the news that they could now think about joining me here. She was delighted.

"Great!" she wrote back. "We shall be glad to come!"

Now it was up to me to get the appropriate paperwork done and look for a place where to live. A week later though, I had another letter from Mother.

"Ilgvars will not be coming…" she wrote. "He has befriended an Estonian woman and they are both planning to go to Australia. Since other countries also have started to take in the refugees, they have decided to go there."

I was quite pained about that. One would have thought that, being the oldest son, he now would have the responsibility for the family, since Dad was not here anymore. Obviously that was not what he wanted. He wanted to be free.

Actually, I had already noticed my brother's inclination for the lighter side of life while we all still lived in Germany. He often went out in the evenings to dance. I also remembered his stories about the time he had spent at the boarding school in Latvia; stories about playing cards, going to the nearest town to live it up with girls and asking Dad for more and more money. I could understand about those times. People do all kinds of things when they are young, but I thought that now it should be different.

It also pained me to hear from Mother that Ilgvars had opened the parcels that I sent before she got to them, and had taken out the cigarettes and the chocolate for himself, perhaps to coax his girlfriends. Obviously

he did not care that they were meant for Mother to exchange for extra food for them all. He wrote to me that he needed some shoes, but said he could wear only good leather shoes!

"Don't send me any cheap stuff, I cannot wear them!" he had added as if I were a millionaire. I sent him the leather shoes, even though I could ill afford them, but never even got a word back from him. It was painful to see what kind of a person he had become, not caring about anybody else but himself. Perhaps it was better that he went his own way.

Soon after, another letter came from Mother, telling excitedly, "Can you believe it!? I have received an offer to go to Canada! The Canadian officers, who have seen my leather work here at the refugee camp, are interested in having me go to Canada to teach the craft there! That, of course, would be an excellent opportunity, but I wonder if the Canadian authorities will let me in, when they learn about my bad lungs and my previous tuberculosis? I do not know what to do now. I want to be with you, yet it is too good of an offer to refuse. It would be a respectable position, not cleaning floors."

I did not know what to say, either, not wanting to influence her decision on my account. It did make me sad thinking that if she goes to Canada, we may not see each other for the rest of our lives.

This uncertainty was exhausting and began to wear me down. One day they would come and then again not. These emotional swings did not help my health situation. My nerves were rather frayed already, and all of this drained my strength even more. Regardless of the uncertainty, I worked on the required documentation for their coming, and dear Mrs. Linzy from the Welfare Department was helpful with that. I was very grateful to her for this, and things gradually moved ahead.

It was the summer of 1948, and things in Germany were changing also. Other countries were sponsoring the refugees, each under different rulings. Perhaps only the invalids and those with special circumstances would remain in Germany now? Also the German mark had been devalued, and things were working differently than when I was there.

My most immediate chore now was to find suitable accommodations for me and my family, for that was the main stipulation in allowing them to come and join me. At that time I did not know much about the housing situation in England and had no idea how difficult it would be to find a place. There were no apartments for rent in Birmingham, for the regular English people did not like to live in apartments. People did not live in apartments in the city centers like they did in all of the rest of Europe in those days. Apparently there were some apartments in a

more exclusive part of town, but only wealthy people could afford to live there. Perhaps some older couples or rich ladies, who were alone and had enough money, could do that.

The British wanted their own house in the suburbs. However good or bad the neighborhood, their house was their castle, with living rooms downstairs and the bedrooms upstairs. Each room had to have a fireplace, in which coal was burned, because that was the only heating there was.

"We like to sit and look into the fire," the British people would say. It was nice, of course, but at the same time as they roasted their legs, the cold kept creeping in from all corners of the house, chilling their backs. No wonder so many of them had rheumatism!

I soon found out that for the regular people, who could not afford to buy a house, the only option was to rent a room or two in somebody else's private house with some kitchen and bathroom privileges. It might be the house of a widow, or an older couple, whose children were grown and gone. So this was my only option, but I had never dreamed that it would be so difficult. If there had been only my Mother and I, there would be no problem, but as soon the landlord or lady heard that there was my sixteen year old brother as well, they clammed up.

"You are a family! You need a house!" Yes, very nice, we would love to have one, but where would we get a house without any money? You could apply at the city council, which was just starting to build high-rise apartment houses for families, because the housing shortage in the city was critical, but that would take years of waiting! At sixteen, my brother was too young to live anywhere alone, and there would not be enough money to rent two places.

We just had to stay together! What should I do? Where should I go? I wondered as I looked at the ads in the papers every day and asked people's advice. I went to some of those addresses each day during my afternoon break times. The previous day I had been to a place, which gave me some hope. The landlady was an elderly Jewish woman who had two rentable rooms available and had been more understanding of my situation.

"Yes, I have the rooms, but I have to talk to my husband about this first. Why don't you come back tomorrow and then we can talk some more!"

Of course I did that, energized and full of hope.

It was raining heavily as I came out of the hospital the next afternoon. I had to hurry so I would get back to work in time. The tram, wailing on the old tracks, took me out to the shabby suburb. The streets here were uneven, still covered by cobble-stones and lined with the red brick terrace houses. Large raindrops pelted the window panes, rolling down

like tears. It seemed that the tram was moving so slowly.

Finally I was there. I found the house, where I had been yesterday, but no one answered the door, even though I had been told to come. Then I remembered the landlady telling me that they had a dry-cleaning business only two houses farther down the road. It was not a good neighborhood with the smoke-blackened terrace houses, but it would have to do for the time being.

I found the shop, gathered up my courage and walked in. It was hard for me to ever ask anything of anybody, but now I just had to do it. The elderly Jewish man was there alone. It was probably arranged that way, so the wife would not interfere and take pity on me.

"No," he said. "We have no rooms to rent!"

"But there was the advertisement in the paper!" I argued.

"It was a mistake!"

I talked, explained our situation and at the end even almost begged, but all the previous talk had been forgotten.

"No!" was his answer. "No" to all I had hoped for.

I still tried to talk to him, but my heart sank lower with every word that I said. My throat was dry and tears were there just behind my eyelids. Should I really beg? Then I fell silent, and he had had enough also. He said in just so many words that our fate did not interest him one little bit, and without another look at me, he resumed his work. The iron hissed as he started pressing again, and white steam spewed up to the ceiling, disappearing amidst the row of old jackets hanging there.

I stood there another moment leaning against the dusty counter, still stunned by the cruel news, then realized that there was nothing more to wait for. I managed to whisper a choked "goodbye" to which there was no answer, and then found myself out on the street. It was not raining anymore, but dark clouds chased each other across the sky.

Suddenly, nothing seemed to matter. In reaction to what had just happened, I would have wanted to just sit down right there on the curb and cry. I was so very, very tired. But there was no time for that. I had to get back to the hospital to do my evening shift. Sitting in the tram, I thought how much we had to suffer for anything we wanted in life. And yet, I had to pull myself together. God had looked after us before; I had to trust that He would again.

The following day I would start my new job, and by all rights, I should be out of the Salvation Army house, but our little guardian Major had said that maybe they will let me stay a little bit longer, since I had nowhere else to go. Later in the evening I stood at the bottom of the stairway at the Salvation Army House waiting to find out what the officials of this establishment would decide about me. A radio played

somewhere. The music sounded like a funeral march, and I felt sad, so sad, for again I was without a home—that precious thing that everybody should have. I could see the wind bending and shaking the trees outside. In the same way fate was now bending and shaking me also.

At last one of the officer ladies came out and said, "We decided to let you stay a few days longer until— We would not put you out, even though we do need the place for other workers."

I thanked her, but it did not make my burden lighter. I was "on the wheels" again, and the cruel winds of life were howling around me.

A gray morning had dawned for my first day on the new job, and I felt a bit nervous. How will it be, I wondered? I was also assigned to work in another ward now that was different from my previous workplace. Ward 5 was the women's surgical ward on the first (second) floor and consisted of a large long room with twenty beds in it, plus the two single bed side wards and an enclosed balcony. Still, the regular hospital routine was familiar to me, so I should not worry too much. And indeed, I managed all right.

How good, how wonderful, that I did not have to do the heavy floor cleaning anymore! I thanked God every morning for that, as I remembered the very hard work. Now I saw how the maid did it on this ward. Mary, who did the maid's work here, was a robust but cheerful Irish woman in midlife and we got on well. She was nice to me and we chatted a bit sometimes, but I was careful of what I said, because I had seen that she could burst out in sudden anger, like I had noticed some other Irish girls doing. She did not seem to be so serious about her work. She pushed the bumper a bit one way, then another, not even looking at what she was doing, sometimes stopping and chatting with patients, cracking some jokes and sometimes even whistling some tune quietly, where I had pushed it side by side, covering every inch. And when she decided that it was enough, then it was enough! Well...

Now my work was not difficult, but it entailed continuous coming and going and being on my feet the same as the nurses. That actually was nothing new. I began by gathering up the breakfast dishes on a large wooden trolley. I remember how an old skinny lady often used to try to catch my eye between all the comings and goings.

"Would you get me a lodger, luv? I am freezing!" she begged me with her toothless mouth, hanging on to the handle next to the contraption holding her elevated leg. "I asked the nurses several times, but they are too busy."

Yes, I knew all about the "lodger"! It was a hot water bottle to warm her skinny body and I gladly did that.

The next task was to polish and tidy the lockers by the patient's beds

and help the nurses to straighten and tidy the bed covers before the doctors came on their morning visits. Sometimes they came with the intern and a small group of students, sometimes alone. As they usually came in without stopping, Sister instantly joined the doctor, giving him all the pertinent information about the patient, and she really knew every detail.

I, in the meantime, prepared the trolley with glasses of juice and water and distributed them to the patients. A little later, I served them warm drinks of their choice: malted milk, cocoa or Horlicks, and at noon the dinner was served. I had to collect the large, heated metal trolley at the lift, where it was brought down from the kitchen and designated for our ward. That was no problem at all.

The Sister then would push the trolley inside the ward, roll up her sleeves and tuck a towel behind her belt. Then she would serve each patient individually, for some of the patients were on special diets. Some of the nurses and I would carry the plates around on large trays and settle them on the bed tables in front of the patients, helping them to sit up and propping up with pillows those who needed it. At the end we helped to feed those who could not do it themselves. After that, of course, was the picking up of the dishes again and leaving them in the kitchen for the maid to wash.

After that it was time for my own dinner up in the staff dining room. There I would meet Sandra and Mrs. Avots. Here at the hospital, everybody called her Pauline, only Sandra and I still called her Mrs. Avots honoring the age-old custom of our country. More Latvian women worked at the hospital now, but not all of us could get together at mealtimes. Others worked in different departments: some in the kitchen, some in the doctor's quarters, and their timetables were different from ours who worked on the wards. It was nice to get together, though, even for that short time and exchange our news. We had an hour for dinner, which meant a few more minutes of rest and then back to the wards again.

The first thing after dinner was usually putting away the clean laundry, which had been sent up in huge chest-like wicker baskets. Later in the afternoon was the wash time. I took wash basins to those who had to stay in bed, helping those who needed it, then tidied everything away. I was glad I did not have to deal with bed-pans. That was the nurse's job. Occasionally the patients asked me for one, and I would call a nurse.

After the wash, came the changing and remaking of all the beds together with the nurses. Next was tea time, for which I prepared thin sandwiches and took them around together with freshly made tea and jam. In between, there were some smaller jobs, but after collecting the tea dishes at five o'clock, I was free. It was great that I did not have to work the evenings anymore. Such a blessing! The Ward Sister was nice too, and I was very satisfied with my new job.

I still had to solve the accommodation problem, though. The Salvation Army ladies would not keep me forever, and I had to be sure of the accommodations before my family could come. It lay on my heart as a heavy burden, but it had to be solved. Right after work, I went to follow up on another advertisement that I had found in the paper. It was in a different direction of our town where I had not been before. I took the tram out of the city center and then had to walk up a hill. It was called the Gravelly Hill in the region of Erdington. The houses here were bigger and had three levels. They lined the road at the hillside one above the other.

I found the address and rang the bell. The landlady herself opened the door. She was a rather large woman with shortly cut, grayish hair, a pale mushy face and watery eyes. Her spreading body was wrapped in a big coverall apron and she had a cigarette in the corner of her mouth. That did not leave a good impression on me, but I could not be choosy. She led me along the dark, narrow hallway to the back of the house, her worn out slippers making flapping noises against the dark linoleum tile floor. We came into a small room with an old sofa at one wall, and a table with a few chairs on the opposite side next to the window. The room was small, leaving just a narrow passage between the sofa and the table. The British called this "the breakfast room", where people ate and sat around, if they had time before or after their meals. Through the open door, I could see an even smaller kitchen beyond.

The landlady introduced me to her husband, a thin sickly looking old man, sitting on the sofa. Next to him sat a good-looking, dark haired woman with brightly colored lips. A two-year-old boy rubbed against her legs, sucking his thumb.

"This is our daughter Elsie and her son Bryan," the landlady said. "Our grandson."

Elsie blew a big puff of smoke filling the room with a blue veil.

"Pleased to meet you!" she said (the British common people's usual greeting).

"Please sit down," the landlady pointed to one of the chairs by the table. "And would you like a cup of tea?"

I knew that this was an English tradition to offer tea to a visitor as a gesture of welcome, but I declined. I wanted to get this over with as soon as possible, but they kept talking around and around about all kinds of things, not at all pertaining to my coming here. I was just waiting to be shown the room, so I would know where I stood. It was already dusk but nothing happened. The landlady kept on telling that her daughter's marriage had run into difficulties, so she was staying here with them now also. I rather suspected that she was not married at all.

It was almost dark when the landlady took me up the steep, narrow

stairway at last and showed a room on the next floor. It was not very big and the double bed, wardrobe and a dresser just about filled the room. Not much room was left for anything else, but it would have to do for starters, and the rent would be two pounds a month with the kitchen and bathroom privileges.

"When do you want to move in?" she asked.

"I want to move in right away, but I am not certain yet when my Mother and my brother will arrive. My brother would need another room."

"Oh," she said, "we have an attic. It is full of all kinds of old stuff and furniture, but they could be pushed aside and a corner of it freed where he could sleep."

I should have understood then that these accommodations would be for sleeping only, not for living in, as I learned soon enough, if I could have ever imagined a situation like that. For the moment, I was just glad that I would have somewhere to go and that all three of us were accepted.

Good! It will do! At least now I would have an address to give to the authorities for sponsoring my family.

"I will be here tomorrow evening!" I said goodbye and took my leave, glad that at last I had accomplished something.

That was the night before, but when I arrived at the Gravelly Hill house with my two suitcases the next evening, the lady had come up with different plans.

"Since your relatives won't be coming just yet, I thought that just for a while, you might do without that room that I showed you. You could just as well share a room with two other girls where one more bed is vacant. Only for the time being, of course!" she said. I stood there numbed. What could I say?

"You would not mind, would you?" she added in a voice that was not ready to take "no" for an answer. Exactly the same situation as it had been in Germany during my student days, only this was much worse. Apparently two more girls had come the previous night, answering the same advertisement and she had given "my" room to them! I was so taken aback that I could not say a word.

"Only temporary, you know!" she said, perhaps noting my puzzlement. "And Mary and Reny are nice girls. It will be more fun for you being with the other girls!" she added in an encouraging voice, seeing my darkening face.

What could I do? There was no way back for me. Perhaps everything would sort out somehow later on. The landlady opened the door to another room off the hallway and pointed to a bed in the corner.

"Make yourself at home," she said and walked out closing the door behind her.

I stood alone in the middle of the untidy room and looked around me. The room was in chaos. Clothing and shoes lay everywhere as they had been thrown down, on chairs, on the beds, on the open wardrobe door. The top of the dresser was covered with bottles and jars of cosmetics, with brushes mingling with hair rollers and scattered pins.

I looked around helplessly. Where could I put anything? I opened one drawer, then another. There was not even the smallest drawer in the dressing table that was not stuffed with something. I did not know what to do. I could see that I would have to live out of my suitcases. It had not been this bad even at the camps!

While I still stood there, undecided as to what to do, I heard voices behind the door, and the next moment it sprang open letting in two laughing girls. They introduced themselves to me as Mary and Reny, and I tried to respond positively. It was not their fault that I was in this situation. I mentioned that I was wondering where I could put some of my things.

"Oh, that is not a problem! We will just push our stuff more together. There is plenty of room!" One of them said cheerfully. "Plenty of room!"

Reny, short for Irene, seemed to be the oldest, a real English factory girl, with black dyed hair worn in rollers under a scarf during working hours and heavy makeup around her eyes. Mary was natural, a typical Irish girl with a narrow face and bushy brown hair. They were both kind to me.

"We work in a factory not far from here in Aston," Mary was first to come forward. "Where do you work?" she wanted to know.

"I work at the General Hospital here in town," I answered. Before I could say anything more, Reny cut in with a question.

"Do you have a boyfriend?" she asked excitedly looking me in the face.

I hesitated a bit, having been hit with such a personal question, then said that I didn't. At this, Reny's excitement extinguished. Then they asked me if I would be going out?

"Going where?" I asked, not understanding what they meant by it. I had only just arrived. Why should I go anywhere? I was quite puzzled. It was evening now. Why would I be going out? Only later did I understand that "going out" meant going out of the house to be entertained and to have fun. I kept pondering the subject. Perhaps these girls did not have anything else in their lives but their work and this? It took time for me to understand this kind of a lifestyle and why it was so. What other life could one have in a place like this?

"We are going out for an evening meal. Would you like to go with us?" Mary asked me.

Since I did not have any plans and saw no reason to unpack, I agreed.

"There's a fish and chips shop on the next corner just down the hill," Mary explained. "Reny has a date and I am going to the cinema to see a film afterward. You can come too if you like," she said. Mary was nice; I liked her.

"Well, not this time… I don't think…" I still felt overwhelmed by this new situation, not knowing yet what was what. "But I will go out with you for a meal." I added, not wanting to offend them. Besides, I was hungry.

While we still talked, Reny was busy getting ready for her date, pulling out her rollers, doing up her hair and changing clothes. Then she began the heavy artwork on her face, and she accomplished it with a well worked-out system of her own. Huge black arches for her eyebrows, then liners and lashes, fire red lips, checked closely at the mirror again and again. Finally all kinds of sparkling things were put in her ears, around her neck, and she was ready. At the very last she kicked off her shoes and slipped into another pair, but no stockings! The last check around in the mirror, turning this way and that, and she was quite satisfied with her looks.

"Ready to kill!" one might say, but Mary and I did not say anything. I watched all this in quiet amazement. I had never seen or experienced anything like this. I had never seen any "street girls" except in films, and this poor factory girl looked just like one of them. But, of course, it was none of my business.

At last we were ready to go. Down by the crossroads, a small crowd stood outside the doors of the pub already, and next to it was the fish shop. People came and went, shouting greetings, obviously knowing each other. Nearby Aston was a factory region; I had heard of it.

Many of the workers must be living around here in "lodgings". That meant renting a room in some other people's house. Being a Friday night, everybody was in high spirits. They had received their weekly wage packets and there would be no work tomorrow. That was a good enough reason to celebrate.

Not having been in this kind of a working class environment before, I felt completely out of it, but Mary and Reny saw to everything, while I watched from outside. The fish shop was just a small room that may have initially been somebody's living-room, opening to the street as it usually was in the terrace houses. It was amazing, though, how well things worked. A glass-fronted counter on the right side of the room, behind which the cooking was done, divided the space in two. The left side provided just enough room for the customers to stand in a line and turn around to come out. Through the lighted window, I could see how the fish and chips were fried in big containers of hot oil. A man stirred and turned them around with what looked like a big shovel and at short

intervals lifted out scoops of golden chips and crusty coated pieces of fish. The enticing aroma filled the air even outside the shop, drawing more customers. While the man cooked, a woman kept wrapping up the portions by taking a sheet of newspaper, then a smaller piece of grease proof paper on top of it. A large, crusty golden piece of fish went on it with steaming chips on the side. Then a shake of salt, a drizzle of the malted vinegar, and the next customer could step up. A young lad took the money, so it was obviously a family affair. It all happened very fast, and soon Mary and Reny came out with our packages of fish and chips.

I was quite amazed at this. Food in a newspaper?

"It's all right," Mary assured me, seeing again how puzzled I looked. "There's other paper underneath! The newspaper helps to keep it warm and the smell of it gives a special taste!" she said in her Irish intonation of words.

I paid my share and then wondered where we would eat.

"Oh, right here on the corner, luv!" Reny said. "See, ev'rybody duz!" she added in her Birmingham dialect.

Indeed, quite a few people stood around, leaning against the wall, holding their packages of food in one hand and eating with their fingers. Well, why not? We moved a bit aside and opened our packages too. I watched what the other girls did and did the same. A bite off the crunchy fish, then a golden stick of the tasty potato, all sprinkled with salt and the malt vinegar, and everything hot, as it was just prepared! It was delicious!

"This is the British national food!" the girls explained to me laughing. Whether it was or not, it was really good, cheap and easily obtainable! Some might say it was the food of the common people who did not want to bother with cooking after work, and that was all right too.

For me this was a real experience of being amidst the English common folk for the first time. These people appeared to be different than the ones I had met at the hospital. I looked around with great interest, observing the goings on. Next to the fish shop, the pub's doors stood wide open and people came and went. The lights went on in the streets and the houses around us. The weekend had begun. The girls chatted and giggled with some of the others that they knew. Some young men stopped by and cracked a few jokes with the girls. I gathered that this was a convenient contact place, outside the pub's door, where one could meet new people casually.

I had heard before that English people did their visiting in pubs, not their homes. It was jollier in a pub, of course, and no bother to anybody. No worry about refreshments and no washing of dishes! Only the closest family and friends were invited to the house apparently. And why shouldn't the housewives go out too to have a bit of fun? There were

even some young women standing around the doors with babies in carriages next to them and husbands bringing out glasses of beer for them. Nothing was wrong with that. They were all just having a good time the English way. Older women went into the pub, too—with their husbands or boy-friends—laughing and happy. A pub, a beer, a laugh and someone beside you, what more could you want?

After we had finished our meals, the girls went happily each their own way, but I walked up the hill home. Home! I would have to ponder much longer whether this word was appropriate in this situation, because that place certainly did not have a feeling of home. I had been told to walk in through the back door on my return, which meant going through the tiny kitchen and the breakfast room. I supposed it was so the landlords would see who comes and goes. And they always sat there: she with the cigarette in her mouth, he—gazing at you with a brooding mistrust in his eyes. As if somebody wanted to take something away from them!

I bid them good-night, as I passed through, and went upstairs. The small bulb on the ceiling was not strong enough for reading and there was nowhere to sit in the cluttered room, so there was nothing else to do but to go to bed. Now I understood why the girls went out. This place was only for sleeping and changing clothes, not living. That was the best way for the landlords, of course! They did not have too many people underfoot, and who needed to read? It was just a waste of electricity that they would have to pay for! With a big sigh, I undressed and went to bed.

The following day I learned about all the rules and regulations. The allowed cooking and eating time in the evenings was one hour. The washing of clothes could be done only on Tuesdays and Thursdays at certain times and had to be done in the kitchen. The ironing was allowed for one hour on Fridays, also in the kitchen. No wash could be done in the bathroom or anything left to dry there. And the landlady in her big apron and the old slippers flapped around to see that it was done just so, her cigarette never leaving her mouth.

The next day after arriving, I climbed the steep, narrow stairs to the attic to see what I could do there. The room was large, actually covering the whole width of the house. It had some sloping ceiling, but on each side was a large window, so there was plenty of light. There certainly was a lot of old stuff, broken furniture and what-not, all covered with cobwebs and dust. I could see that there would be a lot of cleaning to do, but that there was a potential of making something quite good. I would have to do something to this room anyway, so Johnny would have somewhere to sleep. The landlady's suggestion to only push some of the junk aside just would not do. Who could live or even just sleep in such filth?

I figured that if I managed to get the room into a somewhat decent state, perhaps I could even live there myself until the time when my fam-

ily came. Then at least I would have a place of my own. I went to talk to the landlords about it and they did not have any objections. Of course, why would they? The room, as it was, was not usable anyway.

"You can keep some of the usable furniture and bring down the rest; we'll put it in the shed," the woman said.

That made me really glad and I was anxious to get to it. I bought some necessary cleaning tools, then carried countless buckets of water up the steep staircase and cleaned and cleaned and cleaned until the room became brighter and brighter. After I removed the layers of cob-webs that had been hanging down from the ceiling almost to the floor, I found that even the wallpapers were still nice, softly blue with some plant pattern. It was such a joy seeing everything getting nicer.

I kept some of the furniture; the rest went downstairs to the bunker. There was a small sofa with thin rococo legs and a broken arm. I could probably fix that and then Johnny could sleep on it. It was short, but I had also slept on a short one in Germany. I had a little money saved. Perhaps I could buy a double bed for Mother and me?

The biggest problem was the floor. It was of unpainted wood that was tainted with all kinds of stuff that was hard to get off. But after scrubbing and scrubbing and using various cleaning agents, it finally began to look better. It took another week of waxing it every day until it started to look like wood and even shined a bit. I also got some white lace curtains for the windows, which right away gave the room a finished look. Since we were so high up, we would not need any heavy drapes, for no one could look in.

When the landlady came up to see what I was doing, she could not believe her eyes. Now she brought her friends and neighbors over to see it too, praising my work.

"Would you mind if I move up here until my family comes and we get the other room?" I asked her then.

"Yes, yes!" she was most agreeable. Her eyes even lit up for joy that now she would be able to also rent my place in the girls' room! The money would be coming in!

I did not begrudge it her, I was so happy that I would finally have a little place of my own. My new bed was delivered too, and I was over-joyed. I noticed that the electrical contact at the wall was broken, but I would ask Sandra's boyfriend to come and fix it for me. Then I could even do my ironing here, and I also bought an electric iron.

Sandra and Robert came over on Saturday, and Robert fixed the outlet for me. I was so happy, and we all went out after that.

But, oh my! When I came back in the evening, I sensed right away that something was not right. As I walked through the breakfast room, nobody answered my greeting. I could not understand what had hap-

pened until a day later. I was balled out for fixing the outlet. The old man came at me like a monster.

"Do you want to burn down the house?" He yelled. "Special permits are needed to use those outlets!" He carried on.

That I did not believe, because there were outlets in all the other rooms, and they were used. Their worry was that I will use electricity, and they will have to pay for it. But I was paying rent, and that would surely cover the little amount I would use! Still, it was not worth arguing.

During the summer we, the Latvian girls from our hospital, got to know some of the Latvian coal miner boys, and one Sunday two of them came with flowers to greet me at my new dwelling, as was our tradition. The landlady brought them up. We visited for a little while, then went out, for the day was beautiful. When I returned, though, again I was approached with fury.

"No boyfriends!"

I understood that, but it should not have anything to do with visitors during daytime and especially if there were more than one of them! Afterwards, there was silence and looks full of hatred. How could I envision that such a normal thing would create such uproar? It was a shame that the beautiful day ended like this. I lay on my bed and pondered what a strange country this was. There was so much I did not know or understand. I suppose, I still had not got it in my head what "being in lodging" was all about.

I had learned my new routine at the hospital, and there were no problems with that, but I realized by now that I could never be a nurse. I absorbed people's pain too much and carried it with me. That was not good for my health. Adding it to my already existing pain of missing my country and the uncertainties about my family's coming, did not help either and seemed to push me to the edge of my mental coping. One could deal with only so much.

A black cloud hung over me, darkening my days. However much I fought it, telling myself how glad and grateful I was having this job, my food and lodging, it did not help. It was all true and yet… something was not right.

I asked myself, what more did I want? Why did I feel so torn up inside? Why did I feel like this? The answer to that frightened me, for I did not want anything… Was I so old that the joy of living had already left me? I felt old. I just wanted peace and quiet. So much had changed since we left home. There were goals then—now there were none. No excitement, no yearning, no dreaming, just trying to survive one day at a time. Everything had paled into a monotonous grayness. It was as if I

was sitting in a boat in an expanse of still water, and there was no wind, no sail and no rudder.

Sometimes I could shake the boat a little, find some joy in watching the ripples and the colors on the water and think that I was happy. But deep down I was not...

At times I was angry with myself for allowing such thoughts to come into my head. Certainly, life was different now, but it was good enough and had to be accepted such as it was with gratefulness. Perhaps I was just worn out mentally from all these constant ups and downs.

To top it off, a letter arrived from Mother.

"It looks like I won't be coming after all, dear. The Canadian officials are promising me all kinds of goodies, saying that they want to get me there to teach my craft."

That, of course, would be better for her, I understood that, but that made my spirits dip again to zero. Then I would be here totally alone without any next of kin. Would we ever see each other again? Mother's only worry was that they may not let her into Canada because of her history of tuberculosis. I wished her well, though, and hoped that she would get there and be happy.

It seemed as if the light had gone out of my days, for there was nothing to look forward to. I just felt tired, very tired. I walked through my days hardly aware of them passing. Why was it so? Nothing gave joy; I did not even want to eat. One day, I cooked some pancakes for my supper because I had always liked them, but when they were there in front of me, I had to force myself to have at least some of them. Something somewhere was missing, but I did not know what it was. The school too was over, and I was almost totally on my own. Previously, when I lived at the Salvation Army, I at least had my friends there, and we could talk over our experiences in the evenings. Now I had no one. No one at all.

At the hospital there was work, people and voices around me, but they did not seem to have anything to do with me. I was there in my body but not in my spirit. Being so much on my own, my thoughts went more and more back to my real home. I had a need to touch and hold on to something that was dear to me. I thought back to that last summer at home and what happened to us. There was so much pain. As I polished the patient's lockers, I saw in the reflections my beloved birch grove, yet knew that it would never be there for me again, and the thought was unbearable.

At home, I loved my room that I had made so cozy and nice, but there was no one to talk to, and I could not find interest in anything. Yet, I did not wish to be with people, either. Some of the young men whom we had acquainted showed an interest in being friendly with me, but I did not want that, either. I had nothing to give them. Sometimes it was

quite frightening to realize how I was sinking into this stagnating fog, not even wanting anything.

July was almost over. I was still fighting my personal afflictions, trying to lift myself out of them. One evening after work I decided to go for a walk. It was such a nice golden evening outside; it seemed a shame to stay indoors. Not far from the foot of our hill, where the factories started, was a long straight canal with a strip of green belt on each side. A narrow footpath ran along the side of it, and I thought that it would be nice to take a walk down there.

Though it was summertime, the wind blew quite harshly, bending the few trees that grew at the edge of the canal. My thoughts started milling around again. I was just twenty-one, but what had happened to my youth?

"Where was the singing joy of the summer?" I asked myself.

It was an autumn song of sadness that the aspen sang, and the willow by the canal moved its long branches as if wiping away hidden tears.

I walked on along the canal. Several low bridges spanned it at intervals and at the end of it a golden sun was sinking down into the bluish mist at the horizon. The factory smokestacks stood like sentinels in the blue shrouded plane rigid and tall. Just for a moment the sun lingered, as if saying the last goodbye, then it was gone.

I turned around and walked back. My legs felt so weak as if I had just gotten out of a sickbed. I seemed to have no weight of my own, and could fly up in the air like a dandelion seed, or just lie down and stay there amongst the grasses at the wayside.

But no! I could not give in! I would not give in! God would give me strength, even though lately all my praying seemed to go nowhere. He will help me, I had to believe that.

My twenty-second birthday passed like any other day, except I got a letter from Mother. She wrote: "I have not heard anything more from the Canadian people, and now have decided to leave it all in God's hands. Whoever will notify me first, that is where we shall go".

That put even more stress on her and me. Time moved on. September passed.

Another letter came from Mother. She still did not know which way she would go, although it was already October. A cold wind blew the rain clouds across England, when suddenly one day a letter arrived, bringing news, "We're coming! We will arrive in England on October 18!"

I was glad, of course, that this was finally happening, and that my family will be here with me. At last we would be together again! There were no celebrations when they arrived. The necessities of life were too pressing. Mother got a job at the hospital too, for we had created a good

reputation for the Latvian women there, and our administrator, Sister Griffiths, was very helpful. Since she already knew that Mother could not do any heavy work, she was given a job in the outpatient department, attending to the doctor's consulting rooms. It was not a hard job like we had had. She did not have to wash floors, just clean the wash-basins, polish the faucets, do a bit of dusting and tidying, then make and serve coffee to the doctors at their appropriate times. She settled into her job very quickly and was well appreciated, especially when it was found that she spoke several languages. She was often called out as a translator, for more foreigners were arriving in Birmingham all the time.

To make it easier, when dealing with English people, we started to call my brother "Johnny", in the English version of his name. He got a job at a small electrical business. His wages were very low, just thirty five shillings a week, but between the three of us, we would manage. He had grown a lot during these two years while we had lived apart. At his sixteen years, he was about half a head taller than I. Here in England, a number of the young people left school at the age of sixteen, the obligatory age limit for staying in school, and then went to work in the factories. Doing piecework, they could make good money and help with the family finances. Mother, however, wanted Johnny to continue his education, even if he had to take evening classes.

I had saved a little money, so I bought some proper clothing for Johnny, for he had nothing except a few things he had found in the used clothing shipments at the camp. They would be all right for working, but now we bought a suit, an overcoat and even a hat, for winter was coming. I was very glad that I could do this for my brother and even more glad to see his happy and proud face when he looked at himself in the mirror. I am sure it meant a lot to him to have decent clothing for once!

## Meeting Ed

Some good things were happening in the Latvian community, too. Quite a few Latvians now lived in Birmingham and its vicinity, so the social life was becoming more active. Once a month a Latvian minister came and held a service for us in one of the churches. People had an opportunity to meet, get acquainted, and hear what happened where and how other people lived and worked. And, of course, we all had a chance to pray together and ask for God's help, for we all needed it badly.

For the most part, we were all pretty messed up people, not knowing what our future would be and still trying to adjust to the different culture and circumstances. Since we all were under a government contract which required us to stay in our appointed jobs, there was not much opportunity to start doing anything on our own, because none of us had

enough money to do that. Of course, it did not mean that one could not try—and some did.

Besides the church services, our Birmingham Latvian group had started some other activities. We would want to celebrate our Latvian Independence Day anniversary on November 18 and entertainment would be needed. Mrs. Roze, the musician, had already gotten together a small group of singers for a choir, and I had formed the folk dancing group. The YWCA allowed us to use their facility free of charge, thanks to our Welfare lady friend. Now we could use the nice hall with the piano for our singing and dancing practices.

All this gave a new lift to our living, allowing us to have something else besides everyday work, and gave us the opportunity to be together with other people. There were three of us from our hospital who took part in the dancing group: Spodra was a newcomer to our hospital, who worked in the doctor's quarters. She and I would dance, and Mirdza would provide music by playing the piano. We were lucky to get the two Latvian girls from the Winson Green Mental hospital to join us also. They were the two sisters—Laila and Brigita, and now we had the four couples that were needed. The three men were from the coal miners, and my partner was my brother Johnny. We were doing pretty well together until one day one of the men backed out, saying that he was planning to emigrate to Canada. True or not, we were one man short, and that would not do.

It just so happened that Mrs. Roze had brought along a young man with her that day who had just arrived in Birmingham and had enrolled in the nursing program at the Yardley Green hospital. Mrs. Roze had wanted to show him what we were doing here in our small Latvian community, and introduce him to us. She had already talked him into joining the choir, and he had consented. The choir practice would start right after our dancing, for the same people took part in singing also.

"This is Edvins Vidners," Mrs. Roze introduced him to me.

"You can call me Ed, "he said as he got up to shake my hand.

He was quite tall and broad-shouldered with blond hair and seemed quite pleasant, but since I was preoccupied with how I would solve my dance group situation, I really did not pay much attention to him as a person. We exchanged a few words, and I returned to my group, but then I had a bright idea. He could stand in for our missing dancer! Yes! What a good idea! When I went to him and mentioned it he tried to get out of it by saying,

"But I do not know how to dance!" to which I answered simply,

"But we are all just learning!"

I don't know where I got the courage, but I did not take his "no" for an answer. I just took him by his hand and drew him physically into

our circle whether he wanted to be included or not. My group was very important to me. I did not give him much time to think about it, either. I asked him to pair off with Laila, whose partner was missing, then gave the instructions for the first few movements (which the others already knew) and off we went. "One, two, three, go!"

There was not too much to know to be able to do folk dancing. We had all learned it at school to some extent. Doing the group dancing, of course, there were the successive movements to learn, but, as I had said to Ed, we were all at the beginning stage here.

Ed seemed to be a bit older, looking manlier than the other young men, who still had retained more of their boyish looks. I did not really take extra notice of Ed; I was just glad to keep my group going. I noticed, though, his strong, brown forearms as we danced around in a circle—for he was right opposite me, wearing a short sleeved shirt. From then on Ed, as we all called him, remained part of our group and he had no problem doing what was required.

The reception of my family by the landlords was quite cordial on the first day. For one thing, the two girls still lived in the bedroom first promised to me, but since I had spruced up the attic room and made it livable, I guess it was just assumed that the three of us would live there. It was all right with me. We would rather be on our own together than split up, but very soon things started to change. Discontent on the landlord's part was growing. Obviously, our presence was now more visible. We had to cook, eat and wash. I could see their faces getting stiffer and harder. A conflict arose after only two weeks, when Mother left a vessel in the bathroom in which she had put some clothing to soak. Of course, she should not have done that for the rule said not to wash or leave anything to dry in there, but the uproar about it was such as if a war had broken out. And it had. A couple of days later, the old man told Mother to look for other lodging!

Really! Did they think that we would be flying around and be invisible? We had a right to live here, for we were paying money for it. In addition, I had made the room livable where before it was not. Now the three of us were living in there, and the room which was promised to me in the first place was still rented out to two other girls.

But of course, their strategy was very clear now. Why keep a family, if now they could rent our room to three or even four more girls and cash in on it? Now it was very clear that their rented rooms were meant only for sleeping over, not for living. It was all planned out so the landlords would get most of the benefits without being bothered by the renters being there. I was terribly angry and embittered about this, especially after I had put in so much work, but of course, they could do what

they wanted. It was their house. I could have never imagined that people could be so evil-minded.

They wanted us to move in a week's time! Where would we find another place within a week if this had taken me months to find!? Oh, God! What would we do? It hurt me so much, but the landlords would not budge, even after Mother tried to talk to them.

"If you are not out in two weeks, we'll put you out on the street," said the old man. That was the harsh, unyielding answer of the people I had trusted.

The last days were very stressful. Nobody talked to us, or even looked at us, even the girls with whom we had had no quarrel! As if we were guilty of some criminal offense! They probably were scared for their own living, so tried to appease the wicked pair.

We scanned the newspapers every day, and found an address in Sutton, another suburb of Birmingham. Mother and I went there right away. It was an older lady, a widow, who was renting an upstairs bedroom and perhaps also the small box-room with kitchen and bathroom privileges. Her son was getting married and moving out. It sounded very good, and we agreed to take it. We had been really lucky in finding this.

By the middle of November, we were in our new place starting a new life. The distance was greater to the city center where we worked, but the bus stop was practically in front of the house. This also was a better area, and the houses were newer and more modern. The rooms were small, but we would manage.

It was already December. The happenings of the last few months had taken much out of me—especially the terrible disillusionment of our previous landlords, when they put us out of our living quarters. I had worked so hard on that room to make it livable. I had thought that finally I would have a place I could call a home, but again I was living in a strange house and sleeping in somebody else's bed. How much longer would it be like this? I was in such a need to have something of my own.

I lay in the dark with open eyes, as often happened now, exhausted but not being able to sleep. I realized that I was overworking myself, for my day started at six in the morning. The journey to town took longer—then working at the hospital till five, after that going to the college three evenings a week, and after that to our dancing practices. I thought of what my teacher Mr. Eggison had said when I told him that my Mother and brother would be arriving.

"Oh, that is good," he said. "Then they will be able to help you, and you will be able to come to college full time! I am delighted!"

"Nothing like that, I am afraid," I had answered. "I will have to help them, not the other way round. And even if it were possible, I could not accept it."

Yes, my future did not look bright. With what I could earn, I could never make it to college, even though for a short time, it had been the bright star in my life that kept me going.

Two evenings a week, after school, we also had our folk dancing rehearsals, which ended at eleven. It was midnight by the time I got to Sutton. I had thought that all these things, which I so enjoyed, would quench the burning pain of my hidden fire, but it did not happen.

I asked myself again and again,

"Why could I not be like others who seemed to be able to glide over everything much more easily?" I kept digging within myself, searching for the right way to live and the purpose, why I was here in this world to do what I was doing.

Why was I so cold inside that nothing and no one could bring warmth to my heart?" For several days and nights the words of Theodor Storm's poem sounded in my ears while I seemed to walk on icy fields with only the stars above me.

*"Schliesse mir die Augen beide mit den lieben Haenden zu, geht doch alles was ich leide unter Deiner Hand zur Ruh' ."*

"...close my eyes gently with your loving hands, let all that I suffer find peace in you."

Then I thought: "Did I really want to close my eyes never to open them? Was it because I was tired and did not desire anything else but only peace for my soul from my Father in Heaven?"

The moonlight shone through the window. It was so light outside, but I lay in bed with tears quietly rolling over my temples and disappearing into my pillow. I wiped them away, trying not to move much, for Mother was asleep next to me. She did not need my pain. She had enough of her own. These tears were for my cold heart, which was not able to love anything anymore and I felt sorry for it.

I prayed to God, yet it seemed that my prayers were not going anywhere but stayed right here at my bedside. Then I prayed even more fervently that God would give me even one heart that would be able to warm me, and then I finally drifted into sleep.

Our dancing rehearsals progressed and we were ready for our first performance at the Independence Day anniversary on November, 18. It would be taking place at the Lutheran church hall, where we also had our monthly services. Quite a few people had gathered, and our performance was well received. Now Christmas would be coming, and we would have to prepare for that also.

Somehow our activities became known to our hospital staff. Since Spodra, one of our group's participants who worked in the doctor's quarters, had to ask for special permission to change her working hours to be

able to make the rehearsals, one of the chief consultants, Dr. Hickman, had questioned her, "What is the activity that you are doing?"

Spodra had explained, although her English language skills were still limited at that time.

"Very interesting!" He had said. A little later we learned why.

Every Christmas, the hospital put on a special show for the staff, and anyone of them could take part in it if they so wished. Usually there were jokes and small skits from the hospital life and also some musical entertainment. To our surprise, one day we received an invitation: "Why don't you take part in our show this year also?" Dr. Hickman, who was in charge of this event, had asked Spodra."I am sure people would love to see something like that. It would be so different from our regular stuff!"

We talked about it and decided to do it. Why not? It would be good for more people to know something about Latvia. The way things were, hardly anybody had even heard of it, and it was hard to explain to everybody what had happened and why we were here.

"Why don't you go home if this country is so dear to you?" they would ask.

I tried to explain to those who were able to understand, but for the most part, the average and lower class English people were not knowledgeable enough to be interested. Many did not even know that there were so many other nations. The only ones they knew about were the Germans and the Poles, because of the war, and they assumed that we belonged to one of those nations.

We promised Dr. Hickman, that we would do our part and practiced even harder. In the meantime, our activities had become known at the other hospitals too, where some of our group's participants worked. People in the leadership began to ask questions about what we were doing and why, and we replied, telling them of the rich ethnic heritage that we felt obligated to keep alive.

For the first time they asked,

"Why do the Latvian doctors have to sweep floors and professors wash dishes? How can that be?"

But that was how it was, at least for now and at least here in England. Right now the qualifications or credentials of our people's professions did not count. We were just imported manual labor without a choice—a mass of people that were viewed as such.

Gradually, perhaps, we would be able to prove our worth, and maybe with these first steps we would be able to show that the name of Latvia had a meaning, that we were part of a nation that did not deserve to be forgotten and wiped off the face of this earth. In many places the authorities and leaders had already noticed the ethics of the Latvian workers; that they were reliable, responsible and hard workers. We hoped that in

times to come, they would discover even more of our good qualities and give us a chance to better ourselves.

Soon we received an invitation from the Yardley Green Hospital also to take part in their Christmas show. The Sister, who was in charge of this project had said, "We would love to see you dancing and to hear something about the Christmas traditions in Latvia."

We discussed it and agreed to do it, but then we would all have to work together to make such a presentation. Since our "show business" was expanding, we needed much more planning. Our choir leader Mrs. Roze, Ed, and also several others, worked at the Yardley Green hospital. We talked about it together and came to a decision that we could do a short story about Christmas in Latvia, interwoven with some singing and dancing.

Now we really had to start working on it diligently, for there was not much time left. Ed had been given the task to put together the text and the program for the Yardley Green hospital show. He in turn asked me to help him with this. Since I had already put on a show about Christmas traditions in Latvia with the Girl-Guides and Scouts at our camp in Germany, soon all of the arrangements were on my shoulders. Still, Ed and I needed to discuss many details and found that we could work together very well. This became our first real moment of getting together—creating a Christmas story!

It was quite interesting, the way it started. Shortly before Christmas, our group had been invited to the Salvation Army house to give a performance of our dancing, because the news about our group had spread, and the ladies there wanted to see it as well. I suppose it was our little Major's doing. The hall was not very big, but they had moved the sofas and chairs to the sides, so there was just enough room. Everybody liked our performance, and our little "Major" custodian was overjoyed of what "her children" had done! She had always had faith in us and had given us the warmth we needed. I recalled that sometimes she would act like a mischievous boy, when she came into our room. Perhaps it was meant to cheer us up, and to show us that they were not all so stiff and uptight like some of the officers were. She would hold onto the ends of two iron bedsteads, which came rather close together in the middle of the room, and swung herself back and forth, mischief sparkling in her bitty eyes behind the gold-rimmed glasses.

"Now! How are my children today?" she would say, a big smile flooding her little face, showing us that she was our friend. We did appreciate her, and it was possible that she had been instrumental in arranging this gathering also.

After the performance, we were invited to stay a while in the large room where we had lived initially, to visit and to feast on cookies and

cocoa.

Ed and I sat side by side on the end bar of one of the iron bedsteads, discussing our plans and exchanging ideas for the text of introduction of our show. He seemed to be a nice person. As we talked, my eyes again and again strayed to his hands. They were large, clean and "honest". Could hands also talk and tell something about the person? Or was it the fairness of his hair looking so silvery against the dark blue blazer jacket, or the white shirt that created this image of honesty for me? I felt good with him. My head, however, was too full of things that needed to be done right now, so I did not think much more about it.

The time for the Christmas show at our hospital had come. It was shortly before Christmas. Excitement was everywhere. The big auditorium was packed with people, and there were quite a few groups of people who would perform. We were in the doctors' lounge, waiting for our turn and feeling quite nervous. After all, this would be our first big performance. Dr. Hickman, who was a very pleasant man and the administrator of this evening's show, came in and tried to give us encouragement. Then we had to go.

"Easy!" I whispered to my group "Be free and happy!"

I led them in a line out on to the stage in front of the glaring lights until we made a circle. From there, we went into the various movements, and everything went very well. Afterward, Doctor Hickman awaited us outside, applauding, as did the audience in the hall behind us. It sounded as if the public had liked us. Of course, our national costumes had something to do with it too, lending color and beauty to the performance.

A bit out of breath, we returned to the lounge. Thank God, it was over! Dr. Hickman came in very happy.

"Congratulations! You did a great job and it was so beautiful! Here is a bottle of wine so you can celebrate your success!" He said, handing us the bottle.

That was very nice of him, but we still had a dress rehearsal at Yardley Green hospital that evening, so we decided to drink the wine later when everything would be over. We took a few cookies that were put out for our refreshment, then got into our coats, and chatting happily, walked outside.

The bus took us farther and farther out of the city center along increasingly darker streets until Ed told us that we had to get off.

Red brick terrace houses lined the street here without any porches or gardens in front. One could see right away that this was a poorer area, where people lived without any frills. Everything was dark, only here and there a little light shone through some gaps in the curtains. The old gas-type lanterns lit the street but were spaced too far apart to give

enough light to the uneven brick paved sidewalks.

Because of the narrow sidewalks, our group had to stretch out in a long line. Ed and I walked side by side at the front, still discussing some of the details in our plans. He wanted me to be the storyteller of the text we had both put together. While talking, I almost tripped, when my heel got stuck in a crack of the pavement. Luckily, Ed caught me in time and then held on to my elbow. We could not afford to have any accidents right now.

As we walked on, I suddenly noticed how we both walked in the same step, even though he was big and I was small. It was such a discovery to me that I laughed and shared it with him,

"How strange," I said, "Up till now, I have never met anyone with whom I could walk that way! Usually I either have to stretch my steps, or else have to keep adjusting my walk with the other person!" and Ed had not stretched his steps.

Ed smiled but did not say anything, just squeezed my elbow that he was still holding. But then we were at the hospital and Ed led us in.

The evening of our actual performance at the Yardley Green Hospital came, and the big hall was filled to capacity. This time there were more of us on the stage, because we also had the choir.

We had decided to illustrate an old fashioned Christmas on a Latvian farm, and I was the first to go out in front of the curtain and give an introduction to this. But, as I walked out and began my story, someone shone a strong, orange spotlight right into my eyes, so for a little while I could not see anything. Looking at my manuscript, I saw only black circles on my paper, but I did not get flustered. It was good that all this was so real to me that I did not have to look at my text on the paper, because in my thoughts and feelings I was already there, seeing the peaceful snow-covered fields with the star studded sky above and the sounds of church bells coming from far away. I knew what I had to say.

I lived my "Silent Night" story as I told it, and our choir sang it in Latvian. After that, some folk songs were sung, followed by dancing and finally feasting and saying goodnight. The applause in the hall did not want to cease. When we were back in the hall, the Matron and the Sisters came to us shaking our hands, tears in their eyes.

"You poor people," they said, "we would have never thought that you carry so rich a heritage, regardless of what happened to you! We hope you will get back to your country someday."

I almost cried too, for I had just been in my beloved country, but now it was no more. But it will be! I believed that more than ever, and hoped that with our songs and our dances we were building a bridge back to our native land. We were shouting its name to the world, not letting it

forget us. Perhaps they will answer some day and will help us to return there. And then we will go back! I believed it; I wanted to believe it!

## The Magic Christmas Tree

This Christmas I did not have to work. Our landlady had said that we could use the living room in our free time, because the bedrooms were small, and there was hardly room there to turn around. With her permission, we decorated a small Christmas tree and put it there for all of us. Mother had invited Edvard, a Latvian man, whom we were acquainted with, to have Christmas dinner with us. She had also invited our landlady to join us, but she had declined, saying that she already had provided for herself. I thought that we should not have invited a Latvian guest in these circumstances, because then she probably would have joined us, and that would have been kinder and more proper at this time. The three of us talked in Latvian amongst ourselves, but we always tried to speak English when she was present.

She had perhaps hoped, that having renters, she would also have some company now that her son was gone, but since we were foreigners speaking a different language, that would probably make her feel even more lonely. I felt sorry for her, but these were days when I was more worried about the loneliness of my own soul.

We were nearing the end of the year, and the hospital was having a Christmas ball for the domestic staff on the 30th of December. It was good that the ball would not be at the Grand Hotel as it had been the previous year. It would be more fitting and also more convenient. Everybody was urged to attend and even to bring friends, for there were more women than men on the staff.

We, girls of our dancing group, decided that we would go to the dance and also invite some of our men. I invited Voldemār, one of the coal miners, who was part of our group and whom I had known the longest. He was a very pleasant young man: tall, dark haired and always in good humor. Not that I had any special feelings toward him. I looked at our team as brothers and sisters who needed to be friendly with each other. Spodra and Mirdza invited Ed.

Something, however, had gone wrong with the communications between my partner and me that evening. I waited all day for him to call, so we could decide where and what time we would meet, but the call did not come, and I did not know his number. I almost did not want to go, but Mother was going, and I went along thinking that Voldemār might just meet me at the hospital.

The dance had already begun when Mother and I arrived. I looked around for my date, but he was not there. I could not understand what

had happened, but later, it almost looked like it had been meant to be, so something else could take place. Voldemār told me later that he had waited for me to call him, but I did not have his number, so how could I?

While I was still deliberating about what had gone wrong, I saw Spodra dancing by with Ed. I knew how much Spodra loved to dance. It was good that Ed had come. The dance ended and a new one began. I was surprised when Ed came up and asked me to dance with him. At first I felt a bit uncomfortable, for he was somebody else's partner but, after all, we were all friends in our group, so there should not be any hard feelings. Perhaps he was doing it to honor me as our group's leader. Ed, however, stayed with me for the next dance also, and the one after. I knew it was not quite right, but tried not to worry about it and just flowed along with the events. I needed to relax after all the stresses from our shows, so I just let go.

Soon there was a pause, and we were asked to come for refreshments that were served next door in the large "winter garden room". This was an elongated hall with glass ceiling and walls, built between the hospital and the nurses' home, so they would not have to walk outside in the bad English weather. It was also a lounge with round tables and comfortable rattan chairs, if they just wanted to sit there, rest or read. Palms and other exotic plants stood all around the room, making it a pleasant place. It was also cooler, which was nice after the warmth of the dance hall.

When Ed and I entered it, it was already crowded with the merry dancers. All the tables and seats appeared to be taken, but then Ed spotted a couple more at the back by the window. He took my hand, and weaving through the crowded room, led me there. Around us was chatter and laughter, and we suddenly felt as if we were on the crest of a wave, too!

Refreshments were brought around on large platters, and we could take what we wanted: small, open-faced sandwiches, mini-cakes, cookies and lemonade. Ed was so full of fun this evening. I had never seen him like that. After we had made our selections of the goodies, we noticed that we each had different things and decided that maybe we should share them, so we could taste them all. We started to feed each other, Ed taking and dividing everything with such seriousness that I could not stop laughing. It looked like it had been his objective. Perhaps he had observed my seriousness or something about me, and indeed, there had been very little humor in my life. It was so good to be laughing freely like this.

Then he suddenly turned and took something off the windowsill, and the next moment a small Christmas tree, about ten inches tall, in a red wooden pot, stood between us on the bench.

Glittering snow covered its green bristle branches and it was beauti-

ful! Before I even had a chance to express my surprise about this, he said ceremoniously,

"And this will be our Christmas tree!" Our eyes met across the little tree. It could be a joke, but it was not. Somehow we both suddenly knew it. A third "somebody" had come between us, putting its arms lovingly around us both.

Realizing this, I felt a bit confused for a moment, and we both could not find what to say, but then we heard the dance music starting again, and the couples streamed back into the dance hall. We got up to go too, for we were almost the last ones here, but then I suddenly looked around. Where was our Christmas tree? I felt quite sad when I did not see it anymore. Then Ed, smiling secretly, opened his jacket a little bit, and there it was, resting at his big chest.

"We will take it with us because it is 'our' Christmas tree!" he said firmly when I began to protest that we could not just take somebody else's decorations. Still, there were quite a lot of these trees on the windowsills, so perhaps this would not be missed much. Ed went to the wardrobe room and hid it in his overcoat, then we went back to dance.

The rest of the evening went by as if in a trance for me, and we stayed together till the end. It was late when we parted outside the hospital gate. The sky was amazingly clear and full of stars. It looked like it might freeze tonight. Mother and I could get on our bus just outside the hospital gate, but there were no late buses going to Yardley Green. Ed told me later that he had walked all the way back to his hospital carrying the Christmas tree in his hand. Something new had come into our lives, something that had never been before, and tomorrow night we would see each other again in Sutton, where we would give a performance at the men's hostel at their New Year's Eve social.

The bus, gently swaying, took Mother and me along the dark, deserted streets out of the city. Only a couple more people were on the bus. The conductor stood near the entrance, resting against the wall, obviously bored or tired. Gazing out in the dark, I still thought about this evening and could not quite comprehend what had happened. The occasional street lights jumped out of the darkness, then again disappeared, but the darkness tonight had its own light. A strange, mysterious light! Was this the light of Christmas? Was this the gift I had prayed for? It was the first night in a long time that I slept a deep, healthy sleep.

It was New Year's Eve 1948. The Latvian men at the agricultural hostel in Sutton Park were hosting a dance and had invited our group to come and help with the entertainment by doing a few dances. We had promised to come, so here we were, all dressed in our national costumes. They had also asked us to bring more women, so the men

would have more of a chance to dance. The hall filled up quickly. Many had come from other surrounding places, wanting to have some contact with other Latvian people.

We danced several dances, and the joy of it grabbed me full force as usual. These men had not seen Latvian folk dances for a long time, so their enjoyment was great. They applauded and asked for more and more. Even a newspaper photographer had come, taken pictures and interviewed us afterward. The next day the pictures were in the paper together with a short story about Latvia and us, the people who had fled and now were here.

After the entertainment, the dance music started and we went out on the floor to get it all moving, for there were not too many couples dancing. The problem was that there were too many men and not enough women. Then one of the men from our group reminded us that we still had the wine the doctor had given us to celebrate our success, and this was a good time to do it. Our little group crowded into the wardrobe room between the rows of overcoats. One of our men produced the bottle and two small glasses. They got filled and the first one was handed to me as the leader. I suggested that the other one should be given to Ed, because he and I were the only ones who still called each other *"JŪS"*, the courtesy form in Latvian to use with people not closely connected to you. The familiar word in Latvian was *"TU"*. There was a fun ritual when making this change, and that was: to fill two glasses, have the two people link their elbows with drinks in their hands, empty their glasses and finish with a kiss, after which they could call each other *"TU"*.

Everybody applauded and thought that it was a great idea. I had thought that we will just toast each other by touching our glasses and that will be that. But before I knew what was happening, Ed had put his elbow through mine, as the tradition called for, and we emptied our glasses. Then a big hand cupped my cheek and firm lips touched mine for a moment. Since I had not foreseen anything like this, I was quite shaken. The others looked a bit surprised too, not knowing what to say or do, until somebody cried out to fill the glasses again, so everybody else could have their drink also. The uncomfortable moment was over.

We went back to the hall where some more people had arrived. Apparently they were some English girls the men had become acquainted with locally, and now there were more dancers on the floor. Ed and I were again dancing together, and the big hand was holding mine. I still felt rather confused after what had happened. Quite a turmoil was inside of me. What did all this mean? But before I could figure it out, an applause dance was called, where any man could clap his hands near a dancing couple and take away the girl. Perhaps that was done so that more men would have a chance to dance. Too many were still standing

at the sides just looking on.

Ed and I had to part now. I danced with one, then another and yet another, sometimes doing only a few steps of the dance, but it was nice to see the men's happy faces. From the corner of my eye, I could see Ed standing at the side, not dancing anymore, and his face was very serious. I was sorry not to be with him, but thought that he would understand that this was a special situation. We had to help our hosts to make this evening a success by giving these lonesome men a chance to have some fun for once.

It was getting very warm in the hall, and we were still in our national costumes. Dancing made us warmer still. During a pause between the dances, Mirdza and I decided to go and change. On our return, I looked around for Ed, but he was not there. Then somebody mentioned that he had probably gone home, and my joy of dancing was suddenly gone.

"Why did he do that?" I asked myself? And he had left without even saying goodbye.

Yet, deep down I knew. We had had our little Christmas tree, a miracle of Christmas for us both and out of it the tiniest shoot had started to sprout, which needed to be protected from the wind of winter. It needed four warm hands to shield it, but I had taken mine away and so had disappointed him. I felt this pain now, perhaps as deeply as he did, even though I had not wanted to hurt anybody. I had just wanted to give joy to others too, but he, of course, did not know that. Perhaps he thought that I was a good time girl who would go with anybody.

It made me very sad, and even though it was very late when we got home, I could not go to bed without explaining it to him. It was getting toward morning, but I still sat there and wrote to him. The little Christmas tree was as dear to me as to him, and the big man with the silvery fair hair and his big, tender hands had captured my heart like nobody else had. I had thought that there was only winter within my heart that no one could melt, but suddenly a vague notion of spring had come into it.

After a few days I received a letter from Ed. He said he was not angry with me and realized that perhaps he had expected too much.

"I just want you to be honest with me and tell me if I and our little tree have a chance to be glad or if we should cry… "

When I read that, I wanted to cry myself. He did not know me yet. He seemed to have made a choice already, but I was not sure of anything. How could I be? We had only just met! He would need patience, a lot of patience! Before a summer can come, the ice must melt and the springtime needs to have a chance to bud and to blossom. What can winter promise to summer before it happens? What could I say or promise him considering the state I was in?

The year 1949 had come. There was another staff ball scheduled on

January 7 at the Yardley Green hospital, and Ed had invited me to come.
We danced under the dimmed lights of the dance hall. Sometimes his
chin lightly touched my forehead, for he was almost a head taller than I.
A strange, sweet trembling went through my body. I looked up at him; he
smiled and pulled me closer to him. A sudden weakness overtook me. I
wanted to put my head on his shoulder and let him carry me wherever he
wanted. The music sounded so taunting, the people swirled around us, and
I just let myself go and enjoy it.

Later, as we sat together at a small table taking refreshments, he
told me, "All these last years I have lived only amongst men, where often
roughness was the rule of the day. I so longed to be away from it and to
find peace once more, a home and someone to love." He looked at me, and
his eyes were full of joy. He apparently thought that he had found all that.

It was a couple of weeks later, when the two-story bus was navigat-
ing the dark narrow streets, taking Ed and me out of the city. Only
here and there lights could be seen in the windows of some shops. Since
Ed's working hours at the hospital were at irregular times, we could not
meet as we would like to. He only had a couple of hours to spend this
evening, but he had come to meet me at the hospital gate to be with me
even for a little while. We both sat on the bus on my way home, even
though he knew that he would have to turn around and come right back
to get to work on time. The bus was full, and instead of sitting next to
each other, we got to sit on the opposite sides of the aisle, so talking was
impossible. People walked through the aisle getting in or out of the bus.
Occasionally we looked at each other and smiled, then again stared out
into the darkness. We did get to sit with each other toward the end of the
journey when the bus had emptied. I pulled a tiny hyacinth plant out of
my bag. The white blossoms were barely opening, but the fragrance was
all around us.

"Take that to our little Christmas tree and take my love to it also,"
I said.

"Thank you, we both will be very glad to have it and will take good
care of it, you can be sure of that." He looked into my eyes and without
words we understood one another. The little tree would speak for us.

It was almost time to get off. We went out to the platform at the back
of the bus. The damp, cool evening air hit our faces and fluttered our
hair. It was wintertime. The sky was full of stars, and it looked as if they
were running past the open door. We had arrived. Only a short distance
and we were at the house where I lived. We stopped and looked at each
other. The wind blew hard, hitting the bare branches of a creeping vine
against the house. The clouds ran past the stars, covering and uncovering
them. We knew we had to part. He took me in his arms and kissed me as

if he wanted to take all of me within him. I let him, but then tore away and, overwhelmed, ran through the gate into the garden.

I stood there by the back door my heart pounding. What happened? What happened? My lips burned and hurt. I put the back of my hand against them. This was our first real kiss, and nobody had kissed or stirred me like that before. My heart beat so heavily, echoing in my temples. I stood outside in the dark and was afraid to go in, in case somebody would hear my heart beating so wildly. Gradually I calmed down and went in. Luckily nobody was there. I happened to look in the mirror and did not know my own face anymore: the eyes were dark and deep and my lips were not my own. Then I wondered what the married people did who kissed all the time? I was still so naive.

The next morning I still had dark patches on my lips, and I put the lipstick on thicker to hide them before going to work. I did my jobs the same as every day but felt Ed's strong arms around my shoulders, and his kiss was still on my lips sweetly enticing and yet scary. I was not aware of much of what happened around me that day; I just felt the winds of springtime awakening me from my icy sleep.

We had only lived in Sutton for a few months when we had to change our lodgings again. The landlady said that one of her relatives needed somewhere to live, so we had to move. Maybe it was so and maybe not. I thought that, perhaps, one more time we had been "too many", and being foreigners, did not provide the company she had hoped for. I could understand that. We were a family and needed a separate place. But where would we get it?

We talked to our Latvian friends at the hospital and found out that several of them had moved out of the Salvation Army and rented rooms in houses that belonged to men from India or Pakistan. They were mostly in the suburb called Balsall Heath, not far from the city center. The houses were rather old, built of red bricks, but some of them were quite large, and the Indian men lived there alone doing their business.

We started looking around in that area and were lucky to find a place. We could even move in right away, so that was a big burden off our shoulders. The house belonged to two men from Pakistan who both traded with clothing. Each morning they packed up their suitcases and then walked house to house, or to markets or small shops, offering their ware. There seemed to be quite a lot of these kinds of merchants in this area. They had to be making out quite well, or else, how could they obtain these houses? Perhaps they had brought money with them?

They did not care about comforts for their living. In their individual rooms on the ground floor, they each only had a bed, a table and a chair and a huge pile of fabrics or clothing on the floor in another empty room.

That way they did not need much room for themselves and could rent the upstairs rooms to those like us, who did not demand much, either.

Actually, we got only one small room, for we could not afford more. Next to it was a large empty room, but that did not have any heating. An iron bed stood there, which Johnny would be allowed to use for sleeping, and that was it. There was no space for another bed in our room; after we had put in our double bed where Mother and I slept, into it, there was just enough space left for a small table with chairs, a dresser and a wardrobe in the corner.

Our landlords were quite nice to us (as little as we saw them). Sometimes we met them in the big old-fashioned kitchen, which served them also as a living room, since they did not have any other. It was quite cozy, especially if they had the fire going in the big, old fireplace with a range inside, where you could also cook. This was where they cooked their curries and baked their special pancakes.

"*Chapati*! Very good!" they would say.

The main landlord was Sher. He was about middle age and had a round face with short, black hair. Being somewhat on the heavy side, he walked and moved slowly. His dark, almost black eyes were always half-closed, as if he was not fully awake. Even when he talked, he did not look straight at you, and only occasionally gave you a quick look sideways out of the corner of those half-closed eyes. It was as if he was hiding something, or was afraid to be open.

The other man was the direct opposite. He was small and thin with big brown eyes in the deep sockets above his lean, bony cheeks and he had an unruly thatch of black hair. He was very friendly and inviting toward us from the start. He loved to talk, even though his English was not very good. With so many lines in his narrow forehead, he looked as if he was carrying the burdens of the whole world on his narrow shoulders, but it was amazing how his face could change in an instant, breaking into a shy smile. And when he laughed, he did it so quietly as if he was ashamed of doing it, even though he also liked to joke.

On the first day already, while showing us the house, he made us feel at home, and that was such a contrast from what we had experienced with the English people.

"You be happy here!" he said in his funny, squeaky voice that made you think of a cat's meowing.

"You want to invite friends, let them come! You want to eat or drink, eat and drink! Everything plenty, everything plenty!"

He talked happily, while opening the various cupboards and showing us what there was, even though we knew that we would not take their food. From then on we called him Mr. Plenty and he happily accepted it.

At first we felt a bit uncomfortable, when we came down to make

our breakfast on Sunday mornings, and they both stayed in the kitchen in their pajamas until noon. Perhaps it was one of their customs. Plenty sat cross-legged in the big chair, his forehead pulled into thousands of wrinkles. While I was preparing our breakfast, he asked me all kinds of questions and tried to make some jokes. When I responded, he was happy as a child on Christmas morning. I suppose he felt pretty lonely, for his whole family was in Pakistan, and he often wrote long letters. But sometimes on Sundays, he made a fire in the old stove and sat in front of it cross-legged reading something like a bible. After we had gone upstairs, we sometimes heard some long drawn out, lamenting sounds, which probably was their kind of hymn singing. We gradually got used to the new circumstances, and it seemed that everything should be alright now.

Another art class at the college had just finished. I came down the circular stairs, and a bunch of laughing young students ran past me. They obviously could not wait to get outside; I must have been going too slowly. I often felt almost reluctant to leave. Our portrait class was at the very top of the building. It was a large room with glass windows in the roof and was divided in two by curtains. On the other side was a life class. When I entered this room in the evenings after work, everything else stayed outside. I got so totally immersed in my work that I only woke up at the shrill sound of the bell sounding all through the building, announcing that the class time was over. Sometimes I got so carried away with what I was doing, that it was hard to tear myself away. But everybody was packing up, the model had left, and I had to leave also, even though I was still full of the exhilarating experience of creating something. This was not only a hobby for me, but the lifeline of my existence at the present time.

My teacher believed in my ability and urged me on. I believed in it as well and hoped that someday I would be achieving more. Perhaps then I would find a release for what was welling up inside of me, demanding to see the daylight.

The big outer door closed behind me. I had just come down the steps to the pavement, when somebody suddenly touched my hand. I looked and it was Ed! He was dressed in his light colored raincoat, his blond hair shining under the street lamp, but then I noticed his eyes. They looked into mine, dark and haunted. He took my hand, but his grip was harsh and almost hurting as he led me across the street. It had rained and the street lights reflected on the wet asphalt.

"It is already so late. How did you so suddenly..." I started to say, fear gripping my heart. I wondered what had happened.

"I had to see you tonight! I..."

I sensed how worked up he was, as if a storm was raging inside of him, as if some questions needed to be answered. We did not get any further, because the tram came, and we had to get on it.

We sat side by side, but it was hard to resume talking. I glanced at him sideways and suddenly saw a stranger. I had never seen him like that before. The intensity in his face scared me, and I instinctively pulled back within myself. He must have sensed it for his lips tightened.

The tram continued on its way, making clanging noises when crossing the junctions in the tracks, and the brakes squealed, slowing down at the stops. The streets were dark with only an occasional old gas light. We did not have to go far, because we lived closer to the city center now. We got off and walked along the quiet street. I tried to talk about this and that, but felt that we were growing further and further away from each other. I knew that was not what he had come for, but the silence was even worse.

Then we were at my house and stopped in front of it.

"Would you like to come in?" I asked, not really wanting it.

"No, I would not!" he answered with even something like defiance in his voice. He took me in his arms wanting to kiss me, but his arms were so strong around me that it seemed he would crush me. Suddenly I was scared of him and tried to get loose.

"Let me go, I need to go!" I loosened myself from his grip.

"Zigi..."

But I was already at the door. I quickly unlocked it and was inside, but Ed was right next to me looking at me.

"Good night," I said in a cool voice, though burning with pain inside.

Then he asked in a trembling voice, "Why are you like that?"

I could not answer him, for my throat was so tight, and tears rose in my eyes. Suddenly all his tension was gone.

"Forgive me..." he said in a low voice, and his eyes were big and full of sadness. He turned around and walked away slowly, his head bent. I closed the door with a heavy heart. What had I done?

Another workday was finished. It had been very hard to keep my composure, my heart being so heavy after last night's incident. As I came out into the hospital yard, the dusk was just setting in, and a wave of cold grabbed me making me shudder. It was no wonder, it was early February, and the day had been overcast and gray. It had suddenly become much colder, and the clouds were low and menacing. I put up the collar of my coat and turned my shoulder against the wind. The uniformed gatekeeper lifted his hand and cocked his eye in a real English way, as I bid him goodnight while passing by. His white, artificial teeth flashed in a

wide smile in answer to my greeting as I walked out of the gate.

Then a surprise! Outside the gate stood Ed, all hunched up in his thin raincoat with raised collar, bare headed. He must have been standing there for quite a while. He looked frozen stiff and small snowflakes sat in his hair. He did not wear gloves either, but even so his hands were always warmer than mine.

He pulled something wrapped in white paper out from under his coat and handed to me.

"A few flowers for you," he said in a low voice.

I opened the paper a little and saw three red, still tightly closed tulips.

"Oh, thank you! But you shouldn't…" I said, for I knew how expensive flowers were at this time of the year, and the training nurses pay was absolutely miniscule.

"Only three," he said. "Those are for you, from our little tree…" and his eyes looked searchingly into mine.

I gave him my hand and smiled. He took it, his eyes full of gladness, and we both suddenly felt good again. We turned against the wind and, our heads down, went up the hill. More and more small snowflakes danced in the air, got in our eyes, smacked our cheeks and got behind our collars, but we were hardly aware of it. Every so often we looked at each other and smiled, and Ed squeezed my hand gently with his big one. I could feel the warmth of it even through my gloves and there and then decided to knit him gloves so he would have something against the winter cold.

Around us, people rushed to get to their warm homes, and the big two-story buses, heavily loaded, drove slowly swaying one after the other out of the city center. The first lights had come on in the city, and against them the dancing snowflakes looked like tiny silvery stars.

The next evening I sat in our small room in the dark; the gas fire at the end wall of the room quietly seethed, throwing a reddish glow over our meager living quarters. In the corner to the right of the fireplace we had built a structure out of our suitcases and covered it with a gray blanket, so we would have somewhere to put a few of our precious decorative things. An embroidered mat, a beautiful wooden candelabra and a bowl with Latvian designs, made by our Latvian craftsmen at the camp in Germany, gave the room a warm and home-like feeling.

On the mantelpiece stood the photograph of my Dad and my three red tulips in a glass. As I looked at them, my heart was heavy. They were not doing well. Was it a bad omen? When I had woken in the morning, my first look had been at them and I saw the buds hanging from the vase limp, almost down to the table. Such a sorry and sad sight! I cut

them short and placed them in a glass hoping that they would recover. It seemed so important that they should survive and come to bloom.

Evening had come. Mother and Johnny were downstairs in the kitchen preparing supper, but I sat in the dark, not being able to take my eyes off the flowers. The light from the fire gently played around them. The blossoms had opened a little but still looked tired and weak, and that made me sad. Will our friendship not last, I asked myself?

I knew that these early blooms were very tender, and if they had been outside for a longer period of time, they did not always recover when brought inside. They just drooped and died. But not mine! Not mine! It seemed that in them was my destiny and I did not want them to die. However much it pained me, I took the scissors and cut them quite short, then set them in a small bowl of water with some leaves underneath where they looked like red water lilies. And indeed I saw how the petals grew strong and shiny, and I knew that they would live, if only for a short time.

There was a lot to do in the big surgical ward where I worked. I was constantly on the go from one bed to the next, distributing food, collecting dishes, tidying the lockers, helping to make beds and completing all the never-ending tasks. Still, I was doing them with joy these days, for springtime was in my heart even though it was midwinter outside.

But if someone started to ask things about my homeland, the old searing pain was back. Not that I wished to hide that I was a foreigner, but, talking and answering the questions, memories would come back, running over me like a burning river and destroying the tender peace that had been so hard to come by.

All the old wounds would bleed, and I would be so full of pain. I felt that I could go down on my knees and knock my head against the shining floor and cry and cry. Then it would take days to get back to normal, for I would see only what had been lost, and even more, what had been done to my people.

A row of nasty days had passed with rain and wind, therefore it was so nice to see the sun shining again, making the whole world seem brighter. There was sunshine in my heart also, and I felt that it had begun to live again. I had not seen Ed for almost a week. Our work hours were so different, but I did not worry about that. He was with me anyway in my thoughts. While working, I talked with him in my mind and felt his presence. A couple of days ago I had written him a letter trying to tell him some of what I felt, so he would understand and know me better. I wanted to bring joy to him. In writing, however, it is harder to

find the right words. I thought the whole day about what to say and what to keep to myself, for after all, we hardly knew each other yet.

Through the glass partition of our ward, I saw old George, the hospital's postman, come along the hallway and went out to meet him. He carried the large wicker basket with mail on his arm and, as usual, took his time finding the appropriate mail. I knew that he liked to stretch it out, keeping others in suspense. Perhaps it gave him a special joy and feeling of importance. But perhaps he just wanted to use the opportunity to linger and to talk to somebody. He liked to get to know people and be friendly with them. George had worked here some thirty years and felt at home here. Who knows, maybe the hospital was his only home? There were many lone people like that who lived in the so called "digs" or lodgings, renting a room in somebody's house, which could be lonelier than a prisoner's cell. Here everybody knew George and was friendly with him.

The hospital was good to their old long-time workers. They were not kicked out when they reached a certain age, but were given some smaller job if they wanted to keep working, especially those who did not have a family or the means to sustain themselves. There was Mary in our staff dining room, half deaf, talking with words and fingers at the same time, half shuffling about because of her bad legs, but she cheered us all up with her happy laugh when we came for our meals. And there was little old Betty, her shoulders bent, perhaps already some eighty years old. She was half-blind and almost deaf, with only a few teeth left, but she still proudly wore her uniform and did something in the laundry room. I met her occasionally in the lift when she went up to the kitchen for her meal or walked along the hallway back to her little room in the domestic's building. I thought it was wonderful to be treated like that. I suppose those were still the times before money became everything.

George had finally picked out the mail for our ward and again went over them, biding his time.

"Ah!" he said, "I think there is one for you also! I can't read it well, but it is your name isn't it?" He handed me a gray envelope, and I saw right away that it was from Ed. I must have blushed, for George smiled knowingly.

"From your boyfriend?" It was well known that he knew all the secrets of the hospital.

"Maybe," I smiled and put the letter into my pocket. Quickly, I distributed the letters to the patients, then went into the bathroom to read my own.

My eyes joyfully scanned the first lines, then... What was this?

"I did not expect you to spend a whole day thinking of what to say to me. If it took you so much effort, then it could not have come from your heart, then that could not be honest or true... I would rather have

the truth even if it would mean the worst for me... If you just say words to cheer me up, it is too great a sacrifice to save one lost soul, and that I cannot accept. Every evening I ask our little Christmas tree how much longer will our good days last? Perhaps Zig will find another lost soul that she will want to save... For you want to save all the lost souls and help everybody..."

"Oh, Ed!" I stood there, choking on my tears as I shook my head in disbelief. How could he misunderstand me so? If he would have perceived anything of my inner being, he could not have said that! How far we really were from each other! And I had thought that I was bringing joy to him with my letter... So much for understanding... Suddenly I was alone in the darkness and cold again. There was no sunshine, no blue sky, nothing.

This letter had knocked me out of that strange, uplifted kind of thinking, where I had been living lately. All that was suddenly gone. I sat in our room that evening and watched the rain run down the windowpanes. It was getting dark, but I did not switch on the light. My thoughts kept going round and round.

"Why did it happen this way?"

Ed obviously wanted assurances from me that I could not give him. My heart had been "on ice" for too long. Yes, I had tried to help people if I saw the need, but this was different. I was not trying to save his soul! I wanted to walk with him, get to know him and perhaps love him. With this letter I had spoiled everything. Instead of the good I had wanted, I had brought pain to him and to myself also.

It was almost noontime the following day, when one of the nurses motioned to me. She said that someone was waiting for me outside in the hallway.

"Someone good-looking!" she chuckled.

I walked out through the glass doors and saw Ed standing by the big window. A hot wave ran over me, and I almost wanted to turn and go back. There was enough pain in my heart already, yet I went up and greeted him.

"Do you think you could come outside during your lunch break? I would like to talk to you," he said.

"I am not quite through yet," I answered. "Another ten minutes."

"That's all right, I'll wait."

It was not long before I finished my work, put on my coat, and we could go. We walked up the hill to the Cathedral Square. How barren everything looked compared to the summertime! Black patches of mud dotted the green lawns; the small trees, which used to give such nice shade along the walkways, stood like angry soldiers in a line, lifting

their pruned, knotty ends of branches like fists against the gray sky. Swarms of starlings circled the tower of the cathedral, and the big trees, surrounding it, swayed in the brisk wind. We sat down on the wooden bench near the church. We did not have too much time.

"I have thought about us a lot these last days," Ed started, and it seemed that it was not easy for him to find the words.

"Me too…" I quietly added, watching the pigeons paddling through puddles picking up crumbs.

"You see… I like honesty and clarity," he continued. "I know that you like to help and do good to all people, but that is also my downfall. Then I think that perhaps I am just one of the many you show your kindness to…"

"But it is not so," I tried to interject, but he did not let me.

"Wait! Hear me out, please! Because of all this, before we go any further in our relationship, I would like to know what you think of me. Do I have a chance with you? I know that I cannot offer you much. Someday you will probably find someone better than me."

"But I don't even want…" I again tried to contradict him but did not get any further.

"I know that I am sometimes too impatient and even harsh," he was determined to say his piece. "People have said that I may mess up my life because of this, and maybe it would be better if I went my own way, for I might cause you pain. But if you are kind to me only to save my soul, then I could not take it."

"But I don't want to save your soul!" I finally got my say. "I don't even know where this "soul saving" saying has come from, and I can tell you that it has never entered my mind to judge your soul! It was good for me the way it was! I felt it big and strong that evening when we first met. I felt trust in you, and that was why I went along with you when you introduced "our" little tree. I thought you knew… You should have known… I was never dishonest with you. I met you with a pure heart and so it is today"

"Then you can at least tell me something," he pressed on.

"No, I can't. I don't know myself what to think at this moment. Don't ask me what I cannot tell you! Why are you torturing me? Why do you want to run ahead of time?" I asked, but saw that he had received his answer. Pain was in his eyes and bitterness in his lips.

"Well, then I do not want to burden you. If I create so much pain for you, then it will be better that I go and don't disturb you anymore. Otherwise you might feel obligated to be kind to me for you want everybody to be happy."

His last words cut me like a sharp knife. He had not understood anything of what I had said. Not anything! My eyes fogged over as I looked

up at the silvery clouds from which a few rays of sunshine were trying to squeeze through. They did not make it. A strong gust of wind shook the trees and flattened the new daffodil shoots down to the ground. I knew I had nothing more to say.

"I have to go," I said getting up and reaching out my hand. "Goodbye. I am sorry that you know me so little."

Just for a moment our eyes met, and his were the eyes of a stranger, full of bitterness. Overwhelming sadness struck my heart for all that had so suddenly happened and turned everything upside down. I turned and went running away. People passed by me, but their faces were like pale moons in some never-never land, for my eyes were full of tears.

I don't know how I got back to the hospital or finished my afternoon's work. Nothing made sense anymore, and it was all the same to me where I was. Only the burning river flowed through me and did not stop.

I wanted to bring joy to the world, sharing the sunshine that was within me, but now I could not do it anymore. Instead of the sunshine, I had brought only darkness. I wished that I could go far away from everybody; that I could go into a forest and redeem my soul.

After this stormy incident, a big silence came into me. It was as if the springtime had suddenly turned into a late winter day, when all the roads are wrapped in fog, and there is nothing to wait for. I sat at home and thought about Ed, thought about both of us and all that had happened. It was a Saturday, and I waited for him all day, though I knew that he was not coming. I had seen it in his eyes after our unfortunate talk in the park.

Evening came, and I knew that he would not come anymore. I had not cried for a long time, but now I let the tears come and wash away all the bitterness and all the pain, so I could come out of it clean and peaceful again.

I had just finished taking around the morning drinks to the patients and took the trolley back to the kitchen, when I glimpsed Ed through the glass partition standing in the hallway by the large window. I turned into the kitchen and was glad that no one was in there. My heart was pounding, but I stood there frozen, staring in front of myself. Why was it that each time, when I had somewhat regained my peace after turbulent times, something new came that destroyed it again and threw me back on the carousel? Why did he come to torment me?

A nurse appeared at the door, telling me that someone was waiting for me outside, and I just had to go and face whatever would be coming. I walked through the glass door but could not lift my eyes to look at him, so he would not see my emotions.

"Zigi!... Zigi..." he said touching my hand.

"It's all right. All right," I barely breathed the words, looking out

through the window at the mountainous clouds racing across the roof-tops, now showing, then again hiding the bright sunshine.

"Forgive me, please! Forgive me… I have been terrible. I don't know what had come over me. I thought that you were just playing with me…" Sadness was in his voice, and he tried to look into my eyes. When I finally glanced at him, I saw how much pain was in his face and realized that I was not the only one who had suffered.

"It's all right," I repeated, but this time I looked straight into his eyes, and I felt that our eyes said to each other more than any words could. "It's all right." I said once more, and felt that all the pain and ugliness slid off me, leaving me cleansed and free.

"I brought you a few flowers. " He took a small bunch of narcissi, wrapped in paper, from the windowsill and handed them to me, his eyes moist with emotion.

"What can I do if I don't know how to fit myself in today's world," he continued sadly. "In the men's world the values were different. You took what you wanted. Now the good I want to do, comes out bad, and then I sometimes get so frustrated that I want to force things to go my way. Then I am harsh and full of bitterness. Only later I see that I bring evil to myself and also to others. But I want to try to mend my ways and not let the evil one out."

I saw how he had struggled with himself, and my heart was full of forgiveness. I wanted to help him to be happy again but still could not bring myself to say anything. But my eyes told him that all was forgiven and forgotten, and tomorrow seemed full of promise again. We could not talk for long. I had to go back to work and Ed left.

That evening on the table in our room stood a vase with the white narcissus, each a perfect blossom as if created in wax, as pure and white as can be found in nature. Their beautiful, cool scent filled the room, and they seemed to be speaking to me, their wise yellow eyes looking deep into my heart. Then I prayed that I, too, would have the wisdom to know how to live my life.

It was a gray day with racing clouds, when Ed and I walked slowly along the empty pathways at the Cannon Hill Park. Strong gusts of wind ran through the bare tree-tops, bending them back and forth. It was a Sunday afternoon, but there were not many who wished to be outside on a cold winter day like this. A couple of people had come out to walk their dogs, which ran across the wet green field joyfully while their owners followed them slowly, their heads pulled into their collars and hands deep in their pockets. Some children fed ducks by the pond, their father handing them bread out of a paper bag. Soon all others had walked away toward the gate, and only our steps made crunching sounds

on the graveled pathway while the wind played in the shrubs beside us.

We turned off onto a smaller path, which led us into a young pine grove. The wind did not touch us in here, and we stopped for a bit, listening to the sounds the tree-tops made. We both felt somewhat subdued today and did not talk much, but just walked, listening to the winter's day and to our inner selves.

It was as if we stood on the opposite sides of a river, each in our own world with the familiar things around us, but between us was the sad river of the days when we had not known each other. Because of this, it seemed that there was so little we could give each other of ourselves.

We would like to get closer to one another but did not know how, being wary of hurting each other. I could sense that his feelings were much stronger than mine—feelings wanting to find a response in me. But I was only just awaking from my deep winter sleep. I was not sure if I could give him what he expected and did not know how to tell him that without hurting him. I kept silent, but we both felt that the unsaid words grew like a wall between us. I knew, though, that words, said hastily, could sometimes hurt the other person more. We did not know each other's vulnerable places yet and how to circumvent them. We had to let the river of time flow until we knew this.

But perhaps we could try to talk more. We came to a bench in a more sheltered corner in the now bare rose garden and sat down. We needed to tell each other something about our childhood days and about our families. Our lives had been so different. I knew only that Ed had grown up as an only child, brought up strictly by his older parents. Now he began to tell me: "My mother had a sewing business, and my father taught woodworking at the technical high school in Rīga. As a boy, I spent a lot of time by myself roaming the city. I loved to find out what was where. In time I knew the city center like the back of my hand. If anybody needed to mend an umbrella, sole shoes or make a key, I could tell them where to go." He chuckled. "Later, in my teenage years, I had to help my mother quite a lot with household chores. My father was not there anymore." He stopped, staring out in the distance.

"What...What happened to him?" I almost whispered, not knowing if I should have asked such a question. He was silent for a little while, then said, "We don't really know... He was shot. Those were chaotic times... The Russians fled and the Germans were coming in. One day he did not come home and nobody could find out what had happened."

We did not talk for a while. Then he said, "I had a grandmother who lived at the seaside town, Liepāja, on the west coast of Latvia. I spent my childhood summers there and we had a great time doing all kinds of things together. I loved to go there. I remember that I travelled to Liepāja by train on my own when I was only seven years old."

"But Liepāja is a long distance from Rīga—half-way across the country! How did your parents let you?"...

"I was not afraid. My Uncle John said that I must be strong like a soldier, for he was one and knew all about it. A couple of times I went to spend a few weeks with him in the summer at his post at another port, where he worked as a coast-guard. I was quite young then—perhaps five or six. Yes, I remember well when he took me on the boat and let me hold the steering wheel! What a thrill that was—pretending that I was a sailor!"

"What about your grandfather?"

"My grandfather was a tailor—a very good tailor. He had even spent two years in America, in New York, and everybody called him "the American tailor"! Grandmother did not go to work outside the home, so she had plenty of time to spend with me. She always found something interesting to show or teach me."

Ed also talked of the rough times he had gone through during the last years of the war, having been drafted into the German army right from his high school bench. He and his classmates had been in the battles fighting the Russians all the way through Poland and Eastern Germany, being constantly pursued by them, and at times surrounded by them.

"After the war ended, I and many other Latvian draftees had to spend another six months at a prisoner of war camp in Belgium. We had been told that we would be taken to a place where we would be released. Instead we were put behind barbed wires... That made us very bitter..." He paused a little while, looking down to the ground in front of him, then continued: "When we were released from the prisoner of war camp six months later in spring of 1946 we had nowhere to go, so we tried to get into the Displaced Person camps. At that time these camps were established all through Germany to take care of the refugees. Some camp commandants, however, refused to take the former soldiers, and that was very hurtful. Perhaps they feared that the military government of the time may not look at it kindly, for we had been together with the German forces. Many people do not understand our situation even now, that to save ourselves from the Russians, our only way was to go with the Germans."

"So where did you go?"

"Well, that is quite a story!" Ed said. "I'll tell you some other time; it is getting too cold."

"Yes, but how did you get to come to England?" I asked.

"The last year in Germany, I served for the American forces as a guard and so did many other former soldiers." Ed answered.

"There was a lot of drinking and living it up with the Americans. I did not want that and therefore decided to go to England to start a new kind of living." Ed said.

"No wonder his attitude to life is different," I thought. I had not

known about all that.

I, on the other hand, had grown up in the shelter of my parent's home, without having been touched by the rough realities of life. Perhaps I had chosen not to see them, always wanting to see only the good and the beautiful and had instinctively tried to keep my world like that. There had been sadness and sorrows, but I had always dealt with them within myself. I did not know how to share with another and how to meet this real life face to face.

But yes! It was getting too cold. We needed to get up and go. Under the shrubs new green shoots were coming up. It meant that spring was on the way! And after the spring will come summer!

As we began to walk again, the same old questions came up.

"Why can't you tell me how you feel? When will you be able to tell me if I have a chance?"

I could not answer these questions, for I honestly did not know. I liked him, he was dear to me and perhaps I even loved him, but the recent up and down incidents scared me. I did not want to promise anything before I was sure.

Suddenly Ed said, "Let's go to Scotland next summer on our vacation!"

Not a bad thought. I would love that, but summer was still so far away.

We walked along the wide main road back to the gate. It had become lighter, but the wind still chased the clouds, throwing into our faces its cool breath, full of the smells of water and damp soil, the promise of spring. Just for a moment the clouds split in two, and silvery rays flowed through them, touching the bare treetops. A swarm of birds flew over our heads into the silvery sky. Spring was coming!

Ed asked me out to dinner at a restaurant one evening, which in those days was really something special. After the war years, people still lived rather "tight", even here in England, and there were not too many restaurants around. It turned out that Ed wanted to take me to the best one in town. Knowing how small his pay was at the hospital, I tried to talk him out of it, but he was not giving in.

For one thing, I had never been to a restaurant in my life. What with the war and then refugee times, there had not been an opportunity, and after coming to England, there never was enough money to squander on a luxury like that. Of course, I had seen films where people ate in restaurants, and I thought of that as we went up the carpeted steps to Pattison's restaurant on one of the main streets in the city center. We sat down at one of the tables. In the corner, somebody quietly played the piano. It was very nice. The waiter brought us the menus, and we started looking at them; then another waiter hurried by and took them away from us

before we had made our selections.

That was strange. We waited and waited, but nobody else came or even looked our way, so we could not catch their eye. Were we being discriminated against because we were foreigners? It was getting very uncomfortable, although we tried to pretend that everything was all right. I could see that Ed was very unhappy and tried to entertain him with a cheerful story, but the discomfort grew for both of us. Finally we did catch somebody's eye and got served, thank God, but the mood of the evening was ruined, in spite of our efforts to save it.

Perhaps it was still the residue of the war and refugee times that made us feel like we did not belong here and could not really relax. Ed brought up the subject of Scotland again and what his colleague at work had told him: the beauty of the land, of the hills and valleys, of lakes and birch groves like in Latvia.

"You would like it there," Ed said, playing with his glass, "and if you will be a good girl, I will take you there!" He promised jokingly.

"That's good," I laughed. "I always wanted to see Scotland!"

"Then you know what you have to do," he continued, and we both already saw the blue sky over the Scottish hills and the birches mirrored in the clear waters of the lakes.

Well, perhaps! Who knows?

As the people began to leave, we got up to go too. The cold evening air enveloped us as we went outside, but up above between the dark bodies of the buildings, the sky was full of stars.

I suppose Ed realized, too, that we needed to get to know each other better and spend more time together. He invited me to go one evening with him to the "West End", the dance hall in town. When we arrived, there was plenty of space in the big ballroom, and we easily found a table. After our turbulent meetings of late, we once again felt happy and free, letting the music carry us. We danced most of the time, just taking short breaks to rest, feeling happy to be near each other, and that was all I wanted right now.

The lights gradually dimmed until only the rotating ball of tiny mirrors was left at the ceiling. The spotlight on the silvery ball turned the dance hall into a fairyland, shedding a myriad of stars over the dancers, making it even more romantic. Ed pulled me closer to him, and his lips touched my forehead softly as I rested my head against his shoulder.

The dance ended, and we went back to our table for a little rest. Ed brought us some drinks. While sipping them, we again drifted into that strange outside-of-time mood, as on that night of the Christmas dance at the hospital. We felt like two big children who had entered a fairy-story land, where everything was possible. Ed seemed to be good at that.

He sat opposite me at the small table, leaning forward a bit, his big hands in front of him. He looked at me smiling, his eyes looking like two golden pools in this strange lighting and his fair eyebrows above them, trembling slightly. Then he asked me if I had ever heard the story about the little magic Christmas tree.

I didn't know it, and while we slowly sipped our drinks, he began to tell me. It was a beautiful story about the traditional old man with three sons who lived in the land of Happiness, where everybody loved everybody and lived in peace. Then an evil ruler sent his armies to overwhelm this small country, and the older brothers went to protect it. The youngest son had to stay with his father, until one night he heard loud noises. The house was burning, and when he went outside, he saw his father in irons, and men in strange uniforms took him away. Then he left, too, and came to lands where only evil ruled. There he was forced to become like they were, only on Christmas night was he allowed to be his old self again. As he thought of his life then, he started to cry, for he could not find what he was longing for anywhere. An old man appeared and asked what was troubling him. The young man told him that more than anything he longed for peace, love and a home. The old man gave him a little magic Christmas tree, saying that if he ever needed advice, to ask the little tree; then he disappeared again.

Now the little tree told him to go and save a princess whom an evil wizard had taken to his abode. He did this, restoring the princess to her father, the king, who gave her to him as a wife, and half a kingdom as well. He was very happy but was still longing for his native land. Then one day messengers came from his homeland, proclaiming that the land was free again, and everybody could go home. The young man and his wife said goodbye to the king and returned to the land of Happiness, where they lived happily ever after...

This is just a short summary, but he sent it to me in a letter also, beautifully written. I will never forget it, for it helped me to understand the deep need Ed had for me. He would finally have somebody to call his own, for he did not have anybody in the world. It made me feel closer to him than ever before, and I thought that at last all my doubts were eliminated.

## The Big Crash

But life is not a fairy tale, and those who like to linger there, sometimes get cruelly disillusioned, when they meet up with real life. I do not know whether for better or for worse, I am one of those people who, perhaps, weave for themselves an unreal picture of life by thinking and believing that life can be good and beautiful, if only we behave that way.

I had tried to keep the bad out of my life, but people are not only good or bad. Both qualities are mixed up in all of us, even though it is not always easy to see. It is hard to accept, that with the good you also have to take the bad, and what is good for one, may be bad for another.

It was a Monday night, and as usual, I was at the college at my portrait class. It was break time, and the students stood around in small groups, talking or walking around to see what the others had done. I had walked around as well, looking at other people's work, but then went and sat down at my desk. I was so very tired lately. Too many activities, I knew it: work, school, folk dancing and now also the choir. But it was hard to give up things that brought so much joy, even though it took away the strength. Besides, I did not have any appetite and was losing weight.

I put my head down on my crossed arms. I was tired, yet my thoughts kept rolling on. Perhaps one of my hardships was also my work at the hospital, where I had to see so much suffering. Death stood just beyond the glass partition, so it could easily stretch out its long bony hand. I had to think a lot about life and death these days. Why was there so much suffering? Why did we cause pain to ourselves and to others? We all longed for peace, perhaps more than for joy or even happiness, but we did not know the way. Sometimes, just for a moment, we would feel happy, but then a shadow would fall on our path, the wind chasing rough sand over it. The happiness was not there anymore; its footprints were gone. We were again drifters without a home, without peace.

Yet, the happiness did not vanish without a trace. Like an echo from far away bells sounding at eventide, it could suddenly come and make you clean. When you are tired and dirty from the road you have walked, a light from heaven can come and give you peace. I still rested on my arms on the desk, and my thoughts just rolled on as usual.

If only we could hold on to more of such times! Goodness given and received. For life is short, and we only have one! This thought was on my mind a lot. There was so much good to accomplish in this one lifetime! If we kept this in our minds, would we not live differently, even though we now were without a home and a country?

But we would return home to Latvia—I knew that with assurance. Even now I could hear the old oak trees and the huge elm trees around the house talking to each other. They all waited for the day when we would be coming home.

At home... I feel the hot midday sun on my forehead as I lie amongst the grasses in the meadow. Sweet aromas float in the air... The sun so hot on my forehead...

Suddenly, somebody touched me and I awoke from my dream. Had I fallen asleep? I lifted my head, and right above me hung the big white lamp. Then I saw Ed standing next to it. For a moment I could not figure

out where I was and what was happening. Then all kinds of disturbing thoughts ran through my mind. Something bad had happened!

"Come quickly," Ed said, "we have to go home!" He was already putting my things in my case.

"But why? Has anything bad happened to Mother or Johnny?" I jumped up to my feet, ready to go.

"No, nothing, but come quickly, a cab is waiting for us downstairs!" He talked fast without looking at me. I stood dumbfounded, not knowing what was going on. I could not move, but Ed was already walking out carrying my things, so I had to follow him. I felt like a child having been spanked in front of strangers, not even knowing what for, and anger was rising within me.

"Why do we have to go right now?" I still tried to question him, but he just rushed down the stairs without answering.

Outside, indeed a taxi was waiting for us, and in it sat Ed's roommate, Robert, and my brother Johnny. I could not understand what it all meant, and became even more confused because nobody gave me an explanation.

"Is it really true that nothing bad has happened with Mother?" I asked, and then Johnny, smiling comfortably, answered, "No, Mother is at home making a supper for us all! Ed and Robert came over with a bottle of wine, but since you were not at home, Ed said that we ought to go and get you. So here we are!"

Now I finally understood, and my anger flowed over.

"And that is why you pulled me out of the class? Shamed me in front of everybody?" I thundered, not knowing what to do, but the taxi was already moving out.

"Well, I just thought that we could all celebrate a bit together," Ed smiled at me trying to pacify me, but as he leaned closer, I knew that he had been drinking, and that upset me even more.

"To do something like that! Handling me like a small child, not even asking me!" I raged on. "I shall never be able to show myself there again!" By now I cried and moaned, taking in the reality of what had happened.

"My whole future is destroyed... all I had ever hoped for... Let me out of here, I cannot stand to stay here!" I fought to get out, but Ed held my arm in a tight grip, and the taxi continued on its way through the dark streets.

"I don't want to ever see you again!" I pushed Ed's hand away and pressed my head into the corner of the cab. Gradually the crying ceased, but in my heart a tight knot of hatred and bitterness had formed. I stared out into the dark and did not say anything anymore. It was no use. Everything was finished anyway.

We were home and Mother received us smiling, hurrying up to set the table for our meal. Soon she noticed that something was not right, though. My heart suddenly flowed over and I said some bad words about Ed. I don't remember that I had ever had such an explosion of words before, nor did I ever do that again. Mother tried to save the situation by asking us to sit down and eat, but nobody cared much for it anymore. Only Johnny ate heartily with his young boy's appetite. This had nothing to do with him, and he probably did not even understand what it was all about.

I sat staring at my plate, not even seeing what was on it, but when I lifted my eyes, I saw that Ed too had not touched his food. He looked my way, his eyes big and full of pleading. All the bravado and intensity had disappeared. I diverted my eyes and looked away. How many times had we already gone through these misunderstandings? I had enough, and hardness came into my heart, such as I had never known before. I lifted my eyes again, stared back at him and let this hardness talk. The words were not necessary. Ed looked back, and his eyes became moist, but I felt that the ground I was standing on had started to sink. I was the loser again.

I suppose it was because I saw how much he regretted it when he had done something wrong, and that made me forgive him again and again.

Robert opened the wine and filled up the glasses. Ed lifted his glass and held it looking at me, his eyes begging for forgiveness. I lifted mine a little and we drank in silence. I saw that I had caused a great upset for everybody; nobody felt like talking anymore, and our visitors got ready to leave. I went downstairs with them. At the door Ed turned and kissed me softly on my forehead, wishing me goodnight. I closed the door and slowly went up the stairs, but my legs trembled as after a long, hard journey.

Too much had happened lately in my relationship with Ed and too many times. After each time it was harder to get my strength together. I was not even aware of how I got through my workday. Thoughts came and went through my mind weaving like shadows, taunting and circling around me. I did not even try to catch them. Some voice in me was saying to leave it alone, leave it alone... and I tried to do that.

Looking from a distance a day later, things did not look as tragic as they had seemed in the beginning. The worked up feelings had evened out and settled down, even though the night before I had felt that my whole world had fallen apart.

What could I do if things like that upset me so terribly? I did not know how to live just skimming the surface. Whatever I did, I was there with my whole being. Was my striving after that idea—the utmost purity

in all things—that seemed so necessary to me, overblown? But I did not know how I could live without it.

The workday was finally over, but I did not feel like going home yet. There might be questions and discussions. I was not ready for that and decided to go and visit some of our other hospital girls who lived not far from our present dwelling place. Since we each worked at a different place in the hospital, we did not have a chance to see each other often, and visiting helped me put my other thoughts aside.

It was rather late when I went home. The evening was damp but warm outside, and it was nice to be out walking. As I went into our room, I suddenly stopped at the door. A huge bouquet of pink roses stood in a vase on the table! Tears welled up in my eyes, and I did not have to ask where they came from because I already knew. Their message sank deep into my heart. Oh Ed! These lovely roses! The tighter buds looked around as if in surprise, the ones slightly open spread their sweet aroma around them.

Then I noticed our little Christmas tree on the mantelpiece, and it made the message complete.

Mother sat on the edge of our bed smiling, and I saw that this time she had shared this tragic incident with us.

"Edvin came and we had a good visit," she said. "He brought you these flowers and wanted to ask your forgiveness for yesterday..."

"But everything is forgiven. It was already forgiven last night!" I said.

"I know. I told him that and... Perhaps it was better that you were not here. We had a long talk and I think I assured him that everything would be all right, but he would have to be patient," Mother concluded.

All the tension was suddenly gone. Nothing had to be said or added. I sank into sleep, the scent of the roses flowing over me like a sweet caress.

The next days passed as if I were living in a rose garden. I knew now that Ed really loved me and felt that our destinies had entwined never to part again. His goodness was around me, and my heart was full of tenderness toward him. I chastised myself now for causing him pain with my explosive behavior, by letting my feelings gush out in that way. That was not wise, and time would have to pass until we would learn to harmonize our feelings and thoughts.

Sunday came, and my roses had opened up in their full beauty. I thought I had never seen roses more beautiful than these, nor dearer to me. Even our little tree seemed to agree that they were the most beautiful. We both could not stop looking at them, feeling the love that they sent our way, and the fake snow on the little tree sparkled with joy.

I had not seen Ed since that fateful evening and wondered when he

would come to see his roses. But in my heart there was peace. I knew that he would come; I only wished that the roses would still be alive so he could see their beauty.

We had bought a radio the day before, which we had wanted so badly, and now our room was like a small happy land. The little tree sparkled, the roses spread their magnificent aroma, and I was happy. The radio played soft music; the gas heater in the fireplace spread its warmth and its reddish light through the room, where dusk was beginning to fill the corners. I felt so good and prayed that Ed too had managed to put down the burden of guilt and was at peace with himself. I wanted so much to cheer him up. I could not stand knowing that he was sad.

It seemed that life had gone back into more normal channels. The days rushed toward spring, and it arrived, but not as I had envisioned. A couple of weeks had passed since our last upheaval at the college, when one morning our mailman George brought me a letter from Ed. He was working night shifts, so I had not seen him. I put the letter in my pocket to read it later at my lunch break, for there was too much to do right now. Finally I was through and went to our lounge, where I could read it in leisure. It was a long letter, and as I read it, it became more and more painful.

"It is night time, actually a very early morning. Everything is so quiet…" he wrote. "I don't know what the matter with me is, but I cannot find peace anywhere… Forgive me for writing and complaining, but my heart is so full that I need to tell someone what it feels and what its burdens are. Since it is all about you, I want to be open and tell you.

At first I was happy when we could meet and spend even a little time together, and after a while, I felt that I had finally found someone so dear to me whom I never wanted to lose again. In my thoughts I had already developed a dream for the future, and that was what I had wanted to tell you that fateful Monday. But then came that lucky or unlucky incident at the college, and that opened my eyes and made me look at things differently.

Yes, on that Monday I had wanted to tell you that perhaps we could, with God's blessing, live our lives together, and then nothing could ever part us except He alone… But now I do not dare to even think or talk about it. I look at myself and see that I am a totally useless person for this life. Perhaps not quite so, but there is a fight within me between the good and the bad, and I don't know who will win.

Before, I was so happy to be with you and your family in your cozy little room, feeling that for a little while I had been "at home". Now I feel like a criminal who has made his entry into a sacred place, where the good people live and who, perhaps, have accepted me out of their

kindness. Now, all that I had envisioned and hoped for seems like a great sin. That is how I feel about it, yet some mystical force draws me to you.

But no, I do not dare to go near you. I am too bad a person for you. I first have to look within myself to see where I must change. If the good in me will win, then and only then will I dare to approach you again. I think that will be the best way, don't you think?

Forgive me for burdening you with my heavy thoughts, but as I said, I could not hold it in any longer. And who else would I tell it to, for I don't have any other dear and close person to share it with... It is almost light. The sun will be rising soon. A new day will be here..."

I sat in my chair gazing at the opposite wall. My surroundings had disappeared. It was as if I was a gray stone, already half sunk in the ground, slowly being covered by moss. Today's pain could not penetrate it anymore, for it was too full of it already.

Visions from a previous Sunday came before my eyes. We had had visitors. Two of our young Latvian men, with whom we had become acquainted, had come to visit. There were many of them here without families, and we always welcomed them to come and enjoy a little family warmth and love. Voldemār and Edvard had brought a bottle of wine and a large bunch of beautiful white lilacs. Mother had baked a cake and made little sandwiches. We all sat around the table in our little room drinking our coffee, talking and feeling relaxed and happy while the white lilacs filled the room with their delightful scent.

Then Ed came. Since none of us had telephones in those days, there were no previous announcements. People just came. We welcomed Ed as usual and asked him to join us at the table. He did that, but it was visible that he was full of that strange intensity again, and it gradually spread through all of us. He did not take part in our talks, remaining distant from us all. He filled his wine glass several times and emptied it in one go, at times delivering some sarcastic comment to what others had said. Our relaxed and happy mood was gone. We all felt a bit uncomfortable. The wine was all gone too, and Ed suggested that they should get another bottle, but our visitors were getting ready to leave. I could understand why and was glad that they did before anything else happened.

The day was a bit overcast but warm, and we all walked out to the tram stop to see them off. I walked ahead with Voldemār, Mother and Edvard came behind us, and Ed walked by himself at the back. When the tram came, the men got on it, but Ed suddenly remembered that he had forgotten his cigarettes at our place. We walked back, all feeling uncomfortable. I could sense that something was happening within him, something he was trying to suppress and the cigarettes were just a reason to come back, perhaps even left deliberately.

It made me very sad. I thought, "Why did he have to lie to me? Why

could he not tell me openly that he wanted to stay a bit longer and talk to me to unburden himself?" That would save us all so many misunderstandings and heart aches, but life was not so simple. I tried not to show my sadness and disappointment, but he must have sensed it and soon left.

After reading his letter I understood better why it had been that way. I understood his suffering, but I also knew that I could not help him. I could not help anybody, not even myself. I wanted to be like a gray rock and let the moss grow over me. To feel nothing, know nothing, for I did not have enough strength to deal with anything more.

Easter came, and the weather had suddenly turned wonderfully warm. The sun walked across the land, making everything sparkling and new. We were not used to such brightness and, going outside, it almost blinded our eyes.

It had been announced that there would be a Latvian church service at the Sutton Park men's hostel this Easter Sunday. My family did not want to miss it, although it took an hour riding on two buses and then walking about a mile to get there. Still, the morning was so beautiful and we got there in no time at all.

When we arrived, the service had already started, and the hall was full. Most of the Birmingham Latvians had come to hear God's word in the Latvian language and to be together with other Latvian people. The pastor's sermon, however, was so monotonous and uninspiring that we did not get much out of it. There was nothing of the joyous Resurrection Day message that people had expected. So the words just flowed over us, while our thoughts went back to the Easter mornings back in Latvia. Here and there people wiped away some tears, and when the singing started again, everybody sang from their hearts.

*"Cēli kā dzimtenes dievnami lai mums ir mērķi un darbi..."*

We started to sing this popular and much loved hymn that we had also sung at my confirmation in Germany (and had often sung at our school prayers as well). Then I choked up, and tears ran down my cheeks. In my mind's eye I saw Dad and Grandpa and Grandma, remembering all the sunny Easters we had spent at home. I cried and could not stop. Hot, long-suspended tears fell on my hands, and my heart was full of sorrow. I bent my head lower, so others would not see it, but then the service was over. People went outside unburdened and free, glad to see the beautiful sunny day.

I quickly wiped away my tears and walked out together with the others. The day was so lovely that many did not want to go home right away, and some of our Birmingham people suggested that we go for a walk.

The huge Sutton Park, several kilometers long and wide, lay before us. This was not a landscaped park, but rather an area pretty much in its

natural state. Some rich person had gifted it to the city, so people could get outside and spend some time with nature. We walked in a long row and spread out over the undulating hillocks, talking and visiting. There was my old school friend Sandra with her boyfriend Robert, as well as people from our choir and its leader, Mrs. Roze. Mother walked with Saša, a man she had become acquainted with while singing in the choir, and Johnny with our good friend Arnold walked behind them. Ed had come also, although I had not thought that he would do so. We had not seen each other lately, and when we walked side by side later, we walked mostly in silence. This was not a day to deal with problems.

The trees around us were budding, and the sun lavishly shed its light over everything. High above in the air, a lark sang its happy song. The air was full of the earthy green smells of spring. We walked along the road, then across the low rolling hills and fields. The new grass sprouted through the old in sparkling greenness. Scattered here and there, were small groves of trees and shrubs.

Easter should be a time to rejoice about all this, and I tried, but my joy lacked uplifting thoughts and my sky was low. I felt so tired. There had been so many stresses since last summer. My trying to get the family over here from Germany, the sordid business with finding where to live and then being kicked out; changing lodgings three times within less than a year in addition of all my other activities. And then these misunderstandings with Ed... The emotional swings were doing me in and taking away my strength. I just walked with half-closed eyes, letting the sun shine on my face and heal me and give me peace, peace, peace.

The warm and mellow days of May wrapped everything in a golden shimmer, and the evenings stretched out long with twilight lingering for several hours. We had choir practices more often now, because there was going to be a song festival in London this summer, a very exciting event to which we all wanted to go. The song festival tradition in Latvia was very old. It had been established in 1879, and it consisted of choirs from all over Latvia learning the same songs, chosen for the program. Then every few years they would come together in Rīga to sing in a large outdoor stadium. There would be thousands of singers in one huge group, with a hundred thousand or more listeners who also had come from all parts of the country.

Now the old tradition was going to be revived for the first time here in England. Not much time was left till the appointed time in June. Sometimes our Birmingham choir went to Sutton to practice together with the men there, or otherwise we met here at the YWCA in Birmingham.

It was a nice late Sunday afternoon when we met there again for

a practice. We sang all the dear, well-known choir songs that were repeated each time the festivals took place, for they were so much loved and depicted our nation's history, our pain and our hopes.

There was the song—or rather a legend—telling about the Castle of Light that had sunk to the bottom of a deep lake, because evil rulers had taken over our land. It stayed there for centuries until young, brave men came and called for the Light to dawn again. And the light dawned, the castle rose and freedom returned to the nation. It brought new hope to our Latvian people whenever it was sung.

There was also the *"Cantata for the Homeland"*, a prayer to God to have our homeland returned to us, free again. And then there was the song called *"My Sister is crying in a far, far away land..."* a song expressing our pain in being exiled.

I loved the songs, but all that they contained was so painful to me that it cut me to pieces. My emotions were hovering on the edge of a razor blade. I suddenly felt so tired and knew I had to leave. I whispered to Mother that I would go home.

"Are you not feeling well? Will you be all right to go home alone?" she asked.

"I'll be all right," I said, not wanting to spoil her evening, for I could see that perhaps for her too, a new springtime was budding. The evening was so lovely. Maybe she would like to spend a little more time with Saša. I went out into the street where dusk was gathering. The air was warm but sultry, full of many scents and promises but also full of nostalgic moods, as it can only be in May.

When I got home and entered our room, it was almost dark. I switched on the table lamp, but somehow the room seemed strangely empty tonight. I turned on the radio. Sounds of a symphony concert filled the room. I loved this kind of music and it flowed around me, but this time it did not penetrate me. Something stood in the way, though I did not know what it was. I began to pace back and forth as if I had to search for an answer. There was a big "WHY" twirling around in my mind! Something strange was happening within me. Looking down as I paced, I saw the colored squares of the worn linoleum on the floor and they seemed to be laughing at me; laughing about my messed up life! Suddenly I felt so sorry for myself. I stopped in the middle of the room and bit my fist, trying to stop the heaviness that was rising up in my chest. My whole life seemed like a broken vessel, and I saw only shards scattered around me. I stared at them, not being able to move.

The music still flowed, hanging in the air; more and more sounds gathered, pressing against me. Somebody was playing a piano. I did not recognize the piece, but suddenly the sounds rose—they gushed into

me—and all my hidden hurts were in those sounds. More and more they crowded within me, until it became one huge ball of sounds and hurts. I fell on my bed and cried together with the crashing sound of music. I cried and cried, not quite knowing what it was I was crying about. It was about everything that was so wrong.

Gradually I calmed down somewhat, switched off the radio and lay down on the bed. Everything was silent again. I would try to sleep. Suddenly a trembling went through my body. It stopped for a moment, then came again and shook me even harder. I could not stop the shaking. Then a pricking pain in the region of my heart! What was happening? Suddenly I was afraid for I was alone! There was no one at home and who knows when somebody would come? Just thinking about it, the trembling became stronger, and my heart started to pound. I tried to relax and sleep, but the waves of trembling shook me more and more. I bit the pillow to stop my teeth chattering.

I don't know how much time had passed since I had been lying there. It felt as if each new trembling put a tighter ring around my heart. I silently cried and prayed that somebody would come.

Finally I heard the door shutting downstairs, and Mother and Johnny came into the room. With difficulty, my teeth chattering, I told them what had happened. Mother was very concerned but did not know what to do. She gave me one of her tablets, but my heart started to work so hard that I felt it might burst.

It was midnight when the doctor finally came, but could not find anything physically wrong.

"It's nerves," he said, gave me a sedative and told me to stay in bed for a couple of days and rest.

At last the evil hands released me, and I gradually drifted into sleep.

The next morning I awoke tired and weak as if I had been through a difficult illness. Johnny and Mother had to go to work, but she said she would call Ed and ask if he could possibly come over for a little while and see how I was, since he was still working nights and would be free in the daytime. I protested against it and thought that would not be fair, since our relationship was in such a mixed up state, but Mother just waved goodbye and was gone.

Silence was around me. I looked at the ceiling. It was getting lighter and brighter in the morning light. Somewhere the sun was shining. My thoughts started working but did not seem to go anywhere. Somebody had cut the connections, and only heaviness was in my chest. I closed my eyes and tried to not think of anything. Perhaps I snoozed a bit...

Suddenly I heard the door open quietly, and Ed came in with the morning's breath on his hair and his clothing.

"Good morning, little buddy!" he said smiling. "What is happening here?"

"You should not have come," I started chastising him. "You have worked all night, you need your rest!"

"There will be time for that!" He was cheerful and kind, just like a nurse should be with his patient, and all day long his quiet loving care was with me.

I felt so grateful to him that my eyes often veiled with tears. Nobody in my life had ever showed such tender caring, except sometimes my Dad a long, long time ago, but in a more hidden way. Everybody else was too wrapped up in their own affairs to pay such special attention to me and I had to manage things by myself the best I could.

And now Ed was here in place of Dad. He really put on the act as if he were my Dad treating me as a child, jokingly coaxing me to eat the little sandwiches he prepared for me, telling a children's story. His warmth was all around me, wrapping me like a comfortable blanket, and as he sat on the side of my bed and looked at me, his eyes were moist with unexpressed love.

It was already afternoon when I finally got Ed to agree to rest a little, for in the evening he would have to go back to work. Since there was no other place to sleep, and the bed was wide enough, I moved closer to the wall so he could lie down next to me. He loosened his tie and then lay down on top of the blankets on the outer edge. I closed my eyes, too, but could not sleep. Perhaps later I had snoozed off, when I awoke hearing someone at the door. It could not be Mother, it was too early.

I did not move and then heard someone opening the door and looking in. Then just as quietly the door closed. I believed I was hearing our landlord, Sher's, heavy steps going away along the hallway. He saw us both sleeping. What did he think? I did not feel good about this, but there was nothing I could do.

Ed was sleeping peacefully. I lay next to him and listened to the ticking of the clock. The afternoon was almost over. He would soon have to get up.

Gradually I recovered from the fearful happening but still felt weak and sometimes light-headed. Ed came to me almost every day and spent all his free time with me. He was so good and brightened my days with his cheerful presence. I was getting stronger, and we both cooked rice pudding in the large kitchen. The pot got fuller and fuller, but the rice was not tender. We stirred the pot in between laughing and exchanging kisses, but in the end, the pudding was burnt. Perhaps we cooked it the wrong way, not using enough water? Anyway, these days

were full of quiet warmth and gentle sunshine. We did not try to solve problems or question anything, just lived on the surface and for the time being that was good.

The doctor decided, though, that I ought to go away for a few weeks to a convalescent home to rest and recover. Together with the hospital service officer, called the almoner, arrangements were made for my travel and stay. I was sorry to leave Ed. During these last days we had come closer to each other in a different way. I had seen how good and caring he could be toward those he loved. I felt good and safe with him, but when I was alone, fear and that dreadful sorrow was with me again, so I knew I had to do what the doctor ordered.

At my visit at his office, the doctor had asked what was eating at me that made me so sick. Then I told him how much I loved my country and how much I was hurting for its cruel destiny. I told him also how much I desired to be back there, but for this he had no sympathy.

"You have to forget that you will ever return there! You are living here now," he said harshly.

"But then there is no point to continue living!" I answered, full of pain.

"You'll live!" he said just as harshly while writing out a prescription.

## To Exmouth

I left the next Monday morning. Mother and Ed came to see me off at the station, pretending to be happy and cheerful to make me feel good, but I knew that Ed would be sad when he could not see me. But I knew, too, that he fully understood my need to go away to get better. We waved to each other until the train went into a tunnel. I closed the window and leaned back in the corner of my seat. Outside the window were fields and meadows, trees and houses, but we moved past them all. I relaxed, letting my body melt with the rhythmical swaying of the train, closing my mind to everything.

The journey was long, because I had to cross almost half of the country, going from the Midlands to the southwest corner of England. When I got to the small seaside town of Exmouth, it was already afternoon. A taxi took me to the St. Luke's convalescence home, which stood on the corner of a street facing the sea. The sky was gray, and heavy clouds raced across it, making the sea, too, look gray and dull.

The room where I would stay was on the second floor. It was a large long room, very much like the one we had had at the Salvation Army. Here too, the whole end wall was of large windows. I was glad about that, for I could view the sea even from my bed. There were five other girls sharing this room with me.

Night came, but I lay there for a long time not being able to go to sleep, listening to the sea. I was not used to the sounds it made, but perhaps this was the therapeutic part of being by the sea. The listening to the repeated sounds, prevented me from thinking deeper thoughts, and it finally rocked me into sleep. Maybe that was why the British believed so strongly that one had to go to the sea to really relax and recover.

During the following days, I learned to know my roommates and the order of things at this place. It seemed to be some kind of a church-affiliated establishment, but I never inquired about it. Together with my roommates, I went for walks, but sometimes I went alone. I spent a lot of time at the seaside. Often I went out even when the weather was bad and sat in one of the glass-covered shelters along the promenade facing the sea. As I kept watching the waves, they seemed to pick up my thoughts and carry them high above the raging waters, then laying them down to flow with the foaming mass to the shore, before crashing against it, breaking up in a million pieces, then dispersing, sliding in shallow washes over the hard sands and then ebbing back to the sea. And the ebbing water took my thoughts back into the sea, and they were no more. The beach was left hard and clean.

Somehow this watching of the waves, as they came and swelled, burst and returned, their constant repeating of this action, gave peace. I understood now why they sent me so far to be at the sea.

In the late afternoons, I usually sat at the seaside writing letters to Mother and to Ed. I talked with him in my thoughts and in between looked out into the distance where the clouds hovered above the horizon and the sun slowly sank into the blue veils of mist, finally disappearing over the quiet waters. A couple of fishing boats floated in the bay, then one after another returned to the harbor. So also my thoughts always returned to Ed and to both of us, but I did not try to go any deeper, for then my chest got heavy again. That was how I spent my days here. I just let things happen around me without being involved. Every morning I had a letter from Ed, full of encouragement and tenderness, and they helped me to get through these days.

The early afternoons and nights, when we had to sleep, were the hardest for me. All was quiet and I could not do anything to fill this time. My thoughts milled around without being able to really touch anything. I tried to sleep and not to think, but all kinds of crazy images seemed to gather around me in an ever-closer circle, going round and round. Then one night I had the shakes again, and my heart raced, making me weak. I tried to relax and lay quietly, but it was getting worse. I almost wanted to go and look for some help, but the house was all dark and silent, and I was reluctant to wake anybody and cause a disturbance.

I sat up in my bed and looked out to the sea, where a small light in

the distance lit up and disappeared. It was guiding the ships in the dark of the night, and I prayed that it would show me as well where I needed to go and how I should live, so as not to cause pain to myself and others. I sat like that for a long time listening to the sea and gradually calmed down. A wind had risen and moved the curtains. I lay down and my savior, sleep, at last took me to never-never land.

I walked along the sea a lot. When the sun came out, it was so beautiful, but I did not know how to really rejoice like I used to. A hand of sadness touched everything. If I could only feel joy again, be enthused about something and warm my soul somehow! But a strange sad emptiness was in me like a dark hole that no sunshine or beauty could penetrate.

I struggled to get out of this emptiness, trying to turn my thoughts to the times when I had felt strong and fearless and happy. To be good... What was good? Perhaps I wanted too many answers, the same as Ed, when he asked me questions I could not answer. Maybe I had to relax and wait until time itself would tell.

Often I felt like a boat without a rudder. It was not enough to have a compass if you did not have a rudder to steer with. Sometimes, if you were lucky, the winds would turn and take you to a coast where you could get a new rudder. Then you could go out again and forget all that had been. Perhaps it will be so with me?

If only I would know what it was that was lacking in me! Maybe hope most of all. I, who had always tried to encourage others to have hope and trust, now had lost it myself. Even from God, my greatest hope and source of light, I felt far away, separated and forgotten. I knew that it was not so and yet there was something standing between us. What had I done that had caused this? There was doubt and uncertainty, yet I believed strongly that I would regain it all: the faith, hope and love and yes, harmony within myself.

Days passed, and indeed, I began to feel better. I started to see what was around me and even to be glad about what I saw. Perhaps it was because the weather had turned warmer. The sun was so bright, and the sea expanded to the horizon as blue as the sky, so it was hard to tell, where they came together. White clouds, looking like white sails, drifting across the sky far away above the horizon, seemed to invite me to travel along with them.

My roommates and I went down to the beach and took off our shoes. The sand had not warmed enough yet and felt cool under our feet, but it was nice to feel it sift through our toes. We walked against the sun, and only a couple of feet from us the water washed up over the sand, carrying white fluffy foam edgings, playing around and then flowing back to the sea. A fresh breeze blew through our hair, flapping it around and bringing new life into our bodies.

Gradually I got to know my roommates better. Each morning we went for a long walk on the beach, sometimes even to the high bluff at the other end of the bay. On our way back, it became our regular routine to stop at the small cafe at the edge of the beach. We sat around the table drinking coffee and eating crisp meringue cakes, filled with whipped cream. There were jokes and laughter. I didn't always think they were so funny, but I laughed along with the others, letting myself drift with the happy mood. While talking, bits and pieces came out about people's lives, and it was interesting to listen and to imagine how my new friends lived.

There was Doris, a young woman with crinkly, fair hair and a round face covered with freckles. Her looks were natural like a country girl's. She did not have much to say of her own, nor had much of a personality. Perhaps it had been suppressed, because anything she said apparently was what her husband Denis had said, had wanted or didn't want. At times it even seemed that she was scared of this Denis. She was ready to do anything, only so that Denis would feel that he was the boss.

They had been married for two years but lived with his parents in their household, because they could not afford to buy a house of their own.

"I would like to have a baby," Doris told us, "but it has not happened yet. My mother-in-law is the boss around the house, always checking everything and watching my every step. My family lives in another part of England, but I have not seen them since the wedding. Denis doesn't like to travel, and I am not allowed to go alone."

Poor Doris! No wonder she was here.

Lucy was a bit older, maybe a little over thirty, with dark hair, a narrow face and large light blue eyes. Her loud laughter often filled the room. She laughed so easily about anything, often adding some funny saying and then being the first to break out in hearty laughter, which caused us to laugh with her. Lucy's voice was low and husky, perhaps because she smoked, but around her eyes and mouth were a lot of small laughter lines. She did not talk much about herself, but I guessed that her life had not been quite as easy as her laughter might make you think. If she heard of anyone's hardship, her face and eyes were full of great compassion. Yet, she did not linger on sad things, but soon found something to laugh about again. We were glad to have Lucy, who kept us on a lighter note, and I sensed that she had a lot of hidden wisdom.

My eyes slid over the other faces as we sat around the table and stopped at Vera. She must have come from a higher class in society than the rest of us. Thin-boned and rather tall with a fur jacket around her slim shoulders, she sat right opposite me, her eyes following Lucy's story. Her light brown hair framed her thin, fine-boned face, and even her

fingers were thin and fine. A wedding ring and an engagement ring were on her finger, but the last one almost covered the first. She was divorced, that was the only thing we knew. Had it been now or earlier, she did not say. She could have been around forty, but her face was still nice and attractive. For the most part she only listened and smiled quietly, only occasionally making some comment. I liked Vera.

The other two were young girls about eighteen or nineteen. Jenny was a pretty girl with a pale face and large brown eyes. One could even say that she was beautiful with her blond, drawn back hair and full lips. She cared about her face a lot, spending a long time each morning painting her eyebrows and lashes. Jenny was a pleasant girl but still only a child, even though she was engaged and showed her ring to everybody. It seemed that her life was an empty book, for she did not talk about anything else but her boyfriend.

There were many such girls in England, usually from the lower class, who left school as early as they could, then worked for a little time in some office or a factory, intensively painting their faces but even more intensively looking for a husband. When they found someone pleasing and willing, he was soon roped into buying a ring. That was the first great victory, with which to shine in front of their friends, causing them to be envious and hunt for their own victims with more enthusiasm. It seemed that love was not the most important factor, getting married was. Then sooner or later the wedding followed, with bridesmaids, photographers and the rest of the pomp. The bread winner had been secured.

Now they could take a breather. They did not have to paint the face anymore, and after a little while, when a child was born, it did not seem necessary to take the rollers out of the hair even in the daytime. The only thing to remember was that on Friday night, when the husband would bring home his pay packet, to take it and put it in a safe place. Perhaps she would be gracious and give him back a few shillings for his needs. Then in the evening they would both go to the nearest pub for a "pint" and a chat with the neighbors. The baby may sit outside the door in his pram chewing a potato chip, and everybody would be happy. Sometimes more young mothers, with their babies in prams, would stand outside the pub's door sipping their beer and doing their visiting, while their husbands visited with other men inside. Yes, there could be all kinds of living.

I don't want to say that this characterization would pertain to everybody, but on the average, as I saw it then, this was how the common people lived, and in their view it was perfectly all right. Maybe Jenny was not in this category, and I hoped she would be happy. After all, perhaps it was easier to live and to be happy if one knew less and deliberated less. She did not seem to ask much of life, nor question it.

Alma was a real working class girl. And yes, there was quite a distinct class system in England in those days. She appeared to have grown up pretty much on her own and had probably learned of the realities of life early.

"My parents own a Fish and Chips shop in a suburb, where the factory workers live." She told us.

I could well imagine that. The terrace houses lining the streets, next to the uneven pavements; the gutters scattered with papers and cigarette butts. Everything in these factory areas is soot-covered, and on every other corner there is a pub with a Fish and Chips shop next door. I could picture it so well, because there were a lot of these areas all around Birmingham.

People gathered there especially on Friday nights to celebrate the end of the work week and to have some fun. They lingered in the warm fish place, which smelled of hot oil and fat, while the chips sizzled in the large cooking vessels and in another swam golden pieces of fish. I thought that this was the most popular food in England.

Still, to run these shops took a lot of work, and very often the whole family had to take part in doing it. That had been Alma's case too, but living mostly on fish and chips had messed up her stomach, so now she was here.

She was the only one, whom I did not like much, with her spiky colored hair and her lax manners. When we walked along the street, she reminded me of a cat. Her eyes were greenish too, and they roamed about all the time under half-closed lids as if searching for something. When she spotted a young man coming toward us on the street, she whispered something to Jenny and then laughed loudly, swaying her body like a snake, perhaps to draw the man's attention to her, her eyes keeping him captive. I found that so repulsive, that if possible, I stayed behind the group. I was ashamed of such behavior, but then, perhaps she did not know any better. I could just say to myself, poor girl!

I also got to know Anna, an Austrian girl. She did not live in our room, but we found common ground right away, both coming from a different background than England. Anna was going through a divorce and suffering terribly. It was hard for her to talk about it, and she experienced severe gastric pains. Sometimes we sat in the lounge chairs in front of the house, talking about Germany and the war, and she told me about that period in Austria. She was a nice, serious girl and I liked her a lot.

One evening she came down to the lounge with her zither and played and sang some of her Austrian folk songs. The zither was so much like our Latvian folk instrument kokle and gave a similar sound, except the zither had more strings. It was all so beautiful, but made me think of my home country and brought tears to my eyes.

The days seemed to pass faster and faster. Perhaps it was because I spent more time with others. It did me good, because I did not have much time to dig into my thoughts. My face had become brown, being in the sun and wind so much, and I had even learned to laugh and be cheerful. I loved the sea breezes; they filled me with new vigor, and I let them play around me on my walks. I had thought that maybe I would get home after two weeks, but the doctor and the head of the establishment had decided that I needed another week, as had been initially scheduled. And indeed, the third week helped me to get stronger and more stable.

The last day before leaving came. The weather had turned cooler and grayer. Low clouds dragged across the sky, pulling white veils of rain behind them, which swept the land and dipped into the unruly waters of the sea.

Later the rain stopped and we went on our last walk along the sea. The sky was still gray, but the clouds had lifted a bit higher. A strong wind blew, and I could feel its saltiness on my lips. It flipped my hair around my face, yet I turned deliberately against the wind and delighted in its strength. We walked as far as the other end of the bay, where the waves crashed against the high bluff furiously, splashing over the railings and even onto the street. We stood watching the wild play of the sea, a sight you could not get tired of watching, but heavy raindrops began to fall, and we had to hurry home.

I was on my way home again, and fields and hills ran past the window of the train. The sun shone and the sky was blue, but big white clouds roamed around, covering and uncovering its brightness. I sat in the corner by the window, warmed by the sun, but there was a thought that warmed me also. I was going home! The only one in the compartment, sitting opposite me, was a man reading a newspaper. I listened to the rhythmical sound of the wheels on the tracks and let myself be swayed along through time.

The scenery outside was changing. More and more hills appeared in the vicinity. They were such strange hills—round with bald tops, and I wondered why. The slopes and foothills were overgrown with shrubs and trees, but their tops were bare with no vegetation. There was something very sad about their appearance, I thought. The sun shed its light over them, yet it could not warm them enough. Was it not so with me also? I felt very much like those bare hill tops. No flowers or trees or even shrubs wanted to grow there. It was so with our human lives also. People, too, would rather live in the valleys. Life was easier and more comfortable there. Climbing hills took effort. Some strove a bit higher, but very few wanted to go to the top. As I looked at the hills, it dawned on me that something similar was happening with me. I had wanted to climb my

hill, but had to change my mind. Perhaps reaching up too high was not good. Others would not want to follow you there, leaving you lonely. A silvery mist covered my eyes. They were two big, hot tears.

Oh, no! I surely was not going to start crying! I was going home! I thought of who was waiting for me there, and right away everything seemed better.

"Faster, faster!" I wanted to urge the train. It whistled as if it had heard my command and took on a more cheerful sound.

And then I was in Birmingham, and loving arms greeted and held me.

The time had arrived for the first Latvian Song Festival in London. It was June 18, 1949. The members of our Birmingham choir gathered at the station the day before, all in high spirits. There were about a dozen of us, and it was a cheerful crowd. My whole family was going, and Ed also had made last minute arrangements at work to come.

London received us with its noise and crowds of people. The taxis sounded their horns, the big two-story buses slowly moved through the crowded streets. There were lights and billboards, everybody was rushing somewhere, and the air was filled with the smell of car exhaust.

The place where we would stay was ten levels deep under London. It was in a bomb shelter left over from wartime, for none of us had money to pay for hotels. When we got down there, using a special lift, our voices resounded strangely in these long, wide concrete tunnels with the low ceilings. On each side of them was a row of bunks. It made you wonder how the people felt who came here when the bombs were falling above the ground, and the buildings collapsed and burned. It must have been terrible, but when we saw the bombed sites in London, there was no comparison with the destruction of the German cities. There were fewer buildings standing in Germany than had been bombed in London. We, however, did not have time to think of that now. We had to rush to a rehearsal.

The concert took place at the Kingsway Hall in Holborn, a region of London. Our choir members, all dressed in our national costumes on this festive day, came out of the subway station on to the street, where people looked at us with curiosity. Being in high spirits, we did not mind. On this day London belonged to the Latvians! When we got to the hall, in the streets around it, only the Latvian language was heard. It was wonderful, for this was the first time that so many of us had come together in this country. When we lived in the refugee camps in Germany, all squashed together, sometimes we were tired of each other, but now, since we were dispersed all over the country, each Latvian face was dear to us, as well as each word, heard in the Latvian tongue.

The huge hall was filling. Excitement and expectation was in every face. When we stood on the stage, singing the beloved songs about Latvia and the freedom it had enjoyed, I felt goose bumps all over my body. The words took on their meaning as they had never done before. There was so much emotion that I could hardly keep from crying. This was the day and the time when we proclaimed anew that we were Latvians.

It was getting hot, standing on the stage in such close proximity, and we women, in our heavy woolen national costumes! We had been on our feet for quite a long time, listening to the lengthy opening speech of our ambassador and also waiting while the men's choir sang. There was no seating for us and I began to feel lightheaded. I had to use all my willpower to keep from fainting.

Then we sang the last song, *The Cantata*. The esteemed musician Alberts Jērums was directing this song and he was wonderful at his job. Even the smallest movement of his fingers received the right response from the singers and his face expressed the story of what we were singing about.

The organ played softly, leading into the solo part of the soprano. A well-known soloist, Ludmilla Sepe, started *"The Prayer"* in her beautiful voice, *"Dievs, Tevi lūdzam, ak Dievs jel klausi… Ar savu visspēcīgo roku novērsi Tēvijai ļaunu…"*

"Lord, we humbly pray, Lord, hear our plea; with your all-powerful arm remove the evil from our country…"

The words of the prayer floated up to the vaulted ceiling so clear and full of heartfelt faith and trust. I did not think that there was a heart that was not silently praying with her. One great prayer rose from this gathering of people, one heart and soul of a hurting nation.

The prayer ended and the choir resumed in jubilation, their hearts full of new faith and hope.

*"Tev, dārgā tēvija, tev dziesmas lai spēcīgi skan! Lai skan! Lai skan! Tev, dārgā tēvija…"*

(For you, dear fatherland, may our song joyfully sound! Let it sound! Let it sound!")

Then it was all over, and people streamed out of the half light of the hall into the sunny streets of London.

Late in the evening, after we had returned to our underground "hotel", we were still so full of today's excitement that nobody wanted to go to sleep. We sat around a table at the one end of the tunnel drinking black coffee out of thick mugs, discussing the day's events. But then somebody began to hum a tune, others added the words, and before long we were all singing again, for the Latvians loved to do their talking in song. They had done it for centuries; it was part of their living. More and more songs followed, many sung in harmony with joy in our hearts. They rose up to

the low ceiling and then disappeared in the emptiness of the long tunnel, which had never heard songs like this. It was almost morning when we finally ended the singing and lay down on the thin, naked bedding to get some rest.

Our traditional Midsummer Fest was just a week later. June 23 is the *Līgo Night* and June 24 is John's Day. It was the age-old celebration by the Latvian people of the summer solstice, supposed to be celebrated with bonfires, singing and dancing. Our circumstances had changed drastically, but even though it was not the same, wherever Latvians lived, they tried to remember this festivity in some way. Saša, Mother's new boyfriend, had invited us to the celebration at the house where he lived. It was in the Birmingham suburbs in another part of town. Saša had been an army officer like my Dad, but now he was a cobbler. As a matter of fact, that house was full of cobblers.

This enterprise had been started back in Germany, in Luebeck. I don't know who had put this crew together, but they were all mostly former soldiers, released after World War II. It could have been a member of the British army who had seen a potential here for a future business. The Latvian men had been trained in making special orthopedic footwear in Germany and later, as a group, brought to Birmingham. The owner had even provided this big, old house with rooms to rent for them, so they could still be together, and it had worked very well.

The house was in an area that looked like it was left over from grander times of living. The huge houses stood amidst large trees in their gardens, separated by high walls, all neglected and uncared for. Perhaps the present owners could not afford to keep them up, and time did its work, eating up the woodwork. The big gardens were left to overgrow with thistles and weeds.

However, for people who had lived in the cramped refugee camps, this was good enough and even luxurious, for lodgings were hard to come by. The men had done the most necessary repairs on the house and had cleaned up the part of the garden closest to the house. They had even made a volleyball court for recreation and dug up a small vegetable patch in the back of the house, yet there was still more land left further down with a pond and some large fir trees. That part was covered with nettles and blackberry bushes, which nobody wanted to touch.

The men had also fixed up a bonfire for later this evening, when we would celebrate our traditional *"Līgo"* fest after it got dark outside. Somehow I could not quite get into the spirit, even though this had been my favorite festival in Latvia, because the proper *Līgo* night had been two days before. This was not a celebration you could move; it had to be on the proper date. Instead, I had to think of how we used to celebrate it

back home, and it made me sad that it was all gone. We did go outside for a while and sang the old *Līgo* songs at the bonfire, but I did not feel much like singing.

In the house, tables had been set with food and drink in one of the large downstairs rooms, and a little later, one of the men came downstairs with his accordion. Now we could also dance, and the atmosphere was cheerful. The large glass door was open to the garden, and the scents of the summer night flowed inside, mixing with the smoke of the cigarettes (for everybody smoked in those days). I danced a lot, for there were only a few of us women here tonight, so I danced with everybody—but mostly with Ed.

When we relaxed from dancing, the accordionist started to softly play some nostalgic tunes from the wartime. These men, who had been through the fires of war, still had it in their blood. They had wanted to protect their country but had lost. The sadness and the bitterness were still with them. That was probably also the reason why they sometimes tried to console themselves with drink. Occasionally there was too much drink.

"...good bye, good bye, my white birch grove..." another sad song started and it touched my heart right away. I knew that song so well. The young men had sung it in Rīga as they marched, leaving for war. I did not want to dance anymore and went to sit down in the big armchair in the corner. Scattered and wilting, on the floor lay the grasses and wild flowers—our *Līgo* night's blessings. Nobody danced anymore. The cool of the graying morning streamed into the room through the open door.

"...and do not cry if I don't return... so many stayed in the killing fields..." somebody picked up the words of the song and others joined. But my eyes filled with tears. My Dad did not return and many others as well... It was suddenly cold. One of the men brought me a glass of wine trying to pacify me, but I just shook my head. He tried to coax me, but then Ed came up, sat down on the other arm of my chair and said quite cockily, "I shall take care of my girl myself!"

"I am already taking care of her!" said the other man who had brought me the wine.

They continued to banter, jokingly fighting over me, and I just let them be. Both had been drinking some, as had everybody here tonight.

But suddenly I had enough of it. I was tired and wanted to sleep. Upstairs was a room with several beds, which had been prepared for the visitors who would want to rest. I lay down on one of the beds without undressing and pulled the blanket over me. Only now did I realize how very tired I was. Ed soon came up, too, as well as a few others. He lay down beside me and crept under the blanket. His hand was hot as it touched my body, but I pushed it away. I felt as cold as the gray morning

light coming through the windows. I kept pushing his hand away again and again. We struggled like that for a bit, then at last I felt him drifting into sleep.

I lay there with open eyes and watched the morning light in the window become lighter and lighter. The birds awoke and began to chatter and sing. The first reddish reflection of sunshine touched the ceiling. I must have drifted into sleep at last, but soon the others started to get up to go to breakfast downstairs, so I got up also.

It looked like Mother and Saša had stayed up to watch the sun rise, as the old tradition required. When I saw them, they both looked happy and cheerful. Perhaps they had found their own magic blossom this night. I did not feel so good, and my head ached even though I had not had much to drink. I wanted to go home and was happy to get into my own bed and go to sleep.

Ed worked days again and came to see me one evening. The summer evening was so nice and mellow that we did not want to stay indoors even though it was already dusk. We walked to the nearby park, where the quiet chatter of the birds came from the big trees, but soon there was silence. We sat down in the grass, still warm from the sunny day, although the evening's moistness was already in the air.

We had not talked about ourselves for quite a long time. Ed had not pressured me anymore about how I felt toward him, but I thought that the letters we had exchanged while I was away had brought us closer together, even if nothing was said in so many words. I knew that he had not done it because of my illness and also because he had seen how it upset me. I could not be pushed, he understood that now. Mother, too, had explained it to him on that night, when he had brought the roses and I was not there. Years later I found a letter she had written to Ed after that dreadful incident at the college. Actually, it was a short story she had written about a fairy with a crystal heart that would break if not handled with care. I had tears in my eyes when I read it. It was so amazing that despite our rather aloof relationship, Mother had understood and described my inner being so well.

I was grateful to Ed for not questioning me, because right now, more than anything, I wanted to retain my peace and my health. I also knew that he had become very dear to me. I wished that I could share that with him, but I was not used to sharing my feelings. For years I had not had anybody close to share them with and the words just would not come. I sat plucking at the grass and did not say anything.

"Try to talk to me," Ed said in a quiet voice. It will be easier for both of us," he urged me gently.

"I can't. I don't know how..." I got up to my feet, already getting

disturbed.

"Well try, I will help you if need be."

"I can't. I just can't!"

We started to walk, and then I began to think how many times in the past things had gone wrong in my relationships, because I had been too afraid to show my feelings, or had not said what I thought and felt. I started to talk, very hesitantly at first and with long silences, but then gradually it got easier. I told about the hard days of leaving home, about the sorrow I still was not able to put aside. I told about Dad, and very hesitantly, also about Ilmār, my first love, whom I lost to the war. I talked about the refugee days when I often felt as if I was frozen in ice and that everything within me was dead. I also shared with him my joy of creating and my hopes of achieving something in the field of art. But you cannot do anything with an ailing heart. You have to free it to start a new life. And I did want a new life! I did! But I needed more time, so I could go to meet it full-heartedly.

"Don't ask me anything more now," I said, "I will tell you myself when the right time comes, and perhaps it will not be too long till then."

Darkness was around us, and I could barely see Ed's face anymore. He had been silent all this time listening quietly, only occasionally asking a question.

"Thank you for telling me all that," he said taking both my hands, his voice full of warmth. "You see, it was not so hard after all."

"You know, it really helped," I cheerfully acknowledged.

"See? Now you will have to promise that from now on you will tell me all that depresses you and then we will be good friends."

"I promise," I said half-jokingly, and he pulled me to him and kissed me lightly. We walked home, both unburdened. A new moon was climbing up above the rooftops and one after another the stars came out.

When I got back to our room, I had a surprise! We had a visitor - my art teacher Mr. Eggison from the college! That was really something unexpected.

"I was worried about what had happened to you, when you were not at the classes for such a long time. I thought I should come and find out," he said.

I liked Mr. Eggison and had compassion for him, for he was an old man and seemed to be rather lonely. He loved to chat, and sometimes during the class I even felt a bit uncomfortable, when he lingered with me longer, because some other students might have wanted his help. Still, there was nothing I could do about that. He had told me a few things about himself. I knew that he lived alone with his very old father who treated him badly, because of some old family misunderstanding, even

though he looked after him and provided for all his needs. The father also had not wanted him to become an artist. Finishing our talks, Mr. Eggison always asked about Mother, my brother and the work at the hospital, for he knew of my situation here.

I did not know how to react to this situation, because it was so unexpected. He and Mother seemed to be in some deep conversation, for Mother liked to talk as well. When I came in, we greeted each other, exchanged a few words, but then they went back to their subject. I sat there but was not even aware of what they were talking about as they did it in low voices. I had my own thoughts after talking with Ed. Hour after hour passed.

Mother made some tea, but even so, we began to fight sleepiness. The old gentleman, however, did not sense any of that. He sat with his head bent, deep in his story, staring at the table. Perhaps he was happy that he had someone to talk to, and we did not want to interrupt him. He really must have been very lonely. Finally he did get up to go, but it was already one o'clock, and we had a workday waiting for us.

The next morning our landlord Sher gave us a notice.

"You have too many and too late visitors" he said. He added that he was expecting more family from India and that he would need all the rooms. This last statement could be true or not. I thought it was just added on so as to soften the blow.

The main reason was probably that Ed was coming so often now and at different times. Perhaps Sher also wondered what was "going on", since he must have been the one who came to the door, when I was sick and saw us both in bed. Then there was the late and lengthy visit of my professor last night, which we could not prevent without, perhaps, offending the old gentleman. It must have clinched his decision to give us notice.

It was too bad that we had come to this, but nothing was "going on". It had not even entered my mind that anything could "go on"! We were not in such a relationship. Now we were "on the wheels" again, as we had come to name another move. We were very concerned, because we knew how difficult it was to find a place for the three of us. Johnny was still too young to live by himself, and his wages were not enough to sustain him, nor were Mother's and mine. Our wages were low, so we could not afford to pay very much.

We tried asking around in our neighborhood if there was a room anywhere to rent, but again we got the same answer as before,

"There are too many of you!"

We went from one place to another asking, explaining, begging, but no results. A week had passed, but we had not found anything. Our hearts were heavy. It was Sunday and Ed came over. He knew of our

problem and was concerned, too. Lately he had also thought of leaving the hospital, for the pay was so small for the training nurses, and the hours were long and irregular. He was not afraid of working hard, and was willing to do anything to earn more, and to have more time to be with me. That, however, was not so simple.

It was a warm day in July when Ed and I set out for another expedition in search for new lodgings. We went into the local store to ask if they knew of anything, but they just shook their heads. There were so many people in this area from India and from Ireland. They bought the large houses and then filled them with their relatives until they almost burst. No, we did not have much hope of finding anything here, but we kept going along the street slowly, evaluating each house as to whether it would be worthwhile going in and asking. If we saw a window without curtains, we thought perhaps no one was living there and went inside to inquire, but the answer was as before,

"Sorry, we have nothing!"

After dealing with this for a little while, we lost our fear and shame. We had to find something and started to knock on each and every house on the street. Our level of hope was very low by the time we got to the last house before the crossroads. This red brick house was even larger than the others. We stood at the big front door and had already knocked several times, but everything was quiet and nobody came. As we turned to leave, a youngish man came out of the gate with pruning shears in his hand.

"What do you want?" he asked us kindly.

"We need to rent some rooms," but he too, shook his head saying that he did not have anything. But then he remembered something,

"Wait a minute! My mother owns the house on the corner across the street, and she rents rooms! She does not live there herself but has a family there who takes care of the rentals. Why don't you go there and inquire?" He urged us on.

"Well thank you! Thank you very much!" I said.

"Actually, I think that somebody just moved out of there. Go and talk to Kathleen," he said, "She is in charge of things over there."

We thanked him again and could not get across the street fast enough. And indeed, there were two good sized rooms for rent! One, the living room, was on the ground floor—the right hand corner of the house—with two windows, each facing a different street. The other room was upstairs, facing the back garden on the east side. However, we would first have to speak to the landlady herself. Kathleen called her up, and she was willing to see us at five that afternoon. We took down the address, thanked Kathleen and hurried home with the good news. The rent was three pounds a month, higher than we had projected, but we would

have to manage somehow.

We rushed home with the good news to share them with Mother, and I went downstairs to make some coffee to celebrate this, but when I came back with a tray in my hands and stopped at the door, I heard Mother saying, "...then it will work out good. You and Johnny will be able to sleep upstairs and Zigi and I will sleep downstairs..."

I went inside and looked from one to another.

"What was that?" I asked. "Is Ed going to live with us also?" It had never crossed my mind that it could be so, and felt unpleasantly surprised that I was put in such a position. But Mother had it all very clear. In her mind it was all worked out already.

"Well, you both want to be together and then you won't have to go anywhere. And anyway, sooner or later you will want to get married..."

Even that had been decided without asking me. I stood there dumb-founded. When had all that been discussed? And without me? Every-thing in me was rising against it. I felt as if I had been put in a cage. I had wanted to tell Ed myself, when my time had come, not like this... It looked, however, that everything had already been decided, and I did not want to say anything to cause unpleasantness or to create new problems.

"Ed will go and look for another job tomorrow. Then toward the end of the week we could move perhaps," Mother added.

I was still confused. Perhaps Mother could see more clearly what I could not see yet? Maybe her decision was good, but maybe not. Mother was a practical woman, and this kind of arrangement certainly would be practical, but there was so much more to it. It was my whole life! How could she make such a decision so lightly?

I also did not know how much Ed had been involved in this decision-making. We had never talked of marriage, and I had not even thought about it. I was not sure if I would even want it, because Ed was some-times so unpredictable. Anger was rising within me toward Mother that she had put me in this position without talking with me and without get-ting my permission. Perhaps she had suspected that I might not like this arrangement and would raise opposition. Then it would all fall apart. But we still had to see the landlady; only then we would know what would happen.

The landlady, Mrs. Floyd, lived in a large red brick house on Bris-tol Road. This was an area where rich people lived in their big houses, hidden in the gardens with high brick walls. Still, as we walked along the graveled driveway under the big trees to her house, everything looked so forlorn and sad. There were no flowers anywhere, only the bare tree trunks stretching up high above the roof, keeping everything in shade.

When we were let into the entrance hall, it was dark, and I could smell the cool mustiness of an old house. We were led into a large room, where an elderly woman rested on a couch, supported by pillows. A fire burned in the fireplace even though it was summertime, but it made the room warmer and more pleasant. Mrs. Floyd was perhaps in her sixties, a small thin woman with grayish hair and a pale face. She greeted us, talking with difficulty, and invited us to sit down.

"Please excuse me if I don't get up," she said. "I have asthma rather bad. I do have a daughter living next door and she comes and looks after me."

In a few minutes the daughter did come in and brought us some tea, as is the British custom. I let my eyes roam around the large room, noting the somewhat faded rug and the decorated ceiling. The old furniture and even a concert piano at the other end of the room were nice, but everything was covered or piled up with things that were faded or dusty. Poor lady! No wonder she had asthma, living in an environment like this! Here she was, in the big house, alone and probably lonely. When she talked, I sensed that she had probably come from the so called "common people" or a bit better, but had come into money by marriage or some business deal, and now had the big house and all the stuff. But what did it help her… and yet she was kind to us.

We drank the strong tea, chatted and then Mrs. Floyd wanted to know something about us. Mother told her about the war and the refugee days and that now we worked at the hospital. Mrs. Floyd looked satisfied with what she had heard, and as we parted, she said that we could have the rooms. In addition, she even lowered the rent to two and half pounds, considering our situation. We were very grateful to her for that, and as we parted she said,

"I wish you to be happy in my house." Perhaps she felt some joy having helped people like us. But we hurried home, filled with joy that we would have a home again and even a more comfortable one than before.

## To Varna Road

In a week's time we were settling into our new residence at 40 Varna Road in Balsall Heath. It was a white, two-story corner house with a narrow strip of a garden around it and a low white fence separating the house from the street. In the back of the house was another much larger garden, secluded by a high brick wall. Some vines and shrubs climbed up the walls, and several fruit trees grew near the edges. The back garden was quite large and was divided into two parts. The smaller area, directly behind the house, was sectioned off from the bigger garden by wooden fencing that was overgrown with small, white climbing roses. It

looked so pretty! An archway in the wall of roses led into the larger part of the back garden.

Grass covered the area near the back of the house, and clotheslines where stretched across it, where the tenants could dry their washed clothing. Mother was very happy to see the untended vegetable patch in the middle of the larger part of the back garden and right away asked Kathleen if she could use some part of it, because she loved growing things. She was allowed to use half of it and could not wait to start digging. We younger people figured that the far corner of the garden under the apple tree would be a great place for sunbathing. Seeing all this, we were delighted with our new home.

Ed arrived, too, and told us that he had found a job at the Gas Works distributing the meters. The pay was not very much, but it would do for starters. When most of the work was done and things were tidied away, we sat down to a belated dinner.

I felt so strange, seeing Ed sitting with us at the table in the living room, knowing that he would be staying here and be here every day. He had just bathed, his hair was still wet and combed smoothly, and a fresh smell of soap came from him. He wore a light blue, short-sleeved T-shirt, which showed his brown muscular arms. Ed had done a lot of sports and basketball playing in the past and his body was strong like an athlete's.

His being here made me feel like a young wife, seeing her new husband in a home situation for the first time. Only I was not a young wife and felt that I had been put into a situation where I should not really be.

After we finished the dinner, I put the dishes on a tray and carried them along the lengthy hallway to our kitchen at the very back of the house. Actually, it was just a small nook at the end of the hallway, just inside the back door, which led out to the garden. There was an old gas cooker and a boiler for doing laundry next to it. At the end wall, there were cabinets above and below a narrow counter, and two sinks were by the window for doing washing. The room left between the cooker and the sinks was barely enough for someone to turn around, and we had to share this kitchen with two other tenants. One was a young Irish family with a baby girl, who lived in a room next to ours on the ground floor, but we did not see them often. The other tenant was an elderly Irishman, living in a room with a door right opposite the small kitchen area. We were not bothered by such triviality as sharing the cooking space with them. We each just cooked at different times and it worked fine.

I had already started to wash the dishes, when Ed came out too, a pipe in his hand. He turned his head aside, blew out a big puff, then put the pipe on the windowsill and picked up a dish towel.

"What are you doing?" I asked in surprise.

"I will help you. Then you will not have to be here alone so long

and we both shall be able to rest and relax," he said quietly and began to wipe.

I watched him work, and my eyes became moist with emotion. Nobody had ever cared for me that way, with such tenderness and understanding. Perhaps only Dad did that a long time ago, when I felt his caring ways touch me in a special way. Now I felt this touch again, and my heart flowed over with warmth and gratitude. Ed saw me being so moved and put his hand to my cheek.

"No... There's no need to..." he said quietly smiling.

I smiled back at him and we continued working in silence. As we finished, the last rays of sunshine touched the wall in our small kitchen. We hung up the towels and went back to the living room. Our new life at Varna Road had begun.

The upstairs room was arranged for Johnny and Ed. Actually, there was not much to arrange. There was our large bed; the wardrobe and a chest of drawers were already there. Both men had only a minimum of belongings, so that made it simple. All the living and eating would happen in our living room downstairs, which was comfortable and even cozy. At the one end of the room was a gas fireplace, in the middle a table with chairs. On the left, at the inside wall was an old convertible sofa where Mother and I would sleep. A long sideboard was in the outer corner between the two windows, where we kept our food and dishes. A wardrobe stood in the right-hand corner next to the door, and a faded grayish-blue, patterned rug covered most of the floor, except the edges. For us, this was a paradise!

In the alcove of the larger window, facing the side street, we put our big trunk and covered it with a dark gray blanket. There, on a white embroidered mat, in a place of honor, I put our little Christmas tree and both of our photographs facing it. Small shelving with some books stood in the alcove to the left of the fireplace, and on its right side we covered an orange crate on which to place our radio. Next to it, on the right hand side of the fireplace, was a big arm chair that became Ed's favorite place to sit, even though the springs were not too good anymore. We just put a pillow underneath and it was fine.

In the evenings, when the day's work was done, Ed sat there quietly smoking his pipe. I used to tease him at those times, saying that our personal chimney was smoking, but as I passed by, he would catch my hand and pull me down on his lap, putting the pipe away. I curled up against his wide chest and felt that this was the best place on earth. The warmth from his body flowed into mine, and I could hear his heart beating so close. He kissed me lightly, and while the dusk wrapped everything in its darkening veils, we dreamed our dreams of a future together, and our

love matured like a flower looking into the sun.

August had come, and everything would have been good, except that I could not sleep well. All kinds of nightmares bothered me as soon as I closed my eyes. Perhaps it was because we had had some sad happenings in the ward lately, and all that stayed with me. I was torn by thoughts—why was there so much suffering in the world? I saw people come into the ward, looking happy and healthy. It seemed that nothing much could be wrong with them, but then the same person had a surgery, and I saw him or her spend their last days there. It was so unbelievable, so senseless. Fear and despair walked at my side again.

"What is this life we are living?" I asked myself again, as I had done many times before, but in the night I dreamed of a black dog biting my hand. I felt his wet teeth around my fist. Frozen in fear, I waited for him to bite me. I wanted to flee, but could not move. I wanted to cry but couldn't because my chest ached from the heaviness of unshed tears. Again and again this dog returned and afterward I always felt sick and weak. I tried to forget and to ignore this, but now I even sensed its presence during the daytime. There he sat in his tussled coat and waited, his tongue hanging over the sturdy teeth. Then something happened that really struck me.

Usually I knew all the patients quite well. They were all kinds of people. Some made friends easily, since the ward was one large open room, where they could see each other. The curtains were drawn around each bed only if it was necessary—when a patient was having a treatment, an examination or after a surgery—also when they were very seriously ill. Some were more reserved, but I had a good relationship with them all, except sometimes I would get too attached to some person and that was not good.

Everybody in the ward knew Lucy. From her first day there she created a special aura around herself. Her big rounded body in the flowery robe, her bushy black hair and smiling face could be seen here and there at one bed or another. There she helped someone to get a book or a magazine out of the locker, there she helped someone to have a drink or said a few cheering words to someone who looked sad. She helped me to give out the drinks when I came with the trolley and helped to pick up the empties. Everybody loved Lucy.

"All right, all right! Auntie Lucy is coming," she would smilingly answer, if someone had a need, and soon everybody called her "auntie". In those days people stayed in the hospital longer than they do now. The day came, when all the tests on Lucy had been done, and she had the surgery the day after. She recovered from it and soon began to walk around, for the surgery had not been a heavy one.

But then one morning, as I came in, I saw the curtains pulled around Lucy's bed. At first I did not pay much attention to it, thinking that perhaps she was having a dressing changed. Later, as I went around with the drinks, I opened the curtain a bit and saw Lucy lying there with her face flushed red. She opened her eyes a little and tried to smile.

"A little temperature…" she said with red and chapped lips.

Dinnertime came, and we started to take the food around, when suddenly one of the nurses came and said something to Sister. They both hurried and disappeared behind Lucy's curtains. Soon the other nurses hurried back and forth as well. A call on the telephone. The doctor hurried in. An oxygen tank…

We were all silently concerned. One of the junior nurses took over the dishing out of dinners, and continued as if nothing had happened. That was the etiquette. No emotions, no excitement, so as not to alarm other patients. I carried the trays around automatically, all frozen inside, waiting. The other women ate their food silently, throwing fearful looks at the curtains where great activity was taking place. The Staff Nurse hurried back and forth with medications, injections and other things, then made another call on the phone.

The dinner was finished. I went around with my trolley collecting the dishes. I was almost at the other end of the ward, when I heard movement behind me. Looking back, I saw the doctor, the Sister and nurses coming out from behind the curtains and walking out of the ward. They did not talk or look at each other, and from their backs I could tell what had happened. Behind the curtains was silence. Auntie was gone.

I suddenly felt unsteady on my feet, and there was ringing in my ears. Black patches alternated with arrow-like flashes of light in front of my eyes, and I felt hot, so hot. I ran out onto the balcony, feeling dizzy and fell into a chair. I felt on the verge of fainting, when a couple of nurses ran out, too, and tried to help me by pressing my head down between my knees. The day was cool, and gradually the ringing in my ears stopped. I could see clearly again but was cold—so cold—and my limbs felt frozen without any strength. The Sister came out also and said, "I think that you need to go home, dear. I shall call the taxi." And I walked away with no other thought in my mind except that Lucy was gone. There was a life, and now it was not anymore.

A few days passed until I got myself together again. When I went to see my doctor, he told me, "After all that has happened, I have come to the conclusion that you are not suited for hospital work; you should leave it and look for something else. First, though, we have to get you on your feet again. I am writing out a sick leave for you and the hospital will make arrangements for you."

Since Mother also was due for a week's vacation, the hospital ar-

ranged for us both to go to Bournemouth on the southern coast of England. The following Saturday we got on our way.

Being August, this was the height of the season, and in Bournemouth people were everywhere, everybody looking cheerful and relaxed. It was holiday time, the highlight of the year! People milled around the vendor's stands and the game machines that stood near the pier and on the promenade alongside the beach. It seemed that money had been saved for this all year. And so it was! One had to buy joy and entertainment for any price, so there would be enough of it for the rest of the dreary days. At this time, people allowed themselves what they probably had denied themselves all the rest of the year. They lived in an elevated atmosphere, having left the burdens of everyday life miles behind them.

Bournemouth was a pleasant seaside resort town, built on the side of a high bluff with a lot of trees and even some palms. But that was not what many people looked for. It was the holidays! People flowed along the streets, milled around, looking at the souvenirs, and the little stores were full of them. It was really surprising, as if they had never had a chance to buy anything! They even suffered the pushing and shoving of the crowds gladly—for this was a holiday!

The souvenir and knick knack stores were the fullest, where everybody was trying to find some curious little thing to take home to a relative or friend, for such was the tradition. This gift shopping created almost an atmosphere of Christmas. People's eyes shone in delight, handling the various things and comparing prices. They looked happy and wanted to bring happiness to others. Or was it so? Perhaps it was just a special need to let themselves go for once without worrying about tomorrow.

Not all were shopping. They just seemed to like mixing with the crowd, perhaps wanting to feel part of these elated masses. We went out a few times, too, just for curiosity's sake, and it was interesting to watch the people and try to guess what it was all about.

Whenever the sun shone, the beach was full also, especially with families and children. The young people tried to get a suntan as quickly as possible, so they could parade before their friends when they got home. The older people did not get into the sand, although they had taken off their shoes. Instead, they sat in the lounge chairs at the side of the beach or on the benches along the promenade, watching the sea and everything that happened around them. The older men, their hats lowered over their faces, read newspapers. Others had pulled the papers even lower and snoozed under them, while the old ladies at their sides clicked their knitting needles as furiously as ever. The knitting in England was

so much a habit that they did not even have to look at it, their eyes flitting around and taking in everything that was happening.

The mornings were usually sunny and hot, but in the afternoons big blue clouds often appeared, covering the sky and suddenly it was quite cool. People quickly packed up then, leaving the beach almost deserted. Only some children still ran along the water's edge, and perhaps a couple of young people walked there locked in embrace, the whole world forgotten, leaving four imprints of their feet in the wet sand. But the sea swelled, the waves came bigger and higher, washing it all away. When the waters receded, it was as if no one had ever been there.

We used the beautiful weather, spending as much time as possible on the beach. It felt so good to lie there in the warm sand, watching the sea through half-closed eyelids, listening to the rhythmical sounds of its flowing and ebbing. I would look at the sky while letting sand sift slowly through my fingers. If only it were possible to let all the worries and sorrows sift through my fingers like that! But no, I did not want to think of that or anything, just feel the sun's healing warmth and savor this time of peace.

Except, when evening came, all kinds of needless thoughts and feelings invaded me again, and I sank into them like mire. I had to think about Lucy again, and perhaps it was not only about Lucy, but about all our dying... Sorrow surrounded me like the waters of the mire, and there was nothing to hold on to. I wanted to be home with Ed, to curl up in his lap and feel how peace came into me. Some strange feeling of safety flowed out of him and the unwelcome, weird thoughts did not have power over me anymore.

As the days passed, I began to feel better. We sunbathed, took walks and enjoyed the fresh sea air, but only half of me was there. The other half was at home with Ed. He wrote to me every day, letters full of love and encouragement, but we longed for each other's presence. We counted the days till we'd be together, and I knew now that my home would be wherever he would be. I was glad when the train was racing across the fields and meadows again—going north, taking us home!

I did not return to the hospital. As soon as I thought about it, something within me rose against it, and I knew that I had to follow the doctor's orders and look for a different kind of a job. I handed in the necessary forms at the Labor Exchange but knew that it might take time, and I wanted to use it to strengthen myself mentally and physically.

Ed worked at his new job distributing the gas meters, and if he happened to be anywhere close, he would stop by to have some tea or spend his lunch hour with me. He did it more and more often till it got to be a habit with us. Those were such pleasant times! The house was quiet. We

sat opposite each other at the table sipping our tea and listening to the radio softly playing the newest tunes.

"Again, this couldn't happen again..." somebody sang in a velvety voice, and we felt as if he was singing it only for us.

> "... this is just once in a lifetime,
> This is a thrill divine...
> What's more, this never happened before,
> though I have prayed for a lifetime
> that such as you would suddenly be mine,
> mine as I'm holding you now,
> and yet never so near...
> And though this couldn't happen again,
> we'll have this moment forever,
> but never, never again..."

This was our song, and when the song was finished, we both had tears in our eyes. We hugged and held each other, wanting to protect ourselves from anything coming between us. The only thing we wished for was that we could always stay together.

The summer was almost gone. It was a late Sunday afternoon when Ed and I came in from the garden after spending the last part of the day enjoying the sunshine. I suddenly remembered something and stopped on the path.

"You know?" I said, "I think that I finally know the answer to the question you asked me so many times."

We stopped on the pathway facing each other. The sun was just going down over the tree tops, and the birds said goodnight to each other in the apple trees. Ed was silent for quite a while. He just looked into my face with searching eyes.

"Are you sure?" he said, not taking his eyes off me.

"I am sure," I answered.

He still looked into my eyes, as if wanting to assure himself that it was really what I wanted, that I was not just favoring him. Then I saw his eyes filling with a warm, golden light. He had received his answer. His arms went around me till I thought he would crush me, but I knew that with this I had promised myself to him for life. Without rings, without champagne, the sunset betrothed us on a quiet late summer evening. With his arm around me, we turned and walked into the house.

On quiet evenings on the weekends we often sat in the big chair, the dusk thickening in the room and talked about how we would try to save some money for starting our life together. Then in the spring we would get married and maybe go to Scotland for a couple of weeks.

But it was only autumn and the waiting became harder and harder now that we had promised ourselves to each other. The gas fire seethed in the fireplace, shedding its warm light over everything. White snowball chrysanthemums stood in a vase on the table looking so white against the dark background.

We loved to sit in the dark, just watching the flames and did it often on weekends. Mother was out with Saša, and Johnny was somewhere with his friends. We were alone at home. In time, it seemed, the golden flames got into our blood making our hearts beat faster. Now that I had promised myself to him, it became harder and harder for me to resist the hands that wanted me so badly.

"We must not... We have to wait..." I would whisper and free myself from the impatient hands.

"Why? You know that you are my girl and always will be." I could hear his heart beating wildly and his hands were hot around me, drawing me closer.

"Come to me," he whispered in my hair, then found my lips and I was sinking, sinking...

But I still had my dream that every girl has about her wedding day and I did not let myself get lost completely. I gathered my wits about me and tried to be sensible for both of us.

And the thread of excitement snapped, the hands released, the golden flames died down. Peace was around us again but not as it had been before. Somewhere something was still smoldering. Going upstairs, Ed squeezed my hand lightly, gave a sad smile and said in a low voice, "I'm afraid I will never understand you..."

The next evening after dinner was finished, Ed sat in the big chair as usual and smoked his pipe, but he was silent and looked somewhere away through the rings of smoke he was making. I tried to talk to him and asked if he was not feeling well, but he said that he was all right and tried to behave normally. I could see, though, that this pretending did not come easy to him, and he soon went upstairs.

I sat alone in the big chair and felt sad, as if I had lost something very precious and dear to me. I would have liked to talk and be close to someone, but no one was there. After a while I went upstairs, put on the light and saw Ed lying on the covers undressed. He lay on his back, his chest moving quietly up and down under his folded hands. I did not know if he was really sleeping or not. I stood there for quite a while looking at him, and deep sorrow rose in my heart. I knew that I had hurt him even though he tried not to show it, because he did not want to upset me.

I put out the light and went downstairs. The room suddenly seemed cold and lifeless. Neither the fire in the fireplace, nor the warm light of the lamp could warm me. I sat in the big chair again and thought about

Ed and us both. It made me so sad that I wanted to cry. What should we do? How would we be able to wait till spring, when it got harder with every day?

If we were not all living here together, it would have been easier, at least for me. But then we would not have grown so close, and perhaps I would not have given him the promise I gave. Did Mother know this and had thought that I needed a push when she made the decision to ask Ed to live with us? Or was it to her own benefit to get me situated, so she could proceed with her own life? I will never know it, and it did not count anymore anyway.

Perhaps I was very selfish, thinking that I could wait till spring, but what of Ed? I did not know what he was going through, what fights he had to win within himself, but I sensed that it was much harder for him than it was for me. I did not want to hurt him, but was so afraid of what could happen if I gave in to him. Besides, what of my dream—of being pure for the man I loved on our wedding night? What of my dream?

Then, however, I remembered the words he had said last night. They still sounded in my ears, and only now did I begin to grasp the meaning of them. Poor Ed! He had been so good to me and had given all of himself during all this difficult time while I was sick. He had been loving, tender and understanding, yet now, when I could give him something back, I did not want to do it because of some selfish thought. Yes, this thought… this white dream, which now would never come true… My heart ached quietly as if I was standing at a small, white grave. But I knew what I had to do, so somebody, who was very dear to me, would be happy. I knew that it was my time to give.

Ed lay sick for two days with severe gastric pains. He slept days and nights curled up from pain, taking the medicine the doctor had prescribed. I went up now and then and asked if he wanted anything, but he declined everything. I just left him some milk in case he might want to take some.

The house seemed so quiet and filled with sadness. I walked around the room and stood at the window for a long time looking at the gray sky. The trees had lost their leaves. The wind bent and plucked at the dry, left-over summer flowers in the front garden. It was autumn. In me too, the wind blew harshly, and it seemed to rain and rain.

A new morning had come. Still half asleep, I heard that the door opened and closed quietly. I opened my eyes and saw the whole room full of silvery sunshine. At the side of my bed stood Ed, cleaned up and fresh.

"You are better," I smiled and stretched out my hand to him.

"Yes, I feel quite good today," he smiled too and sat down on the edge of my bed. "And how did you sleep?"

"Oh, good, good... But are you not going to say good morning to me?" I asked.

He bent down slowly and gently kissed me on my forehead, on my eyes, nose and lips, and these kisses conveyed a deep tenderness and a strange kind of peace. But I sensed that there was also pain and self-denial in this peace. I knew that he was ready to do anything for me, but did I have a right to accept such a sacrifice? I pulled his head down to my chest and whispered, "Oh Ed, dear Ed..." a big lump rose in my chest, I could not talk. We held each other and in this embrace was a deep understanding, and assurance of faithfulness for life. We had finally made our peace, and in the warm morning light gave in to what needed to happen.

Later we sat at the table having some coffee. The sun still warmed the room. On the table in a vase stood four large, white snowball chrysanthemums that Ed had brought me the previous weekend, knowing how much I liked them. And now I thought—they were the token of his love; they were in place of my white wedding dress, which I would now never wear.

We looked at each other, and our eyes were moist with emotion.

"Sweetheart..." Ed said in a low voice, and his big hand touched my cheek, "You are not sorry, are you?"

"No, no!" I shook my head and smiled, but my eyes veiled over, and I hid my face against his chest so he would not see it. He stroked my hair with such tenderness. I knew that he was happy, and I did not regret anything anymore.

Each year on the anniversary of that day Ed brought me the white snowball chrysanthemums. It was our own private celebration, which no one else knew about.


It was not so easy for me to find another job. Even though my high school diploma covered a wide spectrum of subjects and showed top marks in each of them, people at the Labor Exchange did not know what to make of it. In Latvia, I would have been able to enter the job market easily with my present knowledge; here it was different.

"What did you major in?" They wanted to know. "What job experience have you had?"

What could I offer them? I had no idea, because I had not had an ordinary life. The war—all that time as a refugee—had disrupted everything.

"I could do all kinds of work, if only somebody would show me what I had to do!" I told the interviewer at the Labor Department.

In England, however, things were different in those days. For the most part, young people started working from the age of sixteen, when by law they could leave school (which many did), so I was already too

old. Too old! I was only twenty-three! Still, the employer would have to pay me more money, according to my years, and that was not a good deal for them.

I went to several interviews, but it was the same thing all over. They did not know what to do with my excellent diploma.

"If you could do typing or stenography…"

"Sorry, but I do not know how to do those things."

"Could you work in a chemical laboratory?"

"I would, if somebody showed me what to do, I would learn." But that was not good enough.

My steps became heavier as I went back to the labor department again and again. Was I really no good for anything? I wanted to work, whatever it might be! I looked in the newspaper, and found an ad for a job which might suit me. They needed seamstresses at a factory, where they made raincoats. I answered the ad, and what a surprise, I was called to an interview and was accepted!

It was all very strange to me, when I entered my new workplace. Actually, I had never been inside a factory in my life and felt like the proverbial "white sparrow". I looked around with interest, taking it all in, but saw that I, too, was being observed by the workers there. I was led into a large room where people were standing by long tables. It looked like they were measuring and cutting the fabrics to patterns, but in one corner of the room stood ten sewing machines, where the new workers were trained. There were six of us who wanted to learn, and an old skinny woman showed us what to do. I had never used an electric machine and it seemed to run by itself as soon the pedal was touched, but I soon learned to handle it. We had to sew different types of seams and sew the whole day.

The radio played music and the speakers carried the sounds all through the five story building. From the floor above us came a constant sound of roaring and grinding of the sewing machines. I got a glance of this room when I passed by on my way to the canteen at lunch time. It was a huge room full of sewing machines. The working women sewed, at times shouting to each other over the roar of the machines. Laughter sounded now and then in response to something funny that was said. Looking in from outside, it almost appeared like a big game. But I knew how much work had to pass through their hands to reach the amount of work they had to produce in a day, and the machines roared on as if a hundred saws had been put to use.

Suddenly a siren sounded! It was even louder than the rest of the bellowing noise, and everybody dropped everything in an instant. The machines stopped and the workers streamed to the dining hall. I sat down at the window to eat my sandwich and from there I could see what was

happening all around. It was interesting to watch this colorful crowd. There were young girls, middle-aged women, and even some older women with gray hair. For the most part, they chattered cheerfully—there was joking, teasing and laughter. They looked as if they knew each other and felt good at this place. Would I also become one of them? Somehow it seemed so unbelievable. But then the siren sounded again, and it was time to go back to work.

The afternoon seemed to stretch out into eternity. I was sewing the same seams over and over. My shoulders and back ached from so much sitting and leaning forward. They hurt more and more as time went on. It must have been from the unusual work. I waited for the evening. It was already dark and the lights came on in the other places, but our corner was dark. Only the small lights at the machines stayed on. Our supervisor was not around, and the young girls, sitting opposite me, did not work anymore but painted their eyes and lips, talking quietly.

At last the siren blasted through the building again and the workday was over. I thought this had been the longest day of my life, but in time I would surely get used to it. So now I was a factory girl and moved with the crowd toward the gate. The moist evening air surrounded me as I came out on the street and I took a deep breath savoring it.

The street lights were on everywhere. I took my place at the end of the line at the bus stop, but felt so strange. People milled around me, but I felt as if I was on a lonely island and around me was just emptiness; as if I was not in the right place, but did not know where else to go. So I stood there, not thinking or willing anything, just waiting where fate would take me next.

It was my third day at the factory and the supervisor was satisfied with my work. She said that toward the end of the week I would be able to move "upstairs", but I would have been willing to go right away. I was so tired of playing around with those scraps of fabric.

It was moving toward lunchtime. Now and then a voice sounded over the intercom, calling some person, or the telephones rang. Our supervisor was called, and she left, but after a few minutes she was back.

"The personnel manager wants to see you in her office," she told me.

I went but could not figure out what the reason might be. Had I done something wrong? The manager, Mrs. Smith, was a kind-looking lady with an intelligent face.

"Take a seat," she said, pointing to the chair opposite her desk, "and don't worry, nothing is wrong," she assured me, perhaps sensing my concern.

"I received a call from the Labor Department," she said. "They told me that they have found an office job for you, if you would like to go to an interview this afternoon."

That was an unexpected surprise, but I was quite puzzled as to what I should do. I had only just started this job, how could I run away like that? But Mrs. Smith smiled and urged me to go and try for it. Then she continued, "When I accepted you, I saw that you did not come from the usual circle of factory girls, and I am sure that you can do something better. I wish you luck! If things don't work out, however, just come back to us," she said. "You can leave right now," she added and I thanked her.

Still rather perplexed, I walked out onto the street. A little later a bus took me out of the city center toward the Aston region. I knew that area a bit from my short stay at the lodging in Erdington only a year ago.

I did not have to go far, and got off the bus, following the directions the manager had given me. It was a regular industrial working class area, which had surrounded the city center since the olden days. The dusty, red brick terrace buildings stretched along both sides of the street like walls, without a tree or a shrub, and the pavements were crumbled and uneven. Yet people lived here and, perhaps, were even happy.

I found the appointed street and it was just as gray and dreary as the rest of them. I looked for something resembling a factory with a sign reading "The Universal Plating Co.", but the buildings all looked the same. I almost passed it, when I noticed a small plaque on a gate with that title and then also a larger, partly faded sign on the brick wall. Undecided, I stood there not knowing what to do. The place looked shabby, and I almost did not want to go in. But since I had come this far, I took courage and walked in, even though my hopes were dashed already.

I opened what turned out to be a back door to a small room, and then a dark hallway led me into a large room with various kinds of machinery and some big vats. Men worked around them, wearing big leather gloves and aprons in front of them. I did not see any office-like opening and asked one of the workers, "Can you tell me where I can find the office?"

"It is right next to where you are standing, just go up the stairs," he said, showing me a narrow stairway that I had not even noticed.

Upstairs, I walked into the bright office room where three women worked at their tables. When I told them my business there, the oldest one got up and knocked on a door, presumably leading into the manager's office.

"Come in, come in!" a voice behind the door answered, and as I walked in, I saw a big, rather heavy set man, sitting at the desk and talking on the telephone. He glanced at me, and without words, motioned for me to take a seat. Then the door behind me closed quietly. After a couple of minutes, he finished the phone call, apologized and got up to shake hands with me. He seemed to be a pleasant man.

Before we started the interview, he asked me to excuse him for a few minutes. "I am sorry! I am needed downstairs to take care of something urgent in the works room. I shall be back soon."

"But of course!" I answered.

I sat in the comfortable chair and looked around. The room was not large but was modern and nicely decorated, which you could not have guessed judging from the looks of the outside. Would I succeed here, I wondered?

It took a bit longer than he had anticipated, but finally he was back and sat down in his comfortable chair. Mr. Fisher was a big man, perhaps a little past middle age, with a round face and black, smoothly-combed hair. His face was a little deeper toned, and from the way he talked, I detected, however slightly, that he was not English-born, either.

"Well, what can you do? What have you done?" he asked. "Actually I expected to have a man to assist my chemist in the laboratory... I see that you have studied chemistry?"

"Yes, but only on a very general level. Still, I could learn if I were shown what to do!" I said.

At that he looked thoughtful. I thought that it would be the end of our interview, but he kept talking and asking questions and observing me at the same time. Since I felt sure that nothing was going to come of this, I talked openly, telling about the war and the refugee times and how it all disrupted my plans for further education. I told him about working in the hospital, as the government required, and that now I was considered to be too old to start anything new.

"What a shame that you cannot type and do stenography," he said regretfully.

"I could take some classes and learn," I said, "I had already thought that it might be useful."

"Well, in that case... I was just thinking that our manager could use someone in his office someone who answers the telephone, receives new orders and... can you draw?"

"Oh, yes! I can draw very well!" I answered joyfully.

"The machine parts that are sent here for plating are very specific. They need to be drawn and the areas to be plated have to be specially marked. And, if in time you could take over the manager's correspondence, then, I think it could work out very well."

"I definitely could do that," I assured him, hardly being able to believe what I heard.

"Of course," he continued, "at least in the beginning, I could not pay you very much. Say, three pounds a week, considering that you have no experience? Then later we would see. What do you say to that?"

"I am glad that you want to at least give me an opportunity to prove

myself. I will try to do my best; you can be assured of that." I said, and he smiled.

"I know... I too was not born here. I come from Yugoslavia and know very well how it is when you are in a strange country. I have several Poles working for me, former Polish soldiers. I think the people from Europe are different than the people here. They are more responsible and do a good job. Ah... I think that we will do well. So, do you want to start on Monday?" he asked, leaning across the desk.

"Certainly!" I smiled happily as I got to my feet.

"Wait!" he said. "I am sure you would like to see what we have here? Come with me, I will show you!"

We came out into the larger office room, where the women were talking to an older man in a white coat.

"Ah, Mister Hunt!" the director exclaimed. "Come and meet your new secretary! I am sure she will be a great help to you!"

Mr. Hunt apparently was the main manager of the plant, right after Mr. Fisher, who was the owner and director of the company. I could see that Mr. Hunt was rather surprised about this development, even though he tried to hide it making some kind of a joke of it. I could sense that he liked to joke and also tease the girls, although his hair was somewhat gray and a bit receding at the temples. He had big gray eyes and every so often a mischievous glint could be seen in them as we all talked. He had a small mustache on his upper lip and his speech had a rather strong "Birmingham" accent.

Then Mr. Fisher took me to show me his kingdom. I saw how proud he was of his achievement. Downstairs the works area consisted of two large rooms, formed by combining two regular family houses standing back to back, so there were entrances on two parallel streets. The previous backyards had given room to expand the combined works area that was taken up by large vats filled with dark fluids. This was where the chemical processes took place, mainly to plate bicycle parts with nickel. In another place, chrome plating was done to various machine parts.

On our way, we met some of the Polish workers and were introduced. There were Leo and Jack, former soldiers of the Polish army that Mr. Fisher had hired in order to help them to get started in this country. Finally, we arrived at the other end of the establishment, to the small room where I had come in.

"This would be your office," Mr. Fisher said. "There is not much here, only a desk, a few chairs and a gas fireplace, as you can see. The room should really be fixed up and made nicer," he said, but I did not care about that. I was so glad that I would not have to go back to sewing.

When I was out on the street again, my head was pounding from what I had experienced. I could not believe that I had really been offered

a job! Somewhere in my mind, I had an inkling that Mr. Fisher came up with this job, perhaps because he felt sorry for me and wanted to help someone in my position. Maybe he did, or maybe not. I certainly was not going to question him about that.

At home everybody was very glad at my unexpected news of landing this job, for nobody had been pleased about my work-ing at the sewing factory. Still, I had felt that I needed to do something, and had not wanted to wait any longer.

The new job did not turn out as well as I had expected mainly because there was not enough to do—the days stretched out so long. I understood, though, that it might take time for things to adjust. In the meantime, I tried to get as much understanding about everything as I could, so I could be more helpful. I got acquainted with the workers who explained what they were doing in more detail, and good relations were formed. Also Mr. Hunt told me various things, but I had a sensation that he did not take me too seriously. Yet, with each day I learned more and he began to change his mind.

I also started to take classes in the evenings in typing and stenog-raphy at the private Pitman College downtown. My art classes had to be postponed for some later time; otherwise it would be too much for me. When I did not have much to do in the office, I practiced my typing, which I found quite interesting. It would be a new skill for me.

At lunch time I went over to the main office. A small kitchen was next to it where the women, or should I say "girls", as we called each other, made tea. We sat together eating our sandwiches, drinking the tea and chatting. I mostly just listened and observed, although the others were kind to me. They asked some questions, but since our backgrounds were so different, we soon ran out of something to say. Still, I was con-tent to just be an observer, and it was interesting to listen to their chatter. I gradually came to a better understanding of how they lived and what they were about. I had always been interested in personalities and why people were the way they were.

Doreen was the pretty dark-haired girl with brown eyes and a pale, well-kept face. She was Mr. Fisher's secretary and was the biggest talker. The subject was mostly her fiancé, called Frank, who was one of the Pol-ish workers here at the plant. The main subject was how much they had put in the bank. That meant—how much she had got from his pay packet and put in the bank for their wedding, or how she had bought something for their future life together.

It seemed to me that her attitude to all this was very prosaic and calculating, but apparently it was done following the old English tradi-tion of how things should be done so everything would be "proper" for

the bride-to-be. She talked quite openly about all the aspects of married life, how it would be, and what her father, mother and sister thought about how they should live. The only one who did not appear to have any say in all of this was the groom. His only duty was to give Doreen three quarters of his weekly wages for the needs of the wedding. The wages in those days were paid in real money and put in a special envelope, so Doreen, who worked in the office, took out the appropriate amount ahead of time to save Frank the bother.

One day I got to meet Frank and was more than surprised. My first thought was: could the good looking Doreen with the good manners, attractive dressing and acceptable education not get anybody better? Not that I meant to put Frank down, but they appeared to be the least suited couple I could imagine. There he stood at the door of the office in his gray overall suit, an old cap on his head, short and not at all good looking. His face looked gray and crinkly, and I wondered what on earth they might have in common? Also, his English was poor. How would they communicate? What kind of a marriage would it be?

It was possible, however, that Frank was a good man with other good properties and most likely he would be a good provider for Doreen's needs, because doing piecework in plating the bicycle parts, he was earning good money. Yet it was unbelievable that this would be a compatible couple. I felt sorry for Frank. It seemed to me that he was manipulated. Listening to others talking, I learned a lot about the English ways, and that in the English society it was an accepted view, that when the girl reached the marriage years, she had to find a husband. If she was lucky to find someone willing, she should get him to buy her the ring as soon as possible and then hold on to him till he took her to the altar. What happened afterward was not so important.

Sorry to say, this was the image I got from Doreen talking so coolly about her intimate affairs. The only thing missing in all her talk was love. I could only guess that love had nothing to do with it, if only the other things were correct for the friends and family. Again, I wanted to say, poor Frank! He was already under her thumb, and dear Doreen would see to it that he stayed there!

When Doreen did not talk, the tall, bushy-haired Peggy told about her boyfriend Bernie, what he had said or done. She laughed often and loudly, talking with a discernible Birmingham accent and one could tell that she came from a simple working class home. But it was exactly this straight forwardness and simplicity that made her endearing and I liked to listen to her happy laughter.

Peggy and Alice, the oldest of the three, loved to discuss the previous night's comedy shows on the radio and could not stop laughing at the jokes they had heard.

"Did you hear that? What did you think of them?" They asked me, but I had not listened. To my mind it was rather sad that people needed these artificial jokes to make them happy, but of course, I kept that to myself. I was not a humorous person.

I liked Alice the best. She was the main bookkeeper. Small and thin, she could have been in her late fifties. She was friendly and kind; she talked and laughed, but there was also a serious side in her, and she fiercely loved her husband and their only son. I liked to listen to the girls, but soon the lunchtime was over, and I went back to my little room.

Sometimes Mr. Fisher stopped by on his tour through the works. We chatted a bit. He asked how I was doing. Sometimes he would seat himself on the corner of my desk and would loom over me. I did not like that, but often he was away from the plant for long stretches of time, leaving everything in the hands of Mr. Hunt. When he returned in the late afternoons, he sometimes brought with him a guest, some blond, good looking woman. Then he asked Alice to make them some coffee, and occasionally, suppressed laughter could be heard from his office. When after a while they left, the room was full of blue cigarette smoke and the leftovers of some sweet perfume.

Alice, who was the closest to Mr. Fisher and had been with the company from the beginning, told us later,

"He married a rich, older English lady, who helped him to establish the business, but now the marriage is not going well. I don't think they live together anymore."

So everybody had their worries, however rich they were. For anything gained one had to pay a price; and it was not always true that you could buy what you wanted with money. But such was life and we had to accept it.

Our life settled into a regular routine again. Every morning we each went to our workplace: Mother still went to the hospital, Johnny to the electrical shop, Ed to the gas works and I to the plating company. The evenings were short and passed quickly, having dinner and getting ready for the next day. Quite often now, Saša was a guest at our house on weekends, and we all sat around the fireplace in the evenings, toasting bread against it, spreading the toast with pineapple jam and eating it together with the coffee Mother had made.

It was so pleasant to sit in the half darkness of the room and let the gas fire spread its warm light around, knowing your loved ones were close by. We had already accepted that Saša would be part of our family and were glad that Mother had found someone to share her life with again. I watched the light from the fire play around the flowers on the table, and, against the dark background, they looked like a painting.

Then I thought, could one wish for more happiness than this? Yet I was not always so happy. There was a time each month when I worried and then with each day worried more.

Ed had got himself another job at the gasworks, where he would earn a little more money for our future. It was a very heavy job, shoveling coal and feeding the big stoves at the gas works in great heat, but he was young and strong and did it willingly. He also had to work nights, so we did not see much of each other. Perhaps in a way that was good, but sometimes I missed him very much.

After a couple of weeks working there, Ed told me, "I was reprimanded last night at work! It was for working too hard!"

"How is that?" I could not understand.

"Well, there are seven of us on the job. The last two days, I had felt that the guys looked at me sort of funny. We take turns feeding the stoves and drink tea in between in the side room. When I came back to the room after working, one of the fellows said to me: "Do you want to put us all out of work?"

At first I did not understand. Then he said that I was working too hard and fast; if I carried on that way, there would not be enough work for all of them and some of them might be let go!"

"Really? I would have thought that they wanted you to work harder!" I was surprised as well.

"No, no! Now I see how socialism works! I could do alone what the seven of us do now, but the job has to be stretched out to fit seven! We cannot let the boss see that we don't really need so many workers on this job. No wonder that we have so much time for drinking tea!"

That really was a strange way to accomplish something. It was quite the opposite of our Latvian work ethic.

Another month had passed and again I had worries of possibly being pregnant. I sat alone in the half dark room, and sadness was in my heart. I did not want to cry, did not want to tell anybody, not even Ed, but tears filled my eyes as if saying goodbye to something. I looked at our little Christmas tree and saw one tiny star glistening in it. It made me think of a forest, thick with snow, and that soon it would be Christmas. Yet my thoughts weighed me down, and I felt like I had to walk through deep, deep snow. Then I thought—had I not deserved even a few brighter moments?

I could not hide my worries from Ed for too long, though, for he read each tiniest shadow from my face and did not let me off until I told him. Now we both had a burden on our hearts, and he tried to pacify me the best he could. Such tenderness was in his big hands, and his eyes looked into mine full of sorrow, yet also full of love. A day passed and

another, then finally we could breathe again. At least this time our sins were forgiven.

Shortly before Christmas, Mother presented us with unexpected news.

"I've got something to tell you," she said one day. "Saša is buying a house and has asked me to come and live with him, and also Johnny would have a room there. Having a house, he will need someone to look after it and I would be glad to do that. Then I shall not need to work in the hospital anymore, and I think it will be just fine."

Apparently the reason for all this was that the big house, where Saša and the other cobblers lived, was going to be sold, and they all had been given notices to find other places to live. This was a tough thing, for we knew so well how hard it was to find suitable lodgings. One of Saša's friends there also had a wife and a little two-year-old boy, so who would take them to live in their house? Since Saša and the man who had the family had saved some money, they had decided to buy a house together, and by borrowing a little more from a third man, who also had an old mother living with him, they could just manage the down payment. They had already found a house in the Birmingham suburb of Kings Heath, which was not too far from their workplace.

"I think I should accept his offer," Mother said. "You will be getting married and will want a place of your own anyway, so it would work out well for us all. Saša said that if all goes well, we could move in before the New Year!"

Yes, I could understand that, and why should she not have a life again after all these years of suffering, not knowing anything about Dad? Saša was a good man: quiet, serious and responsible but with good humor. Mother was forty-seven years old and Saša was eight years younger, but at that age, the difference does not count as much anymore. Saša also had been an army officer, and they got on well together.

No, I had nothing against it. It probably was a good solution for us all, except that would mean that I would be staying here alone with Ed. He was closer to me now than anybody else, and yet, there was much that I did not know about him. Perhaps it was a rather silly thought, to suddenly be afraid to leave Mother's secure lap. Whatever happened, I would have to face it alone. But then I looked at Ed and knew that everything would be all right.

Christmas came and went quietly. On Christmas Eve, which for us Latvians, is the most sacred part of Christmas, Saša came to be with us. While Mother was busy in the kitchen, we decorated our small Christmas tree, and he helped in making a star out of some wire and a garland of tinsel. He was a pleasant person, very much his own man, perhaps because at the age of thirty-nine, he was still a bachelor. He had

bushy red hair and thick eyebrows above his light gray eyes. The strong features in his reddish face told that this was a man who knew what he was doing. His walk and demeanor were direct and purposeful as that of a former soldier, his hands revealed the hard work he was doing now, but they were very capable and knowing hands.

At last everything was ready and it was time to light the Christmas tree. I did the lighting, and with each candle lit, it became more and more beautiful. We sang the old well-known Christmas songs, and our newly-made star glistened at the top of the tree, conveying the great wonder of the love which was given to us on this night. My heart overflowed with gratefulness, and for a moment, tears filled my eyes, making the candle lights join up in one great tree of light. Ed's and my very first Christmas together!

Afterward we exchanged gifts. It was not anything much, for none of us had money, but that was not the point. Those were gifts which came from the heart. Then I took Ed aside to the alcove by the window, where our little Christmas tree stood on our makeshift sideboard all alone and lonesome. Yet, I had not forgotten it. I pulled a tiny baby Christmas tree out of a bag. It was exactly like the mother tree, with white snow on its green bristle branches and a little red wooden pot. I put it next to the larger tree in remembrance of our very first Christmas when we met. We both stooped down by the table and looked at our tree, remembering the happiness and also the troubles we had had during the previous year. The little tree seemed to be talking to us also, bringing us greetings from that evening a year ago when it became "our" Christmas tree. Ed put his arm around my shoulder and kissed me on the forehead.

"It is our Christmas tree and it always will be," he said.

We looked deep into each other's eyes and knew that it would be so.

Later Ed told me: "You know, I have never known a Christmas like this. My parents were not religious. Yes, they had a celebration with a nice dinner and some friends or relatives, but I was not part of it. I was just there, a child who behaved. There was no Christmas tree, no presents. I remember that my Uncle John was there also and made me stand and act like a soldier…"

That made me very sad. There had been no warmth in his family.

"My mother was very strict. When I was sent to do some shopping, I was not allowed to make a list. I just had to remember. If I had missed something, I had to go back," he said. "And if I was told to be home at five, it had to be five! No excuses!"

There was no forgiveness. He said, sometimes his mother would not talk to him the whole week, if he had done something not to her liking. It was hard for me to imagine that sort of living. Yes, discipline was neces-

sary and also training the memory was good, but did it have to be so harsh?

"My parents did send me to the best school in Rīga. It was a classical high school, heavy on languages with five or six of them. It was a co-ed school, but the classes for girls and boys were separate. Quite a few sons and daughters of prominent people went to this school. I found wonderful friends there."

Ed must have really liked it there, and I loved to listen to his stories of the pranks they had played on their teachers.

"My best friend from the very start there was Viesturs—Viesturs Baldzēns. His family had a farm in Piebalga, a region northeast of Rīga, but during school time, he stayed with us in our apartment. Then in summertime we both went to the farm and worked. It was great for us to be together in the fresh country air and develop our young bodies and muscles. We both liked to play basketball and growing strong was important. I loved to be on that farm and being together with Viesturs. We had a lot of good times."

He sat there, reminiscing a bit, then picked up where he had left off.

"My other closest friend and classmate was Ali Strunke. He was the son of the famous Latvian artist Niklāvs Strunke. I am sure you know of him, don't you?"

"Of course! He had a very unique style. I liked his paintings."

"I liked them, too. It was interesting to see his father's studio when I visited. Ali was such a great guy with a lot of humor and it always was fun to be with him. We both were together also during the war, because we had been drafted into the German army at the same time right after our graduation from high school. He later found that his parents had fled to Sweden and joined them there. In our graduating class were eleven of us boys and we were all close. A few of us got out of Latvia, others stayed. Viesturs stayed. I don't know what happened to him…"

Ed ended telling his story, still being moved by the thoughts of his old friend, and I could empathize with him, because I had lost my best friend also.

The last day of the year of 1949 had come, and it had been a busy day for us all. Mother and Johnny were moving to Saša's house, as had been agreed. All day things were sorted—what they would take and what would be left for us. We only had the bare minimum of everything, anyway. They had to be divided carefully so we would each have some of the necessities. Everything was packed, and it was time for saying good-bye to Mother and my brother Johnny. A friend had offered to take them to Sašas house in his car and he took them away. Now they were gone, and the house was suddenly so quiet and empty. Ed had already left for work, for now he worked nights at the gasworks to earn

a little more money. The room looked different and kind of unfamiliar with things removed here and there and nothing in their place. I adjusted everything the best I could, but there really was not much to do.

I sat down in the big chair, but the silence around me had its own voice. This would be the first New Year's Eve I would be spending alone... Quite alone...

It was almost ten o'clock and I wondered what Mother and Johnny were doing now in their new home. Suddenly I heard a knock on the door, and Johnny came in bringing with him the cool breath of the winter night. By now, my little brother had grown into a handsome young man of seventeen.

"Come on, Sis, get ready quickly and let's go to town!" he said in a cheerful voice and was already at the wardrobe taking out my best dress.

"What are you doing?" I said perplexed, still not quite making out what he meant by what he had said.

"I promised Ed that I would take you out tonight, so you would not have to sit here alone," he said, and then I understood. Dear Ed!

"Let's go to Mecca to dance, but be quick, so we can still catch the last bus to town!"

I still tried to argue, but he already had my dress and shoes out of the wardrobe. I gave in, dressed quickly, and half running, we made the evening bus.

Mecca was a dance hall in the city, and this evening excitement was everywhere. The hall was decorated with balloons and colored streamers. The spotlights, turning at the ceiling, flooded the big room with changing colors. A band played on the small stage in brilliant light, and a young girl came out at intervals and sang.

The hall was full of cheerful, smiling people, and around the sides were tables in an intimate half-light. We mixed into the crowd of happy dancers and flowed along with the music in the relaxed atmosphere. Johnny was a pleasant partner, and even though he was young, he knew what was necessary to create a nice carefree mood. I knew that he liked to go out, and to be with girls and live it up a bit.

We both liked to dance and did it almost non-stop. I was glad now that Johnny had brought me here tonight. Music and laughter was around us, but higher up, under the vaulted ceiling, the space was filling with blue cigarette smoke. Up there was a large net with colored balloons also, to be released at the midnight hour.

Suddenly the lights dimmed; the hall was in half darkness. The music stopped and so did everybody else, standing still and listening. Somewhere a clock rang, counting out the last seconds of the year. And then the New Year was here! 1950 had arrived!

The lights were switched on again. People hugged and kissed, wish-

ing each other a happy New Year and we did, too. Voices and laughter sounded all around. Then the balloons came floating down over peoples' heads and, squealing and pushing, they tried to catch them.

The band started to play again, and it was the old traditional song *"Auld Lang Syne"* that everybody knew. People crossed their arms in front of them and joined their hands with others, stepping back all the time as more people joined to form a circle. It must be an old custom to do that while singing this well-loved song.

The New Year had been ushered in. We were out on the street again, where the cold winter air wrapped around us. We walked quickly, gripped by the cold after just leaving the warm dance hall. At this time of the night the city center was usually deserted, but not tonight. Quite a few people were in the streets, coming or going from somewhere. Most likely, those were people who had been celebrating somewhere the same as we had. More lights were on and the festive spirit seemed to be everywhere.

At the City Hall Plaza, a whole crowd of people had gathered and were singing and dancing even without any music. There were ladies in fur coats, factory girls without stockings on their feet, gentlemen in evening dress and Irish workers with colorful neckties. They all mixed together tonight, the rich and the poor, without distinction, joining their hands and singing *"Auld Lang Syne"*, repeating and repeating it.

We would have to wait quite a while for the night bus to take us home, so my brother asked,

"Do you want to wait, Sis? It is getting real cold, we will freeze. What if we just walked? It is not really that far!"

"Let us walk!" I agreed, shivering.

We walked along the wide Bristol Road that was well lit and there was no traffic on it, but the side streets, branching off, became darker the farther we got away from the city center. Here and there we passed a pub, where people still lingered outside. They sang and shouted good wishes to one another, not being able to part. A little farther, we passed a lone drunk. He walked along carrying a bottle in his hand and talking to himself. We smiled at him and he stopped and smiled back happily.

"Hi!" he said to us, wanting to have a chat. But the cold was freezing my feet quite badly through my high-heeled shoes, so we just walked on, clinging together to keep warm. The white neon street lights shed their light across the empty street, and an almost empty night-bus passed us by, but then we were already close to home and finally in the warmth.

The gray days of January came and went, cold and dreary. Everything was so bare outside. Ed worked shifts, so we did not see much of each other during the week, but the weekend was our celebra-

tion time. We both cleaned and polished our "house" until everything was spotless and shiny. After a bath and some clean clothes, we could relax and start enjoying our weekend. A faint aroma from the furniture polish was still in the air. The gas fire hissed quietly, and on the table were flowers and fruit. No matter how little money we had, we always bought some of those. We were happy, because now we had peace, love and a home that we had always dreamed of. We sat in our big chair and celebrated the twilight hour, Ed smoking his pipe, my head resting on his shoulder. In silence we watched the darkness creep into the corners, then slowly it covered everything. Only the bright, warm circle of the fire was left.

Sometimes a young black cat sneaked into our room and stretched in front of the fire, and we let him be there.

We also talked about our future, and decided to have a wedding in March, so that our union would be sanctified before God and the people also. We had very little money, but we would do what we could and it would have to do.

After Mother and Johnny left, our landlady Mrs. Floyd invited me to come to her to talk over the new situation. In a delicate way, she also suggested that we should get married fairly soon, so people would not talk.

"We have already made arrangements to get married in March," I told her, and she was very kind, wished us happiness and even offered for us to pay less rent. That was really generous of her, and we were very grateful for the lucky circumstance that had led us to have this place.

Johnny stopped by to see us quite often on weekends. Sometimes our friends from the choir came by and knocked on the window next to the outer door. Then we would drink coffee and talk, sharing our experiences of our daily lives and most often ended up singing together. We Latvians all felt like family.

## Our Two Weddings

Time gradually moved toward spring. We celebrated the tulip fest and the narcissus fest, our special days from the year before, when we had gone through all that turmoil and yet had come through it. We had also made an appointment with our Latvian minister for our wedding to be held on March 25, as well as an appointment at the Registrar's Office for the same date. In those days, our Latvian minister was not licensed to register weddings. On Saturday we went to town to buy our rings. We easily found one for me that fit perfectly, except that it was difficult to get it off afterward. Ed, on the other hand, could not find one big enough to fit his finger.

"We will just have to make one for you," The sales person said, tak-

ing the measurements. "It will not take us long."

How great was our disappointment, when only two weeks before the wedding, the minister sent us a message that he would not be available to perform our wedding on that date, because he had to go to a conference in London!

"Could you have the wedding the week after?" He wrote.

That really upset us, for we could not change the Registrar's appointment. If we did, we would have to wait for quite a while again until we got another date. As a result, we had two wedding days—one before the Judge on March 25, and the other before God on April 1, 1950. In England a lot of couples chose to get married before the end of March because then they could get back taxes for the whole year. That was a great help for the new couples, and would be a great help to us also.

It was a rather warm and overcast spring morning on March 25, when we went to town to the Registrar's Office to be married. Saša and Mrs. Bērziņš were to be our witnesses and awaited us there. Several couples were already in the waiting room, some brides very smartly dressed in nice suits with corsages and flowers. We were just simply in our Sunday's best, for we did not have any other special clothing.

Our turn came, and we walked into the large room with tall windows. The sun had come out for a moment and shone on us while the Registrar welcomed us and started the ceremony. Then we had to repeat the words he asked us to say. I listened as Ed talked and his voice sounded unusually deep. He was promising to love and to take care of me for the rest of his life. Suddenly the immensity of this promise sank into me. This was forever, and there was no way back! I felt something like a touch of eternity in my heart, making this moment so great and unique. We were promising ourselves to each other for life!

We put rings on each other's fingers, and with that, the ceremony was over. The Registrar congratulated us and wished us well. We signed the register and the marriage license. Then we were on the street again and mixed into the crowds of the weekend shoppers. Saša and Mrs. Bērziņš went home, where Mother was preparing a dinner for us all, but we had to go and order flowers for my wedding. I wanted lilies, but it was not so easy to find them. They had all been reserved by churches for

the Easter Sunday, just two weeks from then. Finally we did find a shop, where they took our order.

Then we were on our way to Saša's house. The bus slowly navigated through the crowded streets, taking us out of the city center. Farther out in the suburbs, daffodils bloomed in front of houses, and the trees and shrubs were full of swollen buds. Since the bus was rather full, we did not get to sit together. I sat on the left side of the aisle; Ed sat on the right, a row ahead of me. I saw his shoulders and the back of his head with the brown hat and thought that this person, this strange man over there, was now my husband, and I was his wife. That suddenly seemed so incredible, so unreal; we were bound for the rest of our lives! We really did not know each other that well yet.

I would have liked to touch him, to have him look at me, so I would be assured that he was not a stranger, but my beloved. Of course, I did not do that. I sat quietly in my seat, turning the gold ring on my finger that felt so new and unaccustomed there. I was thinking that this was the first hour of my married life. Through the window, I could see the sun trying to break through the clouds, making everything lighter and brighter. When we arrived at Kings Heath and got off the bus, the sun shone richly over the trees and houses and the sky was blue.

Mother awaited us with a good dinner, and we could get to it right away. The table was set up in Johnny's room, which was the largest on the ground floor. There were flowers in a vase and red wine in glasses. We drank to our happiness, hoping that we would have it, and enjoyed the nice food.

After eating though, we wanted to leave. This was our day, and we wanted to be on our own. We had planned to go to the West End to dance in the evening, but we still had the whole afternoon. Outside the day was so beautiful, the warmest one so far this spring. It would be a shame to spend it indoors. We got on a bus and went to Cannon Hill Park, not far from Kings Heath and partway to our house.

Once in the park, we walked hand in hand along the paths, enjoying the warmth of the sun on our faces and hands. Blossoming cherry trees arched their branches above our heads blessing our day. Crocuses and daffodils bloomed under the trees. All of nature was waking up for a new cycle of life, and so were we—the birds in the trees singing our wedding songs.

Having walked the whole length of the park to the other end, our legs were quite tired. Suddenly we had an idea.

"Let's go to the cinema!" We almost said it in unison, thinking of the large "Bristol" cinema that was quite close by.

"Good idea! We can rest up and see a film!" I said.

That was not a regular thing people did on their wedding day, but

so what? This was our day. We could spend it the way we wanted! Feeling like big children, who had taken liberties to go out on their own, we bought the tickets at "Bristol" cinema and walked in. They were showing a film with Doris Day, whom we both liked. "The Lullaby of Broadway" was a lighthearted, happy story. Lights flashed on the screen, there were songs and music. We watched and enjoyed it, but it was like it was all at a distance, for we were too full of our own feelings about the happenings of this day.

The evening of our first wedding day had come. We sat at a table at the West End dance hall downtown. The dancing couples moved past us. We had been dancing quite a lot already and began to feel the effects of the long day. It was good to just sit quietly, watch the dancers and only now and then exchange a few words. We did not need many words. We understood each other without them.

All of a sudden, I remembered that we had sat here a year earlier, when Ed told me the story about the young man and his Magic Christmas tree. I felt a deep tenderness welling up in me as I remembered this, when he opened up to me in this special way for the first time. Instinctively I reached out my hand and put it on his big one that was lying on the table right in front of me.

"My dear hand," I thought... but before I had even finished the thought, he pulled his hand back and said, "I don't like people petting in public!"

I was aghast! It was like a smack in my face. I had only put my hand on his here in the half-darkness, where all around us young people were kissing and embracing. A big lump rose up in my throat. I felt unduly reprimanded. Luckily Ed asked me to dance again, and I could hide my face from him, since he was much taller than I. We danced, but big hot tears welled up in my eyes and rolled down my cheeks. It was sufficiently dark, so that nobody could see them. The ceiling projector made the colored lights to change and slide over the dancers, all the time and I just let the tears roll. Great sadness filled my heart as I thought, "Have I already lost before I have even started my new life?"

I could not even wipe away my tears, for then Ed would know that they had been there and I did not want that. I gritted my teeth and tried to cut off this kind of thinking. We continued dancing, and Ed did not notice anything wrong. The tears gradually dried, just leaving stiff tracks across my cheeks, but the heaviness in my heart did not disappear.

"So this is what my wedding day is like," my thoughts would not stop. "What will my whole life be like?" I wondered as I turned, following the dance rhythms automatically. "Why, why did you do it to me, Ed? My dear, dear Ed..." I asked within myself silently.

I felt his shoulder close to my cheek, the well-known scent of his body, and the held back tears hurt even more, though I knew that he could not have done it to me deliberately.

When we got home, however, he noticed that the joy of this day was not in my eyes anymore in spite of all my trying not to show it. He took me in his arms, and wanted me to tell him what had happened, to which I just shook my head. I did not want to accuse him, and I knew that the hurt would pass as everything in time did.

"Tell me!" He held me and did not leave me alone, and finally with great difficulty, I mustered a few words. He held and kissed me on my eyes and my forehead insisting that he had never wanted to cause me pain. The great stone lifted from my heart, and nothing stood between us anymore. I smiled through tears, which had welled up in my eyes again, but this time they were the tears of gratefulness that Ed had taught me to talk and share my sorrows. After that, I took off my new wedding ring and put it back in the box. I also told Ed that I wanted to be by myself this last week before the forever and ever... He had a hard time understanding that.

"But what difference does it make?" he said putting his arms around me.

"It does to me," I half whispered, and he gave in and went upstairs.


The following week was full of activities. I went over to Mother's every evening after work, to help with food preparations for the wedding reception that was to be held at her place next Saturday. The guests had been invited, as many as we could squeeze around the tables in Johnny's room. We figured that twenty one was the limit, but at least our closest friends would be there. When I got home in the evenings, all kinds of surprises awaited me. Those were wedding gifts, brought by our friends! Things that would be very useful in our future life, like blankets, sheets, dishes and other things. Almost at the last minute, quite by accident, we found out that Ed's uncle was also in England and lived in Bradford, a mill town farther north. Many Latvians lived and worked there. We were glad that we had managed to contact him, and he promised to come to our wedding.

Saturday came, the day of our real wedding. It was April 1, 1950. The ceremony was to take place at six-thirty in the evening at the Bishop Ryder Lutheran church in the city, where our Latvian monthly worship services were held. There was plenty of time till then, but many more things had to be accomplished. First Ed and I went to town to get the flowers for my bouquet that we had ordered the Saturday before. But when we arrived at the shop, the flowers were not there, and nobody knew anything about our order.

"All the lilies are reserved for the churches for the next Sunday's Easter service and there are none we can spare for you!" was the answer.

I was so upset that I almost cried. We went from one place to another, but the answer was the same. Neither anger, nor tears, nor arguments helped. There were no flowers for me. I was beginning to panic, when I suddenly remembered a small shop in one of the narrow side streets and indeed, that was where we got them, my white lilies!

Happy that this problem was solved, I went home to put the flowers in water and then right away got on the bus to Mother's house to help with the last preparations. Ed stayed in town, for soon he would have to go to the station to meet his Uncle.

It was already late afternoon, when finally I was on my way home. The bright morning sun had disappeared, and the sky was overcast and gray again. I felt rather tired after working non-stop all this week, and it was good to take a little breather even on this short trip on the bus.

At home, I was awaited by Ed and my new relative, the brother of Ed's mother, who also had been an army officer. He was rather short and stocky and had a smoothly shaved head. Ed introduced us, and I was glad that he too would now have someone of his own family at our wedding. Then I saw the half empty bottle of cognac on the table and was not happy about that. They had been drinking.

We all sat down and Uncle filled the glasses. He said this meeting should be celebrated and passed a glass to me as well, but I declined. I did not like such strong drinks and was rather concerned when I saw that Ed had been drinking quite a bit as well.

"Why don't you go upstairs and start dressing?" I urged him, but he just laughed.

"There's still plenty of time and it will not take me long!"

I went upstairs to what would be our bedroom, and where I had brought up all my clothing yesterday. I laid out my national costume on the bed. It would be my wedding dress tonight, and Ed would wear his new dark suit. That would have to do. We had no problem with that. The wedding was expensive enough to even think of anything else.

Finally we were all ready. Mother and Johnny came too, all dressed up nicely for the ceremony. It was time to get on our way. We had arranged to go to the photographer before the wedding, so our guests would not have to wait after the service, and we all got into the taxi. Ed was a bit "high" and started giving commands to the taxi driver that embarrassed me.

"Why did they have to drink so much knowing what was ahead of us?" I thought. We were at the photographers quite a while, though, and I was glad about that. It gave time for the effects of the drinking to subside. Ed was his own self again.

At last! We were on our way to the church. The dusk was gathering

in the streets. People hurried along this way and that with heavy shopping bags in their hands. Long lines stood at the bus stops as it usually was at this time of day on Saturdays, because on Sundays everything was closed. Only the "News Agents"—shops that sold newspapers, magazines, cigarettes and sweets—were open on Sundays. It was so strange to think that we were not part of the crowds today but sitting here in the black limousine going to a wedding. Our wedding! Was it really true?

All this week had passed by being so busy that we had hardly had a chance to see each other, let alone experience those quiet times that we so enjoyed. The driver slowed down as we neared the church. He wanted to get us there at the precise time, and he did.

In Latvian weddings, the bride and groom are led into the church by a leading couple. We had chosen Saša and my dear friend Mrs. Avots to be our leading couple. They awaited us at the door and right away led us into the church, walking with the rhythmical sounds of the organ. Ed and I, with my hand through his right arm, followed them to where the minister stood in front of the altar. As in a dream, I sensed the people sitting in the half-dark pews looking at us. I was so keyed up that I trembled, and even the flowers in my arm trembled. I felt Ed's body tighten next to me. He must have felt my trembling and he pressed my arm closer to his body. There was comfort in that, and the trembling ceased.

We were at the altar, our leaders receding to the sides. These would be the final bonds tying us together, so we would become one before God for all time. I looked at the golden flames of the tall candles, and my heart lifted up in one great prayer to God that He would be our strength and our help in whatever we would have to face. The prayer rose up, disappearing in the dark vaults of the church ceiling, as dark and mystifying as the future that stood before us. Yes, I was afraid of what the future would bring, I had to admit. I knew it would not be a path scattered with roses.

I tried to listen to the minister's words, but they slid by me. Only the words of my prayer to God were still with me.

"Abide with us, Lord Almighty!"

Then we had a surprise. Our friends from the choir had prepared a song especially for us. It was a prayer written by a Latvian poet and a Latvian composer.

"For every hour, I thank you, Lord,
For every breath,
For every living day..."

It seemed that every word was meant especially for us. The sounds rose up to the ceiling, touching and moving us to the depth of our hearts. This seemed to be the most poignant moment of this evening, when we really felt in the presence of the Lord Almighty.

Then the "Yes" words were said and the rings exchanged. High up in the vaults the music started. It was Handel's "Largo", played by our dear choir master, Mrs. Roze. The ceremony was over. We turned and began to walk the first mile of the rest of our lives together.

At home the party was like parties usually were, with eating, drinking and later also singing. Toasts were offered and drunk to our health and happiness, the glasses lifted up many times, wishing us happiness in our married life. The room was packed, but at least we had our very closest friends there. Ed and I sat at the end of the long table, but now and then I seemed to step back within myself, silently asking if this was really my wedding? It seemed so unreal, this crowd, this gayety. I would have liked to go somewhere quiet to think about it. I had never been a crowd person, but now of course, I had to stay here. I saw that Ed was drinking a good deal again, but on an occasion like this, it was rather difficult not to. People kept touching our glasses and then you had to take at least a sip.

It was well after midnight, when we finally went home on the nighttime bus. I was glad that it was all over now, and there was peace and quiet again. Ed went upstairs, while I prepared the bed for the Uncle on our sleeper sofa, where Mother and I had been sleeping all this time. Then I quietly went up the stairs, too. It was dark in the bedroom. Only the street lamp let some light in through the window, so I could see a little. Ed was in bed. I softly called his name, but there was no answer. He had fallen asleep.

I did not switch on the light, but slowly undressed in the dark, so as not to disturb him. A quiet sadness entered my heart. I lay in bed with open eyes and saw the ceiling becoming gray from the morning light. I thought how different this day would have been if we had waited... I knew that on that autumn day when I gave up my dream, but it was not so easy to forget. A silent ache was in my heart that it had not been possible, but it was in the past now.

It was rather late in the morning when we awoke, and the sun shone right into our faces. It was so warm and my eyes were still full of sleep, though I could hear the morning noises outside and sensed that Ed was awake too.

"Good morning, sweetheart," he said, and I murmured back the greeting, still full of sleep. The sun was so warm on my eyes that I could not open them. Then I felt Ed reach out his arm and slowly pull me close to him.

Already a while before our wedding, we had figured out that we would not have enough money left to go to Scotland at this time,

but we thought that we could, perhaps, go to London for a few days. We had seen an advertisement in the Latvian newspaper that a Latvian lady, living in the suburbs of London, owned a large house there, offering it as a guest house to tourists, or travelers for a reasonable price. Ed had written to her, saying that we were two tired travelers who would need a room, and could she accommodate us on the given dates? The answer had come back positive, so we were all set.

Actually, we were not too well set, for our saved money had shrunk considerably, but since we had both asked for a week off from work, we did not want to waste the time, either. We borrowed five pounds from Mrs. Bērziņš and then we could go. The first thing next morning, we took Uncle Jon to the station and put him on the train, after he promised us that he would wind up his affairs in the north and come to live with us, so he would not be alone in the world. Then we got on our train to London.

When we arrived at the guest house, the owner was surprised to see us, a married couple, for she had expected two men. Ed had not been too explicit about this in his letter.

"I am so sorry! None of the small rooms are available anymore! All I have left is a large room with six beds, but since this is not tourist season, I am not expecting anyone else, and you can stay there if you want to."

We accepted, for there was no other way.

"Would you sign the register, Mrs. Vidners?" The lady asked me, which sounded so strange, since nobody had called me by that name yet. I had an urge to look over my shoulder to see if there was not another person who might answer to that name. I was also hesitant about signing my name for I had not practiced it, and the owner probably guessed our new family situation. Then she took us upstairs and showed us the room that was large but very bright and clean with white covers everywhere.

In the afternoon we went to acquaint ourselves with the city. We walked along the wide streets, passing the large store windows full of all kinds of beautiful things; the big city droned and buzzed around us. We walked like Hansel and Gretel in the storybook, hand in hand, looking at all this big, colorful world, being happy that we did not need any of those things. We had enough with what we had. Perhaps the very fact that we did not have money to buy anything showed us what was important and what was not.

I liked London with its big old buildings and the crowds of people streaming past us. So many different faces just caught with a glance, and sounds of different languages reaching our ears! We walked and walked until it was dusk in the streets, and the street lights came on blooming like big red roses. They reminded everyone that the evening was nearing,

and it was time to return home.

When we got back to the guesthouse and walked into our room, a surprise was awaiting us. Our two beds had been pushed side by side, and my pillow was covered with a lacy pillowcase. In addition, a pink blooming hydrangea plant stood on my nightstand. I felt very much moved by this act of kindness, and the big room looked more like home right away.

We needed to eat, and Ed moved the small table from the window alcove closer to the fireplace. Then he put a shilling into the gas meter, and pleasant warmth began to radiate as I set the table for our supper. I had bought some lamb chops for our Sunday dinner, but since Mother invited us back to continue feasting on the leftovers from the wedding party, we did not get to eat the chops. That was why I just fried them in the evening to take them with us the next day on our journey. They were Ed's favorite food, and we could not afford to waste them. I had also brought some rye bread and butter, which would make a meal. When Ed went downstairs and brought up two mugs of hot tea, there was nothing more to wish for.

We sat at the small table in front of the fire and ate the chops with our fingers. A piece of bread and the hot tea to go with it tasted wonderful. We laughed and joked.

"If anyone could see us now!" Ed said. "Like real country bumpkins, come to town with their own food!" But what was it to us? We did not care what the world would make of it. We were happy!

When everything was tidied away after the meal, we did feel tired after the long and colorful day. The white beds were so inviting with the clean, nice smelling sheets. We got into them and were in each other's arms.

The following days were cool and overcast. We spent them mostly in the museums and art galleries until our heads began to spin. In the evening we walked around Piccadilly and Leicester Square, where the large cinema fronts glittered in lights. Small cozy eating places coaxed the passers-by to come in.

We flowed along with the happy crowds, feeling as upbeat as they seemed to be. We did not have the money to go into these luxurious cinemas, where you could see the plush carpets, plants and soft intimate lights through the open doors, but we went into one of the small eating places around the corner from the square. The chef, in a tall white hat, stood in the window, frying sausages and enticing people to come in and taste them. It was late afternoon, and we were hungry. The food really smelled good. We went in and we ordered sausages, eggs and the thinly cut potato strips, the same as the other diners. It was a warm and cozy place, where one could sit and eat while watching the people passing by

outside. They were mostly young people, young couples with their arms around each other, but there were some older people also, perhaps visitors to the city. To finish off our meal, Ed ordered a piece of cake for me as a dessert, then quietly smiling, smoked his pipe and looked on as I enjoyed it. He knew that cakes were my weakness.

By Wednesday evening we had visited most of the important places we had wanted to see, and in the afternoon it had started to rain. We had thought of spending the whole week in London, but checking our finances before retiring, found that they had shrunk amazingly. We had not even bought anything or done things that might be costly!

"I think we should go home," I said. "We have seen a lot. We have enjoyed ourselves. There will be other times to come and visit again".

"Yes, I agree," Ed said. "All things considered... the wisest thing would be to go home and spend the rest of the days there."

All of a sudden we wanted to be there, in our own place, with our big chair where we could sit by the fire; where our little Christmas tree stood on the small table in half-darkness giving a glitter or two from its snow-covered branches. Yes, we would go home tomorrow.

In Birmingham the weather had turned. The north wind again shook and swayed the trees and shrubs. The sky was again overcast with clouds, low and heavy as lead. It looked like winter was on the doorstep, not spring, the wind being so sharp and biting. We, on the other hand, were in our warm room by the fire, making toast and enjoying our suppertime in firelight. The springtime was in our room together with its magic.

Summer came and went. It had delighted us with the white climbing roses, blooming all around the garden, but now they were almost gone. The apple trees, too, had exchanged their delicate blossoms for branches full of apples. So often during the summertime we had spent sunny Sundays lying under their green canopies, sunbathing and exchanging kisses, which filled us with a heavy sweetness like honey bees with honey. Still warm from the hot sun, we had to go inside to do what we had to do. It was our first summer together.

Autumn came, and the rays of sunshine were long and golden, but they did not have the warmth of the summer anymore. When they filtered through the branches of the apple trees and fell on the grass below, a lot of leaves lay there already. The roses had finished blooming and small reddish fruits had developed in place of the blossoms.

The dazed summer days had left something in me also. I knew that I was carrying a new life and was happy about it. Earlier, we had talked about saving up money and getting situated nicely before having a family, but with our meager wages, that would take years. I would not want to wait for years. Ed felt the same way and was loving and caring. It was

all right. Things were not so important. As long as we could get by, we would make it work.

In the evenings, sitting in the big chair, we tried to imagine how it would be, when we will have a little child of our own. It had to be a boy, a little Eddy with blond hair. My heart warmed at this thought and was full of tenderness, but we would have to wait.

We were happy at home, yet sometimes, we had a great urge to get out and see something else. We would count up our pennies to see if we had enough to go to the small local cinema. It only cost a shilling there, and that was such a treat! We felt like children who had found a piece of candy on the street. When we came home after the film, our steps echoed on the frozen ground, and the cold breath of the night crept through our clothing. A few dry leftover leaves scuttled along the gutter pushed by a breeze. Up above us were the big, bright stars of a cold autumn night.

Ed had found another job and now worked in a factory making meshed metal guards. He did not have to work shifts anymore, as he did at the gas works, and could be home in the evenings. I was very glad about that, for I wanted him near me, especially at this time. When I wrapped my arms around his tall body and rested my head on his chest, I felt that I was at home, and that nowhere in the world was it so good.

"You are my home," I said to him. And he put his protecting arms around me, kissed me on the forehead and smiled quietly. He had never told me in so many words that he loved me, but I knew it without words. Like my Dad had said—love had to be felt. We shared everything now, sometimes just sensing each other. How good that Ed had taught me to talk and open up! Life was so much better and easier.

And yet, and yet... If I want to be totally honest, there were times when I drew back within myself. Just a few small splinters now and then, especially when Ed had been drinking.

Ed's Uncle Jon, his only relative here, had been living with us since he came to us a couple of weeks after our wedding, and we got on very well. The landlady, Mrs. Floyd, was kind enough to allow us to use another small room for him, charging only ten shillings a month, which was very generous. Altogether, the three of us earned about ten pounds a week: Ed got four pounds, I got three pounds and Uncle also three or a little less. Our rent was two and a half pounds or fifty shillings a month, a pound being twenty shillings. The Uncle was delighted to have his own small room where he could rest or go to bed as early as he wished. Before, up in Bradford, he had lived in a men's hostel without any privacy at all.

Uncle Jon was a good man, usually quiet and self-contained, but always friendly and kind toward me. A fun ritual developed between us as time went on. Every evening, after getting home from work, even before taking off his coat and hat, he would first come to the kitchen to

greet me. Each time I already knew beforehand what he would say when I heard his steps in the long hallway, so I awaited him with a smile.

"Good evening, Zigi," he would say, "and how are you doing?"

"Good, good!" I would answer.

"And how is your love life?"

"Also good," I would answer, laughing.

"Then everything is all right, so what are you shouting about?" he smiled too, then turned, and chuckling to himself, slowly walked away along the hallway.

After dinner, while we still sat around the table, Uncle liked to smoke his cigarette, but first he cut it in smaller pieces and then put one piece into a short cigarette holder.

"You don't need that much at one time," he would say, but it was probably to save some money, so that once in a while he could afford to by some cognac. And he would drink only Martell, nothing else would do. On the workday evenings, he sat there in the corner of the sofa like an old tree stump, dressed in his gray cardigan, smoking his little stub of the cigarette and talking slowly. Uncle Jon still had a shaved head. He was not fat, but his body had settled within itself, and his walk was heavy. He looked like an old man, although he was just over fifty, but he had lived through a lot and had also lived it up a lot and had remained a bachelor.

Uncle Jon had spent most of his life in the army, having joined it at an early age. Sometimes on weekends when we sat around, he would tell us more about the old days when he had been in the Czar's army, learning the military skills. That had been before Latvia became an independent state. Later he had taken part in the liberation of Latvia from its enemies, when the independence of the country was proclaimed. It was very interesting to hear about it all. In the later years after that, he had served in the coast and border guards chasing the brandy smugglers off Latvia's western coast.

Ed also remembered and told me how forthcoming he had been in his younger years. Now he was an old man with bent shoulders and stiffness in his legs, who worked in a factory sweeping floors. He knew very little English and was glad that he even had this job, so he could earn his daily bread. That was the most important thing, and between the three of us, we could manage all right. Often, I made a large pot of sauerkraut soup with meat in it. That, eaten together with rye bread, would provide a meal for us for the whole week.

During the week we each went to our job, but weekends were our own special time of celebration. Not that anything that special happened. I think it was the feeling we created in our home. Everything had been cleaned spotless (both of us sharing the work)—then it was bath-time. It felt so good then, changing into clean clothing for the weekend. In

those days in England you could only have one bath a week in the one bathroom that we had to share with other tenants; therefore it always was special. There were flowers and fresh fruit on the table, the symbols of our celebration, and nothing was lacking. We were the richest people on earth, even though the only thing we owned was the double bed I had bought before Mother came from Germany, and toward the end of the week we had to count our pennies carefully, so we would have enough for our bus fares to work.

Uncle Jon said that we did not know how to live. Why did we waste money?

"Why do you buy flowers and fruit?" he said.

Why indeed, but that was the only daring thing we did in our lives, and people needed joy to be fully alive. That was why our home was what it was, full of joy and love. We did not have to feel deprived.

After having cleaned our "house" on Saturday mornings, Ed and I would go to town to do our weekly shopping. First we went to the larger department store in town that carried more of the continental foods, which you could not get in the small local shops. We liked salted herrings, various sausages and rye bread. These were the times before supermarkets or self-serve stores. The next trek was to the Bull Ring market on the edge of the city center. We walked through the rows of tents and carts full of fruits and vegetables there, checking the quality and the prices until we found what we wanted.

The market was an interesting place. It had an atmosphere of its own, as most markets do. The people milled around like ants in an ant-hill, but nobody minded the pushing and shoving; they even seemed to enjoy this togetherness, apologizing and moving on. It was nobody's private place; it was everybody's place, the vendors shouting their slogans and praising their products amidst the crowds.

"*E-ya!* Fresh tomatoes! The best in the world!"

Everything was "the best in the world", which nobody believed but took with a smile. It happened quite often that you saw the vendor put nice apples or tomatoes in your bag—you were not allowed to touch anything yourself! But at home you found that he had smuggled in something of lesser quality also. How they did it was a mystery.

When we had got all that we needed for the week, Ed turned to the flower sellers, who usually stood under the overpass with huge baskets of flowers at their feet, shouting their sales pitches and holding out bunches of flowers to passersby.

"You take your time and pick out what you want," Ed would say, standing by and smiling while I tried to find the nicest ones, but mostly also the cheapest, for I did not want to wreck our budget. When all that was done, we headed back to our tram stop. Even though our bags were

heavy and we were tired, our hearts were happy. On our way we had to pass a bakery, and Ed would say, smiling,

"Now why don't you go in and get something for yourself." I usually bought just one little cake for myself like an éclair or a cream puff, for the men did not care for sweets. Then there really was nothing more to wish for.

Uncle Jon too, wanted to celebrate sometimes, and those were the worry days for me. He would give Ed money to get the cognac, and then Ed would have to keep him company, whether he wanted to or not. Usually it started on Saturday afternoon or evening and continued till Sunday noon, but occasionally till Sunday evening. That made me very unhappy, but what could I say? The old man also needed some enjoyment once in a while, for he did not go anywhere, nor had any friends. When he had had a few drinks, he became more talkative, and his old soldier's stature came alive for a little while until his body became tired, his shoulders sank, and he asked Ed to help him up the stairs.

Poor old war horse! He did not have anything in this world but this bit of drink, which made him remember the man he used to be. I did not begrudge him that, but I would have preferred that Ed did not have to drink with him. The old man also had arteriosclerosis in his legs and Ed had to give him injections for that. He had done a lot of living it up in his heyday.

After some rainy days, it was a clear autumn day once again. The sun had come out for a change and was warming my back through the kitchen window, while I stood at the stove cooking our dinner. Potatoes were cooking, bubbling and raising steam; in the skillet, the pork chops were getting golden brown, spreading a delicious aroma in the area. It was to be our special Saturday dinner.

I knew that in a moment or two, the door opposite our kitchen area would open, and Jack's big body would appear in it with a smiling face under the dark, half-gray thatch of hair and bushy black eyebrows. He was another renter, and we actually had to share this tiny kitchen nook with him. Jack, however, did not do much cooking. Being a bachelor, he just used it to boil some water for tea and occasionally fry some sausages, but he loved to talk. I suppose, while living alone, that was a necessity, so as soon as he heard me working in the kitchen, he came out and gave me a greeting. I already knew what would come next, for I had heard it many times.

This was a ritual Jack had invented. With a serious face—as serious as he could make it—and, as if he was going to reveal the biggest secret in the world, he would say in a hushed voice, "Zigi, you know what?"

"What?" I asked, smiling, knowing already what he would say.

"Mary had a little lamb, but she also had a bear. And everybody saw

the lamb, and nobody saw the bear!" That may have been a song he had learned in his childhood days in Ireland. Then he laughed with such an abandon that I had to laugh too.

"Now have you ever heard anything like that?" he would laugh gasping for breath.

"No, never! And that is why you repeat it to me every evening," I answered.

So we often chatted and joked while I worked in the kitchen. Jack also knew all of the newest gossip concerning of what was happening in the house, for he often visited with Kathleen, (the caretaker of this house) who also was Irish. She had her own apartment on the other side of the house. He would tell me his news in a whispered voice, even though nobody else was around. There were not too many renters, anyway. One older woman had a room upstairs and a young couple with a baby lived next to us on the ground floor

Funny Jack! But Jack was also a naughty boy, and we all knew it. His mind was more set on fun rather than on working, and he was often "ill". When I asked him if he had worked, he just stood there in his crumpled shirt, leaning against the door and silently chuckling to himself.

"I had to go to the doctor, you know?" he said in a weak voice. "I don't think I am very well," he added, trying to keep his big face straight, but I could see the mischievous sparkle in his eyes. He pushed his fingers through his bushy hair and shoved his hands into the pockets of his pants. They barely hung on his hips, held up with a belt under his big belly.

Jack was a simple soul and lived simply—not much thinking about tomorrow. He did not have any relatives and he did not horde things. Just a few shirts and something warmer for the winter; that was all he needed. He worked only so much as not to lose his job. That was why he went to the doctor so often, to get a note saying that he really was ill and could not work, which was required by the government. He must have had an Irish doctor who would give him these sickness notes. Of course, it was so much more pleasant to sit in a pub, where golden mugs of beer were passed around the table and many a wonderful tale was told.

"There is so much a person can learn!" He would say. "And then there is the laughter! A person could not live without good laughter!" That was Jack's view of life.

After a little chat, he went into his room and came out a few minutes later with smoothly combed hair and a white nylon scarf wrapped around his neck, probably so others would not see that he did not wear a collar and a tie, which was a must for any full-blooded Englishman and even more so for the Irish when they went to the pub Then he put on his jacket, called out a goodbye, and cocking his eye at me, walked outside

through the back door. I just shook my head, smiling to myself. But who knows, maybe he was wiser than the rest of us. He did exactly what he wanted to and "never mind" the rest.

The dinner was almost ready when I heard steps in the hallway. It was Ed. Smiling, he came up to me and kissed me, still full of the cool breath of outside. Then he put a tall package wrapped in white paper in my hands. When I opened it, there were four huge white chrysanthemum blooms, like balls just rolled in fresh snow. The small, curved petals half covered each other in rows and rows, leaving pale green shadows between them. My beautiful flowers! I was so moved that tears came into my eyes.

Dear Ed, he had remembered this day, our proper wedding day! Perhaps he did understand what I gave up for him that day a year ago. We stood in the small kitchen hugging each other, and our eyes were moist. This was and always will be our true wedding day: without ceremonies, without feasts, only with a soft scent of white chrysanthemums on a sunny autumn day. Thank you, Ed, thank you for remembering!

Christmas was nearing again. The ground was frozen and echoed under my steps as I hurried to catch my bus on my way to work in the mornings. In the evenings the sky was already dark, and the stars in it were large and cold. The days were so short. Everything outside was bare and had shrunk within itself in the cold of the winter. Even the soot-covered houses seemed to have become smaller and grayer in the area where I worked. A sharp wind swept the streets, chasing empty cigarette packs along the gutters. There was no snow to cover this winter starkness as there had been in our native Latvia, where the land was covered with snow, soft as a white blanket all winter long. There was no relief here. People stood in lines at the bus stops looking ill-natured and hostile, or rushed past with lowered heads, guarding themselves against the wind.

Regardless of all that, Christmas was coming, and that changed the mood. In the city, shop windows bloomed like colorful gardens with all kinds of attractive things beautifully displayed, enticing people to come in, and they did. Like bees in a beehive they flowed in and out through the glass doors of the department stores. They did not mind being pushed and shoved around the gift counters of toiletries, scents and especially toys. People crowded there the most, wanting to get closer to see the displays and check the prices.

The crowds were everywhere, but now they were happy crowds with people's eyes full of anticipation of bringing joy to their loved ones, and a little while later, they would come out with larger or smaller packages in their hands. And the faces were smiling again, for Christmas was coming. Even just seeing these colorful things lifted your spirits. These

were the days when the regular folks in England did not have too much, having just recently come out of the constraints of war, so anything was truly appreciated.

In our house too, preparations were made for celebrating this wonderful event by continuing our old traditions as far as possible. And we too, the same as everybody else, were dreaming of a white Christmas. We heard that the film called "Holiday Inn" would be shown in our small local cinema and went to see it one evening. How wonderful it all was! We loved to hear Bing Crosby sing "I'm dreaming of a white Christmas". Our hearts were so full of joy, for we knew what those white Christmases were really like. Happy memories came to mind of Christmases in Latvia. That was a treasure we could take with us into the future, and we expected a lot from it. Not things, or riches or fame, but that our love would grow and would be in us always.

The last week before Christmas, Ed's workplace had a Christmas party for all the workers, and we decided to go and have some fun. I put on my mauve colored taffeta dress that I had made the previous year. It looked so good on me, but I had forgotten that I was bigger now since I was expecting the baby. Standing at the bus stop, I started to feel uncomfortable and whispered to Ed to stand in front of me, so I could undo the side zipper of the dress and breathe easier.

The evening turned out to be quite fun. We danced, but every so often the music stopped and some fun activity took place. It was a real "English" party. Various talents were called out to give a performance either singing, or acting, or telling a joke. A short young man attempted to sing the very popular song *"Mona Lisa"* and just about tortured it to death, but the applause was great, and there was a lot of laughter.

A joke was played by the company, causing a lot of whistling and cheering from the public. All the expecting fathers were called out and given pacifiers as a gift for their coming babies together with good wishes. Ed also was honored with one. It was a typically English celebration, but we did enjoy it.

On the last day before Christmas Eve, which happened to be on a Saturday, Ed and I walked through the Bull Ring market doing our final shopping. Needless to say, there were more people than usual. The weather was awful. Wet snowflakes, mixed with rain, fell on our faces and sometimes even into our eyes, so for a moment it was impossible to see. The asphalt under our feet got blacker and muddier. We tried to navigate around the biggest puddles and now and then wiped the wetness off our faces, yet today it all seemed more like fun, for it was going to be Christmas! The joy of it was everywhere around us.

When we had bought everything we needed, we looked for the Christmas tree. I sorted through a heap of them trying to find the nicest

one. Not a big one, but a nice one, and my heart was full of joy like it was in my childhood days. After that, Ed bought me a nice pink cyclamen to put on our table, and then we could go home.

Our very own first Christmas! It was Christmas Eve, and the whole house was filled with the smells of my baking the traditional small bacon rolls and other things. All the other food for the cold table had been prepared before; only the Christmas tree remained to be decorated. Our living room was sparkling clean, and each little thing seemed to have put on a festive mood in anticipation of the sacred night. Even our old bluish rug had taken on fresher color, warming itself in the reddish glow of the fireplace, for Ed had scrubbed it on his hands and knees. The room was bathed in a pleasant silence, except outside the rain threw heavy drops against the window panes.

I took the decorations that we had and put them on the tree with the white candles between them. On top went the silver star that Saša had made for us the previous year. When that was done, I stretched the silvery, translucent angel's hair over everything and then it was finished.

I looked at our initial little fake Christmas tree standing on the small table by the window and saw two tiny sparkles of its snow winking at me. It, too, will have a second little one this Christmas. I had already bought it. This tree was still our joint heart and soul for it had brought us together. I stooped down in front of it and gazed at it with love and gratitude in my heart. I told it that the following year there would be another little head at this Christmas tree, and it looked like it smiled happily back at me.

Then I heard a knock on the door and went to receive our guests: Mother, Johnny and Saša. At that same moment, Ed and Uncle Jon came down the stairs dressed up for the celebration. When everybody had settled down, I started to light the candles on our Christmas tree, and Ed switched off the lamp. With each lit candle, more light came into the room and also into my heart. The star sparkled at the top of the tree, and the angel's hair looked like a shiny silvery veil over everything. We watched this beauty for a little while, each having our own thoughts and feelings, but all of us knowing that this was the sacred night when our Savior was born.

I began to sing *"Silent Night"*, my most favorite Christmas song, and the others joined in harmony. Since we had sang it in the choir, we knew all the parts, and it sounded wonderful, our voices rising as we went through the verses reliving the wonderful words, which we had known since childhood. Afterward, we sang other beloved Christmas songs, while the candle lights threw star-like shadows of the tree branches on the walls and the ceiling. Looking into the lights of the candles, my heart was one huge prayer that our Father in Heaven would grant us His

light on our future paths also.

Our path after the New Year, however, was not so bright. In the middle of February, when I went for my monthly checkup, it was found that I had high blood pressure. The doctor said that I needed complete rest and ordered me to stay in the hospital for two weeks.

"Why can't I rest at home?" I argued. I did not want to be away from Ed.

"No," was the short answer. "This is important."

I had to stay in a smaller building called the Annex, situated next to the main Sorrento Maternity Hospital, and my days consisted of just lying in bed and resting. Quite a lot of blood was taken for tests, and the bad part of it was that the Sister in charge, who drew the blood, was not good at it. She would poke and poke, and by the time I went home, both my arms were black and blue. There was also one more thing. In the English hospitals they did not tell you anything about your condition. There must have been some improvement, and I was allowed to go home but cautioned sternly not to do anything for another two weeks. Apparently the high blood pressure had something to do with my kidneys.

"Promise that you will rest…" said the doctor. "Remember, it is very important!"

"I promise!" I answered sadly.

So here I was, sitting at home in the big chair, looking around and thinking about all the things I had planned to do before the baby arrived in the beginning of May, but now I could not do anything. It was hard, and I asked myself repeatedly what had I done to deserve this?

Mother came to see me one day.

"My poor girl," she said, looking at me with a worried face and tears in her eyes when she first arrived. "I am so sorry that things are not going well for you! I came to see if I could help you with anything."

"I do have some clothing I put in to soak, and there are a few groceries I need, but maybe I'll manage somehow…" I said, though hoping that perhaps she would help. It was so hard for me to leave everything to Ed, and I ended up doing what needed to be done, even though it was not good for my present health situation.

As we sat talking, I wanted to tell Mother of my worries and fears for my baby and myself. I really wanted to bare my heart to her this time and perhaps get some comfort, but after a couple of sentences, she cut me off and started to tell me her own story. I interrupted her flow of words in the beginning and tried once more, asking her to listen to me, for I had such a need to unburden myself, but it was no use. She was so wrapped up in what she had to say, that she did not even hear me. For the first time real bitterness rose up in my heart toward my Mother. I closed up and did

not say anything anymore. After she had talked for a while, she got up, satisfied with what she had done, and said, "Well, I'd better hurry home. I put some peas in to soak last night. I'll have to get them planted!"

She had no problems, and she obviously did not have time or interest for mine All the business of helping had been forgotten. I was sure that my Mother loved me in her own way, but she was always so full of herself that she did not have room for me. Well…

I put my head down, so she would not see the hurt in my eyes. A little peck on my cheek and the next moment she was out on the street, walking away happily. I stared after her and swallowed hard. We had never been particularly close, and she had admonished me about it, but how can you share anything with another person if they show no interest and do not want to take time to listen to you? And especially at this time! How could she not see?

I had never bothered her with my problems before, even as I was growing up, but this time my heart was so full of sorrow that I really needed her love and understanding. As I watched her go, I was sad and knew for sure that the only person in this world who truly loved me and on whom I could rely on was Ed.

I did get better and went back to work for a little while. I actually wanted to stop working, but Mr. Fisher was going away and Mr. Hunt's back had gone out, so they begged me to stay at least a couple of weeks longer. Not even to work, but just be there; for by now I knew quite a lot of how things worked.

## Ulī is born

March arrived with fresh spring breezes and warm, sunny days. Everything was budding and blooming outside. This spring was so beautiful, only I did not see much of it. Easter was nearing, and we had already planned how we would celebrate it, when suddenly a dark curtain fell over everything. At the checkup, my doctor told me to come to the hospital the following day to stay. She also told me that my baby would, most likely, have to be born earlier than expected. I still tried to bargain with her, "Could I not at least spend Easter at home?" but she answered kindly yet sternly.

"There will be other Easters to celebrate. We will expect you tomorrow morning at the Annex. Goodbye."

I went out into the quiet sunny street and walked away slowly, thinking how I would tell this to Ed? Tears filled my eyes, even though I did not know exactly what was happening. I suddenly felt very lonely. This big "unknown" was before me and there was no escape.

Ed was gentle as I knew he would be. Although he was worried too,

he did not let me see it but tried to comfort and cheer me up. The following morning I was at the hospital as ordered. I lay in a bed in the Annex again, near a half-open window. It was a room with three beds in it, and the other patients had had their babies already.

A branch full of pink blossoms was almost leaning in through the window, and I could hear the birds sing in the large trees outside. The fresh scents of the budding leaves and the sprouting grass floated in. Everything out there was so beautiful that I felt like crying. I had become so "soft" lately, but I had gone through a lot these past few months.

It was Easter morning, and I could hear the sounds of church bells coming in through the open window. Somewhere in the hallway nurses were talking. A spurt of laughter, then suddenly silence. A moment later, the Staff Nurse escorted in all the main doctors. In the Annex were people like me who had problems before the birth, but also young mothers with babies who had some problems. The doctors visited all the beds checking the medical progress on the charts, exchanged a word or two and moved on. They also came to my bed, and the main doctor Hallam asked me, smiling, how I felt.

"I don't really know," I said. "They give me pills and I sleep most of the time."

Our "house doctor" then told her in a low voice what was given to me and how often, and everybody smiled at me kindly. Then they turned and walked out, but I could see them stop in the hallway discussing something, after which Dr. Hallam said something and for a moment turned her head and looked at me.

It was almost lunch time, when our young house doctor came in, took a chair and sat down by my bed. He looked at me with his dark kind eyes and told me something in a low voice. It was something serious, but it seemed to me that he was talking about somebody else, not me. Perhaps I was not quite awake yet. I tried to listen more carefully, and this was what he said: "We just concluded that we cannot wait any longer. Your baby has hardly grown in the past weeks. If we do nothing, the poison, which your kidneys are producing lately, will kill the baby… You understand… It is for your good, so, the sooner, the better."

"What will you do?" I whispered.

"We will induce the labor, and the baby will be born prematurely."

"When?" I asked, still feeling that the talk was about someone else.

"Tomorrow," he said looking me straight in my eyes and not averting them, and suddenly I saw in this look with great clarity that it was me who he was talking about.

He squeezed my hand and smiled at me warmly. "Don't worry at all. We will take good care of you!"

Then he was gone. I stared at the white wall, empty of thoughts or

feelings. It was cold. I looked at the window and saw that the blue skies had disappeared and the sunshine had left the blossoming branch. A silent grayness was everywhere. The wind had come up, shaking the thin curtains and blowing into my face a cold, damp breath, but I lay there motionless and just closed my eyes. I did not have any physical or emotional strength to deal with anything anymore.

The following morning I woke up with such a cold as I had never had before, and nothing medical could be done at this point. Again, all kinds of medications were given to me, and the next couple of days went by like a nightmare, sleeping and waking and sleeping again. By Thursday morning my head was finally clear. This would be the day they would take me to the main house of the Sorrento Maternity Hospital, where everything would be done that needed to be done.

I waited the whole day for somebody to come and take me over, but evening had arrived and it was already getting dark outside, when at last somebody came for me. Wrapped in blankets, I was wheeled across the yard. From the shrubs and the flower beds came the cool scent of the fertile earth. Several tall fir trees towered over the big main building, and above them I could see the first evening stars. I breathed the fresh evening air deeply and wondered when I would feel it on my face again, and how I would be, when I would leave this house and everything would be over.

We had gone up to the second floor. I lay alone in the large dusky room, covered and strapped to a table-like bed. Silence was around me. No people, no sounds of any kind. I felt like a trapped bird with tied wings knowing that I would not escape this. I did not even have a wish or the strength to do it. I lay there and waited; waited for what had to come. Turning my head, I could see through the window the dark tips of the large fir trees against the reddish evening sky and prayed to God, releasing myself into His hands. There was no other help for me.

Then the doctor came in, together with a nurse, both dressed in surgical outfits, and began to busy themselves. My time had come, even though this was only the first step in a long succession of medical procedures. They told me that they also had to turn the baby around.

Ed came a little later and was allowed to stay after the visiting hours. I was still on my own in the large room, but was now in a bed. He kissed me, but we did not talk much. What was there to talk about? Ed looked at me with large, sorrowful eyes, for he could not help me in this. I tried to show a more careless face, but that Big Unknown was before us, and it seemed that was the only thing we had right now. I started to have the first vague pains, and Ed stroked my hand lovingly. He stayed until the sleep time, but then he had to go. I put my arms around his warm neck, hanging on to him, but I knew that he had to go, and I had to stay.

Again I was alone in the big, dark room. The street lamps threw spooky shadows on the walls, and the pains grew stronger. The night passed as a nightmare with sleeping and waking and everything getting mixed up with the pains. At intervals I was given a small glass of a bitter liquid to drink. After drinking it, I again fell into the dark nothingness but could not quite make it, for burning sparks shot me up to the top of a carousel wheel, where I would hang until everything spun off into a colorful ball.

The morning passed. After dinner, which I did not touch, I was taken to a smaller room, where the sun was pouring in through the big window, and it was very hot even though the nurse pulled the curtains tightly shut. I was lying on a narrow table, and the pain was bad, so bad that I thought I would drown in it. I tried to bear it, but then suddenly everything seemed to explode into one fiery ball.

"Nurse!" I cried out, and the next moment there was the Sister, the doctor and the nurses around me, but then I sank into darkness and oblivion.

As if through a wall, I heard voices again. Somebody said something to me, and I did what I was told. The next moment I felt something warm slide out of my body, and a tiny voice began to cry. The nurse cried out cheerfully,

"It's a little boy! You wanted a boy, didn't you?"

"Yes," I sighed happily and nodded, but I was still not quite there and could not open my eyes. When I did open them, I saw a big lamp above me and that outside the windows was darkness—the whole afternoon had passed me by! The nurse had already wrapped the baby in a blanket, and I barely got to see a little ear and some dark hair before she whisked him off to the premature babies' ward, where he would be taken care of. I was asked what name I wanted to give him, and I said "Uldis" as Ed and I had decided.

While I was still being tidied up, I heard Ed's voice in the hallway and the nurse telling him that he would have to wait just a little longer. When everything was finished, I was given one more shot in the arm, wrapped in blankets and wheeled to another building. Ed walked next to me with flowers in his hand.

I was put in a clean warm bed with curtains pulled around the cubicle. Right away the nurse put Ed's roses in a vase and placed them on my nightstand. We were alone finally. Ed kissed me gently and then sat down at my bedside holding my hand in his.

"We have a little boy just as you wanted," I breathed happily, but sleep was overtaking me so irresistibly that I just managed to whisper, "Sorry, my dear, but I am so... so... tired..."

"You just go to sleep and don't try to talk. I will sit here by you."

He stroked my hand with his rough, hard-working fingers, and in a few moments I was dead to the world.

When Ed came to see me the following evening, I was much better and asked if he had seen our baby. He nodded, tears veiling his eyes, and said that he had just been there at the premature baby ward.

"I don't want to alarm you dear, but he is so little, so very little..."

"I know, only three pounds and fifteen ounces, but he will grow. The doctor said that the beginning will be the hardest, but he will grow and be like everybody else," I assured him, and my heart was full of love for this little person, whom I had not even seen properly. I would have so much liked to have him with me, but I knew that it was not possible.

I was in the Isolation Ward, which housed mothers and babies who needed special care. The long room was partly partitioned with walls where curtains could be pulled across the front portion, but usually they were open, so I could see the nurses walking by and hear what was happening in the other rooms, but had to stay in bed.

I heard the babies being brought to the other mothers for feeding, and I had such a yearning for my baby that tears came into my eyes. The afternoon came and I could not stand it any longer. It was very quiet in the ward, and I asked the Staff Nurse if she could call and inquire how my baby was, for the doctor had told me that I could do it any time.

She said she would do it, but I waited and waited. Hour after hour passed. When I saw the nurse and asked her about it, she was evasive and said that she had tried to call, but the line had been busy. I panicked, thinking that she was hiding something from me. My little, tiny baby! Something must be happening that they did not want to tell me! That was it! Tears overwhelmed me. I pulled the blanket over my head, so no one would hear, and bawled like my heart was breaking.

Somebody, however, had noticed that everything was not right with me. The Sister came and asked, "What has happened? Why are you crying?" Still sobbing, I told her everything, and she went to investigate. It turned out that the nurse had not even called, having forgotten or did not consider it necessary. I was very upset about that.

"I shall call them right away! Don't you worry!" the Sister said and went to her office to make the call to the premature baby ward that was in another building. After a few minutes she was back and told me that everything was all right.

"When you are more rested, I shall take you over in a wheelchair to visit him!" she said, but that did not happen either, and I did not see my little son until the day when I went home.

Gradually I got better, and one day I had a lovely surprise. The ladies from our Latvian organization had sent me a beautiful bouquet of white lilac with other spring flowers to congratulate me on the birth of

our baby. The card said: "To mother and son". I read it and it made me cry. Was I really this mother they were talking about? I could hardly believe it.

Ed came to see me every night, and that helped a lot to get through this difficult time. At last the day came, when I could leave the hospital, but I had to do it alone. Since our baby was so small, he needed more special care and had to stay at the hospital longer until he would weigh five pounds. I was sad but had to accept it. The main thing was that he would be all right.

On the day, when I was released, Ed had come to fetch me, and before leaving, we went over to the premature baby's ward to see Ulī. We had given him this shortened version of his name because Uldis just did not sound suitable for such a little guy. The nurse picked him up from his cot and brought him to the glass wall separating us. Now I could see my child for the first time, and it was so unbelievable that he really was mine. And yet, as I looked at the little face, I could see the likeness of Ed, and he was mine! Emotions changed from love to worry and fear how we would cope with so small a baby, but his little face was still with me a long time after we had left the hospital.

It took another couple of weeks for me to get stronger, and then I started to go to the hospital every day to feed him. When I finally held him in my arms, his small head leaning on my breast, I felt at last that we belonged together and this had not been a dream.

It was already the beginning of May, when Ulī could come home to us at last. I was so excited but also worried how I would manage to take care of him. I waited nervously all day for the ambulance to bring him, but it was late afternoon when they finally arrived. I held my precious little bundle in my arms and was beside myself with joy.

Now what should I do? Perhaps first take off his little coat that I had knitted? I put him on the sofa and pulled off one sleeve, but then, how to remove the coat from under him? I turned him to one side and the other, but it did not work. I was so afraid to move him in case I broke something. By this time I was in a panic and all wet from perspiration, but something had to be done! I tried again and carefully lifted him a little while holding my hand under his head and removing the coat with the other hand. It worked, and nothing broke! Now I had more courage, and until the evening, when Ed came from work, I knew how to handle him quite well.

After that, a long succession of days and nights began, when I hardly did anything else but feed my baby, change him and feed him once again. Since he was so small, he had to be fed every three hours, but he was not strong enough to feed for long and kept falling asleep. I had to wake him to continue feeding after a little rest, but the feeding times stretched out so long, that one almost ran into another.

Sometimes, getting up in the night, I was so tired that I felt dizzy and light-headed. It also happened that often, while I was changing him after a difficult feeding session, he would bring everything back up. It was a tough time for us all. Ed, through all of it, helped however he could. He held the baby up over his shoulder and rubbed his little back for the air to come up. In time things improved though, and we did not have to wake up so many times in the night.

Outside were beautiful sunny days. The little white climbing roses bloomed again and their sweet smell filled the air. The birds sang all day long, running up into the blue sky. This early summer was so beautiful. It seemed that God showed us His love through every flower and opening bud. We had managed to get a second-hand pram and Ed had spruced it up. Now I laid Uli in it and put him out in the garden in the fresh air, where the sun and the soft breeze could play around him. It was good to see how he was growing and becoming stronger.

I was so happy and felt like a summer myself, fulfilled and content with my small family. We were making out all right. I made a nice blue satin quilt for Uli's crib and made a few sets of smaller clothing out of very fine fabric. In my spare time, I knitted more things that he might need. Yes, one did not need to spend a lot of money to be happy. Ed was caring and loving, and our life continued in peace and cooperation. Since we did not own anything, our life was simple and uncluttered. We just had to take care of ourselves.

The only thing that still worried me deep down was my previous illness. I was afraid that something still could go wrong. I read something that scared me, and each month I had to go to the hospital for tests. I learned that the illness I had was called toxemia and it was still with me. I felt as if I lived on borrowed time, as if this happiness was only on loan and could be taken away at any time. There had been so many disappointments that it was hard to believe that happiness could truly last.

We did have a big scare one time when Uli was about three months old. He was running a fever, and we had to take him to the hospital and leave him there. It was terrible. He was still so small and we worried so much. I was beside myself in case he did not have enough strength to overcome this. Yet he did, thank God!

The summer days became shorter, and the first autumn flowers opened their golden blooms in the gardens. A change came into our lives also. Saša had paid off the money to his partners who helped him to buy the house, and now it was his. Since his partner had bought his own house and had moved out, he had vacant rooms. He and Mother proposed that we might move there, so we would all be together.

It was a rather hard decision to make, for we liked this place, where

we had lived for two years now and had spent many happy times. Yet, there was a rumor that the lease on the house had almost expired and it might be sold. After a family conference, we decided that we had to move, if we wanted to be sure that we would have somewhere to live in the future.

A golden late summer sun was setting behind the tree-tops, when the parting time came. It was the beginning of September, 1951. Stocks still bloomed in my flower bed by the front window. I picked one and breathed its wonderful, cool fragrance, then went indoors to see if anything had been forgotten. A light dusk was gathering in the room, and a sad silence seemed to lay over everything. There was our big chair and the sofa where we had slept; there was the bluish gray rug over which the warm glow of the fire spread in the evenings. Our black orphan cat loved to warm himself in front of it. We had not owned anything here. Everything was just as it had been when we came. Only the shadows of the past days would perhaps linger for a little while, and then they, too, would be gone. Goodbye to the place, which will always have a deep meaning for us, for this was the place where our life together began.

## To Station Road

We arrived at Saša's house on Station Road in Kings Heath. A long row of red brick houses lined each side of the curving street like two red walls. These were very much like the terrace houses, except they were bigger, with an attic room on the third floor, and in the front of each house was the tiniest front garden at the main entrance, where a few steps led up to the front door.

From there, a long hallway stretched to the very back of the house into the breakfast room and the tiny kitchen beyond it. Three doors opened from the hallway to the right. The first was to the front room, where Uncle Jon would live. Next was the opening to the stairway, leading upstairs to the other two floors. The second door led into the dining room that was facing the back of the house with a French door opening to the narrow, brick-paved yard. That was now my brother's room. The last door opened to the right, just before entering the breakfast room, and led through a short hallway out to the back yard.

Kings Heath was one of the many former villages which had once surrounded the city of Birmingham. In time, as the city expanded, they joined it as suburbs, yet the old village centers were still there. Small shops lined both sides of the main street, catering to whatever the local people might need. There were the butchers, the bakers, the greengrocers and several grocery stores. It was still the time before supermarkets. Several clothing, hat and shoe shops sported colorful displays in their windows. There were also two flower shops, a yarn shop and the Woolworth's store.

At the city end of the village was a large cinema, called the Kingsway, only one block from where Station Road entered the main Kings Heath Road. In the middle of the village were several pubs; a couple of churches stood on some of the side streets. The bus service to the city was very good. On the whole, Kings Heath was quite a pleasant place, and two nice big parks were at each end of it. Still, the living at Station Road was something quite different than what we had been used to.

Saša still needed extra money to pay the mortgage, so the house was filled to the limit. We did not have a private life or any say about anything anymore. We were given the large front room on the second floor, facing the street, and once we finished working on it, our room looked nice. We redecorated it with pale peach colored embossed wallpaper and made more storage units and night stands by knocking together several wooden orange crates. I covered them with the same leftover wallpaper, lining the insides with white, and making white muslin curtains in front. In the larger unit, there was even room for some books, so everything gradually looked better.

We still had our double bed, which was the only thing we owned besides Ulī's crib, and Mother and Saša had bought a wardrobe, a dresser and a table with chairs for us at a second-hand store. That was nice, and the room was quite spacious, but we had only one room. The tiny kitchen and the adjoining breakfast room at the end of the long hallway downstairs were for everybody's use. The breakfast room had only a large table and chairs in it with a built-in wall cabinet for dishes.

Eleven adults and our baby son, all Latvians, lived in the house, so on late afternoons the breakfast room was like a marketplace with people milling around. Three single men lived in the large attic room above us and two more men lived in the smaller room opposite us.

My brother Johnny lived in a room downstairs, facing the garden. He often suffered from gastric pains. Perhaps the stress was too much for him, working days and going to school in the evenings to study electrical engineering. Many times he wanted to quit, but Mother would not let him, urging him to think about his future.

Uncle Jon lived in the front room on the ground floor directly below us. Mother and Saša made do with the smallest room in the house. It was just a box room, usually used for a baby or as a storage room, situated at the end of the long hallway on the second floor, adjoining the tiny bathroom. Only a single bed fitted in there, a dresser and a small table by the window. One could not think of a more crowded situation, but then, nobody owned more than the bare necessities.

The single men worked night shifts at the large Cadbury chocolate factory. They began to rise in early afternoon one after the other, for there was only the one small bathroom with a toilet in the house. Then

they came downstairs, cooked some simple food like bacon and eggs or sausages and beans and sat around the table chatting and cracking jokes.

While they still sat there, Mother and I had to start cooking the dinner for our men. Saša, Johnny, Ed and Uncle Jon came home around the same time, soon after 5 p.m. I sat Ulī, who was now six months old, in his pram in the corner of the breakfast room and went into the kitchen. The men talked to him and tried to make him laugh. The older man, Ludvig, especially was fond of him. He often picked him up and talked with him, showing him different things around the room and telling him what they were. This man's wife and son had been left behind in Latvia when he had been drafted by the Germans (and had ended up in Germany when the war ended). Because of the Soviets, they never got together again, like many other of the former soldier's families.

In the small kitchen, steam rose from the boiling pots, rising to the ceiling. It condensed on the cold, painted brick walls, from where it ran down to the brick floor, for there was no ventilation. At times Mother opened the kitchen door to the outside, and a whole cloud of steam escaped. The cold damp air rushed in right away, creeping around our legs, and the door had to be closed. It was late autumn, and this was no luxury house.

Heaps of fallen leaves lay under the big tree in the narrow back-yard, and the wind swept them around and around. They were not golden or red but greenish gray, turning an ugly brown as they dried out, shriveled and got smaller and smaller. I mourned the bygone summer in our rose garden. This was so ugly. An uneven brick pavement covered the narrow space between the house and the neighbor's fence, and a couple of shacks had been added at the back of the house. Those were another toilet and the coal bunker. A tiny patch of grass was further down beyond the old shacks, and at the very end was a small hothouse. Clotheslines stretched from one end to the other in the narrow yard, for there were no washing machines or driers in those days.

The white chrysanthemum day had come. Ed brought them to me and I was so moved that he had remembered. In this sea of people, our room was now like a small quiet island, where we could have some alone time. But not even that always... Mother sometimes quietly opened the door on Sunday mornings, when she heard Ulī making some sounds as she passed by our door. She wanted to see what Ulī was doing, and entered, sometimes knocking, sometimes not. We did not like that. We wanted to snooze and enjoy our Sunday morning. There were plenty of other times when she could visit. We did not really have any privacy.

The men were satisfied with their jobs working for Cadbury's, even though they had to work nights. They did piece work and earned good

wages. They urged Ed to apply, too, and he did. Cadbury's was fairly close to Kings Heath, while the place where he worked now was quite a bit farther.

He was accepted, but his job was not at the assembly line where the work was easier, but consisted of carrying sacks of the raw crushed chocolate on his back. I don't know if it was by his choice to earn more money, or because he was a bigger, stronger man. Now he also had to work nights, and that was the hardest part of it. During the week we hardly saw him at all, except for the very short while after he got up before he ate his dinner. Then he had to leave. While he slept, Ulī and I spent the time downstairs in the breakfast room and kitchen, where I did my chores—mostly washing Ulī's napkins and preparing meals for him. I took Ulī along also when I went shopping or for a walk in the park.

Since there were so many people living in the house, there were often birthdays to celebrate. Food had to be prepared for the parties, and homemade beer was brewed that was stronger than the regular beer. It got to the men's heads, made their faces flush red and their bodies heavy. There was singing, of course, without which a party would not be a party for the Latvians. At first there were folk songs, then other best-loved melodies from the times back in Latvia, but soon there were only the soldier's songs that had been sung during the wartime. They were about fighting for their homeland, about yearning to see their beloved girl and about coming home when the war was over... Of course, none of that came true...

Then followed the stories about the futility of the war and the friends they had lost. It was inevitable each and every time, when they had reached this stage. Men with tears in their eyes asking each other, "But man, do you remember? Do you remember the icy river we had to cross? The Russians closing in on us and Russians on the other side too! There was no other way but to go into the river, cross it and then lay in the snow without moving till darkness came. I was frozen to the ground when we had to move..."

"Yes, yes... I was there too. My bones are still aching at night. But do you remember..." another agreed.

Then Ed joined in: "I was there too! I thought that I had lost my best friend there! We had been in a big battle with the Russians. Our whole unit was dispersed, and we were looking for each other. It was an early winter morning and I was entering a remote German village. Then I saw someone in the distance on the empty street. He was walking towards me. It looked like Ali, but he looked strange, for he did not have his black-rimmed glasses! His coat was torn! As we came closer and recognized each other, we ran towards each other and hugged and hugged,

tears running over our faces. 'Edi, you are alive!' He cried. 'And you too, Ali!' I cried also. We were so glad to see each other."

There was more talk of one incident and another. They all remembered, and it turned out that in many instances they had been at the same place and now walked again across the snowy fields and knelt beside a fallen friend. It was all still fresh as if it had happened yesterday. It was an open wound. A sorrow for lost friends and lost battles, for the homeland not saved.

Now and then, there was also a memory of veiled sunshine, a memory of someone's love, a young love, hoping for a future together which was not possible anymore. It all had to come out. But there were also other memories. Then the men's heads lifted up and the backs straightened out as the old fighting spirit woke up in them. As they sang, it seemed that they were listening to their own steps as they once walked off to war with their heads held high. They were Latvian men, many still boys, right off the school bench, including Ed. They had believed that they were going to fight for Latvia and had hopes, such hopes for its freedom... Now they were left with the bitterness and shame of how it had all ended, for it was not up to them only. When the Germans gave orders to withdraw, they had to withdraw, even when they had to leave their own country.

But that was a long time ago. About seven years. I could well understand their pain and frustration, flowing out at such times, but wished that they would not talk about it so much. Yet this was an unalterable part of these days, these times, so they drank and sang and talked till the morning, each trying to gush out their pain which they could not do when they were sober. It was in vain to urge Ed to come up then; he did not hear me. One such night, when they were celebrating again, we had our first argument about drinking. I felt him sliding away from me and tried to prevent it, but my hands touched emptiness. Helplessly, I withdrew into myself saying nothing anymore.

Christmas of the year 1951 came through rain and mud, but we prepared for it as usual. I counted my shillings carefully, figuring how much I would be able to save from my housekeeping money to buy some gifts for the closest in the family. I spent time looking in the village store windows, pondering, where I could get the most value for my money. The giving spirit sang within me, but I could not spend much, for I did not work outside anymore. It was not the time of credit cards yet, and it was not a time, when young mothers left their babies with someone else to raise them and to look after them.

The last week before Christmas, Mother and I spent cleaning and washing everything as it was our custom to do. It seemed that by putting

much effort into cleaning the outside, we cleansed our insides, too, wiping away the cobwebs of what was not necessary and sparkling up what was good for the Christ Child's coming.

It might sound strange that I mention God so often, because we were not religious people. We did not go to church, except now during our time in exile, when the Latvian minister came once a month to give us a service. Then we felt it our duty to go, but partly it was also to keep in touch with other Latvian people. To keep up our national ties meant almost as much as keeping in touch with God. However, the spiritual need was in us and God was very much alive in the midst of us—but only privately in our hearts. We needed Him in our lives to survive.

As we worked, trying to spruce up Saša's old house with the long dark hallways our efforts did not show up very much, but the curtains at the windows looked brighter and bouncier, and the old, second-hand furniture showed a slight glow after being waxed and polished. Ed was good in helping Mother and me in doing this, even though the other men and Johnny, too, went out to have their own fun. That was probably the difference between Ed and the other men. He had had to help his mother a lot during his growing up years; he understood women's work better. He could not leave us working alone, even though he had done his shift at the factory the same as the others. He stayed behind to help, and we very much appreciated it.

Mother and I cooked and baked, and the house was filled with our traditional Christmas smells of the small bacon rolls (pīrāgi), which were a must. Otherwise it was usually a cold table with all kinds of traditional goodies for this evening, so nobody would have to cook.

I was so happy to decorate our Christmas tree, for this was our son's first Christmas, even though he did not understand any of it yet. He stood in his crib at the railings watching me as I put the candles in the little holders and handled the shiny colored balls. He liked those and stretched out his little arm pointing to them.

"I - ii!" he said, and I picked him up, took him to the tree and let him touch them. That made a smile break out on his little face.

When everything was ready, I dressed Ulī in his new, white knit suit, and we tried on his little white boots for the first time. That was a big surprise for him. He sat on the edge of our low bed and tried to touch them with his little hands. Then he leaned forward, possibly to put them in his mouth as small children were apt to do with anything new that came into their view. I had just turned away for a second to reach for something, when I saw him suddenly lose balance and fall forward. I tried to catch him but did not quite make it. He fell down on the floor and started to cry, but my heart almost stopped, fearing what might have happened to him. I picked him up, but there was just a small bump on

his forehead, and he soon settled down. Thank God, our bed was so low, otherwise it could have been worse!

The door opened, and Ed came in and scooped Ulī up in his arms. Behind him came Mother, Saša and the other residents of the house. We were the only ones having a Christmas tree, so I had invited everybody to come and share the Christmas Eve celebration with us. The room was full. People sat on the chairs that Saša had brought in and on the sides of our bed, which alone took up a good part of the room.

As I lit the candles on the tree that stood on our table next to the fire place, Saša turned out the ceiling light, and the small candles, twitching and slightly smoking, spread a gentle circle of light around them in the darkened room.

We sang the well-known Christmas song "O come, all you children...", and everybody's eyes, full of joy, were gazing at Ulī who looked around full of wonder, his little mouth slightly open. He looked at the Christmas tree and at the people around him. They all looked different than on workdays. Everyone was spruced up in their best suits and new shirts and ties. The men sang in their low voices, and their shadows loomed big on the walls behind them, but in their eyes one could see that they, too, were moved by all this. For some of them this, perhaps, was the first Christmas for a long time that they spent in the midst of a family.

Mother and I had already set the table downstairs in the breakfast room, so that right after our short sacred celebration at the Christmas tree, we could go downstairs and partake of what the good Lord and our hands had provided. Drinks were handed around to toast Christmas, and the food tasted even better. After eating, however, the men got restless, and Saša suggested going down to the local pub to find out what was happening there tonight.

Saša was not one to drink much, but he liked to go down to the pub on weekends, where other Latvian men from the vicinity gathered, too, to visit, crack some jokes and talk politics. This was an established routine from his bachelor days, and nobody could keep him from that. On Saturdays the pubs were open from twelve till two in the afternoon and again from six till eleven in the evenings and the same on Sundays.

The British pubs were more like meeting places, with several rooms for different kinds of clients, rather than places to get drunk. There was a special lounge with comfortable chairs and tables where men brought their wives or girlfriends to spend some fun time. They had a few drinks, chatted and sometimes even sang. Saša had asked Mother along, too, in the beginning, but she soon found that the heavy cigarette smoke made her cough, and did not go anymore. She also felt that she did not need this kind of fun, and stayed at home instead. Of course, she would have rather liked that Saša was with her too, but she knew that this was a time he needed for

himself, since he had worked hard during the week.

After Saša's suggestion, the men were all eager and happy to go, putting on their overcoats and getting ready. Ed dressed, too, and said that he would go with the men for a little while. That made me sad, but I did not say anything. He had also been working hard and needed some relaxation.

Suddenly the big house was so quiet. I carried Uli upstairs and looked at the Christmas tree standing there alone and kind of sad. A light scent of the burnt wax was still in the air. In the corner was a heap of the torn papers of the presents. Suddenly, it all looked so forlorn, but I did not want Christmas to be done with already. I lit two candle stubs near the top of the tree, took Uli in my arms and sat down in a chair to watch them. I wanted to be glad and still feel the goodness of Christmas, but something heavy and hard was lying on my heart. As I stared at the golden flames before my eyes, they grew bigger and brighter until two big tears rolled down my cheeks. I pressed Uli to my chest and rocked him softly, but my heart was silently crying.

"Then this is what our Christmas is like... Our daddy does not need us..." I thought to myself, yet hoped that perhaps he would come before the candles finished burning. But I was waiting and hoping in vain. The last drops of the wax fell down onto the green branches, freezing there like tears, and when I blew out the wicks, they sent up spirals of smoke in the air as the last farewell to Christmas.

I put Uli in his crib to sleep, but then remembered that our original little tree had not received its gift yet. I found the brown paper bag with the baby tree in the red pot and put it on the mantelpiece. Now our tree had two babies. Standing in front of it, I told it my sorrows, and it looked kindly back at me. Was I asking too much, wanting Ed to be with me tonight? Perhaps. I swallowed hard, then slowly undressed and went to bed.

Waking in the night, I heard voices downstairs, and the bed next to me was empty and cold. So the men were still celebrating... I curled up and pulled the blanket over my head. It was better not to think. Morning came. The men still sat around the table, tired and just half awake, and the large tub of the home-brewed beer in the corner was empty. Their foggy eyes roamed around the room as if looking for something, while unsteady minds groped for the new day. The bodies were heavy, asking for rest, and one after another, they went upstairs. Only the sweet sour odor of the beer and the cold stink of the cigarette smoke were left in the air.

Whatever was left of our pre-Christmas efforts had been turned into a war zone. Puddles of beer were on our festive table, cigarette butts had been quenched on the sides of the plates next to some unfinished food. Soiled, the same way as the white table cloth, was my clean and bright Christmas joy, and nobody could retrieve it. But in truth, nobody even wanted to. In the afternoon the celebration continued, the way the men

were used to doing during their rough times. The day passed like a nightmare. Such was our life at Station Road.

The New Year had come. It was 1952, and January was halfway gone, when I discovered that something had happened; something that had not been thought of or planned for. Every passing day and week convinced me that my suspicions were true. The worries turned into fear, and fear into panic when I thought that I would have to go through the suffering again, that I had gone through just recently with Ulī. Would I be able to come through it? What would happen to my Ulī if I didn't? I felt like one condemned to death. I tried not to think, to be calm and accept whatever my fate would be, but then again panic would seize me with its burning hands, and I cried, moaning and rocking myself in anguish. I felt like hitting my head against the wall, so the outer pain would help me forget the inner suffering. I did not want to die yet and prayed to God, but there was no help anywhere.

Ed and I looked into each other's eyes, trying to comfort each other, but with each day we became more sad and silent. Only Ulī smiled cheerfully standing in his cot and holding onto the railings. It was good that he did not have to know of life's difficulties yet. He had just cut his first teeth, and the little hand was constantly there, rubbing against them. Tears came to my eyes looking at him and thinking what would happen to him, to us all if... if...? For a new life had announced itself.

I finally pulled myself together and went to the doctor. He redirected me to the local prenatal clinic, and thanks God for that! A very nice lady doctor took away all my terrible fears that my illness might be repeated.

"Each pregnancy is totally separate," she explained. "Since your overall health is good, there is no reason why you should not look into the future with joy and have a good, normal pregnancy!"

This took the heavy mountain of grief off my heart. The only stipulation was that I should go to see my former doctors at the hospital and also that the birth would have to take place at the hospital. Women without health problems were usually delivered at home by a midwife in those days, if the situation was applicable.

I was so embarrassed to go back to the hospital the first time where I had only just recently finished with the testing after my illness. But one way or another, there was nothing I could change, and now I did not want to, either. Now that my worst fears were put to rest, I was even beginning to rejoice about the new baby. I very much hoped that Ulī would have a little sister and was pretty sure that it would be so.

The winter days passed, rainy and dark. Time slowly moved toward spring. The March winds blew clouds across the still gray

sky, but there was a different smell in the air. I took Uli to the park every day, pushing his pram along the paved walkways. The big trees stood there dark and bare, wet from the many rains, but in their top branches the wind sang a different song. Narrow streams of water ran on both sides of the pavement, cheerfully bouncing over the tufts of grass or left over brown leaves, carrying the smells of water and earth—the first messengers of spring.

They brought to mind the far away spring times in my homeland, and I stopped for a moment, closing my eyes. As the cool damp breezes touched my face, I saw it all in my mind's eye, the same way as in those long gone spring days under skies much like today's. I had risked the flooded river to get to the forest on the other side, in search of the first spring flowers that grew there. Yes, I remembered it well. It was the very last spring at home, so very long ago. Six long years, and now I was a wife and a mother, not a girl with a head full of dreams.

I hoped that I would be able to implant the appreciation of nature in my children as well. I wondered if they, too, would find joy looking at the pink evening clouds, or smelling the spring in the air, or holding the first spring flowers in their hands. Would I know how to teach them to hold on to these riches of the heart, which no money could buy? Or would they walk in different ways, growing up here in this strange land?

I pushed the pram up the hill. Beyond the bare branches of trees, a golden sun was close to setting. Spring was coming but the days were still short. It was time for us to get home and start dinner.

On the thirtieth of March, we celebrated Uli's first birthday. He was a little smaller than other children his age, but was sturdy enough and would, perhaps, soon catch up with them. He walked around our room holding on to the furniture, and we all enjoyed watching him.

Lately I had acquired a friend. A Latvian girl from another town had come to Birmingham and worked and studied to be a nurse at the General Hospital, where I once worked. We met and got acquainted at one of our Latvian church services, and now she often came to visit me on her free days. Her name was Aina, and she did not have any family here; they were all in Latvia. I loved to have Aina visit me. She had the most hearty and infectious laugh, and when she came visiting, we would talk and sometimes laugh about practically nothing. She helped to lift me out of my seriousness, and that did me good. It was also good to talk to someone my own age, because Mother and I never managed to do that kind of talking.

Also Mrs. Avots, one of our foursome who initially came to England together with us, had become a very close friend of mine, and now I called her Aunt Paula. She was such a wonderful, empathetic person;

there were not many like her around. She still worked at the hospital as the Matron's personal maid, but the Matron and all her personal friends looked upon her not as the servant, which she still was, but as a respected person and a personal friend. For Aunt Paula was a lady, and nobody was in doubt of that.

With her caring nature and the genuine interest about anything that was happening to me, she had been like a second mother during the years since we came to England. I could talk with her about anything, and she would listen not only with her mind but also with her heart. I was sorry that I had never been able to develop such a relationship with my mother, but she was different, and we could not reach each other. She was a good person, but lived within her own world, and did not have much time for others. She did not have it for me, either, and I did not turn to her with my problems anymore.

Summer came with blossoming days, and our life flowed like a wide, quiet river. The hot yearnings of youth had stilled. We did not have to rush anywhere, for life was good right here. Even though our circumstances were far less than many others might desire, we were happy and content. Neither did we ever think that we were poor. We had all we needed, and what we did not have, we could do without. I walked as if through a sunny, green valley and was happy. This was not the magnificent highway I once had wanted to walk, to achieve success in my art, but in this walk was quiet contentment and assurance of love. One did not really need much to be happy, and I could attest to that.

Ed was loving and caring, and we spent most of our free time together. On Sundays all three of us would go to the park. Sometimes Johnny or Uncle Jon joined us. We would sit in the grass under the huge chestnut tree in the park and enjoy the nice summer day. After the chestnut trees shed their blossoms, it was time for the rhododendrons to lift their beautiful clusters of blooms in a magnificent array of colors. Ulī walked around in the grass, inspecting everything he saw. He was almost a year and a half old. After my great fears at the beginning of facing a repeating illness and even dying, my fears had been laid to rest. I deeply enjoyed my motherhood, feeling the new life in me growing day by day. I felt like a blossoming summer day myself, carrying my burden toward the harvest time.

The roses finished blooming in the gardens and parks. Their tender petals slowly dropped, making little heaps of them on the black earth under the thorny branches. Some late buds still tried to open, but the nights were getting cold. Walking in the park, golden leaves fluttered down from the birch trees, shimmering against the late summer sun, then settling down at my feet. For a moment I felt sadness for their fate, as always when I saw some life ending, but I knew that was how it had to be. Each living

was also a dying, and each dying was a new beginning.

## Māris is born

Autumn was coming, and my burden had become heavy, but I carried it with joy, for I was healthy and able to carry it. I relished my motherhood this time twice as much, perhaps, because the first time it had not been possible. Even my doctor was glad when I went to the hospital for my checkups. She told the nurses how different two pregnancies could be. This time everything was so good but last time—

"You were really lucky to have your baby alive that time," Dr. Hallam said, and only now did I get to know how serious things had been and was doubly thankful to God who had seen me through.

Autumn was here, and the leaves were falling in heaps and heaps, giving the last farewell to summer. God had been gracious to us, giving us these peaceful and golden days. I sensed His hand in everything and silently thanked Him for the joy and peace of these days. Together with the fruit in the trees, my time had come also to deliver, and I received it gladly, not fighting the pains that came and went. Luckily it happened on a day when I had gone to the hospital for my checkup. Ed had come with me on the bus and he only had to go back and get my suitcase that I had already packed. My time had come.

The baby was born early next morning at 3.20 a.m., exactly on the due date, when it was still dark outside the windows. The Sister wrapped him in a blanket and held him over her shoulder. I saw him squinting and squinting his little eyes as if trying to see where on earth he was? Yes, I had another son instead of the little girl I had hoped to have, but it did not matter now. I was very happy anyway that everything had gone so well, and my heart warmed toward him already. I named him Māris, and he was healthy and big, weighing eight and a quarter pounds He was laid into a little cot in my room and I almost laughed when only a little while after the birth I could hear a ticking noise. I thought that it might be a clock, but it turned out that Māris was sucking his little fingers, trying to have his first meal. I stayed in the hospital, actually at the Annex, for ten days recuperating after the birth of my baby and then was ready and anxious to go home.

Ulī was taking a nap in his crib when Ed and I came quietly into the room with the new baby. I stood by his bed and looked at his little pink cheek. Perhaps he felt my presence; he moved and opened his eyes. For a moment he looked at me as if he did not know me, then closed his eyes again. I began to think that he had forgotten me, but then he sat up and rubbed his eyes with his small fist. He looked at me again, and a slow smile spread over his little face.

"Ulī… mama is home…" I said, and the next moment he was in my arms. I pressed him to my bosom, kissed his soft hair and was so glad to be home with my family.

On the floor at the end of the crib I saw a little pile of Ulī's dirty napkins and a few of his clothes. Mother must have forgotten to take them downstairs and put them to soak. But, of course, she also knew that I would be home now, and perhaps had assumed that she should not have to bother about my things anymore.

During the next few days some visitors came to see my new baby, and I proudly showed him off, even though he was wearing the little flannel jackets that I had made for a baby girl with edges crocheted with pink thread. But it did not matter in the least. I was only sorry that I could not spend too much time with Ulī yet. Perhaps his little heart did not understand why he was not the one and only to sit in mama's lap. But how to explain it to a year and a half old child, that right now the little brother needed more of mama's time? Still, soon I would be stronger and then it would be different.

It was a Saturday evening. On the table were flowers and fruit, and everything was sparkling clean in our room. My little boys each slept in their cribs, and the house was quiet. I lay in our wide bed. The small lamp on the nightstand spread a circle of its warm, cozy light around the room. Everything was so good, only our daddy was not with us. Earlier I had felt a stab in my heart, when he said earlier that he would like to go out with the men this evening. I would have liked so much for him to be with us, but then I realized how selfish it would be to insist on that. After all, it had not been an easy time for him, either: working, looking after Ulī and everything else. Everybody needed some change once in a while, no matter how dear their family was to them.

A little sadness still sat in the corner of my mind, but I quenched it and urged him to go and to enjoy himself, assuring him that I had nothing against it. And I didn't, either, anymore. He had hardly gone anywhere lately, nor had he been drinking. No, I did not mind at all. I said a quiet prayer and switched off the light.

This was the fourth Christmas for our original little Christmas tree, which had brought us together. Now it had three little ones standing around it on our mantelpiece. When I was in the room, my eyes would often linger on it, for it was the symbol of the quiet miracle which had happened that night, and of all there was between us now. We did not own money or things, or even this one room that we presently rented, but in it lived love and contentment and two little boys bringing joy to our hearts. No, we were rich enough.

Perhaps a rich person did not get as much pleasure out of a whole

week's living it up as I did on Friday nights, when after a hot bath, I could stretch out between the clean sheets in my warm bed, and a pleasant tiredness would fill my body. I had put a mug of warm milk and crackers at the bedside before, so I could feast a little. It was good to know that the week's work had been done, and everything around me was clean and tidy. The little boys slept sweetly in their cribs. I looked at their peaceful little faces, and saw their hands sometimes move a little in sleep, then all was quiet again. Uldis was talking quite a bit already, and we thought that it was time to call him by his full name, for he had developed well and was quite sturdy now. Māris too, started to make funny little sounds. My sons...

My thoughts went over the week's happenings, while I partook of my simple evening snack, then I opened my new edition of the Women's magazine that I bought each week, and that was my weekly treat. There was a little of everything that made up a woman's specific life, and I learned a lot that I did not know yet.

Every two weeks, Ed had to work the whole night on Fridays, and then I read until sleep overcame me. On other Fridays, he would come home at ten, have his own bath (for there were no such thing as showers, at least not for the common folks, in those days), and then came to bed next to me, still warm from the bath, and I would slide into his arms, happy and content.

These weekends were like small beautiful islands in our otherwise rather monotonous everyday life, which was not without some problems and small irritations, but I tried to keep things on an even keel. Mother and Saša had gotten into the habit of going to the local cinema once a week. It was just one block from our house, and they showed a new film every week. We were also very tempted to go, wanting a little diversion in our lives, and sometimes we sneaked off after the children had gone to sleep, whispering to Uncle Jon or Mother to look in on them. They were very good children, and there was never any messing around after they were put to bed at a certain time. They had been trained that way, and there was never any problem.

Like two big children, we hurried with great anticipation across the street, where the cinema stood at the back of the square—with lighted titles and ads of the current film on its front. It was cheap entertainment, but even then we felt a bit guilty for wanting it for ourselves. However, people, could not live just by working the whole time; these visits to the cinema threw a little diversion in our gray working days. Otherwise we hardly went out anywhere, and could not go because of the children. We had never heard of babysitters in those days. The families took care of their children themselves. When the Birmingham Latvian Association had a dance or other kind of a social, Saša and Mother always went, for Saša was the treasurer. Mother, however, never offered to stay at home with the

children, so that we could go sometimes as well, and I never asked her for such a favor.

The January of 1953 came with gray, dreary days and cold winds. Sadly, it did not start on a happy note for us, either. On January 3rd Uncle Jon suddenly passed away. Since he had not come out of his room at his usual time to get ready for work, Ed had gone in to awaken him and had found him dead in his bed. He had just quietly gone to sleep. His work in this world was finished. There had been quite a few heart problems amongst Ed's relatives, and Uncle Jon had them already when he came to live with us. Ed had taken him to doctors, who gave him medications and prescribed injections in his legs for the clogged arteries. Ed, having been a nurse, could administer those easily. Obviously it had not helped. Uncle Jon was only fifty-four years old.

Now he was gone, and it was a hard blow to us, for we had all come to love his quiet presence. Ed was especially stricken, for Uncle Jon had been his only relative outside Latvia. We both also felt somewhat guilty about the not-so-nice exchange of words the two men had had not too long ago. I did not really know what it was all about. I had entered the room when both men were shouting at each other. I had never seen Ed so angry. He was quite pale in his face.

"You apologize!" He shouted, but Uncle Jon just sat there fixing his cigarette butt into the holder and did not say anything. I did not know what the reason had been to start this conversation, but Ed told me later that the Uncle had called me *"nelga"* a common name for degrading somebody. I was rather surprised about it, because I always thought that our relationship was good. It was not all that important to me and I never learned why he had called me that. However, this Latvian word *"nelga"* could also have other meanings. It might be that someone is stupid, inept, but it might also mean that one is not standing up for oneself, and allows oneself to be used. I did not take it to heart, but even though I tried to pacify them, the rift remained, and I felt guilty too, because it had been about me.

Poor Uncle! I don't think that this incident crushed him enough to take him to his grave, but it was sad to think that it needed to happen at all. But who could know the ways of life and death? The old warrior had now joined the other ancient warriors up there beyond the stars. I thought, perhaps he had felt that in this world his fight was irrelevant and without meaning anyway. The foreign land had broken his spirit and his pride. May he have peaceful rest now!

Although we had just recently laid Uncle Jon to rest, we had a more joyous event soon after. We had already made arrangements with our Latvian minister for christening Māris at the end of January and did

not want to change them, for this was a time when he would be here in Birmingham. We had planned to have the christening at home. On the appropriate day we cleared the breakfast room, putting the big table in Johnny's room in preparation for the subsequent party. Then we set up a small sideboard for an altar with a white cover, candles in our nice carved wooden candelabra, a bible and flowers. We had invited our closest friends and they came. There was quite a crowd and just enough room to move around in the breakfast room.

Sorry to say that our little man got so upset, seeing all these strangers who wanted to greet him and look at him, that he almost got hysterical—for he had not seen any other people but us so far. He was four months old by now, but since it was wintertime, he was mostly upstairs in our room in his crib. It was hard to pacify him even after I took him upstairs, but finally this was done. Aunt Paula was his godmother and two of our best friends were the godfathers.

After putting the children to bed, we had a nice celebration party as was the custom. Mother and I had set up a table with all kinds of Latvian goodies to treat our friends, and of course, there were also a few drinks to wish our little fellow health and happiness.

The English weather can be very harsh in wintertime with a lot of rain. The hardest thing for us now was drying the children's nappies (diapers) and clothing. We did not have a washing or drying machine and, with two young children, I did plenty of washing by hand every day. Whenever it was not raining, I would put the clothing outside on the line in the yard, but they never dried there completely even on dry days. The air in England was moist. Often Ed held the nappies against the coal fire in the breakfast room, after he got up in the afternoons, while I cooked his dinner. Then I continued doing it through the evening till they were done, but I used the rack, just turning the clothing constantly. After that, everything still needed to be ironed. The dampness was always the worst thing in the winter time, and we were glad when it was over.

Spring came waving with daffodils and tulips; the chestnut trees blossomed and shed their candle-like clusters. The summer was again upon us, fragrant and green. Little Māris was a good baby. When the weather was warm enough, I put the playpen in the back garden on the small patch of grass, and he played there happily, while Uldis played with him from the outside. I did my washing in the kitchen, so I could see them and talk to them in between going in and out to put the clothes on the line.

One evening Ed said to me, "Seeing that you are all day and every day in the house with the small children, you should really have some kind of a diversion or activity for yourself that you might enjoy," for I

never went back to work after I had my babies. It never even crossed our minds that somebody else should look after them, and I would not exchange raising my children myself for anything in the world. However little money we had, we managed. During the very lean times, I had learned to make do. Ed got paid every week, like most workers in Britain did in those days. Since we did not own anything and did not have any other commitments but our rent, it was easy to figure out what we could and what we could not do or have.

"Why don't you start a folk dancing group again?" Ed said. "You need a little time out too! Since I am working days now, I could look after the children in the evenings while you are at the rehearsals."

Ed was on a different job now. He had hurt his back, carrying those heavy bags of unrefined chocolate and after recovering he now worked on shoveling the clay-like chocolate from the trolleys to other receptacles. That too was very heavy work, but he did it to earn even a little more money for his family. The advantage was that he could work days now—a more normal situation—and we were both glad about it.

It was very good of him to make such a tempting offer to me. After some deliberation, I agreed and we formed a new group. Everybody was very enthusiastic to dance again, but of course, it was a somewhat different group of people than we had had before. Of the girls there was Mirdza, Aina, Valentine and I. The four boys were Arvīds, Augusts, Alberts and my brother Johnny. We danced at several of our Latvian socials, but were also invited by various other groups to take part in their celebrations—indoors or out. Amongst them was also an invitation by Cadbury to dance at their International Festival. At this time we could be more flexible, because we had a good accordion player, Jānis Ķīvītis. Ed came with the children, too, when we were performing, and it was nice that our whole family was involved.

Ed also got more involved in our local Latvian activities. A Latvian organization, called *"Daugavas Vanagi"* (The Hawks of Daugava—the largest river in Latvia), had been established right after the war by the former Latvian legionaries, initiated by their former leader Colonel Vilis Janums. Those were the men who had been drafted by the Germans to help fight the Russians during WWII. After the war ended, they had been sent to a prisoner of war camp in Zedelgheim, Belgium, because they had fought on the "wrong side" although they had only fought against the Russians. While in this camp, they made a vow to help those who had been wounded or made invalids during the war, as well as to help the families who had lost their breadwinners. They vowed to do it after they would be released and they kept their promise. Later many of these men went to England and there the organization continued to do what

they had promised. There it was also known as the "Latvian Welfare Fund". In time it grew and expanded its work with its center in London and branches all over England, and later all over the world, wherever Latvians lived.

The previous winter, a branch had been established in Birmingham also, and Ed had been one of the initiators of the Birmingham group. They had also wanted to develop more activities for the Latvians in Birmingham and the vicinity, so people could get together. There were many former soldiers who lived alone, scattered amongst the British in the countryside. They needed to make friends and to know that they belonged somewhere.

Now that the summer had come, it was time to start thinking about celebrating our great Midsummer Fest—our ancient Latvian tradition— and Ed was in charge of it. He thought that our folk dancing group could be a good asset for entertainment at the festivities, and also our performances could draw more people for our local socials.

Our group discussed it and decided that it would be fun to perform at the Midsummer Fest, but first a place had to be found for the celebration, preferably out in the countryside. Somebody told us that there was a Latvian man who apparently rented a large, old mansion with big grounds halfway between Birmingham and Coventry. That might be a perfect place for this celebration. The following Sunday we decided to go and check it out.

It was a nice sunny afternoon, when our little family of four started on our way. The bus took us out of the city along the Coventry Road. We passed Elmdon Airport, which in those days consisted of only a couple of shacks and two small runways. Farther on, the countryside opened up with fields, meadows and farmhouses, hidden in the trees. It took about three quarters of an hour to get to the small village of Meriden, where we got off the bus. Not far from the bus stop, we saw a roundabout with a monument in the middle of it. It looked quite old and weather-beaten.

Ed stepped up to look at it closer and read the inscription.

"Would you believe it?" He exclaimed. "We're standing at the very center of England!"

And indeed we were! As we walked on, the aroma of flowers and grasses was overwhelming. We had not been out in the countryside for a long time, and seeing the flowers at the roadside, the same as in our homeland, was very moving to me.

We found the big white building a little farther on down the road, half hidden by a row of big trees. It stood on somewhat higher ground than the road. After mounting a few steps up the embankment, we were in a fair-sized meadow with trees and bushes adjoining the side of the house.

"This could be an excellent place for our celebration, if we could

make a deal with the owner," Ed said.

Two young men played table tennis outside, and we heard them talking in Latvian. Another two played volleyball a little farther on in the corner of the field. They most likely lived here as renters.

"*Labdien!*" Ed said. (Good day!) Do you know, where we could find the landlord of this place?" Ed asked the young men.

"Yes, go to the stables on the other side of the house. He is catching piglets right now!" one of the men said and they both laughed. That left us wondering if they were joking.

"Catching piglets?" That sounded funny, but we did as we had been told. But then! I could not have been more surprised! In the stable door stood an old acquaintance from our times in Germany in 1945, right after the war! It was Žanis! The always smartly dressed, self-assured young man, who had courted my cousin Ruta at the time, was now working with pigs! I could have never imagined him doing anything like that, but here he was! It really was Žanis, and he was as surprised to see me as I was to see him.

We greeted each other, and a little later we got to hear more about him, when he took us upstairs to his apartment. There we also met his lovely wife, Laura, and a life-long friendship was formed.

"I am still working shifts at the coal mines," Žanis told us, "but am going to quit soon. I have other plans in mind."

He was a businessman at heart, one who could sense where money could be made. He had rented the big Meriden Hall, which gave him a good income from the renters and a free place to live for himself and his family. The young Latvian men who rented were his friends, mainly people who had been involved in sports and had gladly helped him to spruce up the old place. Since he also had stables on the property, he had started raising pigs and selling the piglets, which again gave additional income. Yes, Žanis had big plans for the future.

"As soon as I leave the coal mines, I will finish with the pigs, too, and start a lumber business instead."

It was nice to hear, and Žanis was as jovial as ever. We received the permission to have our festivities here, and were also offered a room to stay the night with our children during this event. Žanis and Laura also had two little girls, Solveig and Karmen, each approximately a year older than our boys, who were two-and-a half and ten months.

Our Midsummer night celebration was a great success, and had drawn a big crowd of Latvians from the surrounding communities, especially from Birmingham and Coventry. That had been the purpose of the organization, to have the Latvian people come, meet and then organize their own activities where they lived. These socials would also provide money for the welfare work.

After this Žanis said, "Why don't you come and spend your vacation time here with us? It will not cost you anything and we shall be glad to have you!"

"That would be lovely!" Laura chimed in. "It would be fun for the children to play together!"

"That would be wonderful!" We gratefully accepted, because we did not have the money to pay for any hotels. We would have just stayed at home.

Those were truly fun days for us all. In the mornings, Laura and I washed the children's clothing and hung it up on the lines between the trees. She even had a simple washing machine that made the job easier. Then we picked up some blankets to spread on the ground, and together with the children, went to the meadow at the side of the house. Trees and shrubs separated it from the neighbors and the road, so we had complete privacy. We could lie in the sun and visit while the children played next to us. The red and white clover grew amidst the grasses like it had in Latvia. It was so pleasant to be here and to enjoy the summer and freedom as opposed to our crowded living at Station Road. It was also so enjoyable to be with Laura. She was so easy to talk to, and we both already felt like old friends.

Ed helped Žanis with some jobs. The place was big, and there was plenty to do. One night they both stayed up to watch another sow having her young ones. Meantime, Laura and I enjoyed the good weather and each other, spending time outdoors in the meadow. Uldis played with the three-year-old Solveig, who was a pretty girl with pale skin and curly red hair. She was Laura's oldest daughter. Māris and little two-year-old Karmen sat on the spread out blanket next to us, playing and crawling about. Karmen had dark curly hair and hazel eyes and was as pretty as her sister, only in a different way.

Māris very much wanted to walk. He was so bouncy and healthy. I took him by his hands and taught him. What a joy it was for the small fellow! And one day he got to his feet by himself. We watched him stand there slightly swaying; then he lost his balance and fell down on his bottom. That, however, was the beginning, and even before we returned home, he made his own individual steps at ten months old.

In the evenings, when the children had been put to bed, we sat with Laura and Žanis upstairs in their living room, talking till all hours.

"My father was a baker back in Latvia," Žanis told us. "It was in the port city called Liepāja on the west coast of Latvia, and he was an avid businessman, even though he had not had much schooling."

Now Žanis was following in his father's footsteps, having an eye to see where business could be built and advanced. He said his greatest

joy was—to find something small that he could make bigger and better.

"When I have a pound, (meaning British money) I do not think, what I could buy with it, but how I could make two pounds out of the one." It sounded like he was not afraid to risk, and his head was full of ideas for bettering himself and his family. We had never met a person like that, and it was very interesting.

Yes, Žanis knew how to live, or rather, how to make something out of life, and that can sometimes mean more than the school education for a particular person. He learned from life itself, and we had to laugh and wonder about his escapades, when he told us of the situations he had sometimes got himself into.

These were great evenings that we spent together, and our friendship deepened all the time. Our vacation time, however, was almost over. We were all sorry to part, but on the last evening, Žanis suggested that we celebrate this new friendship and go to the Elmdon airport, where a nice new pub had been opened.

Laura's mother also lived on the premises and promised to look after the children, who were already asleep. It was already rather late, but we got dressed quickly and off we went. The drive was fun too. Laura and I sat in the back of Žanis' small van, sitting on some overturned boxes, which were not very stable and moved as we went around the corners. Žanis would just shout, "Hold on, girls!" and we did the best we could.

I could bet that Žanis was the first Latvian who owned a vehicle in this region. At the Airport, Žanis parked his little van between the expensive-looking cars, and we walked into the brightly lit bar. Inside, music and the cheerful chatter of voices mixed with the tinkling of glasses—and above our heads, of course, the cigarette smoke was collecting.

We found a table and ordered drinks. I don't know if everything we talked about was so funny, but we laughed a lot and had that great feeling, when people feel free and are having a good time. Then suddenly, the big lights dimmed and we heard someone shouting, "Time, please!" and everybody knew that it was time to go. We scrambled into the van again and drove home singing happily.

The summer was ending. The petals of flowers fell. Those that still held on reached toward the sun in their last thrust to show their beauty. I too, wished that the summer would not leave us yet. I went to the park with the children almost every day. Māris sat in the push chair and Uldis, holding on to it, walked at our side. Once again after a long time, I perceived all the beauty around me like in the old days. The waning summer talked to me from the flowers and trees; it came from the songs of birds.

"We are leaving, leaving…" they seemed to say.

It was the eternal cycle: the sorrow of leaving one season and the joy of welcoming the next one. I perceived such supernatural beauty in everything. It flowed into me and filled me, as if God himself had come into me and filled me with this indescribable sense of happiness. I had experienced it once before during war time when the bombers had buzzed in the air, but around me had been beech trees in their burning autumn glory.

I understood that it had nothing to do with what was happening, or what I had or did not have. It was a moment of eternity when God said, "I am! Look at me!" and that was so wonderful, that nothing else mattered. I felt only this deep happiness of being grateful that God had opened my heart to His presence without my having done anything, except being glad and grateful for it. Later I thought about it. Was it because our life was so simple and uncluttered that I could perceive everything like this?

Autumn had come again with cold winds, and the rain drops kept hitting the window panes day and night. It was another weekday evening. Outside was pitch darkness. The children slept upstairs, and the whole house was quiet, because the men were at work, and Mother and Saša had gone to the cinema.

I sat alone downstairs in the breakfast room at the large table. Various pieces of cloth were spread out on it, and I tried to figure out how to make a little suit for Uldis from what were once his dad's best pants. It was good English gabardine, washed, ripped apart and turned inside out. That should still be good enough. The cold crept around my legs, coming from the window and under the doors, making me shiver time and time again. The fire in the fireplace had gone down long ago, for we had to save coal.

The gusts of wind became stronger, shuddering one door, then another. It got quite scary. I had a feeling that at any time one of the doors could open, and somebody would walk in with stealthy steps. Frozen in fear, I listened, but everything was quiet. I slowly opened the door to the hallway, but it was dark and quiet in there. I should at least put on the light, it would be safer, I thought to myself, even though we had to save electricity too. I listened some more at the  bottom of the stairs to see if the children perhaps were stirring, but everything was quiet, and I went back to my work.

I kept turning and measuring the pieces of fabric one way and another until I finally got what I needed. But time and time again my hands rested on the table doing nothing, and I looked at the black window-panes, where the rain flowed and flowed.  I felt that this was a moment when I had to stop and look at my life. Where was I? Everything was

going well, only...

Then one day a problem arose in our complacency. Uldis got sick though he had been very healthy so far. We were overwhelmed with grief, seeing him in his bed breathing with great difficulty. The doctor had been and said that he had asthma. Asthma? I had thought that only old people had asthma, but now it had happened to our child and at such an early age! He was not even three. We wondered why he had this, and the doctor explained that, because of his premature birth, the breathing vessels in his body were smaller and more delicate, and every infection made them even narrower, making his breathing more difficult.

We stood at his bed and watched how he labored for every breath, crying out and moaning, his little face red from the great effort, but we could not help him. The only thing to do was to give the medicine at the appropriate times and wait until the spasm would be over. But it was so hard to wait, seeing and hearing his struggle.

Evening came, but there was no improvement. I finally went to bed, but lay there with open eyes. Ed was not sleeping either. This helplessness was so hard to bear. Hearing the child's gasping, made my heart shrink in fear. Ed tried to comfort me, but we both felt the pain. I gathered all my senses and prayed to God, biting my fist to keep myself from crying.

At last the morning came, and finally he was better. Praise the Lord!

Another year was almost gone. It was the last day and last evening of 1953. I sat alone in our room, and the house was quiet—the only sound was the clock counting out the last hour in this year. Ed was at work, and our little boys were sleeping. I don't know why, but I have always had a desire to stay awake to see the Old Year out and welcome the New Year in. It had always been important to me to take this time to look back at the road I had walked and think about it.

I went to the children's beds and looked at their peaceful faces. They had grown a lot this year. Māris was such a bouncy baby, all peaches and cream with blond hair and blue eyes. He had also been a very happy and contented baby, playing by himself and being no trouble at all. He was so "cute" and outgoing that he opened everybody's heart wherever we went. I thought that this attention might hurt Uldis, for he was not so forthcoming, so I did not encourage it. Both of my children were equally dear to me, and I wanted them to love each other. It bothered me that people in the house paid more attention to one rather than the other, and was anxious that it might foster jealousy.

Poor Uldis, his illness created problems time and again. It usually started after he got a cold. He started to wheeze, and that left him pale and drained. The doctor said that he would outgrow this, but when he

had these spasms, they lasted for two or three days, and those were always hard for all of us.

Still, God had always looked after us and had been with us in our ups and downs. Our greatest wish now was to have our own place, however small, but one where we could be on our own. Times, however, were hard. There was very little money that we could put aside, even though we lived very frugally. We did not want to borrow money, so our only hope was the city council flats or houses they had started building in various places in town. We put in our application, but a lot of points were needed to qualify, and the waiting lists were long. We had hoped that we might qualify on account of Uldis' illness, but our points were still not high enough.

A wish for our own place was now the only thing I asked of the coming New Year. As the children grew bigger, it was hard to raise them the way we wanted while living in a crowded situation, where everybody taught them something different. We had discords even with Mother sometimes, when Ed reprimanded the boys, but Mother tried to make excuses for them. On the whole, she did not interfere with our life much. In fact, we could have almost been strangers. Even though we lived in the same house, we each spent our time in separate rooms and met only when preparing dinner, and then there was no time to talk. She was not interested in the children much, either. We each lived our separate lives, but at least we had a place to stay and we made the best of it.

Now, standing by the window and watching the fireworks shooting up and exploding in the dark sky, I thought about it. Then the church bells rang in the New Year, and I sent my prayer toward the dark sky out there, as dark and impenetrable as our future. 1954 had come.

## To Almeley

My days were now so busy with the children and the housework that the spring had passed before I knew it had come. Summer again was on our doorstep. We heard that the Latvian National Council of Great Britain had rented or bought a big mansion near the village of Almeley in Herefordshire, close to the Welsh border. It was to be a place where the Latvian people would be able to have larger gatherings, summer camps for the children and a place for spending vacations in a Latvian environment. Especially, it would be perfect for celebrating our Midsummer Fest in proper surroundings!

Since our friendship with Laura and Žanis had continued, he suggested that we should go and check it out, and that he would take us. That meant there would be Laura and I with all our children. (Laura in the meantime had acquired little Edvard, now six months old, so all together

there were five of them). Ed could not come, for he could not have a vacation at this time, and Žanis could not stay either, but they wanted at least Laura, the children and me to have the fun of being out in the country.

We packed and got underway, and what a journey it was! As soon as we got out of the city, little Karmen whined, "Mummy, I need to go!" Then, one after another, the children started to need to go potty. We had to stop again and again. When we got to the Malvern Hills, another problem came up. Māris suddenly turned pale and green. We stopped again till he recovered, but then the others got sick too. More stopping and stopping again! Then came the highest hill, and the little van began to labor. We had to get out and walk, only Laura and the baby stayed. The rest of us got back into the van after we reached the top of the hill.

Going down on the other side was easier, of course. The narrow winding road took us through many small sleepy villages with postcard pretty cottages, sunk in flowery gardens, surrounded by trees. Some still had thatched roofs, and they all had small windows. In some other place, there would be a small stream cutting through the village with a low stone bridge across it. As we went on, the fields gradually became more open and the land leveled out.

After a while, we got to a bit larger town, and going through the narrow streets, lost our way. We needed to get to Leominster and asked several people how to get there, but nobody knew of such a place. At last somebody caught on, "Oh, you mean Lemster! Why didn't you say so? This is Leominster!"

How could we know that it was pronounced that way? He gave us instructions where to go, and we happily got through the town and also found the village of Almeley. It was not too far from there.

Here it was—a small village amidst the meadows and fields. The few houses at the crossroads sat quietly dreaming, warming themselves in the afternoon sun. Orange and yellow cress climbed up the trellises at the walls, and lupines and roses surrounded them. Everything looked asleep. We saw no people. The lone oak trees spread their green canopies over the silent gardens and houses.

As we went on, a low stone wall appeared on the right side of the road. Ivy and creeping geraniums covered it in places, dusty from the graveled road. Clumps of red poppies and purple lavender grew inside the cracks where the stones had fallen out. On the other side of the wall we could see gray stone crosses and plaques, crooked or straight and tended and untended ancient grave sites. An unpretentious gray stone church sat in the middle of this forlorn-looking place as it had done for centuries, with its plain square tower and without any kind of beautification. It seemed to represent life itself—its harsh reality. The church stood there reminding us of our living and dying, the worldly and the eternal,

and uniting both. A hazy sunshine covered everything, giving a feeling of silent waiting, and this waiting had no haste. It looked like nothing here had haste, and that was good. That was why we had come here.

After going through the Almeley village, the road continued through fields and soon came to a side road where a small sign read: "The Nieuport House".

"This must be the place!" Laura said.

Two stone posts still showed where the gate once had been, and next to it was the guardsman's cottage, overgrown with weeds and hollyhocks now. The Nieuport House must have been the home of some wealthy family once, but since these places take a lot of upkeep, the families of today cannot afford to keep them. Now our Latvian organization had rented or bought it and wanted to spruce it up for the Latvian people. Somehow the proper title "Nieuport House" did not quite stick with the Latvians, but the simple name of Almeley did. So from the beginning on, it was just Almeley, and the Latvians came to love it.

After driving through the gates, we saw greenish-gray oat fields in their early growth, extending for some distance on the left side, but on the right were fenced-in meadows, where cattle grazed. Not far from here was a farm, hidden in the trees, and as we learned later, this farmer was leasing and working most of the Latvian property's land. Only the grounds, surrounding the buildings and the core of the property, were left for the use of the guests, and that was plenty.

Coming closer to the mansion, the road led us in a curve through a thicket of dark green firs, like driving through a welcoming gate. Upon coming out on the other side, the red tile roofs of the buildings came into view through the luscious canopies of the surrounding trees. More of the thick fir trees grew alongside the road and through them we caught glimpses of the stables. Later we learned that during the war they had been converted and used as a military hospital. Now the plans were to adapt these rooms for the use of old people and invalids, who might want to live out here in a Latvian environment and be taken care of.

Finally, the curved drive led us past some hundred-year-old oaks and guided us into the parking area by the main entrance. As we found out, this was the main entrance, but it was situated at the back of the house and was not very impressive. The front of the house was on the other side and was much more imposing, with its whole structure facing the south with a view of the lake and the forest beyond.

It turned out that the setting up of the house was in its first stages of preparation to receive visitors, and the furnishings for the guest rooms were minimal at this time. We happened to be their first visitors, but we did not need much, as long as we had somewhere to sleep. Our rooms were sparsely furnished, but the windows faced the front, with a view

of the lake, and that was more than enough. Here, the three levels of windows opened to the loveliness of Almeley. Beyond the rounded front lawn, four terraces, one lower than the other, led the eye down to the lake, which lay there quiet, surrounded by trees and shrubs. A dark fir forest enclosed the lake on the far side where it mirrored in the quiet water. A row of dark green junipers grew densely on each side of the terraced areas, creating a separation from the rest of the land, making it look more formal.

The manager of the property was Mr. Skujēvics, a very distin-guished-looking older man with gray hair and a short mustache, perhaps in his sixties. We learned later that he had been a high ranking official at the ministry of finance in Latvia during its years of independence. He was very nice and helpful to us in every way. He had lost all of his own family and was on his own. Now this was his home, where he lived and served for the rest of his life, taking care of the administration of the property.

The housekeeper was Mrs. Marija Ķeņģis. She was a large woman and reigned over the house and the workers like the general of an army, being everywhere and seeing everything, giving her directives in a loud voice. She certainly knew how to handle the job, having specialized in home economics back in Latvia at the *"Kaucminde"* Home Economics Institute. People, coming here as visitors would have a full board, so that meant a lot of planning and a lot of meals to prepare.

We took our things up an impressive curved stairway made of heavy old oak, and went to our rooms to get settled. Really, there was not much to settle. We each had an iron bedstead, a couple of chairs and a small dresser, but we understood the situation and were just happy to be here. After all, this was a historical moment: our own Latvian country home— and a mansion at that! Anyway, we would be spending most of our time outdoors, and downstairs were huge lounges furnished with big old chairs and sofas for sitting indoors. Even a piano was there, all of which was probably left by the former owners. Large glass doors opened to the front lawn with a view to the lake.

It was the month of June and the days were beautiful. The air was so fresh here, far away from the large cities and full of all the scents that the green earth could muster. We went for walks or spread out a blanket on the front lawn and played with the children. It was fun watching Solveig, Karmen, and Uldis running around, hiding from each other behind the shrubs and making up their own games. Laura's little Edvard, our god-son, was just learning to sit up by himself, but often rolled over and needed to be propped up again. Our Māris was a year and eight months old and tried to do roll-overs on the lawn.

Of course, we also walked down to the lake. Trees and bushes surrounded it, leaning over the water in places, some even dipping their branches in it. Reeds and yellow water lilies grew under them, and ducks liked to hide in their shade during the midday sun. The children loved to watch them. A small landing with a wooden walkway extended over the water for those who wanted to swim. Even several swans lived in the lake, and it was great to see them glide regally across the water, their heads held up proudly. The biggest of them, called "Peter" by the locals, was the bravest one. He swam over right away, and the children had such fun feeding him the bread that Mrs. Ķeņģis had given them from the kitchen.

It was so good to lie in the grass by the lake without any thoughts or worries of tomorrow, and it was a paradise for the children. The weather was good, too, so we were doubly blessed. No planning for meals either! That was a special bonus for us mothers. The fees for staying here were very low in these days, and we could afford them.

Only a couple of days were left till the Midsummer Fest celebration, so people at the House were very busy with preparations, wanting this first celebration here to be great. A lot of people were expected, and some started arriving in the next days from various parts of England, but most came on the *Līgo* day, the 23rd of June, because the evening of this day was the high point of the celebration. Some raised tents in the adjoining meadow, where a clump of trees partitioned it off from the front lawn area. They called out to each other cheerfully: "Hey! Nice to see you! Let's get together later!"

"Hello! Have not seen you for ages!"

A happy mood was everywhere. Verses of *Līgo* songs could be heard here and there, and the excitement was growing. Our people and others from Birmingham arrived by a hired bus: Mother, Saša, Ed and Johnny, as well as others from our house. Žanis came also, and it was nice to see them all. Now there were people and activities all over the place.

Mother, Laura and I went with the children to a nearby meadow, picked flowers and made wreaths to wear on our heads later that evening. Ed and Žanis brought us some branches of oak leaves, and we made wreaths for them also.

Our ancestors had believed that this was the night when John, the son of God, rode around the countryside on a black horse, bringing blessings to people who waited for him while burning fires on the ground, or lifting up high on posts barrels filled with wood and tar. People then gathered around welcoming him by singing the special *līgo* songs. It was the celebration of the summer solstice when it barely got dark on that night in Latvia, then began to get light again right away. But it was more than that. It was a magical night, full of mysteries; a joyful celebration

of the high point of growth of the season, invoking blessings in special songs for good crops and herds, which would provide for their families during the coming year. Young couples were urged to go and look for the magical golden fern-blossom that would bloom on this night only. It was also to honor all men called "John". Even though the times had changed, people tried to continue the old traditions from way back.

Some people may call it St. Johns Day, but I have never ever heard of such an association, at least not in Latvia. It has been established by research that the Latvian Midsummer Fest has nothing to do with the church or Christianity. (Wikipedia)

As the dusk set in, the celebrations began with Mrs. Ķeņģis and Mr. Skujēvics acting out the roles of the Hosts, called "John's Mother" (Jāņu Māte) and "John's Father" (Jāņu Tēvs) for this evening. The visitors, called "John's children" (Jāņu bērni), arrived singing traditional līgo songs, crowning the hosts with oak-leaf wreaths and throwing flowers and grasses over them as blessings. In Latvia people used to go from farm to farm in the rural areas, repeating this old tradition in each place, feasting on the special foods that were a part of this celebration and praising the hosts, then moving on with others joining them. There was the special homemade caraway cheese, beer—especially beer and often home-brewed!—and the small bacon rolls, pīrāgi at every house.

Here in Almeley the celebration happened in one place, of course, and when the official part with the feasting was over, everybody could do what they wanted. People settled down in small groups on spread out blankets, near some trees or shrubs, singing, and in between songs, feasting on the food and drinks they had brought along. Some food was served inside the house also, where beer was available, and the kitchen provided hot sausages with sauerkraut and other things.

A little apart from the main house, a bonfire had been set up near a large oak tree and it was just beginning to send smoke and red sparks toward the darkening sky. People sat around here, too, watching the flames, and perhaps remembering how it was back home in Latvia on this night. There was even dancing on the front lawn later, and spirits were high.

As always, I needed to get away by myself for a bit and think about all this. Ten years had passed already since we had left our beloved country, and now we were here celebrating and even being happy… Had we already forgotten? I was sure that was not the case, but perhaps we had learned, that pining for our homeland constantly was not a good thing either. We had to live where fate had brought us.

I remembered the words my doctor had said to me some years ago when I almost had a nervous breakdown from pining for my homeland. He had said then, "You have to forget about going home. You will never

get there. It is a fact you have to accept. This is where you are, and this is where you have to live."

"But then there is no point to living," I had answered, deeply pained by his words.

"You'll live," he had said harshly, not even looking at me as he finished writing out a prescription. There was nothing for me to say after that. I thought that he did not understand. But now I saw that he had understood. He knew that a person could be as strong as he or she needed to be. Soon after that I had met Ed, and that was a new reason to live.

## To London?

The year 1955 did fulfill our wish for a new place to live but in a totally unexpected and different way. One Sunday afternoon in May, when Ed and I rested on our bed reading and Ed was leafing through the newest issue of our Latvian newspaper *"Londonas Avīze"*, he suddenly laughed and said, "I say, wife!" (he never called me that as a rule!) "How would you like to go and live in London?"

I looked at him completely puzzled. What was he talking about? But he just continued to read out loud, "The Latvian organization, *"Daugavas Vanagi"*, is looking for a caretaker for their property at 72 Queensborrough Terrace, London W2, preferably a married couple. Please send application..."

"That's good!" I answered jokingly, not taking him seriously. "Let's start packing!" I gave a laugh and went back to my reading, yet my thoughts kept creeping away from my book.

"What was it that was said there?" I went over it in my mind. The seed had been sown. "Yes, come to think of it, I would like to live in London," I thought, and all of a sudden it was not a joke anymore. After a little while, I asked Ed to read it again.

He began again at the beginning, but the only thing that really stuck in my mind was that there would be free living quarters for the caretaker and his family! Fantastic! What a thought! What an adventure that would be! My "little wheels" started turning faster and faster from one thought to another.

"But why not?" I asked myself. "Ed would not have to dig the clay-like chocolate in the great heat anymore!" I felt quite sorry for him lately. He looked so thin from the heavy work and the sweating, even though he never complained.

"Could this be the opportunity we had been hoping for?" my thoughts kept rolling on. "I could work, too, and at the same time look after the children. They were not so small anymore; Uldis was four and Māris would be three in the fall..."

Ed happened to be thinking along the same lines, and all these thoughts now made us more and more excited. We started to talk more seriously of all the aspects, which in the beginning had seemed like a joke. Of course, we may not get accepted even if we applied, but why not try? We could not lose anything by doing that! After having made a decision, Ed wrote a letter to the House Committee.

A week passed. Our excitement had died down, and all that seemed like a dream we had dreamed. It also seemed so unbelievable that life could be different than it had been these last years; that something could really change! Then one day, a letter came from London, inviting us to an interview a week later. Now we were really excited and decided that we had to go.

It was a cool gray day in London, when we got off the bus on the wide Bayswater Road near the Queensway, and slowly walked to the indicated address. We still had plenty of time. Seeing that it was a Sunday, the streets were empty. A sharp wind blew sand along the pavement like slithering serpents. Empty paper cups rolled in the gutter. It was quite chilly even though it was the beginning of summer.

Cars ran in both directions on the busy Bayswater Road, one of the main arteries entering the city center from the west. Large five- and six-story apartment buildings and hotels with balconies lined one side of Bayswater Road with a nice view of the large Kensington Gardens on the opposite side of the road. Through the iron railings, we could see a children's playground quite near just inside the Kensington Gardens with a gate opening to it, and I was glad about that. Farther beyond we could see walkways, large trees, patches of grass, and even some ponds. As we found out later, the Kensington Gardens were huge, stretching for quite a distance at the one side of Bayswater Road and joining up with the well-known Hyde Park farther on. The Bayswater Road ended at the Marble Arch—the gateway to the city center, only five minutes on the bus from where we were.

We found that Queensborough Terrace was quite close just across the road, being one of the many smaller side streets branching off the Bayswater. It was a quiet street and not very long. Narrow six-story buildings stood one next to the other like a row of soldiers, all constructed almost the same way. Only the color of the paint and a few extra decorations showed where one ended and the other began. The entrance of each one was marked by two thick columns, forming a small porch, and next to it was a low iron fence. Behind it, narrow curved stairs led down to the half-basement level, where most of the hotels had their kitchens. This was the so called "back door", through which most of the deliveries were made.

We found the building easily. On the big outer door we saw a small copper plate that read, *"Daugavas Vanagi"* and "The Latvian Welfare Fund". This was the place. Ed pressed the bell. A little while passed until somebody came and opened the heavy door a crack. Through it, we could see an older face with white hair and black-rimmed glasses.

"Yes?" he asked, eyeing us with mistrust in his eyes.

"My name is Ed Vidners and we have come here for an interview," Ed answered.

"Come in then," he opened the door a bit wider and let us in.

We walked through an inner porch, and then through another door with a glass upper part, and came into the inner hallway. A huge mirror covered a good part of the wall on the left, and a long heavy side table stood in front of it with some letters scattered on it. The air smelled stuffy and a bit like mold. Everything seemed so dark, dusty and dreary that I almost wanted to turn around. It gave a feeling as if nobody lived here, but from the downstairs came a muffled sound of voices.

The old man introduced himself as the present caretaker, Mr. Ādler. He said that he and his wife had been doing this job, but it was getting too hard for them. Since the organization needed an office manager, he and his wife, who was also a bookkeeper, would be ready to take on that job. He pointed to the offices which were to our right, opposite the large mirror.

Mr Ādler talked very slowly, separating each word, like an old person who did not have to hurry anywhere. He also moved slowly, and I wondered how he could take care of the big house. Then we noticed that he wore a leather glove on his left hand, so he was also an invalid.

"I shall take you upstairs," he said slowly, his face wearing the same wooden expression without any visible emotion. One might call him a proper bureaucrat, even though we did not know anything about his past. A stairway, covered with a rather worn, red-patterned carpet, led up straight from the small main hallway. Mr. Ādler went ahead of us, and we followed him up one flight of the stairs. After two shorter turns in the stairway, we came to a large double door. Mr. Ādler opened it and let us into a large room with a high ceiling. It looked like it covered the whole first floor.

"You may sit down while I go and call the head of the committee. They are having their monthly meeting downstairs, but they are expecting you," Mr. Ādler said and left.

We looked around the room with interest. At the center of the left-hand wall was a fireplace with a large mirror above it, and in the corners of the room were some sofas with old-fashioned stuffed chairs next to them. Portraits of some Latvian statesmen and famous writers hung on the walls next to the fireplace. The far end of the hall was taken up by four tall windows (partly covered by dark red velvet drapes) opening

as doors to a narrow balcony facing the street. In the corner near the windows, stood a piano and two tall, old-fashioned display cabinets with some mementos showing through the glass.

Everything here seemed so unreal, as if we had come into another time. Even the air seemed old as if the day was taking a nap. It felt as if the flow of time here had no consequence. I walked around the hall, looking more closely at some things, my steps sounding loud on the smooth parquet floor.

Quite a while passed, but nobody came. When we had looked at everything, we sat down in the old soft chairs with the worn velvet upholstery. Looking around, I thought how different I would make things here, how I would clean and polish and bring new life into the old house. Yes, that was exactly what I would want to do: to turn this dusty, snoozing place into a lively and comfortable one, where people would want to come and have a good time. Let us leave this half-dead mausoleum in the past! These challenging thoughts already weaved and fluttered in my mind like a flag of battle. I felt my whole body getting ready for a challenge of new activities, for up till now our life had run in a very narrow channel.

Just then the door opened, and in came a middle-aged man with partly gray, wavy hair and big hollows under his sun-browned, high cheek bones. We shook hands, and he introduced himself as Mr. Kursietis, the head of the house committee.

He talked quickly, sometimes even falling over his own words, summarizing what they would expect from the new caretaker.

"Our goal is to liven up the old place, spruce it up and establish a club downstairs, where people can meet and also bring more income to the house. That is why we want younger people who can do it."

That, however, was only a project. Besides that, it would be up to us to keep the stairs and hallways of the six-story building clean, as well as the three bathrooms, three guest rooms, the big hall and the three offices. We would also have to receive the mail, answer the telephone, and receive the overnight guests, for whom three rooms were kept vacant on the third floor. Of course, we would have to keep those clean too, change sheets etc. When any socials or gatherings would be planned, we would have to set up the big hall with whatever would be required, meaning: tables, chairs or both and tidy everything up afterward. I would have to serve breakfasts to overnight guests, provide food for special gatherings, snacks for people coming to the club and cater any other food if I wished.

The list was long, and that was not all of it, as we learned later on. The money was not very much either, but there was free accommodation for our family and a possibility to earn something extra with catering the food. That would be up to us.

The caretakers' living room was on the ground floor, right off the

main hallway, next to the other offices, and it had to double as the manager's office also. It was not big enough for the four of us to live in, of course, and I was concerned about that.

"You shall have a large room on the fifth floor for your bedroom," Mr. Kursietis said."Mr. Ādler will show it to you."

When we had received all the pertinent information, Mr. Ādler took us through the whole house, showing us the guest rooms on the third floor and the upper floors where a number of Latvians lived as residents, renting the rooms.

I liked the bedroom right away, for it was quite large and light with a big window at one end, through which we could see the sky above the many roofs. A light blue carpet covered the floor, and there was also a built-in narrow closet with a washbasin in it. That was good, but I failed to think ahead, of how it would be to run up six flights of stairs from the kitchen, which was in the basement, to check on the children in the evenings, or if I would need a piece of clothing. Still, one cannot think of everything. The main thing was to be out of Station Road and to have our own life.

We came down the long stairway, which was narrower and darker in the upper floors, and our guide opened doors here and there, showing us the guest rooms, bathrooms and storage places. On our way down, we met and got introduced to one committee member and then another. It looked like they were anxious to see us, but could not wait until we came down. I wondered why we had not been introduced to all of them at the same time. Then, they too, could have asked questions and assessed us, but it appeared that they were all satisfied. Smiling and joking, they dropped some comments as if it was all already decided that we would come. It was not so simple though. It was too big of a change in our lives, and we did not want to decide momentarily.

"We want to talk it over and think about it," Ed said, "but we will let you know as soon as we have decided."

"Yes, well… Of course, of course… Only try to decide soon!" said the head man of the group."

Gladly, we took our leave and went out into the cool air outside. Our heads throbbed from the tension and all that we had seen and heard. Everything was milling around in our minds. We needed to sit down somewhere and relax a bit. We took a bus to Piccadilly, where we found a nice small pub. A lot of people crowded around the bar at the ground level, the rings of cigarette smoke rising above their heads. Instead, we went downstairs to the basement, where our feet sank into a soft carpet, and only a few people sat at the black tables. It was good and quiet here. The red carpets and red walls, in places interrupted with mirrors or dark paneling, made the room feel warm and cozy.

"Am I glad to move my weight off my feet at last!" I sighed, letting myself down into the comfortable seat. It felt like all the heaviness from my head had spread through my whole body, making it heavy like lead, yet in my arms and legs was a strange vibrating feeling. After all, this had been a very serious experience for us.

We ordered drinks, then Ed went upstairs to a pharmacy next door and got us some headache remedies. We talked for a long time, sitting at the small round table, weighing up all the pluses and minuses of this new adventure. Gradually, more and more minuses were put aside, for we both believed that we could do something good with that place. It was a challenge to our abilities. Ideas and plans of what we could do already were forming in our minds. We felt sure that this was the way we should go. We had nothing to lose, and everything to gain by putting our energies into creating something good and beautiful. We could return to Birmingham and Cadbury at any time if we did not like it. I had only one smoldering concern at the end, and I finally shared it with Ed.

"But what about the drinking?" I asked.

This had been our biggest problem, and for me, the most painful subject in our life together. Sometimes the drinking went too far, causing me great heartache. I had nothing against some social drinking and also understood, that after a hard week's work one wanted to relax together with other men, having a "pint or two". The problem was, when he could not stop in time and wanted more and more. Then I worried myself sick.

"No! It's absolutely clear that there couldn't be any drinking, if all the responsibility would be on my shoulders!" Ed said firmly, and a mountain rolled off my shoulders, for I did not like to complain or talk about it. I wanted to believe him and knew that if he really wanted it, he could do it.

Everything had been talked through now, and the decision had been made. Relieved, we got up and went up the stairs. Would it be good and right for us? Who could say? Coming out on the street, where the first evening lights had come up, I sent a silent prayer toward the darkening evening sky that it would be good! Would that it be right!

# To London

## Part Three

## To the DV House

It was June, 1955 when we moved to London. What a change! In the beginning it was so strange to hear and feel the nonstop drone of the large city around us. We even had difficulty going to sleep, listening to the cars rushing by along the busy Bayswater Road. Yet, in time one can get used to almost anything.

We began to work with great enthusiasm, for the summer season was on our doorstep. A lot of people would take their vacations, and quite a few would be coming to stay here at the Latvian D.V. (*Daugavas Vanagi*) House. The single men, who lived in smaller towns or on farms, where no other Latvians lived, were especially eager to come to spend time together with people of their own nationality.

Often we worked till late at night trying to get more done. First of all, we needed to spruce up the old musty house! The long table in the main hallway now shone and gleamed as a nice piece of furniture should. There was always a container on it with flowers or some kind of greenery to welcome those who came. The dust vanished from everywhere. We painted, wallpapered and I made new drapes and bedcovers for the guest rooms. It all took a lot of time, especially finding the right materials, while trying to keep within the boundaries of our budget.

We had to plan the new club room. That was an exciting project! It would be in the half-basement in the previous library room that was under the stairs at the back of the house. The books were sorted by the librarian, some were discarded and others moved to the billiards room next door. I designed the set-up, the colors and the lighting for the club

room. Ed built the beautiful curved serving counter of black shiny Formica. It came out very good and gave a nice contrast against the yellow and white patterned paper on the wall behind it, with glass shelves for bottles and subtle lighting. The other walls would be a simply patterned medium green with some wall lights. We wanted the room to be modern and also intimate, and at this time, the trend was to decorate walls in different colors. We were very pleased with our efforts, and so were the people when they came to our new club. Now the many local Latvians, as well as visitors, had a place to meet, and there would be income for the house.

My own main workplace was the area that included the kitchen and the dining room, both situated in the half-basement toward the front of the house. Two windows, one in the small kitchen and the other almost next to it in the dining room, faced the service stairway. From the stairway, a door led from outside into the utility room and then through another door into the spacious dining room. Here, deliveries were made for the kitchen and the club. This was where the children and I spent most of the time, they playing and I working, unless I was helping somewhere else in the house. They seemed to be happy enough and soon made friends with a little boy from India, who lived with his family on the other side of the street. His mother, a very nice Indian lady, came over to introduce herself and told us: "My husband is a doctor over here on a research project. Little Ravindra is our only child. He is very glad that he has some playmates now, and I am too."

We liked him also, and he came over often.

Soon after our arrival at the Latvian House, we were informed that the D.V. members' annual gathering was scheduled to take place here in a month's time, and we should be ready to feed and house about twenty people overnight. We were in a panic! How would we do it all? We would also have to set up the big upstairs hall for the meeting. In the evening the chairs would have to be put away and beds set up for sleeping. In the morning, while the visitors ate breakfast, Ed would have to get rid of the beds and change the hall into a meeting room again. It was a tall order, and at first we feared how we would manage it all. But we did all right, and after we got used to the circumstances, we filled even taller orders as time went on. We learned to organize well, sharing some jobs and helping each other as needed to accomplish what was necessary. There was always very much to do, and we were on the move all the time, but that was all right. It made life more interesting, and we were young and able, both being in our late 20's.

After our club was ready, it quickly became very popular. In the evenings, and especially on weekends, there were always people in it. The permanent residents, who lived on the upper floors, also liked to come

down after work to have a glass of beer and chat with others. We knew them all and in time we became friends with most of them.

When light, quick steps sounded on the stairs coming down from the main hallway, we knew that it was Mr. Putriņš, a slim middle-aged man with graying dark hair and brown eyes, who lived on the fourth floor. I did not know where he worked, but he carried an attaché case under his arm. He always seemed to be hurrying, yet as he came down, he always took time to stop for a moment at the dining room door and wish me a good-evening; then, dip, dip, dip, his quick steps resounding on the uncarpeted floor, he hurried on to the club room at the back of the short hallway.

"A Guinness, please!" he would say to Ed, who already had it in his hand, because he already knew that Mr. Putriņš never drank anything else besides, or any more than one bottle of Guinness Stout. Sometimes he stayed a bit to talk; other times he just picked up his bottle and hurried upstairs.

The small, rounded pharmacist, who also lived on the fourth floor, came with light, almost feminine steps. His reddish grey hair was cropped short around his balding head, making his pale round face look even rounder. He, too, used to pop into the dining room right after coming from work. He was a quiet man who didn't smoke or drink, and kept mostly to himself. His voice was soft like a woman's, too, when he asked the important question, "Would you happen to have soup tonight, Mrs. Vidners?" He loved soups. If I said "yes", his whole face would light up in a smile.

"Wonderful! Can I have it now? Right now?" He was already putting away his coat and unbuttoning his jacket.

"Yes, and it's coming right up. Just take a seat, Mr. Bebrup!" I said, pointing to a chair at the large table in the middle of the dining room.

I didn't serve portions, but just set the table as needed and put a large bowl of soup and some bread in front of him, and let him eat as much as he wanted. Sometimes the other inhabitants would join him if they happened to come in and smell the soup. Mr. Ābele, another of our residents, worked at the big Grosvenor Hotel near Marble Arch and he ate there, but he liked to come into the club for a little while in the evenings to hear what was new and chat. He also liked to pull the handle of the gambling machine once or twice. Mr. Ābele was a nice man. He always stopped to talk to me and the boys and sometimes even took them to the park if I was very busy.

Vilis was the only other person who lived on the very top floor, where our bedroom was, and he apparently came from my mother's home town, Valmiera. He had known my aunts and uncles there, so he was almost like one of the family. Vilis was a great auto mechanic and knew a lot about

cars. He also owned a big black Buick and later taught me to drive it in the narrow London streets, making me scared to death. Vilis loved to watch people and to pick up the newest gossip that he enjoyed sharing with others later. It made him feel important. He liked to spend quite a bit of time in the club, especially on weekends, when there were a lot of people. He did not drink much, but he knew many of the local Latvians. That was one way, of course, how one could pick up most of the news.

We had obtained some records of the most popular Latvian songs for the club, and the record player sent the sounds of music all through the basement floor. For us, it was too much sometimes, to listen to the same songs over and over and over, but the people who came to the club loved them. It created a pleasant atmosphere, and brought back memories from the times back in Latvia, where those songs had been sung and had so much meaning. They had a meaning now, too, only different. The sweet and sorrowful memories still lived within us.

Ed worked nonstop. There he was behind the bar, there collecting the empty glasses and rushing through the dining room into the utility room to wash them, there rushing back to the bar carrying new supplies. Yes, it was hard work.

"We really have to think about getting some help on weekends and special occasions," Ed said, and I agreed.

I was busy too, especially on Saturday nights. Some guests liked the little open savory sandwiches, which I prepared as snacks before the club opened.

"Can we have sandwiches for four, Mrs. Vidners?" somebody would come to the door and ask. Another person would come a few minutes later and say, "Sandwiches for six, please!"

Others wanted hot sausages and sauerkraut. Quite a few preferred a Latvian cold table with all the special foods that Latvians liked. On weekends, I usually set it up beforehand so people could just come, sit down at the big table and eat. Again, they could have as much as they wanted for the same very reasonable price. Income for the food was mine; I only had to give account for the breakfasts, which were included in the fee for the accommodations.

Workdays were quieter, but then there was the cleaning and the other jobs like planning meals and shopping for supplies. In time, we found that a Jewish delicatessen in the Notting-Hill neighborhood was a good source for our food requirements, and they were willing to deliver. This was of immense help, saving me time. I would just make a list in the morning, Ed would call the order in, and in the afternoon everything was there. It was a more expensive store than other local delis, but their food was of excellent quality, and I wanted everything to be good for my guests. The meats for the dinners I liked to select myself by going to the butchers.

"Who would have believed that only a few years ago I took you round the butcher shops in Kings Heath and you could not tell one meat from another," Ed laughed.

Because I had grown up in wartime, when meat was very scarce and one had to be very careful about what one bought in order to get the most out of one's coupons, I had not had an opportunity to learn that. Ed showed me the meats and cuts, displayed in the windows at the butcher's, explaining what was used for what. I also had not done much cooking while growing up, for the same reason. The rations were so small that a child would not be given a chance to experiment with them. Yet now I shopped and cooked and even catered parties and banquets! I had learned a lot from my mother, too, when I had helped her to prepare food for our various celebrations. I had done cooking as a teenager on our farm in Latvia, but that was a different situation and a different kind of cooking, using just foods that the farm produced.

Now the work was unending, yet I had a good feeling about it. For the first time in my life, I was able to help to upgrade our family resources. Now I could go out and buy something for myself without a terrible guilt feeling. But strangely, I did not even want anything now. There was also no time for it. One job chased the next one. If I had a little free time, I spent it with the children, even though they were close to me all the time. This was another benefit for me—that I could work, yet also take care of the children at the same time. They were very good at making up their own games and didn't disturb me when I was very busy. In the summertime they played outside on the back stairs, where I could see them, and those were not the days when people kidnapped children. They also did not have piles of toys, so they found ways to play with other ordinary things.

Uldis, our oldest, was four and a half at the time and Māris was three. The boys were especially glad when their little friend Ravindra came over. He was four also, and we sure heard him coming! He was so anxious to tell his latest news that he started to talk while he was still coming down the stairs.

"My... my... my mummy says..." he went on, his large, dark eyes sparkling. He was a very nice and well-behaved boy.

The boys' favorite project was to "cement" the cracks in the stairs, and they could play there for hours, mixing sand with water and filling the cracks, which after a little while would dry and the "cement" would disintegrate. They had to fix it and go at it again.

The first year, while we were still in the organizational stage, it was not quite as rushed, visitor-wise. When I had more time and the weather was good, I took the boys to the park. The big Kensington Gardens was just on the other side of the Bayswater Road. The park was huge, but we

only had to go to the end of our street, cross the Bayswater Road, and there was one of the gates leading into it. Luckily, there was also a children's playground right at this end of the park, with swings, slides and a sandpit. I was glad it was so close, and that we did not have to take the bus to find a playground elsewhere.

While the children played in the sand, I sat nearby in the grass listening to the drone of the large city. It was throbbing like a big heart day and night without stopping. For the most part we didn't even notice it anymore, but at free times such as this, it was quite pleasant to just listen to it and think. The cars flowed along the wide Bayswater Road like life's blood itself. The traffic lights lit up and made them stop at times or change their direction, as life made us do also.

I lay back in the grass and closed my eyes. I thought how different life was here. It was as if I had just awakened from a long sleep and was now full of this electrifying life that was pulsating around me, calling and inviting me to flow along, to become one with it. Yes, I loved London. Perhaps I did not feel like a stranger here because there were so many foreigners around. Nobody looked down on them here like they did in the smaller towns. London was a city of the world, where many roads came together, where people came and went.

Suddenly, what had been far away had become close. Listening to the many languages, nothing seemed impossible. People here were more free-thinking, their horizons wider, and for the first time after leaving Latvia, I felt that I was at home, that I belonged here. I liked the big city with the old ornate buildings, which contained so much history. I marveled at the large parks with the hundred-year-old trees that shed their gentle shade in the grass, displaying their special moods and bountiful colors as the seasons changed.

Just lifting myself up on my elbow, I could see the Kensington mansion behind the iron railings nearby, for this was where the park either ended or began. Across the park, the Albert Memorial's slim spire showed through the trees, and the rounded roof of the Albert Hall could be seen next to it. The Albert Hall was London's finest and most famous concert hall. These buildings told about the days long gone, of the people who once lived and walked here.

Looking at the Albert Hall, I had to think of yet another resident of our house—another single man with very interesting characteristics. It was Mr. Abuls. I had to think how singularly different we all were. I did not know where he worked, but he came home with a dirty face and hands, in heavy boots and an old cap on his head. He had an old jacket on, tied around his waist with a string. He must have been doing some dirty work at some factory or gas works. I used to see him when he came through the dining room first thing after getting home, carrying

his waste basket to empty it in the trash can under the stairs.

"Good evening, Mrs. Vidners!" he greeted me bowing slightly, "I do apologize for walking through like this!"

"But of course, Mr. Abul! It is perfectly all right!" I would answer.

He was always very correct and kind. Sometimes he stopped and we would exchange a few words, if I was not too busy.

"What is new in the music world, Mr. Abul?" I asked, and he would tell me what was the newest in opera and what celebrity would be performing where. But mainly he was a quiet, middle-aged man who kept very much to himself.

Mr. Abul loved music, loved it down to the last cell in his body. You would not recognize him later in the evening if you saw him coming down the stairs, clean and freshly shaven, dressed in a nice black overcoat, shiny shoes and a black homburg hat on his head. A black bow tie and a white scarf around his neck completed the scene. What an amazing changeover! What an amazing man! As if to show the world that "the work may be dirty, but the spirit could still be free and the sky still full of stars," as a famous Latvian poet Rainis wrote once. Mr Abuls did not drink or smoke. Everything that he earned was for music, and this evening Mr. Abuls was going to the concert at the Albert Hall where yet another celebrity was performing. Smiling, he bowed his head in greeting, lifting his Homburg slightly.

"Have a pleasant evening, Mr. Abul!" I wished him, as he headed to the door.

I did not know what he had done before the war, but I respected him because he lived without bitterness. He had learned to unite the two diametrically opposite important things in his life. His love and enjoyment of music wiped out all the ugliness of the other.

A little while had passed since I had lain there in the park contemplating. I sat up and waved to the boys, who stood at the top of the slide, ready to come down. I looked at their happy little faces as they made their journey down triumphantly, only to run back to stand in line at the bottom of the stairs again.

How little was needed for a person to be happy! I thought about it again and again. We did not own anything, but I had work, food, a roof above my head, a dear husband and children, good health and contentment for a job well done. What more could I want? I also did not wish for anything else, nor thought about what might be in the future. Life seemed like a wide river flowing in its comfortable low banks, silently reflecting the heavenly light in its waters and sharing it with the surrounding fields. The river was happy. It could give out of its riches.

The boys ran up to me pulling me by both arms. I had to go and help them to swing, and smiling, I got up and went with them.

During this first period in London I often felt this deep contentment, seeing that our life was getting better; that I could help to build it, and we were surrounded with this pulsating life and friendships. Many new acquaintances were made, but also old friends remembered us and came to visit. Then, after closing up the club at eleven in the evening, we would sit and visit in our downstairs living room. We could forget for a while that it was also our office.

We had completely redecorated it with modern Danish style furniture. There was not much, for the room was not big, but now it looked nice and cozy, with a divan-bed in the alcove on the right for sitting or sleeping if someone was visiting. We papered the alcove in black wallpaper with tiny yellow stars, and I made a grey and white striped cover for the bed. The end wall was almost taken up by a fireplace and the wall to the left had a large window. These walls were papered in yellow with a fine white pattern over it and on the last wall, where the door was, the paper was a gentle silvery gray.

I had searched high and low through all the main stores to find the chairs I wanted. I loved the simple line Danish furniture and at last found a large red armchair for Ed and a smaller yellow-lime colored one for me, which was like a simple wave in which I could rest my body. I also bought a small cabinet for china as well as a writing cabinet in nice light Danish wood.

It took even more effort to find a suitable coffee table, and I went searching around all the big stores in the center of London. I finally found it at Liberty's, but it cost 75 pounds! That was a lot of money! I looked around more, but could not get this one out of my mind. It looked so perfect for what I wanted for our room. Since it also served as the manager's office, where people would come on various matters, I wanted it to be nice. The top of the small table was made of black tiles with nine yellow ones on one end that had black, hand painted faces of the sun on them. The frame was of heavy cast iron. It was perfect, and brought me such delight to see something beautiful around me.

I mused and laughed to myself.

"Can you buy joy?" one might ask, and I would say, "Yes you can! I bought it for seventy-five pounds in London!"

Since I did not have time to paint portraits, I could create something in my surroundings that brought me joy. After all, did I not deserve it for the many hours of working here?

I made some yellow cushions for the couch, and when more friends came, we threw them on the floor around the room and sat there drinking coffee from my small black polka dotted porcelain cups, that I had seen in a shop window on Queensway and had bought. It was such a delight that I could buy a few beautiful things without feeling guilty. Sometimes

we chatted and visited past midnight.

There were so many colorful events and experiences here at the house! And what of the many peculiar happenings! Ed especially had a gift of telling these stories so vividly, and then we laughed and laughed.

"One such incident happened only the other day," Ed said. "One of our permanent residents, an older Miss, had come down to the office to pay the rent. She stood in the door, looking around at our newly decorated room, and said sadly, 'So you did not have enough paper to make it all of the same kind... What a shame...' But we could barely keep from laughing."

If we had made it all in one color, it would be like living in an elevator, for the room was not big, but the ceiling was high. It was obvious that these smaller rooms for the offices had been created by cutting up a larger one, as was being done in many of these old buildings. No, everything here was planned that way, but of course, we did not have to say that.

"Another amusing thing happened not long ago," Ed continued. "A pretty, young blond girl arrived and wanted to stay. I asked her to sign the register and she did. The name she signed was Velta Čaklā, meaning 'Someone eager to work'. That was quite an unusual last name. The fun part though, was that only half an hour later a short man came in, also wanting to stay for a few days. He had a bald head and a face that was round like a moon. He signed his name in the register next to Velta Čaklā, and his name was Jānis Sliņķis, meaning 'John Lazy'. I could hardly keep myself from laughing as the man signed," Ed told us.

This, however, was not the end of Mr. Sliņķis' story, because he came to visit us several times after that. It was amazing how we were often entertained by the mere happenings in the house without even seeking them.

At times, when we had friends visiting from out of town, we decided to go and explore the city by night after closing our own club. Usually they were our friends, Aina and her husband Maigonis, who lived close to London. We did not go to the nightclubs. We could not afford those, but just wanted to potter around and see what was happening in this big, bright city at night.

We milled around Piccadilly and Leicester Square, joining the flow of people who just strolled along leisurely under the city lights. The summer evenings were mild, and the people crowded around the brightly-lit entrances of the large cinemas that surrounded the square. Eatery doors and windows were highly-lit and open, even though it was already past midnight. Nobody had a desire to hurry anywhere; it was good to just be. That was a great feeling. The constantly changing lights of the various signs showed smiling worry-free faces, happy and content for just

having this moment, this night. On the corner at the Leicester Square, a man sold roasted chestnuts from his cart. A warm glow came from the little oven as he put the hot chestnuts in paper bags and handed them out, putting the cash right into his pocket.

We walked to the nearby Trafalgar Square, where huge statues of lions lay proudly on their concrete pedestals next to the playing water fountains. In the middle of the square, the tall Nelson's column reached into the night sky. We had all had a little to drink before we left the house, so the mood was exhilarating. Ed stepped onto the base of the column and sang, "Hey there! You with the stars in the 'one eye'..." and we laughed and talked nonsense like children feeling happy and free.

"Let's go across the river!" one of our friends said. "The night is so nice and mild."

We walked to the Charring Cross station and then farther down to the River Thames. A fresh smell of water and a moist coolness touched our faces as we walked onto the bridge. The River flowed deep down under us, black as the night. Across the other bridge, next to the one we walked on, an electrical train droned by, and more and more of them came, flitting by with their lighted windows. The big city was not sleeping. From far away came a ship's warning. I wondered where it was going.

After crossing the bridge, we came by the newly built Festival Hall on the other bank of the River Thames. This was where concerts and ballet performances took place. It was quite a wonderful building with glass walls facing the river and larger and smaller performing areas inside.

Outside, in the newly established landscaping along the river, stocks bloomed in large concrete tubs, giving out their tantalizing aroma. In strips of grass, stood young white birch trees, swaying their fine branches in the lamplights. Looking at them, I suddenly felt like I was back at home. The birch trees had been my friends since childhood days in Latvia. Where was I? The past and the present were suddenly juxtaposed! So strange and yet beautiful! Behind us the modern Festival Hall, but around us birches and the cool wonderful scent of the stocks like I had experienced once at home in Latvia!

Looking over to the other side of the river, the whole lighted panorama of London was before our eyes, mirrored in the dark waters. There was the cupola of St. Paul's cathedral and the spires of other churches, all spotlighted and leaving their images in the water. Once in a while, a dark shadow of a barge would silently slide by, cutting out the lights momentarily.

Back on the other bank, we walked through the narrow winding streets of Soho, London's 'Red Light' area. There were not many people on the streets, but dark shapes of men stood in the doorways under the poorly lit entrances of some obscure clubs. Beyond them were stairs,

leading up or down to who knows where. It was somewhat scary but also fascinating to walk through a place like this—of course, only in the company of others.

Soon the streets were better lit, and not far ahead we saw Piccadilly again, where we had been before. Small Jewish, Russian and Italian delicatessens were still open in the narrow Soho streets, with warmly lighted windows full of big slabs of hot meat and sausages, tempting the late passersby.

"I am hungry!" Ed said, looking into those windows.

"Yes, we could eat, too, after so much walking!" our friends chimed in.

We walked into one of these small delis, where we were greeted like old friends. Soon, sandwiches filled with thick slices of hot salt beef, Russian salad and hot lemon tea were in front of us. It was great! We could not wish for anything more. The owner stood by with a big smile on his round face and even wanted to chat with us.

"Where are you from?" he asked, and we told him.

He asked more questions about Latvia and what happened during the war time.

"Yes, yes, I know... I am from Poland," he said. "I came during the war..."

When we came out to Piccadilly Square again, people and cars still flowed along, but there were fewer of them, and they moved slower. It was almost two in the morning. The fountain, half asleep, still sprinkled its waters at the foot of the famous Eros statue that stood elevated in the middle of the large crossing at Piccadilli, and girls with long hair sat on the steps under it like black silhouettes, hugging their partners, while life still flowed around them.

The theaters had closed long ago, and the taxis slowly drove around looking for clients. Their shiny black cars looked like big black beetles crawling around, the city lights reflecting on their backs. Ed lifted his arm, stopping one of them, and we slid into its warm and comfortable interior. It was enough for tonight.

Another time when our friends had come to visit, just for the fun of it, we went pub-crawling in Soho, where sailors from all kinds of countries milled around, and the cigarette smoke was so thick that one could hardly see the other. We did not go to drink; we just wanted to see what was going on and savor the atmosphere.

In one place we could barely get in, it was so full. We wondered what was happening there. Then we saw someone sitting on a high stool in the middle of the crowd, and we recognized our own local Latvian artist, Bullītis, who sometimes came to our club to draw portraits in pas-

tel. That was what he was doing here too, and the sailors stood around laughing and shouting comments, while one of them sat there posing.

Sometimes after our walks, we went to the small cafe on Haymarket. In an intimately lighted room, small tables sat between tropical plants under which small colored waterfalls played, accompanied by quiet live piano music. The coffee was good and strong there. They also had fantastic cakes or rather "tortes", as they called these very delicate concoctions in Europe—my great weakness! They were served by a beautiful young boy with blond, curly hair, long lashes and... colored lips! But the cakes were fantastic!

Since life at the club and the house had gotten more hectic, we were allowed to take a helper a few hours a week and found a good one right here amongst our residents. That was Edgars Antens, who had already helped us with some painting jobs. He was a vibrant young man, had been a sportsman and was fast and able to do many things. He was single, and during the day, worked at the big Harrod's store packaging cakes. That was not a hard job, so he was glad to spend some hours in the evenings serving at the bar. He liked to be with people and was full of humor. He was the right man for such a job!

That gave Ed and me a free evening together once in a while. We liked to go to the theater or the opera if we could still get last-minute tickets, for we never knew beforehand when we would be able to take our free time. The seats were not always good, and sometimes we were even up in the gallery, but what a treat, nevertheless!

"Have a good time! Enjoy yourselves!" Anten called as we were leaving. "Everything will be all right here!"

So our life was busy but good. The children lived in the middle of it all and were cheerful and content. Now and then, they went to visit in some of the offices, and everybody was nice to them there. On Wednesday mornings they went into Mrs. Blūm's office to help fold the Latvian Newspaper, "Londonas Avize", which was mailed out once a week. That was great fun for them and made them proud for having done something worthwhile. The grown-ups talked with them and made jokes, so they had a great time. The guests and the residents were kind to them also and often stopped to chat. They were well-behaved children and were never any trouble.

When the Latvian sailors came ashore on their breaks, it was a high time at the club. After not having been ashore for a while, they squandered their money at the club or in town during the nights. They also bought the boys chocolate, but in the end there were some who had to borrow money to get back to the ship. One of the sailors sold Ed a beautiful leather travelling bag for a minimal price, and we used it for

many years.

One of the sailors turned out to be a man we knew. His name was Vilhelms Pelns, but everybody called him just Pelns. He had lived above us in the attic at Sašas house and was a sailor now. He brought me a lot of presents from Japan: a whole china tea set and some Japanese pajamas with a robe and slippers.

"Let me pay for them," I said, but he would not have it.

"It gives me joy," he answered. "I have to use the money for something!"

Pelns was a rather strange man—thin and grey in the face. He did not have a family or anybody close. He seemed to just bide his time away with no ambitions or purposes. He lived one day at a time and was even proud of it. He smoked a lot and also sometimes drank quite heavily, but he liked music. He was the only one who had a record player and a few records during our time at Sašas house. I remember how we used to listen to his music on Sunday mornings while still in bed. The boys, though quite small at the time, liked it, too.

He would wake us up with the *"Happy Wanderer"*, and that was a cheerful start for the day. The other records that he played were Doris Day singing *"Que Sera Sera"*, and *"The Black Hills of Dakota"*. They were such happy tunes and we all enjoyed them. Mr. Pelns took a great liking to Māris. The last time he was with us in London, he made a testament leaving to Māris all that he had—if he ever had anything...

Yes, people could live like that too, having no ties, nor a family to care for. Some did not even want to care for anyone. Living for the moment was the name of the game for them.

Sailors of a higher rank lived with us also, sometimes staying with us for several months during the winter, while their ships were in port. They were nice men and we enjoyed talking to them and hearing their stories.

There were not many guests during the weekdays in wintertime, but that was when the Latvian cultural life was in full swing. All kinds of gatherings took place on weekends using our big hall. Our activities had to be tuned to whatever was happening. We had to set up everything, and afterwards, of course, had to clean up and put everything back where it belonged.

On Saturdays the Latvian school "took over" the house, and the children had their fun during the recesses, running up and down the stairs and chasing each other. They were mainly younger children, and our boys took part in it also. It was a good chance for them to meet other Latvian children. Since they had not had much contact with English children, they did not know much of that language, except what they had picked up playing with their little friend Ravindra. At home we talked

only Latvian, but recently we had begun to introduce them to English as well, for Uldis would be starting school next year.

It was really interesting to recount how many different people we came to know amongst those who came to the house. When our Latvian Ambassador, old Mr Zariņš, came to a gathering on some special occasion and we happened to meet, he always stopped to shake hands.

"How are you doing?" he would ask kindly.

He also liked to shake hands with the boys and have a little chat with them. He was a simple and kind man, not like some of a much lesser stature who came up with all kinds of demands, wanting to show how important they were. Yes, we did have our elites, and when they had their gatherings, some of them really wanted to impress who they were (or had been) way back in Latvia. It was interesting to observe the different groups of people who came. Their behavior conveyed so much of what they were about.

How different it was, when the members of the *Daugavas Vanagi* organization came to their yearly meetings. They were mostly the former soldiers of WWII, all ordinary people whose hearts belonged to the organization and the work it was doing, namely to help their invalid friends and their families, many of whom were still in Germany (because they could not work and therefore were not admitted in England). The former soldiers called themselves the "kanaks", which meant the "rough, tough and ready ones", who had gone through WWII. True, they liked to live it up in the evenings, but they were friendly, cheerful and grateful for everything that was done for them. Many of them became our friends, since we saw them from year to year.

Occasionally guest artists came, and stayed with us in the guest rooms, and we saw to their needs, trying to make their stay as pleasant as possible.

There were also global meetings, when prominent Latvian people came from all over the world, and there were many well-known names amongst them. Those were people from Latvia's former government and military, as well as scholars, writers and others who cared about Latvia's future. We felt very privileged to meet and serve them. The thing that they had in common was their simplicity and nobility. I could say that the nobler they were, the more gracious they were to us.

Former Colonel Vilis Janums came and stayed with us for several months, while visiting the many centers of the organization Daugavas Vanagi in various parts of England. We felt honored to look after him during the in-between periods when he was in London. Under his direction, this organization had been created in the prisoner of war camp at Zedelgheim, Belgium, in the winter of 1945/46. He had called his soldiers "sons", and they loved and respected him as their father, because he

had been with them at the Russian front—and all the way through Poland and eastern Germany—as their armies withdrew. Many times he had saved his units from being captured by the enemy. He was a man of great ingenuity—one of the noble ones. When he came to us, the first thing he said to me was: "Please, I do not want any special treatment and would be glad to share meals with your family."

Since it was wintertime, mid-weeks were rather quiet, so we had more time to talk with him as we all sat around the table having our meals. It was a privilege to know him and to be together with his exceptional personality.

It was very much like that when General Rūdolfs Bangerskis came for his visit. He wanted to go to the larger Latvian centers to talk to the people and to find out how they were making out in this country. He was an amazing person—a large man with a distinct military stature that told of his years of military service in the Russian Czar's army. His service had started years before Latvia had become an independent state. Nobody would guess that this big straight-backed man, with his fair, practically unlined face and short-cropped white hair, was eighty years old. That, however, was true, as we found out when we got better acquainted with him. He stayed with us for several months, and on leaving, he gave us two thick volumes of his memoirs as a gift.

Like the colonel, he asked, "Please don't make an exception for me! I shall be happy with whatever you eat and would like to be part of your family while I stay here."

Our relationship grew more friendly and warm as days went by. He even liked to talk to the children and to draw them into conversations with him. Only later did I learn that he was on his own without any family. Perhaps that was why he was glad to share the warmth of ours.

We revered the old General from our hearts, but it was not in our nature to tip-toe and bow, and that was all right for all of us. We respected the high and the low equally and treated them all in the same way. I did not even know at the time that he had been the highest Latvian military and political person during WWII, overseeing the treatment of Latvian military units, who had been drafted to serve in the German army. He never even mentioned it.

It was a real joy to listen to the General as he told us the stories of his long and eventful life. We were glad that we did not have any other guests at this time, so we could spend more time with him. After dinner, we would sit around the table and linger, drinking tea and talking. Sometimes Ed would bring him a glass of cognac from the club. The General liked it, but he never had more than two. A slight pink would touch his fair-skinned cheeks, and his talk would become livelier. I loved to see his light blue eyes that were clear and pure like a child's, illuminating his

whole face up to his high smooth forehead. Here was a noble man, and one did not need to put it into words.

He liked the German song, *"Oh, mein Papa..."*, and if it happened that it was played in the club, he lifted his glass and sang along. When the time came for him to return to Germany, where he lived, he asked if I would pack his suitcase for him.

"That it is one job that I cannot master well," he said.

Of course, I did it gladly and with love. On leaving, he gave us two books of his memoirs. With tears in our eyes, we saw him off like a member of the family. He would always stay in our hearts.

It was too bad that only a couple of years later, somebody ran him down in Germany as he was crossing a street. An old man and an accident... But was it? That was how the KGB got rid of unwanted people...

The former caretakers, Mr. and Mrs. Ādlers, now took care of the office of the D.V. organization, for they were both experienced in administrative matters. People came and went into their office with all kinds of problems, but often the visitors just wanted to visit and talk, ask some questions and hear about what was going on in the Latvian community. These were mostly people who lived too far from the Latvian centers and were alone amongst the British people.

They also loved to go into the "bookstore" that was in a room on the ground floor at the end of the hallway. There they could look at the newest books and have a chat. The bookstore was managed by Edvīns Alksnis, one of the WWII veterans who had ended up in Sweden at the end of the war. He had been one of the 158 Latvian soldiers held in the retaining camps there, all believing that they would be released soon, since Sweden was a neutral country. The Russians, however, demanded that they should be returned to Latvia. Everybody knew that it would be a death sentence for these men, if they were repatriated. When the Communists requested to have them shipped back to Latvia, it caused great outrage in the exiled Latvian communities as well as among the Swedish citizens.

Many Latvians had fled the communist regime late in the year of 1944 by going to Germany. Others had tried to get over to Sweden, because it was a neutral country. Putting their lives at great risk to go across the rough seas in small fully-packed boats, they tried to escape the Communists, and Sweden accepted them. Everybody knew what the fate would be for these soldiers if they were extradited, yet the leftist Swedish government allowed the Russians to come and take them! It was January 25, 1946. Most of them died in the Gulags, far north in the arctic regions of Soviet Russia. That was a very heavy blow to us Latvians, because Sweden, being a neutral country, did not have to do it!

The retained men, including German soldiers, were kept behind barbed wire and were constantly watched. They went on a hunger strike, while the negotiations continued between the Swedish government and the Russians. Some officers and soldiers committed suicide; some injured themselves, yet they were even dragged and carried onto the Russian ship. Mr. Alksnis had stuck a pencil through his eye into the brain and had been too sick to be moved. His life was saved, but he lived with a glass eye and limped heavily, leaning on a cane. We were very sorry for Mr. Alksnis, but at least he was taken care of by being allowed to work at the bookstore, to take care of his family.

Another person working in the bookstore was Mr. Jānis Zariņš, who had been a professional man in the theater back in Latvia. He organized a drama group in London and produced several plays, so we had interesting people around us all the time. My friends, Aina and her husband Maigonis, also belonged to Mr. Zariņš drama group and loved to work with him. We were sad to hear later that Mr. Zariņš had returned to Latvia to work in the theater there, but he was getting on in years, and one way or another, did not get to enjoy it for long.

It so happened that I got involved in folk dancing again. Somebody had heard that I used to lead a group in Birmingham, and the interest seemed to be great amongst the young people. Quite a few of them lived here in London, and I was glad to lead if we could adjust the practices to the times when I was not too busy. Workdays during winter seemed to be the best time, and we could practice right here in the big hall a couple of evenings a week.

We got four boys and three girls together, and I danced too, guiding the group at the same time. If I remember correctly, there was Ināra and Kārlītis, Mārīte and Pēteris, Sandra and Ivars and last of all, Ziedonis and I.

The biggest problem was who would play the music for us?

"Why don't we ask Marianna, she plays piano?" somebody suggested. But Marianna was our Ambassador's daughter. Could we? Should we? Marianna was a large girl, the only child of her distinguished parents, and perhaps was a bit lonely, being somewhat apart from the regular Latvian young people.

"Well, why not ask?" one of the girls said.

It turned out, however, that she was actually glad to join our little group when we asked her. We were delighted and grateful that she had agreed to help us. Now the question remained—what shall we name ourselves?

Various names were mentioned, but they were already used by other groups in other Latvian communities. Then I suggested: "How about

calling us 'Pastarnieki', since we are the newest group?" (Pastarītis, meaning the youngest one). It was not exactly correct, because we were not the youngest, but the newest group. Still, it sounded good and the name was accepted.

Dancing was a nice change for me from the everyday work, and it was something I loved to do. We practiced and then danced at several social functions at the House and also prepared a special show, "The Journey across Latvia". I had already started to work on it for my group in Birmingham. My friends Aina and Maigonis, who now lived near London, helped us in the presentation of the show. He was the commentator and would lead us through the different regions of Latvia, depicting what was special and unique in the particular area, and Aina would sing some solo songs and recite poems related to that place. The rest of us joyfully danced the folk dances that originated from each particular region. It turned out well and we heard good comments.

In March 1956, Mother and Saša had finally decided to get married, so all our family traveled to Birmingham for the wedding. We were very glad about this, for Saša was a good, steadfast man. He would be a good husband to Mother and take care of her. Mother had always been an active and energetic person and was still good looking at 54.

Since this was early spring and it was a quieter time at the house in London, it was easier to get away. Edgar Anten would take our place, so we knew that everything would be all right.

The wedding took place at Saša's house. They had chosen to have the ceremony on the same day when the minister would come up from London to perform his monthly service in Birmingham. The guests were only the closest friends, and everything worked out very well. It was so nice for us to see our old friends after a year and a half, even though we could only stay for two days.

At the end of March, we celebrated Uldis' fifth birthday, and he had to start going to school. We were very lucky that the school was so close, just at the other end of our short street. It was a new and modern school, built in an open area with big trees, surrounded by new high-rise apartment buildings.

I felt quite emotional as I led my young son to begin his life's journey into the world. I felt for him, as if I myself was going to be with people that I did not know and who did not speak my language. My little man—he looked so lonely and drawn within himself, when the teacher took him by the hand and led him away. I thought about him all day, wondering how he was doing and how he felt, being alone in the big wide world for the first time. His English language was not too good, but we had taught him a fair amount during the last year. I should not

have worried, though. He picked it up easily and settled down just fine.

When I walked Uldis to school the first morning, Māris came with us also and was very upset that he had to go back home.

"Why can't I stay too?" He cried and even stamped his foot.

"But you are too young! They will not take you!" I tried to pacify him. "You know?" I said then to him, "We will buy the same book that Uldis is reading at school, and then we can learn to read it at home! What do you say about that? Then you will be ready for next year!" That satisfied him.

I acquired the book the very next day, and from then on, every morning after breakfast, Māris would stand by my chair with his book in hand, waiting until I finished my meal. When I was done, he climbed into my lap, and we could begin. He did very well with reading, but he also loved to look at the pictures. He looked at them for a long while, surveying everything carefully, sometimes even wanting to turn back the page to look at something again, and I let him do it. When he had read enough, he would turn around toward me and say, "Mummy, I want to love you now!"

Soft little hands went around my neck, and a tender, cool cheek pressed against mine. I held him against my heart and rocked him back and forth. Māris was such a bonny and lovable child with his blond hair and blue eyes. He always walked around with his little, soft Pekinese toy dog under his arm, which his godmother Aunt Paula had given him for his first birthday—in time it had become quite flat. I often called Māris a "kitten", since he was so soft and cuddly, and our friend and helper, Anten, made it even one better, calling him 'Mr. Kitten', and soon all the residents in the house called him that, too.

I was very happy to be able to sit with my child like that after breakfast, but then it was time to get up and start working. Ed tidied the club room; I put away the breakfast dishes. Then we both went to clean the stairs and tidy the guest rooms. Ed actually got up even earlier to receive the mail and to tidy the offices before the workday started, but my first job was to make breakfast for the guests and ourselves.

We were very glad to have Anten as a helper and friend. He brought more fun into our lives, because he looked to the lighter side of life. He also liked to fool around with our boys and tease them. One day he said to Māris, "Come, I shall lift you up with one hand!"

Māris went forward, a bit hesitantly, but afterwards he was not afraid anymore. Anten really could lift him up with one hand! Each time he saw Anten after that, he would say, "Lift me up with one hand!" and Anten did, being a strong guy with a sportsman's body. A good relationship developed between him and us, and we worked very well together. His humor also helped us to get over some heavier hurdles.

After working a year at the D.V. house, we thought that we were due for a vacation, and after some resistance, the committee agreed to let us have one. Mother agreed to have the boys for the two weeks, so we could really relax and rest. Those were two wonderful, golden weeks that Ed and I spent at Margate, a seaside town on the south-eastern corner of England. We had each other again, without any cares for tomorrow or the world, just enjoying our freedom and our together-ness. Since it was only the beginning of June, the wind was still quite strong and cool when we went outside, but the days were sunny with blue skies above. We found a place by the rocks, where we were sheltered from the wind, and it was quite warm there. We lay in the sand, soon acquiring a nice tan. As time went on, the weather gradually got warmer.

Not being far from London, Margate was a popular summer resort. Electric trains went back and forth several times a day. Alongside the beach was a nice wide promenade with palms and pavilions, giving plen-ty of room for people to walk, to watch the sea, and to have some enter-tainment. In late afternoons quite a lot of people liked to just stroll there, because it would be too much to lie in the sun all day. Along the other side of the promenade, facing the sea, was a row of small hotels and guest houses offering full board, and they were quite reasonably priced.

One late afternoon, when we strolled along the promenade, we saw a couple of young men in white shirts, walking about and talking to people. We wondered what was happening until one of them stopped by us, too.

"There will be free entertainment in the big Pavilion in half an hour's time," they told us. "Two film stars: Leslie Caron and Tony Britton will be choosing the eight best dressed girls here at the beach! "Come, it will be fun," he urged us.

We looked at each other. Well, why not? We could walk a little bit longer and then go in. I was wearing a crisp light grey dress with a white embossed pattern. It had a fitted, low-cut sleeveless top and a full skirt in three tiers. As a top, it had a short open bolero jacket with cap sleeves. The dress looked good on me, but I never for a minute thought that I might get chosen, yet I was.

Ed and I sat down in the back of the big auditorium. People chatted around us, waiting for what would happen. There were quite a few girls standing on the stage already, but apparently two more were needed. Since nobody else was volunteering, Leslie Caron came down the aisle, looking around. Suddenly she stopped at the end of our row, and waved looking our way.

"Come, come," she said.

I did not realize that it was me that she was calling, until the people nearby, alerted me to it. I still lingered, confused, but Leslie waved me

on smiling, and I just had to go. I did not get first place. That went to a girl in a red dress, with a white poodle on a leash, but I was one of the five finalists. Well, so what? I did not mind one way or another, but the next morning we were pictured on the front page in the local paper.

What we learned about the English people during this vacation was that, even though they were rather serious people for the most part, they did like jokes, especially ambiguous ones. One morning on our way to the beach, we heard some singing coming from one of the enclosed gardens at the Pavilion. We were intrigued, wondering what went on there, so we walked in to see what was going on. An entertainer stood in front of an audience telling jokes, and we sat down at the back to watch what else would happen.

The performer asked the not-so-big audience to sing some well-known English songs and they did. He also said that he needed someone to assist him in the next number, and a young woman went forward.

"Now you sit on my knee," he said to her kindly, and she did that, hesitating and blushing dark red.

Everybody laughed and whistled. Then he asked the audience to sing the very popular song "If you were the only girl in the world and I were the only boy, etc." pausing after each sentence.

"All right! Very good!" then he turned to the girl, "Now, at the end of each phrase, your job is to say: "Without your pants!" That created more and more laughing as the verses continued, until nobody could sing anymore, everything ending in chaos. So that was English humor! Rather daring, I would say!

As in most resorts like this, there was also a fair with some rides, and one overcast morning, Ed persuaded me to go and have a ride on the big dipper. I almost died from the experience! It upset me so much that I never ever went on one again. I felt bad for the next two days. We also tried a ride in a speedboat, but that was not much better. The water sprayed so hard from the fast ride that we could not open our eyes to see anything, and we got out a few minutes later, half-soaked and a half-a-crown each poorer.

Our last escapade was to take a flight over Margate and the vicinity. That was my first flight, but I did not like it. Not in that small plane anyway! Still, we had had a lovely time, and only too soon we had to go back to London and to work.

Life got back to the regular schedules, one job chasing the other, since it was summertime, when most people had vacations. July and August were especially busy. Visitors came from various parts of England and also from abroad, wanting to enjoy London and the Latvian environment here at the house.

I had so many people for breakfast that I hardly had enough seating, but since everybody did not come at the same time, I managed. There were also plenty of guests who wanted to have the dinner and supper, because I made tasty Latvian meals that some people had not eaten in a long time. Here, I especially thought of the single men who mostly lived on an English farm or alone in some lodgings. They would appreciate it. I really had to schedule myself, so as to have everything on the table in time. It was also a bit vexing, not knowing how many diners I would have, but I got used to preparing more food rather than less.

While trying to take care of everything, I had no free time at all anymore. Had to wash dishes, by hand, of course, for we did not have any other machinery to help us but the vacuum cleaner! Had to change beds in the guest rooms, clean the bathrooms and so on. Ed did not have much time to help me. He had his hands full, too, taking care of the club, washing the glasses, cleaning up and restocking. Somewhere along the line I also had to find time to go to the Laundromat to wash our clothes.

The mountain of jobs and requirements was growing, but not the management's understanding of how much two people could do. We could have Anten's help for a couple of hours a week, but it was not enough, and the stress was growing. Nevertheless, we tried to welcome all our guests as members of our huge Latvian family, especially the former soldiers who needed our hospitality the most.

We wanted everything to be good, but underneath, a bit of bitterness had started to brew. The house committee came for their monthly meetings, but never made enough time to listen to us, or to discuss our problems. Instead, they wanted to rush through it, to get to the club sooner, so that they could relax. Maybe they celebrated somewhere else, too, after the club closed, for the next morning they were tired and obviously had hangovers. Nobody had any interest whatsoever to have any more discussions.

"We'll talk about it next time…" was the evasive answer, and the next time it was the same all over again. We could not understand. They were all good people. Of course, having to come all the way to London, they wanted to have some fun also, for at home they worked at their regular jobs. That sounded fair enough, but our problems remained unresolved. We just had to carry on, extending ourselves more and more.

## All Kinds of Guests

The house was full again, and we came across all kinds of characters. We already knew some of the visitors from the previous year, like the little man from Ventspils, who was of a small build and resembled a school-boy. Ventspils was another large port city in Latvia,

and he was proud of it. His name was Ulrich and he had been through the war, but still looked like a young boy with his baby blue eyes and fair hair. Somehow we took a special liking to him. He seemed to be so vulnerable. People in Ventspils spoke a special dialect, and when sometimes he spoke it, he kept us in stitches. He spoke the regular language too, of course.

Then there was the friend of Ulrich's, the Tall John from the Short Street of whatever town.

"I once received a letter addressed exactly that way and it reached me!" he bragged.

"In England? A letter addressed in Latvian?" I thought in disbelief.

Both men lived and worked somewhere out in the country not too far from London, and both were former soldiers. They looked like two comics together—the tall, robust John and little small-boned Ulrich.

We loved Ulrich. When he arrived, he was very shy and polite like a child on his first day at school, not quite knowing what to do with himself. Since he was just a little over five feet tall, he also resembled a schoolboy. His fair hair, smoothly slicked down, and the big blue eyes in his narrow face, looked so much like a child's. He said he had come to spend some time amongst the Latvian people again. He did drink quite a bit, spending much time in the club with others. Perhaps this was the way for him to be as close to his lost homeland as possible, and it was also a time to drown the sorrow of not being able to be there.

When he had been drinking a bit, he was not so shy anymore, at least not with us, and all kinds of amusing stories and sayings came out of him. He told them so seriously, his big blue eyes wide open. Then sometimes he even started using words in his "Ventin" dialect, which made them even more amusing. One evening he came into the dining room with a glass of beer in his hand. He wanted to chat.

"You would not believe what strange things can happen to a man..." He seemed to mumble to himself, his eyes downcast.

Perhaps he needed to be closer to somebody, and we were the closest he could find, because we were always ready to listen to him. So he told us, "One Saturday evening I come home from the local pub. Had been drinking a bit, you know? Half-way back, my legs start to get tired, so I sit down in the grass at the roadside, thinking—I'll rest a bit. A small country lane, you know? I sit there, but then I notice some horses on the other side of the road grazing in the field.

"Goody!" I thought," I'll take one to ride myself home and bring it back tomorrow. So I open the gate and bring the horse out of the paddock. Meaning no harm, you know? But all of a sudden, there's the village Bobby standing in front of me! A policeman, you know?"

And tiny Ulrich stands in front of us, a glass in his hand, with his

big baby eyes open and looking scared as if this was happening at this very minute.

"What are you going to do with that horse, lad?" The policeman had asked.

"So I told him the truth. I thought that the situation was so obvious that any thinking man would understand. Well, he was not a thinking man..." Ulrich gave a sigh.

"No, no," the policeman said. "You can't do that!"

"After that he did some writing in his little black book, and I went home. Well, two years have passed by now, and I have not been called to the court yet, so maybe there will be no punishment." Ulrich finished, giving again a deep sigh, still looking perplexed, but we could not help laughing.

"Ulrich, don't worry! Nobody will come after you now!" Ed tried to pacify him, and he did relax.

He would often come into the dining room in between meals, wanting to play with the boys. He had been drinking some, but I was there to watch them all, for the kitchen door was always open. He would get down on all fours on the floor and tell them that he was a horse.

"Do you want to have a ride?" he asked them.

"Yes!" they answered a bit timidly.

"Get on then!" he said.

Of course, the boys did not have to be told twice, and they all had a ball, frolicking on the floor, riding the "horse"!

A little later yet, after Ulrich had spent more time in the club, he was in the dining room again. As I came in from the kitchen, I saw him sitting on the floor, smiling happily and watching the boys working on his feet.

"What are you doing there?" I asked.

"The horse needs to be shoed," the boys explained giggling, and kept on trying to knock some metal beer bottle caps on to the soles of his shoes.

What next? Perhaps it was not good for the children to mix with people who drank, but there was nowhere else where they could be. They were not allowed to go into the club room while it was open for business, but the dining room was also our living room, and it couldn't be helped. Still, seven o'clock was their bed time, and that was strictly observed, so they were not downstairs later in the evening.

I took the children upstairs to our fifth floor bedroom, where the downstairs noise could not be heard, and everything was quiet and peaceful. We got washed, they got into their beds, and then I sat with

each of them while they said their evening prayer. It was the same prayer my Mother had taught us when we were children. That had been our routine from the very early days, and they knew that then they had to sleep and there would be nothing else. As I look back, they really were very good obedient children, but that was probably also because of our restricted living conditions. Now and then I would run upstairs quickly and listen at the door. Sometimes I heard them still talking a bit, later it was quiet. Our friend Vilis, who had his room on the same floor, would listen in too, especially when I was very busy, or when we wanted to go out. On those rare occasions, we would remind Vilis to watch out for the children and knew that we could rely on him.

One day Mr. Slinķis showed up again. Of course, it was summertime, when those who could, would take their vacation, because in England, the summer weather did not last long. We already knew Mr Slinķis from the previous summer. This time he had brought a companion, who was tall and skinny. They both walked together, reminding me of the two famous American comedians, Laurel and Hardy, that I remembered seeing in films in my childhood days. Since the club was closed till noon, they both came down after breakfast with hats on their heads, as was the custom for men in those days.

"We are going to the Museum right here at the Kensington Gardens," Mr. Slinķis announced to me.

"Oh? Well, have a good time! I hope you will enjoy it!" I answered, and had a laugh to myself. Yes, there was the Victoria and Albert Museum there, but I was sure that was not where they would be going.

Indeed! At lunch time both came home visibly intoxicated, and then they could continue their "studies" at our bar. The fact was, you could also buy liquor in special stores outside the pub hours, and there was one right on the corner of Queensway. But it was their vacation time. They had to celebrate!

"Hopefully they do not celebrate too much!" I thought to myself. But who could discern where the line was?

The following morning, Mr. Slinķis came into the dining room hissing and puffing, red in the face. He started to march around the table, swaying sideways on his bow legs and swinging his short arms back and forth, leaving me wondering what would be coming next? Suddenly he stopped in front of me and spit out his words like out of a firing gun, "Gi' me some work, little girl! Any work! I cannot stand this anymore!" he puffed.

I had just started to peel potatoes for dinner, but while I still looked at him in amazement for such a surprise request, he took the paring knife out of my hand and took my place at the sink.

"Got to get that devil out of me!" was the last I heard from him for

the next half hour. Beginning to work, he settled down and got himself in hand again. It just showed that a real man needed work to be a whole person. All this drinking was for the birds!

For us, the summertime was really like the best show on earth, character-wise.

Ed was very busy in the bar, but there was more to do than just that. Since we only had three guest rooms, they were always full in the summertime. The single men had to sleep in the big hall, where we had set up the metal folding beds in rows. They did not mind, as long as they could stay here, where they could have their drink and be together with other Latvians.

Ed always looked out for our friend, Ulrich. When he saw that he had just about had enough to drink, he urged him to go up to bed. Ulrich, of course, thought that he was just fine and did not need to go anywhere. Then Ed just picked up the little man like a child and carried him upstairs. He put him on the bed and covered him up, where he fell asleep instantly.

On leaving, Ed had noticed the tall older man in the adjoining bed as he was mumbling something under his breath.

"You won't believe it!" Ed said to me when he came back. "There was this tall man, lying on his bed as if he was dead! He was stretched out on his back, still fully dressed in a suit and tie, with his hands folded on his chest. As I passed him, I heard him give a deep sigh and then mumble, 'I hope they will place the wreath at the right end...' Perhaps he was dreaming or thought that he was dead already..."

The following morning Ed got up early as always, to start cleaning up the club room. The spirits had surely hit high the night before. As he walked into the billiard room to pick up the glasses there, he had a surprise. He found Ulrich under the table, sleeping like a baby. He was covered with Ed's big sweater, which had been hanging on the rack in the hallway. This is how Ed related it to me later: "Ulrich, what are you doing there?" I asked him.

"Ulrich opened his eyes and stared around, trying to figure out where he was. Next he looked up. He was still foggy-eyed and stretched out his arm, touching the underside of the table. He checked it out and then said in a serious, wondering voice:" 'This room sure has a low ceiling!' "You're under the table, Ulrich! How did you get here?" I asked. 'I really don't know,' he said, turning his head and slowly getting more fully awake. Then he noticed his covering."

"I'm sorry, Ed! Forgive me for using your sweater. I must have been cold."

I could not help laughing when Ed told me that. It sounded so much

like a kid.

Later Ulrich came into the dining room all spruced up, very shy and looking guilty.

"I guess... I 'bit the berry' last night..." he murmured. "Please excuse me if I did anything... not fitting..." he continued apologizing; his eyes downcast like a child's.

But nobody gave him lectures. We understood these lonely fellows who still could not find a place for themselves in this foreign land.

"Come and eat, Ulrich, you will feel better," I said, putting a plate on the table.

"Well...I don't know if I will be able to..." he murmured, but sat down obediently.

In England the law allowed the pubs to be open only during certain hours, and we at the club had to do the same. The club was open from 12 noon till 2p.m. and from 6 to 11 p.m.

Ulrich came into the bar soon after the opening time, obviously trying to heal his hangover. He ordered a beer, then opened the brown shopping bag that he carried. He took a carton of buttermilk and a box of strawberries out of it. He must have bought them that morning. Then he drank the beer, swilling it down with the buttermilk, chasing it all down with the strawberries. He offered them to us also and was surprised that we declined. What a combination! Ugh!

It really would be hard to believe the weird things we sometimes experienced!

A bit later, when I washed the dishes in the kitchen, there was another surprise. The "dead man" appeared in the doorway, a threatening look on his face.

"You give them back to me!" he said in a deep, angry voice. "I say, you give them back!"

"What should I be giving you?" I asked.

"Just give them back, you know what!" he said, even angrier.

I searched in my mind as to what he might be talking about, because I had not had anything to do with him. He had eaten the supper and gone back into the club. I wondered what it was that he had lost.

"Teeth! My teeth! You took them!" he hissed, red in his face.

"How could I have come into possession of his teeth, and why would I have needed them?" I questioned myself in disbelief. This was incredible! He probably had put them somewhere and could not remember. We found Ed, and the "dead man" repeated the same interrogation. They went to search for them, and of course, in the end they were found, in his coat pocket! Thank goodness!

It seemed that there was no end to these peculiar incidents. We really got to see the intricate make-up of people's personalities and their

reactions to circumstances. It was very interesting from the psychological point of view—amusing and sometimes sad—but all this showed us how different and colorful life, and people, could be when viewed from outside. That probably was the most interesting aspect of our life here at the Latvian House: seeing how people gave away their stories by just being who they were. It was almost like watching episodes of plays happening right there before our eyes, and then guessing what the whole play was about. I think we saw the whole gambit of humanity from one end to the other, from the most simple to the most complicated.

And we never seemed to lack characters! Juris ('J' pronounced as in 'you') was one of them, but a charming one, and we loved him. He lived here in London and dropped in now and then unexpectedly. When he was here, I could recognize his voice amongst the many others coming from the club room. It was Juris, a former officer of the Czar's army, still fairly slim, upright, good looking and charming. He was a man perhaps in his early seventies, perhaps even less, with graying wavy hair and blue eyes. He was our special friend, and we called him "Crazy Juris", for one could never know what he would do next. Hyped and outgoing, brimming over the edges, he never forgot that he was a gentleman, always a gentleman. Even when he drank, he never got drunk. Only his temperament and exuberance rose, and he was always the soul of the party, gesticulating with his hands and arms as he talked. Perhaps it was something left over from his times in the military service when he, as a young and handsome officer, had to entertain the ladies of aristocracy. His extravagant behavior pointed to that.

Whenever Juris came, he would always come to the dining room door first and stop and say, "Kundze!"—(a name used to address a married woman in Latvian), "Allow me to greet you!"

Then he would come in, bow elegantly and kiss my hand. In my childhood days, men really did that as a sign of reverence, especially in the military. If Juris felt more exuberant, he would kiss my hand even up to my elbow, but I would just laugh. I knew him, and he did it with such charm. Perhaps in his mind he had a need to be, even for a moment, in his old elevated status and environment. I was sure he must have been the darling of the ladies in those old days at the military balls. He was still a handsome man, but he certainly had his strange ways of doing things.

There was the time when he arrived in the late afternoon, bringing a few well-dressed men with him, and still in his overcoat, led them into the billiard room.

"Yes, yes, I will play something for you!" I heard him say. But it was not billiards that he was going to play, but the piano that stood in that room. Juris seemed to be so much the product of the Russian culture, and the aristocratic environment there. His temperament, his spontaneous

and exuberant gestures were so much like theirs, as much as I knew of them, so I went to the open door to see what it was about.

There he was, sitting at the piano still in his overcoat with the coat collar turned up. Perhaps he had brought those men from some other club. Then he started. With his arms lifted in a dramatic gesture, he played the first rich accords. After that, he drew his finger all across the keyboard for more effect. Then he started to play the melody of a song. With his eyes closed, he began with deep emotion.

"*Ochi chornayi, ochi krasnoyi...*" (The black eyes, the beautiful eyes) he sang this very old popular Russian song, playing some chords in between for emphasis, then interrupting them with dramatic pauses and gestures with his hands. This was really something to see! His performance was perfect. I could imagine that perhaps in his mind, he was singing it to the ladies surrounding him a long time ago in St. Petersburg. Oh, Juri, Juri!...

He never stayed away for too long but would drop in anytime, perhaps on the way to some errand, and stayed shorter or longer periods at the club. One such evening, I heard raised voices coming from the bar. A moment later Juris came into the dining room, dragging Ed by his arm. His face looked serious and angry, and I wondered what on earth was going on now?

"This Vīdners, this beast!" he said in a disgusted voice, admonishing Ed.

I had just sat down at the table to have a moment's rest and was having a cup of coffee. As it was summertime, I wore a dress with a lower cut neckline for coolness. I looked at Juris and Ed in confusion. What on earth had happened?

"This beast!" Juris shouted. "He does not know anything, not anything!"

"What is it, Juri?" I was really getting concerned.

"He does not know what this is for!" he said, bending down and placing a kiss on the back of my neck."

"Juri, Juri..." what could I say, not being able to stop laughing. That was him, the extravagant cavalier again!

Ed laughed, too, "Of course I did not know!" he said. "I'm glad you showed me, Juri!" then he urged him to go back to the club.

"Kundze! Excuse me!" he bowed elegantly toward me, then turned and went. How could I be angry with somebody like that? Actually, all these things added some spice to our work-loaded life. It was good to have a laugh sometimes in between.

Having so many former soldiers around, the occasional sharing of war stories was inevitable. One evening it so happened that Ulrich was here too when Juris came, and it was the greatest fun to see these totally

different people together. Of course, both had had something to drink, so the perceptions were somewhat elevated. There was Juris—tall, handsome, confident, and there was Ulrich—small, fragile, as if wanting to hide within himself as he walked into the dining room with his usual glass of beer in hand.

Juris was in high gear, telling us about one of his fighting episodes while he served in the Czar's army. He had just stepped with one foot into the furnace room, which opened off the dining room, leaving his other foot where it was, explaining the positions of the two armies. He stood there, gesticulating with his arms, his voice rising as he remembered.

"So we were here, and they were there! And then we went into the battle, swords in our hands!"

Ulrich was standing aside by the wall, his glass still in hand, gazing at Juris with a stiff look, and it was clearly visible how the disbelief grew in his eyes, until he could not bear it any longer.

"What are you talking about there?" He exclaimed. "Horses and swords! My foot! If the Germans came with their tanks, there would be nothing left of you! Not a shred, I tell you! Not a shred!"

Each of them still lived in their own wars. I guessed that whoever had gone through it, could not ever forget it, not all together; just put it aside and try to let it sleep. Of course, nothing happened! No arguments. It was time for another drink and they both went amicably back to the club.

One Saturday morning, Juris arrived unexpectedly quite early and seemed rather excited and hurried. He said that his landlady had asked him to go and get some bread, but then he pulled Ed aside and whispered something to him. A moment later he turned to me and said, "Kundze, please excuse us, we need to discuss something important privately," and they both went to the club room. I did not know his landlady, who was a Latvian also, but had heard that she was a dentist here in London. What their relationship was, I did not know, but their names came up together quite frequently. I assumed that they probably lived at the same place .

Still, that had nothing to do with me, and I went off to do what I had to do. Afternoon came, and through the noise of the club room, I could hear that Juris was still there. He loved to talk and to be with people, and since it was a Saturday, the club room was buzzing.

"What about that bread?" I wondered. "What was his landlady thinking now?"

It was ten o'clock at night, when Juris came to the dining room door and asked me in a lowered voice,

"Kundze, would you happen to have an extra loaf of bread by any chance?" he almost whispered and looked very concerned. "I cannot go home without it…"

It did not look like he had drunk too much either, he just forgot himself when he was in company. I assumed that the lady was quite an authority in their household, and he knew well enough that he would be in "hot water" about this. Perhaps the bread had just been an excuse to get out of the house and get a drink to chase away a hangover?

"Juri, Juri," I thought, "who will eat that bread at this hour, and to-morrow there will be fresh bread!" Still, I gave him the bread and did not say anything. It was bad enough to carry guilty feelings.

Yet, another evening we got to see a different Juri. He came in el-egantly dressed in an immaculate black overcoat, a black bowler hat on his head, a black bow tie under his chin and a white silk scarf around his neck. A light pleasant men's aroma came from his persona. Juris and his lady were going to the Opera tonight. He had not been drinking at all; most likely he did not dare! But then he whispered to Ed, "Maybe just one little cognac for the road…" and then he would have just one.

For us, the biggest escapade was, when Juris arrived one Sunday morning, bringing a whole band of musicians into the lobby of our house. I don't remember if they were Salvation Army, or some other uniformed men. On Sunday mornings, they often walked through the streets in our area, playing popular pieces of music, and people threw them money from the windows. Juris was so excited that he could hardly contain himself.

"Can you believe it? They can play *'Over the Walls of Borden'*! I just had to bring them in so you could hear them too!"

He had paid the musicians two pounds! That was a lot of money in those days, but he was having the time of his life, as they played all the songs he wanted. In the narrow area at the foot of the stairs, the sounds were just booming and most likely could be heard up to the top floor. Juris stood in front of the band, moving his arms as if directing them, overflowing with happiness.

Well, that was one way to live. One should savor and enjoy life! Not many people knew how to do it with such exuberance, or did not dare to let go. Everything else for such people was nothing compared with the moment. That was one theory of life and perhaps wiser than ours, but we were in our late twenties, and only just beginning to build a life for ourselves and our children.

We were glad when the high season for vacations was over, and our life became a little quieter. My thirtieth birthday came up, and it affected me deeply. I could not get over the fact that I was so old! It was unbelievable! Where had the time gone? We did not have a party or big

celebration, only my friend Aina and her husband Maigonis came. We had coffee, cake and a couple of cherry brandies that I liked. There was no time for more, and that was all right with me. I did not particularly like parties and could not remember any celebrations except my third birthday a long time ago.

Our boys' little Indian friend, Ravindra, from across the street, had just started school, but came home one day with tears running down his nice little face.

"What happened?" I asked him.

"The... the... the children said that I had a dirty face..." He said sobbing, and two big tears veiled his beautiful dark eyes. "They said I could not play with them..."

"But that is not true, dear! You have a beautiful face and it is not dirty. They just don't know that you come from a different country, where everybody's skin is darker like that. They just have to get used to you. Don't cry. You can come to Māris' birthday party next Sunday. We would love to have you."

It was the end of September when we celebrated Māris' fourth birthday upstairs in the big hall, and the children had a good time playing hide and seek and running up and down the stairs.

The two other boys at the party were the sons of a friend who worked at the Latvian embassy. He again was a character. We often had to communicate about various functions that would take place at the House to make the appropriate arrangements, but often he called us too many times about the same small detail that had already been established. That drove us up the wall sometimes. We were very busy and would have to run down several flights of stairs to answer the phone on the ground floor, only to hear the same thing again. It seemed that he just called to pass the time or to appear busy, if perhaps, a client had come in.

Our slower days did not last long, though. The Latvian children's Saturday school started, and all kinds of other gatherings were also scheduled. Our assistance was needed everywhere. Then, before we knew it, Christmas was nearing again. We spruced up and decorated the house the best we could.

A tradition had been established to hold a Christmas Fair here at the D.V. house each year on the third Sunday before Christmas. It was sponsored by the Baltic States Ambassador's wives as a charity event, and our big hall was just the right place where to hold it. The goods were donated, and there were a lot of beautiful ethnic hand-made things, like embroideries, knitted gloves and mittens, needlepoint cushions, pictures and a lot of other things. There was a lottery also, and the house buzzed with people. It was a very pleasant event, with musicians providing nice

background music.

Free refreshments were provided by the D.V. women's committee. They were very nice ladies, dedicated to the cause, and always presented a great assortment of home-baked goodies. Their leader was another Mrs. Zariņš, a large woman with down to earth attitudes, and she ruled her flock with fortitude. It seemed to me that the women were a little bit in awe of her when she lifted up her voice, but she too was a nice lady, and all together they made a wonderful contribution to the common good. At those times the ladies took over the kitchen and the dining room, but I had already provided for that and we had a great relationship.

A lot of people came to attend this annual fair, knowing that there would always be beautiful things for sale. Besides, Christmas was only three weeks away and gifts would be needed. Later in the evening, when the opening time came, people visited the club also, and it was an even busier time for us.

On New Year's Eve we arranged a banquet for people our age, with music and dancing in the big hall till midnight. It was quite a success, and then the year was gone.

The year of 1957 started with a new set of events. The Christmas celebrations were behind us, but other festive days followed. January 28th was "Friendly Invitation Day", established by our last president of the free Latvia, Kārlis Ulmanis. It was a special event asking people to remember their former schools by giving them a gift. This day was celebrated each year, usually with a speaker, some entertainment, refreshments and people bringing donations for schools—mainly books for their libraries.

I catered quite a few banquets, weddings and other group gatherings and Ed did the rest of it. It required a lot of shifting tables, chairs etc. More and more people came and used the facilities at the house, and that was what the leadership of the organization had wanted. We had wanted that also, but two people could only do so much for so long. At times we felt like robots, overworked and on call at any hour of day or night. Nobody was interested that things were like this. We had to be "in line", and we tried to be.

In the middle of March, my younger brother, Johnny, and his young bride Lienīte, decided to get married. She was a lovely girl with blond hair and blue eyes and was only eighteen years old. She had trained to be a hairstylist and worked in a beauty shop in Birmingham. Johnny had finished his evening classes and now had a good job at a large electrical firm in Birmingham.

Of course, we had to go to the wedding, but a problem arose just a short time before it occurred. Both boys came down with measles. By the

big day, they were already better, but still had to stay in bed. Luckily, a friend of ours offered to stay and take care of them.

It was nice for us to get out and away for a bit, to have a few free days. The wedding took place at the Kings Heath church, near where Mother and Saša lived. The reception was again at their house, for nobody had money to afford anything else. Still, everything went well, the closest friends were there, and we could even dance a bit in the cleared out breakfast room. We all wished the young couple happiness. They had found a small place of their own not far from Kings Heath and were happy. But we had to get back to London.

Back in our regular environment, we had to be everywhere again—in the club, in the kitchen, and in between, somebody always needed something.

"Mr. Vīdners! Phone!" shouted Mrs. Blūm, sticking her head through the door of her office. And Mr Vīdners ran up and down the stairs from wherever he happened to be, because there was only one telephone on the ground floor and one on the fourth floor.

We needed a break, or we would not be able to make it through the summer. With some reluctance, we were given the first two weeks at the beginning of summer. We made arrangements with Mother that she would take the boys the first week, and they would all go to the Latvian House in Almeley. That would give us a week of complete rest, and then Mother and the children would come and join us at the seaside for the second week. This time we went to Eastborne, south of London, which was a very popular place for the Londoners. The beach there was covered with pebbles instead of sand, but otherwise Eastborne was a very typical English seaside town.

We spent a nice, relaxing time there lying on the beach and, letting the sun warm our bodies. Luckily for us, the weather was nice too, so we could take full advantage of the fresh air. Mother and the boys had had a nice week in Almeley together with friends. Now, when they came to Eastborne, the boys had their fun, playing in the sand at the water's edge or paddling in the shallow water. The pebbles were swept higher on the beach where the waterline ended, leaving the very coastline smooth and safe. Too soon though, our holidays were over, and it was time to return to London.

The tourist season was on. Again, the house was full of people who wanted to stay. We just hurried to fill the big hall with the iron bedsteads. It was almost like a war hospital, but it would be a good income for the house and the organization. If there happened to be a social event, for which the hall was needed, then it got even more hectic, for the beds had to be dismantled and re-installed again in the evening.

Antens would help, but even the three of us could barely make it.

The club room was like a beehive, and both Ed and Antens barely managed to serve the happy revelers. The storage behind the bar was so small that they constantly had to bring cases from the storage place in the utility room under the stairs and in between wash the glasses in the sink out there.

I also had orders one after another.

"Sandwiches for four! Sandwiches for six! Sausages and sauerkraut! Can we have a supper? There are four of us! etc., etc..."

The worn down records sounded over the noise, wailing the songs that people liked the most. "Those eyes, those eyes I shall never forget..." "It was so long ago when we met in spring time..." The guests liked them and listened with tears in their eyes, because many of the men, who lived scattered amongst the English now, had not heard any Latvian language for a long time. No wonder they wanted to hear the songs over and over, although we could barely stand to listen to them anymore. There was one that I liked, though, that had a refrain saying: "The wheel of life is turning, so it has been and will be...

With all that going on, I began to notice on and off that Ed had been drinking a bit, and that worried me. I understood that, working in a bar, it was hard to abstain, for it was a custom here that the clients offered a drink to the barman as well. Ed should not allow himself to take even one drink, because if he did, the second and third would follow. He knew that, yet at times he thought that it was not so bad, and he could handle it.

I knew how it was. People even brought me drinks to the kitchen, although I had said "no". Of course, it was done in friendship, and sometimes three or four cherry brandies sat on the kitchen window sill. Yes, cherry brandy was my favorite, but you could not drink while working. Ed and I sometimes had "words" about this, and after that it would be better for a while. Still, the worry stayed with me, and each time that I saw that he had been drinking even a little, made me feel terrible. It was like sinking into a bottomless ditch. I was scared of what the future would be if it continued.

I noticed that I was getting sharper with the children. While stirring a pot in the kitchen, my mind drew burning circles around my heart. Sometimes I did not even hear what the children were saying or asking, because my mind was too full of the painful thoughts. The easiest way then was to say that I did not know. Then one day my six year old Uldis awakened me from that. Standing in the kitchen doorway, where I was cooking, he said, "Mummy, how is it that you are a grown up lady, but you do not know anything?"

That really hit me between the eyes! The words kept ringing through my mind and into my heart. What was happening? What were we doing?

We had to get out of this terrible cloud, which was beginning to suffocate us. Ed and I talked again. We would need to have more of Anten's help, so we could take a little time for ourselves, and the house committee agreed to it.

We decided to join the London Latvian choir, for we both loved singing. That was a nice break for us, and the rehearsals were held right here in our big hall. Alberts Jērums was a wonderful director and also a very nice person. We knew most of the choir members already, because most of them lived in London or in the vicinity. The songs really gave us the lift we needed.

Christmas was nearing again, and this year we decided to go and spend it with Mother and the rest of the family in Birmingham. She was not feeling too well these days, and we thought it would be good for us to get away for a few days. After all, our family life and well-being were more important than pleasing the society, or earning extra income during the holidays. It was good to see everybody again, and also to visit Johnny and Lienīte in their little nest.

The new year of 1958 had come. I wondered what it would bring us, but the future was hard to see. In the beginning of the year, a letter came from my cousin Ruta who lived in San Francisco, California. It so happened that after I came to England, the rest of Mother's large family had gone to America, because other countries had started to take refugees from Germany as well, England being the first that did this. Mother and my younger brother had joined me in England a year later, but we had not seen the rest of the family for ten years. Ruta wrote that she would love to come and visit us here in England. That sounded great, and we looked forward to seeing her very much.

In view of that, we decided to buy a car, so we could take her around when she came. Ed got his license easily, and then I began to learn to drive also. Ed did not want to teach me, and one of us needed to be in the house anyway, so it was decided that our friend Vilis, the auto mechanic, would teach me. Since we did not have the car yet, I had to learn how to drive in Vilis' big black Buick, which for me felt huge, considering the narrow streets of London. But Vilis was very calm and helped me to get over the initial fear.

We would drive around the smaller streets on this side of the busy Bayswater Road until I got more accustomed to handling the car. The traffic here was slow, because in wintertime the hotels did not have much business. Only an odd taxi drove around, but since five-story buildings lined both sides of the streets, they were full of parked cars. This left only a narrow aisle in the middle for the drivers, and I stiffened up every time some car approached us. It seemed that at any moment we would

collide, but Vilis kept cool.

"Just let it roll, girl!" he would say. "There is room enough." And we did all right. Later on, we even went through the Piccadilly once, and for me that was a rather awesome experience—the people and cars going in so many directions!

I did not quite make it on my first test for the license, however. An old scrawny woman was my examiner and I did not like her attitude from the start. I felt like she had already decided to fail me and that made me feel uptight and nervous. It all ended up when she asked me to do a parallel parking and after that, to back the car around the corner and then continue for some distance. I did that very carefully, concentrating on my driving, until the woman said in her haughty manner: "Madam, where do you think you are you going?"

That was really something! I had thought that she will tell me when to stop, but she did not, and then slamming me with this! As if I was the utter fool! I was disappointed, but in time it became a laughing matter amongst us. I later took the test in Birmingham and did just fine.

We worked diligently at our choir singing also, for there was going to be a Song Festival that summer in Leicester, another town in the Midlands, and our choir would take part in it. Some of the songs tore at my heart, and yet I loved them, for they took us back home. Our superb director, Alberts Jērums, knew how to get the finest nuances out of us. It was a real joy to sing with him.

The weekends were very busy as usual. Artists, musicians and various prominent people came from abroad to visit the larger communities of Latvians and to give concerts or speeches. We looked after them while they stayed in London, and it was very interesting to get to know all these different people. How unique everybody was! Yet all of them were nice, and some of them even became our friends.

Before we knew it, summer was here again. My cousin Ruta came from America as promised, and we all went to the Song Festival in Leicester. There we also met Mother, Saša, Johnny with his wife Lienīte and other friends. They all sang in the Birmingham choir. As always, the Festival was a momentous experience.

Since our annual vacation was due, we took Ruta to see Almeley, and afterwards, went to spend a few days in Bournemouth, on the south coast of England. Mother and I had been there once, before I was married. It was a nice seaside resort, but the bad part was, that almost every day a big rain cloud came up shortly before noon, spoiling our enjoyment at the beach. If it rained longer, we had to go the cinema (the British way of saying this was "going to the pictures", and the American way—"going to the movies"!). There was nothing else to do, except make a

picture puzzle with the children on the floor at the hotel room.

After this, we were back in London, coping with our busy summer schedule. Ruta was in awe of how we managed to do it all. She said that if we worked like that in America, we could have a much better life. We did not mind working, but the worst part was the constant nervous stress.

One evening Ruta brought up the subject again.

"Have you ever thought of coming to America and joining us?" she asked. "You should, you know? All the other members of our large family are settled comfortably in Los Gatos now. It is a small town at the narrow end of San Francisco Bay. You have probably heard that our family was sponsored by my father's cousin, a retired sea Captain, who lives in Los Gatos?"

"Yes, I have heard that," I answered.

"In the beginning, the rest of our relatives were scattered in different places in America," Ruta continued. "It depended on who had sponsored them. Later, my father saw to it that they were able to join us in Los Gatos. My parents had bought a small house for $1500, so our family could help them in their transition to Los Gatos by letting them use our house as a starting point. My father also helped other acquaintances from our home town to come and live in Los Gatos. He sponsored them and helped them in the beginning." Then she added laughing, "During the earlier days of our life in America, one of the rooms in our small house had bedding on the floor all the time, because of the constant flow of newcomers. I am sure that my parents would be willing to sponsor you too, if you wanted to come." Ruta said.

The seed had been sown. At first we thought of it just as a joke, but then the thoughts returned to what Ruta had said. Well, why not? We did not own anything here, and had lived in England for eleven years. Perhaps we could try living somewhere else?

After Ruta left, we talked about it and put in our application to go to America. We were cautioned that we may have to wait for some six years, because America had a quota system. Well, we were not in any hurry. We would hand in the papers, and then, what would be, would be. We could always refuse if we changed our minds.

August came, and with it the time of many vacationers. We were on the treadmill again, running, running but seemingly not getting anywhere. Perhaps our nerves were unable to cope with the constant stress anymore. We began to get upset with the crowded situation and the groups of people who did not want to leave after the closing hours of the club. They would move into the billiard room, expecting Ed to stay up and serve them for as long as they wanted. When Ed tried to dissolve their little parties, they got upset.

"What is going on here? We thought that we were here with Latvians!" They complained.

As if that meant that Latvians should be able to do whatever they wanted and did not have to follow rules. As if the people who served them did not need any rest!

I noticed that Ed was drinking again—first only a little, but then more. I knew every nuance of this and could tell how things were going, and they were not going well. This was my greatest heartache. It made me live in constant fear of what may happen and of how we would get through this summer.

What made me sad and bitter also, were rumors that we had come here to get rich! To get rich! Our wages were so small, it was a pittance! If I remember correctly, Ed got four pounds a week, and I got two, not having been counted as a full-time worker because I had the children. Two pounds for all that work! The only way to make more money was by serving food, but the cost of food was not cheap. If I did not work as hard as I did, there would be nothing. And could anybody work more than we did?

We were glad when the vacation time for the visitors was over. Autumn came, and with it, slower days for us, yet the social season would begin, and then there would be demands and more demands. The most exasperating thing during this slower season was when someone arrived at midweek from some far-off corner of the land and wanted to sit in the club with Ed standing by and entertaining him, while so many other jobs were waiting. If Ed sneaked off a bit, the man was unhappy. He wanted his drink when he wanted it, and he did not want to sit alone, because HE had come to celebrate his vacation.

Autumn had come, and one night we got to experience a real London fog for the first time. A friend had come from Birmingham to visit us. We arranged a free evening and took him to a German club that we had heard about. Apparently, they served very good authentic German food there. It was situated on the other side of Kensington Gardens, not too far from us.

The dinner was excellent, but when we came out after our pleasant evening at the club, the fog outside was like a dense white wall in front of us, through which you could not see anything. Absolutely nothing! Yet we had to get home. The car was parked just outside, but how to drive? Ed had had a couple of drinks; he could not do it.

"You will have to drive!" he said, and I shuddered. It was up to me. There was no other choice, I had to do it.

As I started off, I saw a faint light passing by. It was a bus moving very slowly! I followed it within a close distance, but then we came to the lights. Though they were barely visible, I knew that I had to turn left to go through the park. Another car turned in there and I followed it,

but very soon it disappeared. I did not know where it went, but all of a sudden, all I could see was the white fog, which looked like a steaming soup in my headlights above the hood of the car. Driving in this fog, was really a journey of life or death, because I knew that ahead was the Serpentine, a canal that ran through the park, and the bridge should be somewhere ahead of me. I also knew that the road through the park was winding, but where? I could not remember. With the utmost concentration, I just slowly moved forward. Thanks to great God, we made it home safely, but I felt as if I had been through the mill.

The next morning my right leg was in a painful spasm. I could not move. The doctor came and said that it was from the tension that I had exerted while driving the night before. I had to stay in bed for two weeks until it finally got better.

This made me think of another episode involving my leg, or more specifically my knee. I had had a bad fall from the parallel bars while attending a high school in Germany during the first year of being there. Since it was wartime, there was no medical help then, and the knee never fully mended. If I was not careful, it would occasionally go out of joint. Over time, I learned how to gently move it, so it would jump back into place. It was a rather ugly feeling when it popped back in with a "bump", but I had managed to get it in up to this time. Now it had happened again! I twisted and turned it, but it would not budge. I almost fainted from pain as I tried to do that, and the funniest part of it was that it had happened in bed as I turned over to get up! There was no other option, but to call the ambulance and the emergency crew had to carry me down all those five flights of stairs and take me to the Paddington Hospital.

The ambulance came; I went through the emergency procedures. The doctor arrived, but he could not move the knee back either. We needed x-rays. They were taken from various angles, and the x-ray technician gently positioned the leg for each take; then I had to sit and wait until she developed the films. I sat there wondering how long it would take, but suddenly realized that the leg felt easier. I moved it a bit and it was free and back in place! How wonderful! It had gone back by itself while the technician turned it over for the next picture. When she came back, I told her about it and that was it! I could go back home, but then realized, that I had come practically right out of bed, just throwing on the most necessary things, underwear, a dress, and slippers on my feet! Now I noticed that I did not have my purse either, so I did not even have a comb to tidy my hair. No money either! I could not take a bus, so I walked all the way from Paddington to Queensborough Terrace, perhaps a couple of miles. That would not matter for I was young, but I was so embarrassed to be on the street, looking the way I did. I

supposed it did not really matter what others might think of me. I was glad to be home!

The social life at the house was hectic again. "Mr.Vīdners, here! "Mr.Vīdners, there!" All these things piled up, and I saw that Ed drank more often. Our life was turning into a downswing, and that realization cut me to pieces. We had always been so compatible. Our thoughts, our likes and dislikes were the same. It was this one thing, his drinking, that threatened to destroy our life, and he knew it, yet could not or would not abstain from it. I guessed that he could not, because nothing that I said helped. Then I did not say anything anymore, but the suffering was even greater, because I had to carry this burden alone. There was no one that I could talk to, to unburden myself. I just had to swallow it all, but it was getting harder to do it as the same thing repeated itself again and again.

"If I could have a good cry," I thought to myself sometimes, but I could not allow myself even to cry.

There was too much to do, and people were around me constantly. I could not go out there showing that I had cried. There would be questions. Besides, people liked to see a smiling and cheerful face on a person who served them, and I did not want to disappoint them. After all, they had come here to have fun! At times I felt that my face might crack at any moment and I would drop everything and burst out with a magnificent bawl.

I held myself together with my greatest will-power, but as soon as I was alone for a moment, where no one could see me, I doubled up from the pain that was inside me. Sometimes I went into the tiny laundry storage room, just off the dining room, closed the door and silently moaned. I could not allow the tears to come, because the next minute I would have to go out there again, and everything had to appear normal.

It was a hellish game to play, but there was no other way. There were times when I did not want to come out of my small sanctuary. I thought I would explode into a hundred thousand pieces and wished that I would. Let there be nothing then!

For the first time a thought entered my mind that I could leave, so I would not have to suffer anymore! Bitterness, anger, even hatred arose in my mind. Sharp words flowed through my thoughts accusing, condemning. How much longer would I be able to go on like this?

Then God gave me His answer. He helped me to put the evil aside and to go the way I had to go. I laid my head down on the hard rocks of acceptance and yielded to His will. I had no right to grumble. I had given an oath that I would walk with Ed in good days and in bad. The bad ones had come now, and I had to stay in my place, even if it meant destruction

for us all. I was mainly sorry for the children. Their happy voices were around me, but often I was sharp and impatient with them, while dealing with my inner pain. I did not have any joy anymore.

The autumn rains had started, and that made everything even sadder. The days dragged by like gray, raggedy beggars, and it seemed that I was losing my way in their rags, while trying to search for a better way out, for some hope that only one person—my husband, could give me.

Sometimes during the midweek, when nothing much was happening at the house, I would take time out in the evening to go to the nearby cinema. I walked along the nearly empty streets, where the first evening lights came on. Several times I had met some film stars here, just walking along. Perhaps they lived in some of the expensive flats right opposite the park. Once I had even seen the Queen drive by in her limousine with her bodyguards behind her, and the police stood then on all the corners.

However, I was not interested in seeing anybody now. I did not really want to go anywhere, but felt driven to get out and away from that which hurt so badly. My thoughts were so jumbled. I wanted to escape them, if even for a little while.

On the Queensway, the larger street parallel to ours and only a couple of blocks farther, people walked past me unhurriedly, couples arm in arm, at times stopping at the lighted store windows. There were jewelry, china and clothing shops as well as flower shops, small cafes, and of course, the News Agents shop—the only one open at this hour. Usually I liked the evening lights, but now they did not mean anything. I felt lost and alone in my sorrow about my life that was going astray.

At the other end of Queensway was the well-lighted cinema with large pictures on both sides of the open doors depicting the current show, but it was all the same to me what I saw. When I was inside, I sat in the dark looking at the colored screen without really seeing anything. Nothing could lessen the burning pain in my chest. I was so full of it that there was no room for anything else.

The film finished. I went outside and stood there, still feeling lost, not wanting to go home. I lingered. Not yet. I did not know what to do. Walking slowly, I stopped at some store windows, pretending to be admiring some of the displayed merchandise, my thoughts still whirling, but it was not a good thing to do. I soon realized that I should not stand in one place too long. A man had walked by me several times. I walked on, a bitter lump sitting in my throat. It was dark now, and some of the lights looked so pretty, like full-blossomed red roses, but they did not bring me joy tonight. I saw only my red, red pain. It seemed that it was not worth going anywhere, for I did not have a home that would be a

shelter for me. There was the one, where my husband and my children lived, but my heart was reluctant to go there. I wondered what would wait for me there this time? I did not really want to know.

Still, one could not fool oneself too long with lights like red roses and happy pictures on a cinema screen. The time had come to look life straight in the eye and find some hard ground to stand on.

One day, when Ed had not had anything to drink, we sat down and talked about it for a very long time. Ed acknowledged that he had gotten onto a slippery slope, and we both agreed that to end this situation, we would have to leave here. It had been exciting and interesting in many ways, but we were burnt out from the fast pace of living like this. It would be worse if we stayed any longer. Coming to this conclusion lifted the heavy burden off our hearts, and we felt better. At least we saw the way we should go more clearly, because neither of us wanted to mess up our life altogether.

It was good that when he was sober, Ed always regretted what he had done. We could talk then, and correct our course. However, this time we had to do more. We had to get out of this environment, where the temptation was always there. We had spent some good times here before things got out of hand. If we had not been pushed so hard, perhaps it would not have happened this way. At least we had been able to earn and save some money, for I had done catering for two big weddings and several banquets. We would be better off than we were when we came.

We began to look at houses in the London suburbs, for we had come to love this city. It had a different atmosphere than in the provinces, even Birmingham, which was the second largest city after London. However, the prices were high even for houses far out in the suburbs, and the ones that we could probably afford, would be the ugly terrace houses.

"For that price we could definitely get something better in Birmingham!" Ed said.

"I am sure of that," I agreed.

Our thinking now turned back in that direction.

"Perhaps it would be wiser to go back there?" I pursued the thought. "We would be closer to the rest of our family. We have not had many opportunities to be with them during these last years, and Mother is not too well. I would be so sorry to leave London though..."

Yes, London, the multifaceted and elegant city, where one could feel the pulse of the world. I suppose we were spoiled, for we had lived right in the heart of it these past years. But one could not have everything.

We were also sorry to leave the choir and my folk dancing group, but our minds told us that this was the right way to go. There and then we decided to return to Birmingham. Of course, it could not be done

in a moment. We had to give notice to the house committee, and give them time to find new housekeepers, caretakers, managers—whatever one would prefer to call them.

Christmas was coming again. We spruced up the house for the celebrations, and a large Christmas tree was brought into the big hall. There would be a Christmas service and a party for the Latvian children and their families, as well as for others who wanted to come. There were about fifteen children who had attended the classes, and our boys were amongst them, too.

The event happened very much along the traditional lines, as it had been done in Latvia, in my kindergarten times, and it was a joyous event for us all. Parents came with their children and some had even brought their younger brothers and sisters. It began with the sacred part, the minister giving a short introduction and telling the Christmas story to the children, followed by the joint singing of Christmas songs. The children had been taught to sing one of the most popular children's Christmas songs at the Saturday classes, and it was so moving to hear their young voices. After that, Father Christmas came and the excitement grew. Each of the children had been taught to recite a different Christmas poem for the joy of their parents, and hearty applause followed each child's performance. Receiving gifts and candy was the high point for the children, of course, but the most fun for them was running up and down the stairs and chasing each other. Refreshments had been provided by the nice ladies of the D.V. organization and a good time was had by all.

Our choir wanted to have a Christmas party too, and we set it all up for them in the big hall. There was food and drink and, of course, singing. After we had been feasting awhile on the good food and had had a few drinks, somebody started the tune of one of the songs that we had been practicing. One by one, others joined in as we sat in a mixed row at the table. Each would sing his or her part, and it was amazing what wonderful harmony we could achieve. In between, we put on some records and danced a bit.

Time was already running toward the morning, when a small group of the men started to sing, standing in the middle of the hall in a small circle, their arms around each other's shoulders, their heads bent. Most of the people had had something to drink, and perhaps therefore, emotions were coming out more strongly than they would have otherwise. They sang *"The play of the moonbeams"*—this magical song, which did not allow anyone to hang back. The song started very softly. As it continued, one by one, we got up from the table and joined the group, adding our voices until the whole choir was there in one tight ball. We sang looking at each other, absorbing the other voices and feelings, each experiencing deeply within ourselves the words of the song and the fine nuances of

the music. Matching our voices to each other's, we let them flow into one wonderful experience of music. It seemed that we had never sung this song with so much feeling.

Our choir director had gone downstairs before the singing started, but coming back on the stairs, he heard it and stopped at the door.

After finishing the words of the last line, we all had tears in our eyes.

"A never ending stream of light flows..." The last sounds still vibrated in the air very softly, then silence. It had moved us to our depths.

The director walked up to us, and he too had tears in his eyes.

"If you can sing like that at two in the morning, without a director then... I have no words."

I thought that in singing the Latvian songs, we found reassurance for our identity as Latvians, and the song always united us anew. It lifted our souls into a different realm.

For the New Year's Eve celebration, we arranged a party for the tenants of the house, and almost everybody came. We had food, drink and danced a little, playing records. The famous Latvian playwright, Mārtiņš Zīverts, from Sweden, was visiting with us right then and we invited him to our party. Everybody had a lot of fun when I taught our guest one of our simple folk dances *"Tūdaliņ, tagadiņ"*. Then the clock on the wall showed twelve, and the New Year had come. It was 1959!

It was almost spring when we finally left London. An older couple had been hired to take our place, and we wondered how they would manage to do what we had done, but that was not our business any more. For us, another segment of our lives had ended. What would be ahead, we did not know. We trusted that the Lord would take us where we needed to be.

## In Birmingham Again

We were at Station Road again, at Saša and Mother's house, which we had left four years ago. We would stay here until we could find a place of our own. The house was not so full anymore, for there was no need for them to keep so many renters now. There were only two lodgers now, and since Johnny had married, he did not live here anymore, either. Mother gave the boys the small room on the second floor opposite the room that we had occupied before. Mother and Saša now lived in that room. Since all the other rooms were taken, Ed and I settled ourselves in the large attic room on the third floor. The ceiling was slanted, but the room was large, and I made everything look nice and cozy. That was one thing I knew how to do well.

The evenings were so quiet now. During the first week it even seemed strange that the telephone did not ring, and no one called us or

looked for us. We still had the feeling that any moment someone would call and we would have to jump up and run. Yet, those days were over, and what a relief it was! After a long time, we could finally savor the peace and quiet and feel good.

Yes, the first years in London had been challenging and exciting. It was a shame that it all ended so badly and yet this period had changed us. We had grown in maturity and assertiveness. The next day after we arrived in Birmingham, Ed went to look for job, but it took three weeks until he found one.

"Why don't you try the company I work for?" my brother said to Ed, when he was visiting us one day. "It is a large electrical firm, and they are starting a new department making dishwashers. They are still at the developmental stage, but they will need workers for the project."

Ed went there and was hired. He was very interested to learn everything about the machine from the first stages.

I started to look for a job as well. The boys would be at school during the day and did not need me as much. Uldis was eight and Māris six. Mother still stayed at home, so they would not be unsupervised. If we wanted to buy a house, we would need the money. We had used the earnings that I had saved from my catering to pay back the debt which Ed had accrued while drinking, but I did not want to look back. What had been, had been. We would begin a new life, trusting in the future. If Ed did not drink, which he had not done since our talk, there would be no reason why we could not have a good life again. He was still my beloved.

I began to check the newspaper ads every day and went to various places for interviews. What they asked everywhere was: "What experience do you have?"

Of course, I had none, and I could not lie. One rejection came after another, even though I knew that I could do any of those jobs easily, if I was shown how to do them. But that was not how it worked in this world.

Another unsuccessful day had almost passed. I sat on a high stool in a downtown café, resting my legs from walking so much. My spirits were low. In front of me lay the newspaper with the marked job sites I had searched out. They had come to nothing. I sat at the window sipping my coffee, looking wistfully at the large raindrops hitting the pavement outside. People hurried by with their heads down, trying to get out of the wet as soon as possible, but the black mud on the asphalt stuck to their soles, and the puddles grew bigger and bigger.

Although I sat indoors, I too, felt soaked to the depth of my being. Nobody needed me: not my work, nor my knowledge or diligence. I felt like a foreigner in a foreign land again. I had received the message loud and clear, that it was better to not trust a foreigner. I felt that in every place that I went: if you are not one of us, then you have no place here. I

don't know. Perhaps I was too sensitive. I had felt that I had fitted in fine in London but not in this provincial town. I did not want to go anywhere anymore. This selling of myself was most abhorrent to me. I drank my coffee, watching the rainwater rush down the gutters. I did not want to go searching or even thinking about jobs anymore.

As I sat there and gazed through the window, I remembered how I used to pass by here every day when I worked at the hospital, for it was only one block down from where I was. They knew how to appreciate us Latvian girls there, for we proved that we were good workers. Suddenly a thought crossed my mind. Perhaps I could get a job in the hospital administration? They used a lot of people in all kinds of capacities. Perhaps they could find a place for me, too?

I quickly finished drinking my coffee, found some change in my purse and went outside. Just across the street was a telephone booth. I looked through the telephone book and found the hospital's number. I was lucky to get the person I wanted to talk to. It was Sister Griffiths. She had been like a mother to us, the Latvian women, when we first came to work in this hospital, and she remembered me well even though ten years had passed. Now she was promoted to the Matron's assistant, a very high post.

"Sister Griffiths, we are back from London and I am looking for a job. Could there be anything for me at the hospital?" I asked.

"Come and see me tomorrow," she said.

When I got to the hospital the following morning, Sister Griffiths was glad to see me and had found a post for me already, if I was willing to accept it. No interviewing either, for she knew my work habits.

"To alleviate the Ward Sisters from doing the paperwork, a new post has been created." She told me. "A 'ward clerk' does all that now. It means to prepare papers and receive the new patients, keep the folders in order, receive and file the lab reports, track x-rays, arrange for lab tests, order ambulances, answer the telephone, keep books up to date, etc." She explained. "Do you think that would suit you?" She asked.

"Yes, Sister, and thank you very much!" I was so grateful to her and relieved that I would not have to walk around looking for a job anymore, offering myself as spoiled produce. I knew this place and was certain that I would not have any problem fulfilling the requirements. The only drawback was that I would be working in a ward with patients again, which stopped me from working in the hospital before, due to my sensitivity to their suffering. I would have rather preferred to work in another office. Nevertheless, I hoped that everything would be all right. I was not that emotional child of ten years ago anymore.

I was told that I would have to work in two wards: in the mornings I would work at the private ward 9/10 (the ward consisting of male and

female wards) and the Ear, Nose and Throat Ward 15/16 (again in two parts) in the afternoons. The latter was the ward where I had worked before as a domestic after arriving in England from Germany. These two wards were not as busy as the large surgical wards; therefore it actually was a preferred position.

I thanked Sister Griffiths sincerely and walked out through the long wide hallway, where the well known archways seemed to greet me, and the familiar medicinal odors floated in the air. I had a job! I was happy. The future looked brighter right away, and even the rain had stopped when I went outside. It would be good! Soon we would save some money, and then we would look for a little house of our own, where we could live as we wanted. Time had moved on; many things had changed, and today buying a house was not an impossibility.

Still, more time was needed for that, and a whole year would pass until we got that far. In the meantime, I had to learn to get used to my Ward Sisters and their preferences, since most of my work was with them. The Sister of the private ward dashed around like an army sergeant. Though small in stature, she walked about in big steps, swinging her arms, full of pent-up energy. Her eyes were everywhere; she saw every smallest imperfection and right away made it known in her commanding voice. The nurses dared not stop for a moment.

"Nurse, don't you have anything to do?" The Sister's watchful eyes had already spotted one who had stopped for a moment to chat with a patient, and a whole row of new directives followed.

Of course, "The General" was a teaching hospital, where the nurses worked and learned at the same time, so that they could be Sisters someday, if they chose to do so. The discipline had to be strict, but even so, there could be different ways and approaches. Our Sister reminded me of a small, feisty rooster who pecked and pecked at everybody around her. Yet, she was good with the patients and also with me. She even smiled a little on occasions and always said "please" if she wanted something of me.

The other Sister upstairs was a person that was hard to decipher. If something had gone wrong, or had not been to her liking, her mood could change quickly from the sweetest syrupy kindness to icy cold. It was quite unbelievable to me, but sometimes her iciness seemed like hatred. Perhaps it could be ascribed to what they called an "Old Maid Syndrome?" Yet, she was only about thirty, slim and was a good looking woman, with dark hair and large blue eyes, which could be so kind and understanding, if she so chose. There was something about her mouth though, a hardly noticeable brutal streak, which could change those pretty, kind eyes into icicles in seconds. At those times, I just kept aside and did not ask her anything until the bad spell was over. Perhaps there had

been bad experiences in her life that had made her so. She was always civil to me, though, and even friendlier to me than to others.

In the private ward, there was not so much to do, because it was hardly ever full. To be in this ward, people had to pay the costs themselves, but then they could have the service when they wanted it. The rest of the patients were covered by the National Health Service, where patients had their health insurance deducted from their wages each week, and when they had health needs, or had to go to the hospital, everything was free. The drawback there was that people had to wait for their surgeries or treatments—sometimes for a long time, unless it was an emergency.

The private ward was used for the privileged people who could afford it. Since there were not so many patients, one of my jobs was to arrange the flowers in the mornings, or when they were brought or sent in during the day, and indeed there were many. Each patient had a long bed table at the foot of their bed, and when the flowers were put on them, the ward looked like a flower garden. This ward was in two parts, the male and the female, ten beds in each. A large table was in the middle of each room with cabinets underneath containing all kinds of supplies. I could put flowers on those as well, and I loved to arrange them. During the night, the nurses took them all out into the adjoining bathrooms. In the mornings I re-arranged them, throwing away the ones that were wilted. It was a fun job. After that I did the paperwork at my desk, just around the corner from the Sister's office, in the spacious hallway between the two large patient's rooms.

Quite unawares, the summer had come. Ed got his vacation time, and we went to Wales on the west side of England, which is a nice country with hills and dales. Mostly we drove along the coast, staying in places and camping. Our set up was very primitive. Ed and I slept in our small "pup tent", and the boys slept in the car. That was very cheap. The days were beautiful, and we could spend time on the beaches. The boys liked that best of all, playing in the sand and pouring it over dad's legs, or running into the shallow incoming waves.

We traveled south along the coast for quite a distance, but then one day, when the boys were running back and forth to the water, I noticed that Māris had a few red spots on his back.

"Come here!" I said. "Let me look at you Māri!"

I looked and thought to myself, "This does not look too good."

Then I called Uldis and checked him out too.

"Ed, would you come and look at this!" I called.

He came and recognized it right away, "It is chicken-pox! I had that when I was a child!"

"Yes, I did too!" I acknowledged. "We'd better go home!"

We were sorry to leave, but at least we had enjoyed the one week. The other week we would stay at home while the boys got over their nasty illness.

One beautiful Sunday, when they were all right again, Ed and I decided to take the boys and go to Meriden to visit our friends, the Liegis family. In the meantime, their family had grown. They had another son, Imants, and a baby girl Brigita. It was nice to see them again and hear all their news. The day was so nice, so we all sat outside in the meadow next to the house. Other young people had come from Coventry to relax and enjoy the day, and a volleyball game was going on. I was tempted to join for a bit, too. My playing, however, was short-lived. I had forgotten about my bad knee. As I reached sideways for the ball that came my way, I fell and it was all over for me! I could not get up or stretch out my right leg. The knee was locked in a bent position.

"What a shame!" My friend Laura lamented. "I was looking forward to the whole evening together!"

"I was, too! Sorry, my dear!" I whispered through clenched teeth. The pain was really bad. We had to go home.

It was very sad to have to break up the nice afternoon, but there was nothing else we could do. When we got home, Ed carried me up the two flights of stairs and put me on the bed. The pain was awful, but I had to wait until the next day for the doctor to come. However, he could not straighten the leg, either.

"I am afraid you will have to go to the hospital," he said.

The senior orthopedic surgeon, Mr. Fullford, came at me smiling when I got there. I knew him, and he knew me from the time when I first started to work at the hospital in the spring of 1947. He was the same large kindly man, but his dark hair and mustache had turned gray by now. He had always been nice, greeting me when he saw me, though I was just a manual worker then.

"Hello, hello!" He said. "Now what do we have here?" he asked, as he began to examine the leg.

He tried to gently twist it, but nothing happened. Then everything happened very quickly. I was just on the brink of going to sleep, when I felt my leg being lifted up and then knew nothing more. When I awoke, my leg felt very heavy, but it was straight. It had been put in a metal splint and wrapped around tightly from my ankle up to my groin. No wonder it was heavy.

"You keep it on for a week and then come back to see me," Dr. Fullford said." We will then arrange for you to have some therapy to get it working again. However..." he then paused, looking at the x-rays

again, and said, "The x-rays show that there is a tear in the cartilage, and it has to be mended."

It was too bad that it could not all be done at the same time. Now I would have to wait for the surgery until it could be worked into the operating theatre's schedules.

"Never you mind, love," Mr. Fullford tried to pacify me, "We'll fix you up, and then you will be as good as new! Most football players have this done, and they keep running just fine!" He smiled, squeezed my shoulder and walked away.

I could go back home and did not feel too bad, but it was a job to get up and down the steep, narrow stairs to our attic bedroom. I slid down on my bottom and crawled up pulling my leg after me. In the afternoons, I sat outside in the backyard doing some embroidery, and my shoulders got browner with every day. It was amazing though, how stiff my leg became in that one week! When the splint was removed, I could barely bend my knee at all. Then the therapy sessions started, and those were hard days. After a month of working hard to get my leg going, I received the notice that I was scheduled for surgery the following week.

I did not mind and knew that it was necessary, but had never thought that the pain after the surgery would be so terrible as it was.

"You should try to lift your leg straight up from the bed on the next day!" Mr Fullford said, after he saw me after the operation!

I could not do it. When I tried it, a sharp pain at the knee seemed to cut my leg in half. The therapist came every day and was very persistent. I felt awful. When I could not lift it on the second and the third day also, the therapist started using electric shocks on the muscles of my upper leg. That gave such a jolt to the rest of the leg that it seemed to tear the whole thing apart. After each session, I was soaked in perspiration and tears, which ran down my cheeks even without crying. This was torture, but in the end I finally moved it. Apparently one side of the cartilage had been removed. They called it a meniscectomy.

I was so ashamed of myself, for being such a weakling, because in the next bed to mine, was a young girl, only eighteen, and she had her whole leg amputated that same morning. Yet she was out of bed the following morning, practicing to walk with the crutches. I felt like such an absolute coward in front of Ann, the lovely young being with her whole life ahead of her. But Ann had cancer, and her life was already marked. Yet there was a special light around her as she hobbled back and forth, talking to the other patients and to me as well.

"My leg is not hurting," she said. "Only sometimes my toes..." which she did not have anymore... I felt so sorry for her. She was so brave; I was not.

After I went home, and even when I started to work again, I still had to go to therapy to get the knee strengthened. The leg had been weakened so much, but gradually it did get better, and I could walk almost normally. It never felt quite all right, though, and I had to learn to live with it.

Autumn days came, and it rained and rained. The old house absorbed the moisture. The cold and dampness came through the walls, through the cracks at the windows and under the doors. It crawled in through all the possible places; it was impossible to heat such a big house adequately. Our life had become narrow and unexciting again. Even though we lived with our own family, there were restrictions. Mother complained that the boys made noise after they came home from school and that they left streaks on the linoleum floors with their shoes. That was true, but they were just children. Uldis was seven and a half and Māris was six, and I did my share of cleaning.

We tried to make our weekends a special time for us, as we had always done since Ed and I were first married. I made a tray of nice, small sandwiches and perhaps a cake or ice-cream, made some coffee and took it all upstairs to our attic room. That was our celebration. It was not quite as before when there were just the two of us, but it was still nice. I also invited Mother to come and join us, for Saša had kept his habit of going to the pub on the weekends to be with the other men. That had become a well-established tradition by now, and she was at home alone.

We would ask Mother to join us in the attic, and we would all spend the Saturday evenings together. We would eat and then play games or cards with the children until their bedtime; then they would leave and so did Mother. After that, it was our time when we could be with each other. The iron stove had heated up the room nice and warm. We lay in bed in the dark, listening to the radio, playing the good old well-known tunes. The sounds flowed by like a shiny, bubbling river playing around the rocks, there swirling, there flowing on peacefully in a wide and quiet stream, carrying with it memories and scenes from bygone days.

A soft, reddish light came from the iron heating stove; the raindrops pounded the window and the roof. It was good here in the warmth. We were grateful and content. We did not have a house or a patch of land, but we did have a corner with a roof above our heads, and that had to be enough for now.

## We Found the House!

It was the winter of 1960. Snow covered the fields and roads when we finally found the little house we had wanted so much. It was in Kings

Norton, a newer suburb, farther out of the city, situated on the edge of the green belt. No more houses could be built beyond this street, and even the name sounded pleasant: "Green Acres Road" and it formed kind of a loop in this neighborhood. The houses, built in a more modern style, were the so-called "semi-detached" type, meaning that every two houses were under one roof, with the inside wall in common. The whole street had the same type of housing with small gardens in the front, and slightly bigger ones in the back.

When we first went to look at it, the snow was still on the ground. Ed noticed a small fir tree growing in the middle of the front garden, and exclaimed, "This house must be for us! There's even a Christmas tree here!" It reminded us how our love story was born at Christmas with a fake little Christmas tree, which we still had. That seemed like a good sign for us.

We managed to agree on the price, the three thousand pounds, and paid the down payment, but it was the end of March when we finally moved in. There really was not very much to move. After we put our existing furniture in the various rooms, it looked very empty, indeed. It was good that Ed knew how to do woodwork, and he was quite anxious to do it. He thought that he could easily build some simple cabinets and shelf units for our dining room. The English houses were not very big and did not need too much furniture, anyway.

The main thing was that we had our own place at last! Upstairs were two medium-sized bedrooms and a small "box room." A single bed would barely fit in the latter, and it was usually used for a baby or as a storage room. The bathroom was up there too, together with the toilet and a water heating tank in the corner in an enclosed cabinet. Everything was planned pretty tight. Not an inch of space was wasted. The same was true downstairs. Coming in through the front door, the staircase led straight upstairs on the left side. On the right, the short hallway led to the back of the house, into the small kitchen, (from which a side door led into the adjoining garage) and then out into the backyard. On the right side of the hallway, the first door was to the living room; the next door was to the dining room.

The living room had a large bay window facing the front of the house. The dining room opened to the garden with glass doors, and we liked those nice features. All the rooms had coal fireplaces, except the bathroom and the kitchen. In those we used a small electric heater, for that was the only solution.

A single garage adjoined the outside wall of the house with a door to the coal-shed and the back garden. We did not have much more to wish for at this point. We had the essentials and were very happy. The garden was not big but was sufficient for us. A large tree grew in the far corner

on the left, and under it was a small rock garden. I was happy to see that there were some climbing roses stretched along the back fence.

Inside the house, our steps made noise as we walked on the bare wooden floors, and the cold could be felt on the legs as it came in through the gaps between the floorboards. That was the way British houses were built, so the fire-places would have a draw, but we would change that, as soon as we would have enough money for it. The floors would get carpets, the windows would have curtains and drapes, and we would put electric heaters in all the rooms. It would be nice; we just had to be patient.

Of all the rooms, the living room looked the nicest for the time being. The Danish style furniture that we had bought in London fitted here perfectly. The two small cabinets, one with a flap opening for writing and storage underneath, the other with glass doors for china were just what we needed. Then there was the red armchair with the high back and the simply curved yellow chair, which looked so nice with the black and yellow tiled coffee table in the middle. Under the table was the rug with some Latvian ethnic designs at both ends, which Ed had made, loop by little loop, in the early morning hours after he came home from digging the raw chocolate at Cadbury's. That was when we first lived at the Station Road in Saša's house. The boys were just babies then, and he did not want to awaken us, since we just had that one room. Therefore he stayed in the breakfast room downstairs and worked on it until we got up. When we came downstairs, Ed would still be sitting there at the table, and little Uldis, only two years old, always wanted to help by handing him over the looped bits of yarn. That was why the rug was doubly precious to us.

It seemed that so much time had passed since then. Five, six years? We were not the same as we had been, either. Life had hardened us, but perhaps that was how it needed to be. Everything changed constantly, no one could stay uninvolved, and we had to move with the flow of life. This last change of getting our house was a very special blessing for us. We had longed for it a very long time.

The first weekend after we had settled in, we invited Mother and Johnny with his wife, Lienīte, to come and help us celebrate moving into our new home, if you could call my little open sandwiches, coffee and cake a celebration! I think it was more the thought of making the weekend special that made it so. Ed lit the fire in the fireplace, and it was nice and cozy.

I worked full time at the hospital and also a half a day every other Saturday. Ed did not have to work Saturdays, so he organized the boys to help him, and they started to clean house in the mornings while I was away. We had always shared the housework. When I got home, I

did the things I had always done: washed clothes, especially the woolen sweaters that needed to be washed by hand, did cooking and often also baked something for our evening celebration. It was a good way to finish the week, so we could rest on Sunday.

The boys liked their new school. It was not far from where we lived so they could walk there easily, but we learned only later that the other kids had teased them and even been abusive at first because they were foreigners. However, they had survived it and never complained.

The best thing here was that we lived almost in the country, at the "green belt". Behind the neighboring houses, the ground descended quite sharply, with big oaks growing on the grassy hillside. The boys could run there and play ball with their friends.

Spring was on the way. The snow melted, and the starlings came and whistled in our big tree in the garden. The sparrows chirped cheerfully on the wooden fence, discussing what would be the smartest thing to do now, but in the corner under our tree, the first daffodils began to show their green sprouts. The earth was waking up, though still full of the winter's moistness. But the spring breezes were in the air already, running over the land, telling of the days of sunshine that soon would come.

Now that we had our own house, we looked forward to the spring and had so many projects in mind. We wanted to do all those things that would make it beautiful, but it all cost money, and it was so hard to save anything much from our low wages. We could go forward only in tiny steps, because in those days there was no "hire purchase" or credit. It meant that you needed cash for everything. We had to learn to be patient. Of course, first things first! We got new beds for the boys and a second-hand table and chairs for the dining room, but that had to be all for now.

Gradually the days got warmer, and the hillside behind the houses, on the other side of the street, was covered with bluebells. What a wonderful sight to see them growing so abundantly there! The whole hillside was absolutely blue, and the big oak trees stood in the midst of them in their first greenery, letting the white clouds sail past them!

Then came summer, and the hillside meadow was full of red clover, white daisies and the yellow buttercups. We often went for a walk there in the evenings. On Sundays, when it was warm enough, we would take a blanket, find a comfortable spot in some small incline and lie in the sun. We were so glad to be out of the city, even though it meant a longer commute to work. This was so enjoyable. The oak trees were dark green by now, and small wild rose bushes grew under them, sporting pale pink blossoms. The bees worked around in the red clover sucking the nectar; a cow mooed somewhere farther down in the valley.

As I lay on my back, looking up into the blue sky, again a thought

went through my mind as it had many times before. Perhaps I was at home in Latvia, lying in the grass on the bank of our small river as I used to... Perhaps all this was just a dream... I closed my eyes wanting to savor that unreal dream. But then I heard my children's voices from down in the valley, where they climbed trees, and knew that I was where I was. However, this was good too. We had fulfilled our dream. We had our own house and our children. We were happy.

The boys ran up and tugged at my arms, "Mum, come and play ball with us!" The sleepy time was over. I did not feel too enthusiastic about playing, but then, we did not have too much time to spend together like this, so I went ahead.

During the summer, Ed built us some simple furniture for the dining room using my designs, so we could have storage for our dishes and also some shelving for decorations. We also laid a black marbled linoleum tile floor in there, repeating it in the doors of the new white cabinets. The theme was black, white and pale gray with a few added flashes of color. I found nice wallpaper—light gray with white embossed falling maple leaves. Perhaps I had been a bit extravagant buying the abstract Swedish designer's fabric for the drapes, but the flashes of gold, yellow, brick red and rust with touches of black, gray and a little white delighted my heart and was just what was needed there. I made them myself for the glass doors that opened from the dining room to the garden, and with a couple of green plants and pictures on the walls, I thought the room looked lovely. It was so exciting for me to do this creative work. Since I did not paint anymore, this was a great substitute for it—creating my surroundings.

I made the same kind of drapes upstairs for the boy's room as well. The bay windows of the living room had the same pattern also, except they were in blue shades with additional touches of yellow, black, purple, gray and white, and they looked good too. We still needed the sofa, but that would have to wait until we saved up seventy-five pounds. Then we needed the floor coverings and... No, we were fine. We were in our own much desired home!

It was the time when television began to become popular in England. It was 1960, and some people may have had them before, but we had not seen one. Our first contact with television was when we visited an English friend who had a set. How exciting! The boys were bowled over. A cinema at home! Apparently the programs were shown for only a few hours a day, in the mornings and evenings. This, however, changed quickly as more people bought the sets, but a fee had to be paid for using them, because there were no advertisements included then.

We, of course, did not have the money to buy one, but in time, it became possible to rent a set and we did. It was an exciting day when that

set was brought home! We rented one of the smaller ones, and it was not too good. Sometimes we saw more lines than a movie, but we watched it all with great fascination.

"How can they do it?" the boys wanted to know.

We, of course, were just as ignorant on the subject as the boys were and did not have an answer.

"There must be some very clever people in this world!" was the only answer we could find.

We really looked forward to our evenings now, and the boys were excited to see real cowboys.

"Look, look! There they come riding!" It was fantastic! All those guns and spears! The poor Indians! There was always a downside to it.

It was autumn again, and the boys were back at school. Ed was at his job at the factory making dishwashers and I was at my work in the hospital. On Friday nights, after work, I would usually go to do my big wash at the Laundromat. It was not too far from our house, perhaps a mile. I would pack the clothes in my shopping basket on wheels. They were very popular for carrying heavier things in those days, when not many people owned cars. Next to the Laundromat was a fish and chips place, and I would buy some on my way home, so that I would not have to cook dinner. In England it was quite customary to eat fish on Friday nights. That was a real treat for us. Could one wish for anything more after a long working week, than to sit at the fire, eat fish and chips with our fingers, and watch television? One could, of course, want much, much more, but we knew that it was not in the wanting more, but in the contentment with what one had.

Later in autumn, Ed got a promotion at his work. The dishwashing machines were starting to go on the market, but occasionally they had glitches, needing someone experienced to fix them. Since Ed had been in on the construction side of the machines from the very beginning, he had gone through the testing of the machines and knew all about them. Now he was chosen to be a representative for the firm. He was given a small van to travel all over the country—wherever problems occurred.

Ed, of course, was delighted, and I was glad for his sake. It certainly would be more interesting for him to travel around and meet different people, rather than spending the whole day at the factory. He would be away from home more, but would earn more money and that would be good for the needs of the house.

It would be all right, but only one thing worried me. A more relaxed lifestyle like that might get him into drinking again. He had not done it ever since we returned from London. As he traveled around, he would have to eat out, and the company would pay for that as well as for the

hotel if he had to stay overnight. But when eating, one also needed something to drink; that was understandable. However, if it was an alcoholic drink, one drink could lead to another and the next day more; then bad things could happen. In time, on occasions, I did notice that some drinking had taken place, and a silent fear began to rise within me. I knew that something would have to happen to make him stop.

And the day came when my fears become a reality. When a policeman called me out of the parent's meeting at school, my legs and hands trembled and I could barely speak.

"Your husband has been in an auto accident. He is at the hospital…" He said, and gave me the telephone number of the hospital.

He excused himself and left, but I stood on the spot and could not move. I felt stunned, as if somebody had hit me on the head. Oh God! Oh God, what now? Then a neighbor came out of the meeting and offered to take me to a telephone booth and help me to make the call to the hospital.

My hands trembled and my teeth chattered from fear of what I would hear when I lifted the tube, but I soon heard Ed's voice, and it sounded quite lively.

"Don't worry, everything is O.K.! I'll be coming home now, and it was not my fault!"

I tried to believe him and was happy that he was all right, but somewhere deep down an unpleasant suspicion had taken place. Would this be the pattern now? Hopefully this would be a deterrent for the future.


The winter came with cold days, rain and frost. In the night, the wind moaned around the house and battered the windows and doors. The house seemed to tremble from the heavy gusts. It was so cold everywhere, and during the short evening hours it was not possible to get the house warm with the coal fire. We all bunched together around the fireplace in the living room, closing the door to the rest of the house. When I spent more time in the kitchen on Saturdays, washing the woolen sweaters in the sink and doing the cooking and baking, I wore three sweaters, warm socks and boots to keep away the cold that was coming up from the floor and under the garage door. The small electric heater did not help very much.

"How I wish for a time when I shall not have to bundle up like this in my own house!" I thought to myself.

These small houses did not seem to be strongly built, even though they looked very nice from outside. It was difficult to heat them enough to retain the warmth, and the best thing was to go to bed early. At least it would be warm there. We would definitely have to get some floor coverings before the next winter, for so much cold came through the gaps between the floorboards and through the open fireplaces in the bedrooms.

We just had to be patient. There was not enough money for it all.

Christmas came, the first one in our own house. I did not have to work on Christmas Eve, so I spent the morning baking our traditional Latvian bacon rolls and coffee cakes. The other foods for our Christmas Eve's cold table I had already prepared in the days before. The house was full of the pleasant smells from the kitchen, mainly from the fresh baking. That alone announced that Christmas was here. Ed had built fires in the living room and in the dining room, making the rooms cozy and warm for this Christmas Eve. After the work was done, we all took turns taking a bath, and dressed up for our Christmas celebration.

Together with the boys, we would decorate the small, fresh smelling Christmas tree that Ed and I had brought from the market yesterday. Now it stood on the small table in the bay window of the living room. On the wide windowsill stood our first little fake Christmas tree with a crowd of tiny trees around it, and tonight, as every year, I would add another small tree to it. I stood there reminiscing for a moment or two. So many years had passed since that time! My children had grown so much. There was no one I could hold on my lap anymore... Uldis was nine and a half and Māris eight.

The boys were excited and could not wait for me to open the box of decorations.

"Can we do it now, Mum?" they asked time and again.

There were not too many things, but we had collected a few over the years. There would be enough for our small tree.

"Can I hang up this pretty ball?" Uldis asked.

Māris had found a gold colored chocolate acorn.

"I want to put this on our tree!" he said, already stretching his arm up to put it on the branch.

We all worked around the tree and I put the silver tinsel star at the top, remembering how Saša had made it on our first Christmas together. It still looked beautiful, for I had packed it carefully. I put on the candles, which had to be clamped to the branches carefully so they would not touch anything, while the boys put on the rest of the ornaments. The tree looked beautiful. The three of us stood there admiring it and then Ed came in too, from putting more coal on the fire.

"You have done a great job!" he praised us, patting the boys on their backs.

Then the doorbell sounded and the boys ran to open the door. In came our guests, our family. There was Mother with Saša and Johnny with Lienīte. Lienīte was pregnant and expecting a child next May. That was an exciting event for our family, and we were very glad for her and Johnny.

It was a happy evening for us all, as later we sat around the Christ-

mas tree, watching the small tender lights of the candles burn steadily. Christ was born again in our hearts as we sang our old beloved Christmas songs. Then the boys recited the poems they had learned, and afterwards, we gave out our presents. I was so grateful to God for everything: for my family, for the good food on the table, for our own roof above our heads.

The evening would have been so nice, but then I noticed that Ed had been drinking. He had left the room several times at intervals, but I had not paid attention to it, since we were the hosts and needed to fetch things from the kitchen. He must have gone out to the garage... Pain hit my heart fiercely. He had not been doing it since his accident. Why did he not have a few drinks openly with all of us? That would have been all right, seeing that this was a celebration, but he drank alone, because he wanted more. He thought I would not notice, but I did every time, and that made me shrink within myself.

The Christmas joy was gone, although I tried not to show it to others. When they left, I silently tidied everything up. I did not say anything, but Ed knew that I knew. There was nothing more to say. We went up to bed, and he fell asleep quickly. I lay there with open eyes, as I had done a good many times before, and wondered if this would be the path I would have to walk for the rest of my life.

On Christmas day we were invited to Mother's for dinner, and Johnny and Lienīte were there also. The rest of the afternoon was spent together with the children making a jigsaw puzzle, and a new family tradition was born that we have continued for years.

We celebrated New Year's Eve at home, just our family, lighting the candles again in the tree and touching our glasses of lemonade to wish each other a "Happy New Year". The boys were excited, because this was the first time that they were allowed to stayed up so late.

"Did you hear it?" the boys exclaimed almost in unison.

"Somebody must be shooting the fire-crackers!" Ed said.

We stepped out of the door for a moment. The night was cold, and the stars shone big and bright in the clear sky. Shivering, we went inside again. Ed and the children went upstairs; I stayed behind. I needed to be by myself and sift through my feelings as I started this New Year of 1961. I stood by the window and looked at those bright stars for a long time, my forehead pressed against the cold, moist glass. I had only one wish—that Ed would not drink anymore.

The spring of 1961 came and went with blooming daffodils in the gardens and parks. The breezes ran across the land, swaying the tree tops, playing with the silvery clouds, but still carrying the cool breath of the winter. It was hard for the sun to warm this land, heavy and

damp from the snow and rain. The leaves on the trees were slow to open, but one day they were green again, and the bluebells filled the meadow under the big oak trees near our house. The chestnut trees lifted up their big clusters of creamy blossoms like candles, lit in celebration of the coming summer.

At the end of May, Lienīte gave birth to a little boy and named him Mārtiņš. He was such a beautiful and lovable child with blond hair and blue eyes.

"I am so happy for you!" I hugged them both, wishing them well.

Lienīte handed the baby over to me saying,

"Do you want to hold him?"

"Yes, I would love to!" I answered and she put him in my arms. As I held the small bundle in my arms, strange feelings overwhelmed me. What if I too had another child? Perhaps the little girl that I had wanted? But we could not afford it. How would we live and make ends meet if I could not work? The mind said "no", yet perhaps sometimes it was good to let yourself go, trusting that in the end it would be all right. But I was not raised that way. One had to honor one's duty, and right now my duty was to help take care of the family I had.

I realized more and more that I had to be the stabilizing factor in our lives, the one who had to keep a clear mind when my dear husband's vision was clouded. Sometimes a good stretch of time passed when he did not drink at all, but then again, little by little it started, and then I knew that sad days would follow. It was hard not to worry about what was happening or what could happen, especially now that he was traveling around so much. Sometimes he got home the same evening, sometimes it took a day or two or even more, depending on how far away from home he had to go and how many jobs he had in that vicinity. If he could, he would give me a call at the hospital, or leave a message there if he had to stay longer, but often I did not know, because we did not have a telephone at home. In those days you could not get a telephone so easily; you had to go on a waiting list.

My work at the hospital was easy, but I was in contact with disease and death again. When I first came to England years ago and worked at the hospital, I ended up having to leave it because emotionally, I could not handle it. I thought it would be different this time, but it was not, really. I had hoped that I would be working in an office, not in the ward, but it was not up to me to choose. I needed a job and was glad to take what was offered.

Dealing with all the charts and reports, I knew what the patient's illnesses were and what might happen to them. There were always some cancer patients on my regular ward, staying at the hospital for their radiation therapy (which was the only treatment for cancer at that time). For

the most part, they were sad stories, and again, I was involved with the patients personally. Their sorrow flowed into me and walked with me, even though on the outside, they were just ordinary days for the hospital. I began to feel that the whole world was full of sorrow.

Sometimes, I felt as if a crowd of beggars was following me, trying to touch me with their haggard, bony hands. But there was nothing I could do for them, and despair and fear mounted in my heart for them, for myself and for the whole world. I fought against these feelings, but even though I openly did not give in, they kept me tight as a string. There were also brighter days when we joked and laughed with the nurses, but the evil stood in the corner and waited.

Most of all, my heart ached for the younger people, who had so much living ahead of them, so many hopes and dreams, yet they did not know that soon the gate of life for them would close and everything would be covered by the merciless darkness. I myself started to lose hope sometimes. These dark feelings were like a gray, damp veil, which covered everything—even joy. The death would win anyway, but I had to fight, fight. I did not tell Ed or anybody else about it. I had to be strong and endure what life was offering me at this time. I had to overcome this weakness of mine that had caused me to fall apart once before.

Almost unawares, the summer had come, and with it, the time to celebrate the Midsummer Fest, the most joyous of the Latvian ethnic celebrations. One of the places to gather for this was now the country mansion of Almeley on the Welsh border. In the few years, since the place had been taken over by the Latvians, a lot had been done to upgrade and develop it into a place that had become well-known and loved as a summer vacation place. The old stables, which already had been converted into small rooms by the British government during the war and had been used for a military hospital, were now converted again and made available for the old people who wanted to spend their twilight years in the countryside.

Summer camps had been planned for the children and guest rooms were ready for whoever wanted to come and spend their vacation in the fresh country air. It was a good and convenient place for families with children, for the prices were very reasonable with all meals included. There was plenty of room to run around the spacious grounds, and at the other end of the terraced setting was the beautiful lake for swimming, boating and fishing.

The Midsummer Fest celebration, being the biggest event of the year, drew a lot of people from many parts of the country. Many had their own cars by now, so the crowds grew bigger each year. There was not enough room in the house for everybody, of course, so people brought tents and

put them up in the meadow near the house.

We went too, together with my brother Johnny, his wife and little Mārtin, just a month old. Johnny and Lienīte had recently bought their own little house and a car, for he had a good job now at the same large electrical firm, which had also helped him with his schooling. Now he could reap the benefits.

We arrived at Almeley in the early afternoon, so there was room enough to pitch our tents in our favorite place, near the house, behind a patch of shrubs, under a huge mulberry tree. Mother and Saša came together with their friends on a bus.

The small village of Almeley was not as quiet as before the Latvians had bought the Nieuport House property. On summer evenings, during vacation time when there was not too much to do at the house, car after car went along the narrow road to the country pub in the middle of the village. In England the pubs (short for "public houses") are local meeting places, where people go to visit with each other in a pleasant atmosphere, while having a pint or two and enjoying themselves.

In the summertime, the Latvians all but took over the big lounge at the pub. Mugs of beer were passed around, there were jokes and laughter. Somebody would start to sing and soon everybody would join in. It was an undisputed fact that wherever Latvians gathered, there was singing, at least in those days. The British farmers stood at the bar, quietly sucking their pipes and looking on smiling at the goings-on. It appeared that they liked the songs, and the pub keeper rubbed his hands, moving amongst the guests smiling and eagerly filling the many orders. The money was coming in, and these Latvians were not stingy.

For the Midsummer Fest, however, all the activities took place at the Almeley House. The celebration went on from the evening of June 23, *Līgo* night, to all day of June 24—the "John's Day." This ancient tradition was carried out each year along similar lines, depending on the circumstances.

The times had changed, of course, but the largest communities in their host countries still tried to hold on to the old traditions as much as possible. But after a while the words of the songs began to fade from people's memories, as the oldest singers died off and the youngest did not know them as well. So the celebrations gradually changed in their character also, losing the initial magic that was so tightly bound with the land where it had all started. We did not have that land anymore, yet it was good for the Latvian people to come together—even like this.

The *Līgo* evening was here again. For a little while yet, the last rays of the sun sent their golden glow across the land, then disappeared behind the dark treetops of the forest beyond the lake. Twilight spread over the fields and meadows. The air was full of earthy smells and of

freshly cut grass, but I doubted if anybody was paying much attention to these things. Perhaps it was because the younger people did not have the recollections that we had of what summer evenings in Latvia were like.

Still, on this night the big house and the whole vicinity hummed like a beehive. There were voices and laughter everywhere. A verse of a *Līgo* song would ring out here and there amongst the tent builders. People called out to each other; greeted, hugged, and kissed those that they had not seen for a long time.

"You are here also! How wonderful to see you! Now how long has it been?"

"Oh, I don't even remember, two years, or is it three?"

More eyes searched around for familiar faces. More happy greetings and hugs, voices full of excitement, as it usually was on this magical night.

Then out of the house came our hosts and the symbolic ritual followed on the front lawn, depicting the way it was in the old days to teach the younger ones how it used to be. People gathered around the hosts, while another group of people ("John's children" or *"Jāņu bērni"* in Latvian) came from farther away, all in national dress, singing the *Līgo* songs and carrying armfuls of flowers, grasses, ferns and the "kalmes", a spiky plant from the lakeside. The women and girls wore flower garlands on their heads, made of the wild flowers from the meadows, and carried one for the hostess. The men, especially those named "John", wore oak leaf crowns, carrying one for the host.

Upon arrival, the John's children crowned the host and the hostess, singing the appropriate songs and throwing the flowers and grasses over them as blessings. Then the hostess welcomed the guests, inviting them to come and feast on the special *Līgo* night foods—the home-made caraway seed cheese, the beer and the Latvian special party food, *"pīrāgi"*. The guests sang the special *Līgo* songs thanking the hosts, but the singing did not continue too long, though. Some sheets of paper with songs printed on them had been handed to the closest in the circle, but even so, it ended all too soon.

Were we already beginning to forget our songs? Back home we had sung all through the night and had always found more songs, even making up new ones, which was easy to do if you just kept the rhythm. Perhaps we were becoming too complacent to use our minds fully. That was sad. To me it felt like a slap in our own faces.

"What kind of Latvians were we?" I thought. "Were we already beginning to lose our identity—that deeply ingrained feeling of belonging to our nation? But perhaps not everybody felt this belonging as keenly as I did?"

After the official part, people settled wherever they liked, under

the trees or near bushes, putting down blankets for sitting. Mostly they were small groups of people who had come together and had brought their own provisions with them. It was getting dark, and here and there I could see a light flickering up for a moment. Some laughter or a louder voice rang out somewhere; a beginning of a *Līgo* song sounded. People seemed to be having a good time, enjoying their food, drinks and the warm summer night.

Mother and Saša and their household were also settled somewhere, but I did not want to go and sit. I wanted to roam around, to feel and experience this night.

A bonfire had been built in its usual pace near the large oak tree. Red sparks started to fly into the night sky, touching the canopies with a red glow. Some people sat around the fire talking, some singing or just gazing into the flames, perhaps remembering the times long ago. I stayed there, too, for a little while. The boys showed up for a bit, together with some friends. The fire fascinated them, for they did not have a chance to see anything like that often. They threw some sticks on the fire, watching the sparks rush up, making the fire brighter. Then they disappeared into the night again. They were having a whale of a good time tonight, because no one was chasing them off to bed.

I heard sounds of music coming from the house and walked over there. Microphones had been set up, and people were dancing on the front lawn. Māris ran up to me and tugged at my arm.

"I want to dance too, Mum!" We joined the dancers, and I tried to teach him to waltz.

"One, two three, one, two three…" In the darkness, nobody could see if we did it right or not, but we had fun.

I looked for Ed, but did not see him. He did not care for dancing too much. Perhaps he was inside the house talking with the other men. People went in and out all the time, because more refreshments were being served indoors, but I did not want to go there. I wanted to stay outside on this night, which had been so very special for me back in our country.

Thinking about those far away days made me feel sad. I started walking away into the darkness to be by myself, leaving the fire and the voices of celebration behind me. I stepped quietly in the grass, full of dew by now, but did not get far. Barbed wire stretched alongside the meadow, making me stop. Most likely it was there to keep the animals out, but to me, this brought back memories of the refugee camps in Germany. I stood there for a long time staring into the darkness. Once I had left the lights behind me, it was not quite so dark after all. White mist had risen up at the far end of the meadow, gently wrapping around the trees and shrubs. This was a *Līgo* night, but it was not the same. No, not ever the same as it had been in Latvia. The magic did not work on

foreign soil.

Since this was also the ending of the Latvian children's summer camp, they had prepared entertainment for their parents and others. It took place the following afternoon on the front lawn. This was the John's Day, celebrated together with *Līgo* Night, so quite a few people had stayed overnight to see the performance. The children sang Latvian folksongs and had prepared short skits. In one of them, the smaller children acted out a short poem, where a dog chased a rabbit and a little boy chased the dog. They all ended up running in a big circle. What fun it was for the onlookers, when a little Corgi puppy ran out of the audience and followed the three runners, barking loudly!

Afterwards, everybody wanted to pet and love the little dog, and the children crowded around him, our boys included. It turned out that the puppy belonged to the Latvian farmer who lived on a farm next door.

"This is the last one of the litter of three," he told us. "Actually it is a girl. Would you like to have her? I don't really need more dogs."

"Yes, Dad! Please Dad! Can we have her?" the boys begged, not wanting to let her out of their arms. By now, we too had fallen in love with her, even though one of her ears would not quite stand up. Well, what else could we do? Dad paid the farmer two pounds, and the doggie was ours.

That was a great happening in our family life, for now we had another member to love and to take care of. We called her Suki or Sue for short, and she brought a lot of joy to us all.

At home, we worked on our house as much as our money would allow us. The most important projects were to install carpets in the living room and the boy's room. Not the thick ones, which were too expensive for us, but even the lighter-weight carpets made the rooms feel warmer and cozier right away. Ed also covered up the fire places and installed electric heaters, which were cleaner and gave more even warmth. We saved up enough money and bought a Danish style sofa for our living room, which was just the right thing that we needed to go together with our other Danish style furniture. The abstract-patterned drapes completed the scene perfectly, and I was very happy! My environment meant a lot to me.

I also designed furniture for the boy's room, and Ed built it during the weekends and on summer evenings, when he was at home. He loved working with wood and was good at it. His father had taught woodworking at a technical high school in Latvia. Ed built a desk and a wall unit alongside one of the twin beds that contained a shelf for books. We bought a small wardrobe, and then it was all done. With the mottled rust and black colored carpet and the orange-yellow-black and white drapes,

it was perfect. Ed had also built in an electric heater in the boy's room to make it cozier.

We had already remodeled the dining room the previous year. Our bedroom upstairs was the only one still waiting for improvement. There was no floor covering, and the gaping hole of the coal fireplace did not help either. When we moved from Mother's house, she let us take the wardrobe and the dresser with us. They were second-hand pieces, but served adequately, so it was all right for the time being.

It was the year 1961, and in August we celebrated my thirty-fifth birthday. It was hard to believe that I was so old already. The years had rushed by building up our new life in this country, and it seemed that things had finally begun to stabilize. I baked some cakes and pastries for my party, for I loved baking. The family arrived, as well as my dear friends Laura and Aunt Paula. It was wonderful to have my closest people around me to help me celebrate.

Autumn came with cooler days. The leaves were falling, and school would be starting soon. Our lives ran the regular course with its everyday little cares and worries. There were no problems, but it felt like something was missing. We had done all we could do to the house within our financial constraints, but my spirit yearned for more creative things to do.

"Why could I not be like other housewives, content to just take care of the house and the family? Why did I always have this need to push for something else to fulfill myself?" I asked. I felt guilty for having these yearnings, but it did not help. The desire was still there.

Then a thought occurred to me that, perhaps, I could go to draw portraits again. I talked to Ed about it, and since it would be only one evening a week, he said he would not mind. On the first night at the college, I was so excited rushing up the circular stairway to the portrait class, which was at the very top. Of course, my former teacher, old Mr. Eggison, was not there anymore. Twelve years had passed since I had last come here. Two of the former students, whom I still remembered, were teaching now and they remembered me.

"Good to have you back! It has been a long time!" Mr. Walton said.

"Yes, it certainly has!" I replied.

I was rather doubtful of what I would be able to do after not having done anything in the arts all these years, but once I started, it was not bad at all. After a couple of sessions, Mr. Walton suggested, "Why don't you get paints and start painting, Zig?"

"Do you think I'm ready?" I asked.

"You're ready!" He said.

That got me even more excited and opened a whole new world of

color for me. Mr. Walton told me which color paints I needed to get to begin with and showed me the few basic colors to use. Then he told me to just go ahead. What a joy! I got so carried away with painting that I was reluctant to leave when the class ended. Oh, glory! I never thought there could be joy like this!

I was tired but content when I went down the stairs again. I had received what I needed. When I walked out into the wet streets and on to my bus stop, everything still vibrated within me from the emotional involvement. A damp evening breeze blew my hair, and an odd raindrop or two hit my face, but even that seemed like just a refreshing touch in my dreamlike state of uplifting joy.

Leaning against a post at the bus stop and looking at the wet pavement, where colored lights reflected and changed, I saw pictures that I would like to paint someday.

"Could I?" Closing my eyes, I thought, "But when would that be?"

Shivers went through my body just thinking about it. I saw years and years ahead when my duties would bind me. Not as a burden, of course, but as a gift of love to my family, which I would never want to neglect. Nevertheless, that would take my time and my devotion.

"But perhaps when I shall be old, and the children will be grown?" I still deliberated. Right now, however, even these few hours of delight were better than nothing."

My children had grown. Uldis was ten and a half and Māris nine. I sometimes thought how different my two boys were, in looks as well as in their disposition. Uldis was a doer. He always wanted to help Dad and learn how to do things. Māris was not interested in that. He would rather curl up on his bed with a book, reading, surveying the pictures, absorbing the world in his own way. They both did well at school, and we were glad about that.

Uldis liked to do more complicated structural things. He used to put in an effort to do things perfectly. I would never forget the ship that he once drew. It was when we still lived in London, and he was six or seven years old. He did it using the ruler, drawing each line very precisely. It was a nice ship and almost finished, when something suddenly went a little amiss. Instantly, he crunched it up in his hand and threw it away, even though he had worked on it for an hour or more.

"You could have corrected the mistake!" I said. I felt sorry for him throwing away such nice work.

"No! It was not good enough!" He said, and he did not draw another one!

They were different in their looks also. Uldis had a narrow face and brown hair like mine. He still had his asthma occasionally, and that wore him down when the attacks came, usually each time after he had a cold.

Māris still had his round baby face, his blond hair and a small dimple in the cheek. When he was small, I had started to call him "kitten" because he was so soft and cuddly. Something of that was in him still, but we had grown more distant.

Perhaps it was wrong that I took the advice of someone who had written in the Women's Magazine, that you should not cuddle boys once they outgrew your lap, that they did not like it. Perhaps, but we did not have our former closeness anymore since we did not touch. There must have been something more in touching than just the physical connection. I was sorry to have listened to that advice.

After getting home from school, the boys would go outside and run around and play with their friends for a while until it got dark. That was good, for children need friends and fresh air, but more and more I was on my own. Ed was away a lot on his job, and on weekends there were a lot of chores to catch up with.

On Saturdays or Sundays we still got together with Mother and Johnny and his family, either at our place or Johnny's nice little home. Life was good. My closest friend now was Suki, who would be waiting for me when I got home from my work at the hospital.

I was glad I still had my relationship with my former roommate Mrs. Avots, except now we all called her Aunt Paula. She was such a dear person and practically a member of our family. Her friendship had been such a sustaining power throughout my hard times after we came to England and when the children were small. She was also Māris' godmother and was always ready to listen to my woes.

Lately Aunt Paula and I had started to meet at the hospital during our teatimes. She still worked as the Matron's personal housekeeper, and her room was in the Nurses Home. In the mornings, when she went to the big kitchen to pick up supplies for the Matron's kitchen, she had to walk through the hallway where I worked. Sometimes, in passing by, she would whisper to me to come to her room at tea time. She would often do some baking for the Matron, and there would be enough for us as well.

We would sit in her small room, visiting and enjoying the freshly baked rolls or whatever it was that she had made, sharing our news and sometimes unburdening our hearts. It was good to have someone I could talk to freely, who was always interested to hear what I had to say—and she really listened. Her soft brown eyes looked at me warmly and understandingly, and even if she could not help to find answers, she just patted my hands, and I felt better. She was truly a good and loving person.

Even though she had lost all of her own family, she never complained, but tried to see the good and the noble everywhere. She tried to take the best from life, but also gave back the best that she could. She never forgot the birthdays or other special days of her friends. Everybody

respected and loved her. To me, she had been like my second mother ever since we traveled together to England from the refugee camp in Germany.

Those little visits at teatimes were like bright little islands, and I always returned to work encouraged. I had received warmth and love. I hoped that I, too, could be like that some day, giving comfort to others. But I was more of an introvert, and new relationships did not come to me easily.

I wished that I could have had such a relationship with my Mother, but it never worked that way with us. Mother was a different kind of a person. Not that she could not be loving and kind (like to her neighbors or people she met on the street) but she was always so preoccupied with herself that she did not have the interest to listen to anybody else's problems. But we are all different and can have different outlooks on things. I don't want to criticize my Mother. She was who she was. She needed so much love and attention herself that it did not occur to her that others had such needs, too.

Somewhere in her early childhood she had experienced life's unfairness, which had affected her deeply. There had been five children in the family, all born within ten years. How much time could the mother spend on each little person's idiosyncrasies? This hurt must have been due to her high level of sensitivity, and it seemed that she never got over it. She had told me about it, and I could understand why it hurt her when she was a child, but I often wondered why she would not let it go and leave it behind her.

I was very sad that my relationship with Mother never became better, even though we always tried to include her in our family life, asking her and my brother and his family to come to our house and celebrate the weekends together and exchange news.

Mother came to our gatherings, but did not take part in our exchanges much. She would pick up one of my women's magazines, sit down in a corner and read. Only when it was almost time to leave, would she put the magazine down, suddenly stretch out her arms towards the boys and say, "Now children, why don't you come and give grandma some loving!"

The boys, of course, walked up to her obediently and let her put her arms around them, but what kind of loving could it be, if she did not even have the interest to talk to them?

Another time, she might start talking about her sisters and brothers, who had let her down at a time when she had needed their support the most. That had been in 1940. Her tuberculosis had become active again for the second time and a serious surgery was necessary. It was a very emotional time for all our family. Mother remembered this time with

much bitterness in her heart and refused to forgive and forget.

"I was good to all of them in their times of need, but when I needed them, there was no compassion for me!" Mother lamented about her sisters and her mother.

That was always a painful theme for us. How many times had we heard it already? But she told the same thing again and again, as if trying to convince us to take her side and condemn the others. She told these stories to our friends and acquaintances also, and even to strangers if the opportunity arose, which was most embarrassing. I suppose she needed to show how she had suffered to win people to her side.

It was hard to witness this bitterness. She had stored it for years. We urged her to leave it aside. Even her husband, quiet Saša, sometimes lifted his voice and told her to quit. The men would just walk out of the room, but I had to stay and listen as she tried even harder to convince me that she was in the right and that the others were in the wrong.

Then the bitterness would come out even more heatedly, presenting each painful detail.

"My own Mother said that I needed a spanking rather than compassion!"

But that was our Omi, a down to earth, kind and loving person. I knew that those words were never meant the way Mother took them. Yes, she had received a scolding where she had expected compassion from her family members, but I knew that they were not evil people! They scolded her because they cared! But she could not stop, and continued, "My own sister Irma said that I should have treated myself like a crystal vase on a pedestal, not run around in wintertime selling apples for the farm!"

It was true that she had endangered her own health by taking on a project that she did not necessarily need to. However, these comments had come at a time when Mother was very vulnerable.

"I had gone to see Elzī and Alfred, but when Elzī heard my story, she walked into another room and closed the door!" She argued. "Alfred was the only one who was more compassionate and talked to me."

The fact was that Aunt Elzī, Mother's younger sister, was expecting a baby at any time; she did not dare to be exposed to Mother's illness.

It made my heart heavy each time I had to listen to it, "Forget it, mother!" I tried to pacify her the best I could, but she did not want to forget, she wanted to be justified! The injury had been done; the pain had a right to be there! There was even more pain and bitterness added, because nobody wanted to understand!

One Sunday evening, when she was alone with us, she started on the subject again. Ed did not say anything, but I could see that he was getting annoyed. After a while he just walked out of the room. Obviously, he was

trying to hold himself in check. I tried to end the subject, but Mother would not let go and continued her arguments again even more heatedly.

"But Irma said this, and Elzī said that…"

"Mama, please let go!" I begged her, but she would not.

More time passed. Then Ed came back into the room. I saw that he, for once, had had enough.

"Mother," he said, "if you cannot talk about anything else but to complain about your sisters, then maybe it is better that you do not come. I do not want to hear this anymore!"

Mother jumped up, looked Ed in the face, then without a word, ran out into the hallway, picked up her coat and was gone, slamming the door behind her. Luckily the boys were upstairs in their room playing and did not see this.

Ed and I stood in the middle of the room in silence. There was nothing more to say.

"Should I go after her?" I thought. "Should I apologize, try to pacify her?"

Ed came up to me, seeing my anguish and said in a choked voice,

"I am sorry, dear, that I had to do that…"

"Yes, yes…I am sorry too…" I murmured. But when one is burdened enough, there comes a breaking point.

"No, I will not go after her," I decided. "Perhaps this will make her think and finally understand."

I felt that I had come down hard on her, but I did not feel guilty. People can be provoked only so far without consequences.

During the following weeks I felt awful. Again I was in the middle between my husband and my Mother, like it had been previously when we all lived together at Station Road. The problem was that Mother could not take any deviating view without getting offended. She did not even try to see the other side, and then it was always my job to gently even it out.

Once, when Uldis was little, Mother had bought a nice woolen outfit for him, which I was grateful for. I knew that all grandmas like to buy something for their grandchildren, but why did she have to broadcast it to all of our Latvian friends? On a Saturday night when the men had met at the local pub for a pint of beer and some visiting, someone had said as a joke to Ed, "Well, Ed, you have it made now! Your mother-in-law is supporting your family!"

One can understand what a blow it was to his young father's pride that he was incapable of providing for his family, even though he worked doing a back-breaking job at the chocolate factory. He told Mother not to buy anything for his children anymore, and she was offended again and complained to others that she was not allowed to buy presents for her grandchildren.

Another touchy subject in those days was that she had started to come into our bedroom early on Sunday mornings without knocking first. In passing our bedroom door, she would hear the boys making some noises and come in to visit with them. She would try to be very quiet, but what if we wanted to make love? We never knew when she might walk in. It was hard to think that an intelligent person like her could be so tactless. On one such occasion, Ed had asked her, "Would it not be better, Mother, if you knocked before entering?"

Again a rumor had been spread that Ed did not want her to come and talk to the children, and one more time things were misinterpreted or misunderstood.

It was sad that these things had to happen and yet, one could not live with hatred; at least I could not. I always had to be the one to even out the problems, and gradually everything would get back to normal. We wished only well for Mother, but did not want her to upset our lives, either. We all had to be understanding, forgiving and loving but boundaries had to be drawn.

Ed's work was much more interesting now and was not hard, but he had to be away from home a lot. He traveled all over England in the company's car as a representative and a consultant. Dishwashers were still a new thing in England. He had to instruct the sales people and also go to client's homes, if everything was not working as it should be. Being a new product, the dishwashers were pretty expensive and were owned mostly by rich people. So Ed got to be a "visitor" at film stars' apartments in London and at Lord's and Lady's mansions in the countryside.

When Ed would come home, it was fun to listen to his stories.

"The famous British film star, Jean Simmons, and I were both on our knees in front of the dishwasher in her kitchen, trying to figure out what was ailing it," he told me. We both laughed about it, imagining the scene.

Another time he had had an ambiguous experience, "I was reminded repeatedly by a young rich lady that if I needed anything, anything at all, she would be upstairs in the bedroom..."

There had been an occasion, when he had to go to an older lady's house, and he had asked her, if he might use her phone to call the company about something. Seeing that he was a foreigner, she had asked cautiously, "Do you know how to use a phone?"

"Yes, thank you madam!" He had answered, thinking to himself, "Do they really think that all the foreigners have crawled out of the bushes?"

A few days later, he had been summoned to the main office. Appar-

ently a letter had arrived concerning him. When Ed got home, he told me about it.

"On my way to the office, I tried to figure out what I might have done wrong? I could not think of anything. It turned out that the letter was from the same old lady and she had wanted to express her special gratitude for a very good service. Maybe she realized that her question about using the phone might have been offensive to me."

There was another time when he had been called out to some mansion in Wales to see a Lord So-and-So.

"As I approached the mansion," Ed told me later, "I saw an older man in the yard with a faded cap on his head, dressed in an old jacket, the front fastened with a safety pin, and he had no socks on his feet under the wooden clogs that he wore. I stopped and told him politely that I needed to see the Lord."

"He gave a sniff through his generous whiskers and said, 'I am the Lord!'"

That had been a bit embarrassing for Ed, but later, after the job was done, the Lord had invited Ed to share lunch with him.

"We both sat at the table in the big old kitchen and made sandwiches of salami and cheese. I did not feel ill at ease at all!" Ed exclaimed. "Not all Lords are rich, because it is not easy to keep the big properties going. Not all of them are snobbish either," Ed explained.

Yes, we had seen in many instances that the more intelligent people were friendlier and more understanding than the uneducated ones, who looked upon us as something second best because we were not British.

"The Lord wanted to know where I came from and how I had ended up in England." Ed told me. "We had a nice conversation and parted as good friends."

At the parting, the Lord had given Ed a "fiver" and had said, "Why don't you have a beer on me? And drop by again Ed, if you happen to be in the vicinity; I really enjoyed meeting with you!"

When Ed got home, it was always nice to talk about the interesting episodes that had happened on his journeys. But he was away a lot, and it was hard, waiting and not knowing when he would return.

Often in the evenings, I would stand at the window, wondering if he would come home or not. Suki would be next to me on a chair, her little white paws on the windowsill, watching and waiting, her ears pricked straight up. It was good to have her with me.

The boys had their run around with their friends during the twilight hours. They were not so little anymore, and I let them do it, because they only got home from school at four-thirty. The autumn days were short. The darkness came early, but they did need some exercise and fresh air.

But Suki was the one who always knew when Dad was coming. How

she knew it, we could not figure out, because to get to our house, he had to round the corner, yet she was never wrong. She would suddenly start barking, running around the room, wanting to get out to welcome him. Then she would be up on the chair by the window again, looking out intently. And sure enough, a few minutes later, Ed would turn into the driveway. What a joy it was then for everybody! Hugging and kissing and Suki jumping up and down, wanting to be in on the welcoming!

It often happened though, that he called me at the last minute at work, saying that he would not be home. Then the evenings at home were long and dark. The boys would do their homework in their room, and I would sit downstairs in the living room, knitting or mending. Winter was coming, and it was getting so cold. New sweaters were needed all the time.

We had not experienced as cold a winter in England as the winter of 1962/1963, since the winter of 1946/47 when we were still in Germany, living in the refugee camp in Flensburg. Now we lived in a nice house, but the British houses had not been built for such very cold weather.

All the water pipes were outside the buildings, and even the larger pipes, carrying the water, were not placed deep enough in the ground. Usually the winters in England were not too cold. It froze a little during the night, it snowed a bit, but after a couple of days it melted, turning into slush. Now the cold lingered, the pipes froze and burst open, creating all kinds of problems inside as well as outside the houses.

Since these kinds of houses did not have much insulation or centralized heating, they got very cold during the night. When Ed was away on his jobs, I stayed up till midnight, heating water in the kettle and carrying it upstairs to the bathroom to pour it down alternately into the toilet and into the bathtub to keep the pipes open. If they would freeze, it might cause the hot water tank to burst and flood the whole place. I did not want that to happen. What would I do then? The plumbers were so busy that sometimes people had to wait for days till they came. Central heating was not common in England in those days.

We had installed electrical heaters in the two rooms that we used most, the living room and the boys' room. That would save us from having to go outside for the coal in the cold and wet weather, but electricity was expensive. In wintertime the rest of the house was as cold as a grave. The small portable electrical heater was used for the kitchen and bathroom only while we were there.

When I finally went to bed, I would put two hot water bottles in it, and cover the bed with all we had, even putting our bathrobes on top. For a short while, I would switch on the small portable heater, but I was afraid to leave it on through the night in case anything malfunctioned.

Soon, however, I had to pull the covers over my head so my ears and my nose would not freeze. Even so, sometimes I had to get up toward the morning and reheat my water bottles to be able to continue to sleep. That was a sad story.

Because of the cold, damp weather, we all sniffled and my arm and leg joints were hurting no end, even though I was only in my mid-thirties. The hospital was warm, but my desk was in the wide part of the hallway that was a walk-through area. One large glass door opened to the inside main hallway, but the other, directly opposite, led into the stairway to the winter garden room and the nurses' home. As the nurses changed their shifts, they walked through these doors. Since it was quite a bit colder in the stairway and the door was opened many times, I got quite a lot of draft, especially in the wintertime. No wonder that so many people in England suffered from rheumatism and aching joints: drafts were everywhere. My shoulder and elbow sometimes hurt so much that I had to use my left hand to put the right one on the desk. Still, there was nothing I could do about it, except wait for the spring.

The year 1963 came, but the spring was slow in coming. The days were dull and gray, and there was nothing exciting to plan or to look forward to. Then I thought how ungrateful I was! Was it not what I had wished for most of all, our own place? Now I had it. We had our jobs that provided our sustenance. I even had a chance to paint! And yet, something was still missing.

There was a feeling that life had stopped in its tracks. I seemed to be walking but not getting anywhere. The thought that there will never be anything else in my life, gave me shivers. Just going to the hospital every day and doing a job that did not present any challenge, grieved me. I was grateful that I had it and could help with the family finances, but something inside of me kept me tense and I could not let it go. There was tension in my head, tension in my body. I felt like a tautly tightened string, seemingly for no reason at all. I kept admonishing myself about it, but nothing helped.

"If only everybody could have it as good as we have it now!" I said to myself. Ed was keeping away from drinking, and that was a great burden off my mind. And still, and still... I would have liked to have something to look forward to; to have some hope or challenge for the future.

March came. When I walked to the bus in the mornings on my way to work, the spring breezes blew and gasped in the bare branches of the trees, swaying them this way and that. The fresh and moist earthy smells filled the air, as well as an excitement proclaiming the budding and growing that would soon happen, even though rows of gray clouds still rushed over the land.

## To America?

On one such windy March day, we received unexpected news that knocked us over! It was like lightning from a clear sky! The news was that we could go to America! Our turn had come! Five years had passed since the day we put in our applications. We still lived in London then. With all the changes in our lives during these years, we had almost forgotten about it. Besides, we had not been able to count on it either, because we might not be accepted. It was as if some unbelievable dream was suddenly before us.

To America! We did not know what to think! We had not owned a house at the time when we applied. Now we had spent three years in this one already; had worked and finally had it the way we wanted it!

"And should we now leave it? Leave everything and start again from nothing for the third time? Should we go to a strange country once again and to an uncertain future?"

Those were very hard questions. We lay in bed at night with our eyes open, trying to find answers; trying to look into the future, which we could not see.

"Did we want to go? Should we go? Was this the answer to my thoughts of having no hopes or challenges for the future?" I asked myself.

My argument for going was the bad English climate that was settling in all my joints. And then, this last unusually cold winter and what I had had to do to keep the systems working! I really would have preferred not to experience another one like it, but that was what this country was like. You always had to carry an umbrella and be ready for rain. It was cold and damp most of the time. There had been a few better summers, but there had been some that came and went again with hardly any warmth and sunshine at all.

If we went to California, where all our relatives lived, at least it would be warm. Ed too began to think that perhaps we should go. We were still young enough. Ed would be thirty-eight, and I—thirty-seven. It would be something new and interesting, and would give us new perspectives.

We talked with Mother about this, not wanting to leave her, but she said, "Do not worry about me! I have my own home and a husband who is good to me. We have a good life here and a lot of friends. We shall be all right. But you should go, even just for the children's sake! They will have more opportunities there than here. Old England has been kind of stuck in the mud for some time now."

"Yes!" I said and then added, "Perhaps later you and Saša could join us if the circumstances were right?" That sounded good, and more and more our thoughts turned toward going. My brother, Johnny, said that he

was thinking about going too, because the Brits were very conservative, holding on to the old ways and not wanting to change.

A good example of this was the way that they insisted on having the open fireplaces for warming their homes. The city had built eight-story buildings of apartments for people who had to rent, because they could not afford to buy houses. Many, however, did not want to go and live there! They would not have their open coal fireplaces, but they wanted them, to be able to look at the fire! It had always been like that, and they could not imagine living in an apartment! All very nice, but wouldn't it be nicer to live in a place that would be warm everywhere and at all times? Things began to change after they saw for themselves how much better it was to have central heating. Yes, changes came very slowly here.

We finally came to the decision. Let's go! The Immigration authorities had three requirements that we had to fulfill: either we had to have enough money to sustain us, or have a job waiting for us in the U.S. The third was to have somebody in the U.S. who was willing to sponsor us, so we would not be a burden to the government.

I wrote to my Aunt Irma, my mother's oldest sister, and her husband, Uncle Kārl, not doubting that they would give us the sponsorship we needed. They were like my own family, for I had lived with them throughout my high-school years in Latvia. We received their sponsorship right away. Now it was up to us to get ready.

Uncle Kārl, a former banker, had found a job as a packer at the Mayflower Moving Co. in San Jose, and Aunt Irma had worked, cleaning rich people's houses in the first years. She had been highly appreciated by her employers, for she was a very particular person and nothing but the very best would do. Knowing that she had studied music, her employers had often given her tickets to concerts and even taken her to them.

In the meantime their family had expanded. All three of Aunt Irma's and Uncle Kārl's children had married and had children of their own. It was hard to take that in, remembering my high school years when I lived with them, when we had all been children.

Mother's brother, Heini, and his wife, Austra, had two more daughters born in America, and Omi, who lived with them, helped to raise the girls. Sandra, the oldest, was the same age as our son, Uldis. Dagnija, the younger one, was born five years later. Heini, being a builder, had continued in his profession and had built a big house for the seven members of his family.

Aunt Elzī, Mother's younger sister, had lived in other places in the U.S. at first but moved to Los Gatos eventually. Her husband, Alfrēds Krimuldēns, had been a higher officer in the Latvian National Army

before the war. When the Germans came, they drafted him into their army. Sadly, he had been taken prisoner of war, when the Russians cut off a large area near Danzig in eastern Germany, and they could not get out. The Russians had condemned him to ten years of hard labor in stone mines at a prisoner of war camp in the Ural Mountains in Russia.

Being a younger man, he had survived the terrible years with the help of a lady friend, who had helped him by sending packages of aid. After returning to Latvia, he needed an address to register that he lived in Rīga to be able to find work there. This nice woman, who had been Elzī's and his mutual friend, offered her apartment and they eventually got married and had a good life together. He had been lucky to have such a friend. There were many such couples who were split apart this way, because the Germans had drafted the men and after the war they could not return. It was well known that persecutions would follow them if they returned under the Russian rule. After Aunt Elzī learned about all that, she married a bachelor Artūrs Reinvalds who worked as a carpenter and had a nice house in Los Gatos.

My cousin Ingrīd, the youngest of the three Hincenberg children, lived not far away in San Jose and had four children. Cousin Edvīns lived in Oakland with his wife Inese and their three children. Cousin Ruta, who was nearest to my age and with whom I had always been the closest, was the only one who had moved away and lived in Michigan together with husband Leon and their three children.

Having made the decision about going to America, we put our house on the market, but only a very few people came to look at it. Then we decided that I should start working half a day only, so I could be at home if any buyers came to look at it.

Our whole life was suddenly turned inside out by the knowledge that nothing would be as it was before. It was strange that for all these years here in England, and even after we bought the house, I had never felt really settled. At the back of my mind was always the thought, "but what if we have to move?" That was why I wanted Ed to build all the furniture so that it could be moved, just in case, but it never entered my mind that our move would be across the ocean to the other side of the world. Now the move was turning out to be a reality, and we would be able to take very little of what we owned with us. What an overwhelming thought to me especially! I was here at home more of the time, living with the things I treasured and now I would have to leave everything! All our striving, I mused, will have been for nothing...

Then I thought of quite a number of Latvian people who had already left England for the U.S.A., Canada and Australia, having received news of how much better, more modern and progressive life was there. Eng-

land had been the first country to take in the refugees, but a year later, other countries had offered sponsorships, too. The advantage for people our age, who had emigrated to these other countries, was that they had better chances to continue or complete their education in colleges and universities. We did not have those opportunities in England.

The hard job was ahead of us now, especially me, to decide what we needed to take, and what had to be left behind. On the other hand, there was also a joyous excitement that something was happening with our lives, something new and different! It would be a challenge, but we had decided to risk it.

In June, we went to Almeley for the last time. We wanted to celebrate the Midsummer Fest together with our family and see our many friends for one more time. Only two more months, and we would be gone.

The sale of the house, however, was not going anywhere, even though we talked to our agent several times. We did not want to give it away for nothing either, for we needed the money for the airfare and for starting our life in the new country. We had asked for 3200 pounds. Now we were willing to sell it for 3000, but still nothing.

The month of August came, but the house still was not sold. People were having their summer holidays as was customary in England, and everybody who could manage it got out of town. There was not much hope that anything would happen now, but our requirement was to leave within six months! That meant the beginning of September!

Ed wrote to the American Embassy, explaining our predicament and asking for an extension, but the answer was harsh.

"Either you go now, or we will take you off the list!" That really threw us!

"What now? Wait another six years? No way! That would never work. To settle back as we were and not go?" we questioned. "Perhaps this was a sign that it was not the best thing for us to do after all?"

Uldis was unhappy too. He had passed his eleven-plus exam and had got into the prestigious King Edward School. He did not want to leave it or his friends here.

"You're ruining my life!" he said.

More and more, we came to the conclusion that perhaps it was meant for us to stay, and that we should, but somehow it felt like a nice dream had been taken away from us. Seeing no alternative, we began to settle down again.

Only three weeks were left till the deadline, when something happened that turned our thoughts upside down again. Was it fate or the Hand of God? What should we call it? The coincidence was too strange!

Ed was in London again, because many of the rich people who had bought the dishwashing machines lived there. While he was there, more

calls often came in, causing him to stay longer. Then he would usually stay at the Latvian House, where we had been managers during the fifties. The prices were reasonable there, and the club was still operating, so he could visit with other Latvian people in the evenings.

This time, entering the club room, he had seen a man sitting at the bar wearing the uniform of an American Air Force officer. As they started a conversation, it turned out that he was a Latvian from the U.S.A, stationed in Germany, but spending his week's leave in England.

"I was wondering if you might have heard..." The officer asked him, "I had a good friend when we lived in the refugee camp in Germany all those years ago, and I know that he came to England. I thought, perhaps I could locate him while I am here. It would be so great to get together again!"

"Well, we could ask around." Ed had answered. "What was your friend's name?"

"His name was Mintauts Zvirbulis."

"Mintauts Zvirbulis?" Ed exclaimed. "He is my brother-in law, and he lives in Birmingham, the same as I!"

"Now that is a coincidence!" The airman was overwhelmed by such a discovery.

"If you can wait till tomorrow afternoon, I shall be going home, and I can take you there!" Ed had said.

"Great! That would be just great! I would have never believed that this would happen so easily!"

Ed brought him to my brother's house, and one evening they both came to visit us. We told our visitor about our ruined plans of going to America, because we could not sell the house in time.

"Just as well," I added with a deep sigh. "It would be hard to leave all that we have here; all that we have saved and scraped for all these years."

"Well, what do you have here?" The American let his eyes roam around our small living room and smiled a bit pathetically. "Living in America, you could earn that in a few months!" He said.

He told us more things about life in America and was very positive that we could make a good life there.

"If you are healthy and can work, there should be no problem! The Latvians in America live very well compared to the life in old fashioned England!"

When they left, our minds whirled around everything that we had heard. Could we really? Should we? And suddenly we knew that we had to go! Yes, we would go! We would leave the sale of the house to our solicitor, and my brother would oversee everything. Mother was willing to lend us the money until the house was sold. Uncle Kārl had sent us the sponsorship, so really, nothing else stood in our way. The only thing left

was the packing. We would pack and go!

Mainly that would be on my shoulders, because Ed was going to work till the very last, so that we would have more money. Also, I knew better what we had and what we would need most, as we began our new life in America. These were busy and exciting days. We had to be ready in three weeks!

Mother would take most of the belongings that we could not take, and Johnny would take some also. I packed one wooden crate with some bulkier things, which would have to be shipped over. Otherwise, our suitcases would be the only luggage that we would have. The hardest thing was going through the papers, the letters and all the little things that were meaningful. In the evenings, I sat on a low stool in our small box-room that we had used as a storage room, and the piles of discarded papers grew around me. I looked through them, read some, and with a sigh, put them aside. This had been our life.

The house was so quiet. The boys were in their room, Ed was away. Only Suki was with me as usual. But she too was sensing that something unusual was happening. As I sat there, she climbed all over me, stretched up with her white front paws to my shoulder and tried to lick my cheek. Did she already sense that the parting was near? It broke my heart thinking about it. We all were very sorry that we would have to leave her, for we could not take her with us. It would be very expensive to take her on the plane, but more importantly, we did not know where we would be and if it would be possible to keep a dog there. Tears came to our eyes, talking about it, for she had been a member of our family. It was like leaving a child!

Yet, we had to part. In the last week, Ed had to go to London and he would take part of our luggage to the Latvian House and Suki to our friends, Aina and Maigonis, as we had arranged. They had a house with garden in a suburb of London by now. They also had a Labrador dog, and said that they would take Suki and then see how things would work out; if they would keep her, or find another good home for her.

On the morning when Ed had packed the small van with our things, I went to call Suki. These last days she had followed us everywhere, but was upstairs with the boys now. Hearing my voice, she happily started down the stairs but suddenly stopped in her tracks half way down. The front door was wide open and outside stood the van with the hatch down. I shall never forget the look she gave me. It burned into my heart. I had betrayed my child. Then Ed came in, called her, and they both got into the van.

I don't even know how we got to London in the end. The last day at home was so hectic. It was a nice morning outside, and the boys were having fun with their friends. One of them had brought some kind of a

cart, and they took turns riding in it while the others pushed and shoved and fooled around, until it suddenly went off the pavement, turning over, and Uldis fell out.

Oh, my God! He came in with a bleeding face, and half of his front tooth had broken. How will we go to America now? I had to rush him to the doctor and to the dentist to get things taken care of at least temporarily.

The last night we stayed at the Latvian House in London. Aina and Maigonis came to be with us and said that Suki was all right.

"I wonder if we should go and see Suki for the last time," I pondered, but Aina said "NO!"

Ed also did not think that it would be a good idea, but my heart was aching so badly. I felt like I was in some dark tunnel, and everything seemed unreal. I cried all night for Suki, thinking of that last condemning look, and the whole night was a nightmare.

It was good to get going the next morning. There was no more time to think and brood. I was a bit apprehensive about flying. I had never flown before, except that one time in Margate in that small excursion plane.

"What if we fall and crash into the sea?" I said to Ed, seeking comfort, but he just laughed.

"My dear, people die in their beds every day! Will you therefore not go to bed?"

Yes, of course, he was right, and anyway, everything was in God's hands now: our flying, our future and our whole life. We had to trust Him that everything would be the way it ought to be. Taking courage from this, I stepped into the plane.